G. Roger Smith

May 1957

WAYS OF
WORSHIP

WAYS OF WORSHIP

*

THE REPORT OF A THEOLOGICAL
COMMISSION OF FAITH
AND ORDER

Edited by

PEHR EDWALL
Church of Sweden

ERIC HAYMAN
Church of England

WILLIAM D. MAXWELL
Church of Scotland

HARPER & BROTHERS PUBLISHERS
NEW YORK

GENERAL PREFACE

★

The second World Conference on Faith and Order was held at Edinburgh in 1937. Reflection on its Report led to the conclusion that many, if not most, of the issues on which Christians are divided have their roots in different conceptions of the nature of the Church. A passage in the Report suggested that, besides a direct examination of this doctrinal question, a study of the ways of worship characteristic of different Churches might be a profitable undertaking, and this led some members of the Continuation Committee to press for a discussion of the theological principles underlying what in his Conference sermon Archbishop William Temple had called 'the greatest of all scandals in the face of the world', the maintenance of barriers against completeness of union at the Table of the Lord.

Hence in 1938 and 1939 three international theological commissions were appointed, to study (i) the Church, (ii) Ways of Worship, and (iii) Intercommunion. In spite of difficulties and delays they have carried on their work. Papers were written and circulated. Meetings to discuss them were held when and where possible. In the summer of 1950 each had an extended meeting at which its report was put into its final form, and approved.

These reports, together with a selection of the papers contributed in the course of the enquiries, are now published. It should be clearly understood that their purpose is to provide material for discussion by the delegates of the Churches when they meet for the third World Conference at Lund in Sweden in 1952. Invitations to that Conference have now been issued, and Churches are in process of appointing their delegates. These volumes will best fulfil their function if their readers will remember their purpose, and use them to ensure among the members of the various Churches a widespread understanding of the questions which their representatives will be going to Lund to discuss.

LEONARD HODGSON

Christ Church,
  Oxford
January 1951

5

CONTENTS

*

7

Part III

LITURGY AND DEVOTION   255

EDITORIAL PREFACE

★

The Editors had intended that, as soon as this volume was prepared for Press, their work should be finally reviewed by the man to whom the Commission on Ways of Worship, and, indeed, the whole Ecumenical Movement, owes a debt of gratitude. That intention cannot be realised, for our friend and Chairman Gerardus van der Leeuw has been taken from our midst. He presided at every session of the Commission's meetings until the last morning at Thun in August 1950, when he had to resume an interrupted convalescence.

In Dr. Gerardus van der Leeuw, sometime Minister of Education in the Netherlands Government, and Professor of the History of Religions in the University of Groningen, the Christian world has lost a great and versatile scholar. There is no space here to record worthily what he did in the sixty years of a full life. We might, indeed, be content to say with Thomas Hardy, 'He was a good man and did good things.' His wide range of interests are represented in the Jubilee Volume presented to him in 1950. He spoke as an expert in comparative religion, in theology, in education, in certain fields of literature (for he was one of three chosen from Europe for the recent Goethe festival in America), in religious art, in music, and not least in the field of liturgical study.

Yet beneath this Protean versatility was a man, firmly disciplined by a dedicated will. He was always a rebel against hypocrisy and shams, even as against all that was dull and drab. He had a great love of human kind, and a generous joy in the good things of life, with a positive genius for friendship. For one who so loved his fellows it was natural to hate tyranny. The story of his share in the fight against the Nazi violation of his country cannot here be told. We remember him best as the beloved Chairman and director of our liturgical study in this Commission. He listened patiently, exposed stupidity with a penetrating flash of humour, and rebuked only harshness and intolerance, simply by being himself.

We can only regret that in this volume his visible share appears limited to one paper, which indeed he had no opportunity to revise or to expand. Let it therefore be recorded that the main section of the Commission's Report (pp. 20-36) as well as the memorable final paragraph (p. 38f.) was drafted by himself, and fully considered and revised under

9

his chairmanship. He gave it to us with characteristic generosity and modesty, and was really surprised to find it hailed by many as a turning point in ecumenical thinking. He counted none of it a possession of his own to be guarded jealously.

With all his massive achievement in scholarship and in the arts, the Commission was allowed to see but little of himself. There was always the quiet reserve of a man whose life is not his own. But one had only to work with him in the close and strenuous discussions to see in the background a very great man. Van der Leeuw was big in every sense of the word—big in physical frame, in power and speed of mind, and above all in spirit. We shall like to remember him as truly Coeur-de-Lion. On first meeting him one could almost be afraid. Lions should be safely caged before one ventured too close. But this lion was in leash to the Grace of God. May he rest in peace.

*　*　*

In this volume we present to the World Conference on Faith and Order at Lund in 1952 the all-too slight results of our study, together with a selection of the most relevant evidence which has led to the views reported. The Editors wish to express the thanks of the Commission to various members who contributed papers relating to other aspects of its study. Without the full perspective thus obtained, the work would have been impoverished. The selection here given attempts to show the logical progression of the study as it actually developed.

The Commission had its full share of the common difficulties which beset Faith and Order between 1939 and 1947, during which time solid foundations would normally have been laid. The Commission was set up, in principle though not in personnel, at Clarens in August 1939. The only effective work possible during the war was done in part under the Chairman's personal guidance in occupied Holland, and also by the slow collection of written material upon a tentative programme of study. All the evidence published happens to date from, or after, the first meeting of the Commission in 1947, onwards to the end of 1950. Such material as was not actually presented to the Commission in session was largely foreseen in the instructions given to the Editors.

In the latter part of 1947 the scheme of study was fully revised, and the two groups of papers from which Parts One and Two of this volume are made up soon assumed central importance. This fact in part reflects the circumstance that the Protestant Churches generally, and the Re-

formed Churches in particular, were represented in greater strength than their Catholic and Orthodox neighbours. The older tradition of East and West seemed at first to be overshadowed. The Anglican view found no continuing expression until as late as 1949.

One outstanding fact to which our evidence directs attention is the widespread growth, however tentative in some parts of the Church, of a Liturgical return. It should not be overlooked that the new understanding of liturgical values has been fostered by exegetical, historical and theological study within the separate communions, widened after the war by the renewed possibility of international contacts. The development is further due to the experience of ecumenical thinking and personal contacts during a growing series of ecumenical gatherings, both large and small. We may also feel that the values of the grande tradition had worked silently, and were now beginning to come into their own in places where such renewal might have seemed least likely, even if long desired. Under these various influences the contrast between Word and Sacrament has become at least a carefully studied comparison, and at best a new realisation of a needed integration in our total worship of God in the wholeness of His Church.

At one stage it was customary to seek such harmony in the idea of a sacramental quality inherent in the true preaching of the Word. It has, indeed, been held that this quality offers all the spiritual values of eucharistic worship—that the services of the Word and of the Sacrament are in effect equivalent means to a common end. Against such a view there was, at first, only a reiteration of the Word by some members in a manner tantamount to rejection of the whole validity of the sacramental idea, characterizing all sacrifice as belonging to the Old Covenant, now done away, if not indeed to purely pagan forms. Some of the earlier papers reflect the sacramental theory of preaching in an attempt to ease such sharp contrasts in the Christian understanding of worship. Other members of the Commission, however, as firmly reject any such theory as lacking historical basis.

It is, however, perhaps the most recent and conspicuous development of our common study that many in Lutheran and Reformed circles have left that view, or were even misunderstood entirely by those who assumed them to hold it. In the liturgical return they have begun to recover in actuality the sacramental values once claimed somewhat theoretically, and without clear conviction on either side. This process has, of course, worked in reverse, as the Report of the Commission makes clear. Not the least important evidence comes from the side of Roman Catholicism.

There will always be a meeting and a mutuality in all fellowship that is truly of the Spirit.

So it is that we have been enriched as a Commission by hearing of liturgical developments in the Roman Catholic Church; by some slight sharing in the liturgical treasure gathered by the Berneuchen Bruderschaft in the German Evangelical Church; by the contributions of a member of the Communauté de Taizé-lès-Cluny in the French Reformed Church; and by frequent evidence of the vigorous if still nascent Liturgical Movement in Holland. Our study is far from complete. There is more to learn from the evidence already before us, and more to discover —as we must believe—which our few years and rare meetings have been too short to bring to our notice. Many of us, however, have found what we could not have expected; and in the fruiting of this seed the worship of the Body of Christ must surely be led by the Holy Spirit nearer to truth.

PEHR EDWALL
ERIC HAYMAN
WILLIAM D. MAXWELL

January 1951

MEMBERSHIP OF THE COMMISSION
AT THE COMPLETION OF ITS WORK
AUGUST 1950

★

OFFICERS

Prof. G. van der Leeuw (Chairman)	(*Reformed Church of the Netherlands*)
Rev. Dr. Hans Asmussen (Vice-Chairman)	(*German Evangelical Church*)
Rev. W. Vos (Secretary)	(*Reformed Church of the Netherlands*)

MEMBERS

Prof. Dr. J. D. Benoît	(*Reformed Church of Alsace and Lorraine*)
Most Rev. Archbishop Yngve T. Brilioth	(*Church of Sweden*)
Archdeacon P. Coinidis	(*Orthodox Patriarchate of Alexandria*)
Rev. A. H. Couratin	(*Church of England*)
Rev. Dr. G. S. Dobbins	(*Southern Baptist Convention—U.S.A.*)
Very Rev. Dr. G. Florovsky	(*Orthodox Ecumenical Patriarchate: Exarchate for Russians in the West*)
Rev. Artur Graf	(*Swiss Protestant Church Federation*)
Rev. F. Hambly	(*Methodist Church of Australia*)
Eric Hayman	(*Church of England*)
Rev. Dr. P. Katz	(*Lutheran Church*)
Prof. Dr. W. J. Kooiman	(*Evangelical Lutheran Church of the Netherlands*)
Rev. Dr. William D. Maxwell	(*Church of Scotland*)
Rev. Prof. Alexis van der Mensbrugghe	(*Russian Orthodox Exarchate in Western Europe: Patriarchate of Moscow*)
Rev. Prof. D. Moraitis	(*Greek Orthodox Church*)
Rev. R. Paquier	(*Swiss Protestant Church Federation*)
Rev. Prof. E. C. Ratcliff	(*Church of England*)
Rev. Prof. Dr. Luther D. Reed	(*United Lutheran Church—U.S.A.*)
Prof. Dr. A. E. Rüthy	(*Old-Catholic Church—Switzerland*)
Prof. Dr. M. H. Shepherd	(*Protestant Episcopal Church—U.S.A.*)
Rev. Prof. J. C. Schroeder	(*Congregational Churches of U.S.A.*)

Prof. Dr. Julius Schweizer	*(Swiss Protestant Church Federation)*
Rev. K. M. Simon	*(Orthodox Syrian Church of Malabar)*
Right Rev. Dr. Wilhelm Stählin	*(German Evangelical Church)*
Rev. Dr. G. Campbell Wadsworth	*(United Church of Canada)*
Prof. Dr. R. Will	*(Lutheran Church of Alsace and Lorraine)*
Dr. Nicolas Zernov	*(Russian Orthodox Exarchate in Western Europe: Patriarchate of Moscow)*

NOTE. Some of the above appointed members were not able to take active part in the work of the Commission. Some were appointed in the later stages to replace members who had resigned.

DEPUTIES

Rev. Pehr Edwall	*(Church of Sweden)*
Rev. C. J. Bowles	*(Church of England)*

CONSULTANTS

Rev. Leslie Brown	*(Church of South India)*
Rev. Dr. P. E. Gresham	*(Disciples of Christ—U.S.A.)*
Rev. Dr. W. M. Horton	*(Congregational Churches of U.S.A.)*
Pastor lic. W. Menn	*(German Evangelical Church)*
Frère Max Thurian	*(Reformed Church of France)*
Rev. J. M. Todd	*(Congregational Church—England)*

The above attended one or more of the Commission Meetings either as representing an absent member or as consultants.

REPORT OF THE COMMISSION

*

Introduction

It has always been the work of the Faith and Order Movement to help the Churches to grow in mutual understanding of one another with a view to discovering how far obstacles to unity arising out of differences in faith and order are such as to require them to remain apart. Until the Edinburgh Conference of 1937 no attempt had been made in the Movement to approach this study by way of seeking to enter into an understanding of one another's ways of worship. For some years, however, interest in this line of approach had been growing in various quarters. There were liturgical movements in continental Lutheran and Reformed Churches. In the United States Christians in different Churches were beginning to ask about their worship: 'What are we doing, and why, and have we any history?' In the Fellowship of Unity in Egypt, the Fellowship of SS. Alban and Sergius (Anglican and Eastern Orthodox), and the Scoto-Russian Fellowship of St. Andrew liturgical questions were being raised. Some of these are referred to in the Edinburgh Report, which says:

> The Conference asks the Continuation Committee to take this matter into consideration, and to take steps to promote the study of liturgical questions by the appointment of a commission or by what other method seems best.[1]

In 1939 the Continuation Committee appointed the Theological Commission now making this report, and gave it the following terms of reference:

(a) To study the Ways of Worship characteristic of the different Christian traditions with a view to promoting growth in mutual understanding among the Churches;

(b) To include a study of the place and function of preaching and instruction in Christian worship, and to pay attention to non-liturgical as well as liturgical traditions of worship;

[1] VI, v, 9.

15

(c) To consider not only what are the existing traditions in worship, but also the experiments in 'liturgical creation' which are being made in ecumenical and similar gatherings and in the Younger Churches, and the principles which should inform future developments in the field of worship;

(d) To conduct, as it thinks fit, liturgical conferences at which members may share by experience in unfamiliar forms of worship;

(e) To issue leaflets explanatory of different traditions of worship and to present to the Committee a Report embodying the results of the Commission's work which can serve as material for discussion at a future World Conference on Faith and Order.

For various reasons, not least the unsettled state of the world since 1939, we have not been able to cover all this ground. At our last meeting we were shown proofs of a new edition of *Venite Adoremus*, to be published by the World's Student Christian Federation, which partly takes the place of the leaflets suggested in (e). In the later stages of our work a development closely related to (d) was proposed. It is set out fully in Part III of the volume to be appended to this report, and its practical carrying-out is now in hand. For the rest, our aim in making our report has been to provide material for discussion by the delegates of the Churches assembled at Lund in 1952.

With this purpose in mind we have been led by our studies to divide our report into three parts. We begin with a survey of the present situation, in which we seek to distinguish and classify the different ways of worship which are characteristic of different traditions in the Christendom of to-day. In the course of this enquiry we have been struck by the extent to which a 'liturgical movement' is to be found in Churches of widely differing traditions. This is so clearly an outstanding feature of church life in these days that we have felt bound to devote the second part of our report to a consideration of its bearing on the subject remitted to us. The meetings of our Commission have brought together men taking part in different expressions of this movement. We have learned much from one another, and hope that in this section of our report something of what we have gained may be communicated to its readers.

Another aspect of our study arose from the fact of 'liturgical creations' owing to the achievement of a measure of unity among separated Christian bodies in various parts of the world. An important example is the liturgy of the United Church of Canada. The most recent is that of the Church of South India. The Constitution of this Church provides that forms of worship in use before the Union will continue in use until the Church decides otherwise, and there was no intention of rushing into liturgical experiment. But dioceses in which a number of church traditions are represented found that this provision was not adequate. Use of sectional rites when they met as one body on diocesan occasions seemed to point to the divided past rather than to express the unity of the present. They therefore pressed for a common rite, and the Liturgy Committee was instructed to prepare such a form of service. A draft was prepared, incorporating elements which various traditions had found important, and submitted to every part of the Church, and to scholars in various parts of the world for criticism. The completed service was first used at the Synod in 1950, was approved for optional use, and its translation into the regional languages arranged. This liturgy will be used for two years and then revised in the light of the experience of the worshipping Church. One diocese has produced a book designed to instruct ordinary church members in ways of worship. Essays in the book describe how different traditions in southern India (not only those included in the Church of South India) worship and explain the meaning these different ways of worship have for those brought up in them.

Thirdly, reflecting upon what we have observed and thought in these studies, we have attempted to focus attention upon certain questions which in our opinion are most directly relevant to the purpose for which the Churches will send their delegates to represent them at Lund.

I. *Survey of Present Situation*

As soon as we begin to be self-conscious about worship at all, we have to ask: what *is* Christian worship? Whilst we are actually worshipping the question does not arise, or, if it does, has to be banished again. For the essence of worship is that it is the concentration of all faculties on corporate self-giving to God in response to His love and in praise of His glory. All is centred upon Him, and we only come into the picture at all as living recipients of His living self-communication. That is the heart of the matter. In practice, of course, individuals fall far short of this, but inasmuch as they do so, they have, in that moment, ceased to worship. But once the question has been raised as to the nature of what we do, we cannot go back to those times and places of worship without having at least begun to meet that question with answers which satisfy all that we know of the God and Father of our Lord Jesus Christ, and which make clear what it is He asks of men if they are to 'worship Him in spirit and in truth'.

When we raise the question, we find there are, in fact, different answers given, with equal sincerity, among Christians. We may mention five emphases. These are not always mutually exclusive, but the form which worship takes is very largely determined by the order of importance given to them, and by whether some are omitted altogether. The first two points relate to the modes of worship; the next three are related to the centre around which worship moves. Such an analysis of emphases affords only a rough guide to the present situation. In the second part of this report we shall note many ways in which long-accustomed boundaries are shifting, that many of our problems are found to cut across denominational boundaries, and that views supposedly incompatible are not necessarily impossible to hold in a united Church. Here we offer only a sketch-map of some broad distinctions which in fact exist.

A

(1) *Liturgical worship*—the use of fixed forms, however richly provided with alternatives and variations for the different seasons and commemorations of the Christian year. Usually such traditions are at the same time ceremonial, i.e. using, often extensively, dress, action, colour, lights, etc., as supplemental ways of 'saying' what the liturgy says. In some of the liturgies in use to-day, as for example the Orthodox Liturgy of S. Basil the Great and the Syrian Liturgy of S. James, the essential structure has remained substantially unchanged for fifteen hundred years.

Our study has made clear that the traditional forms of liturgy are throughout scriptural, both in their spirit and in their choice of language.

(2) *'Free' worship.* Other Christians regard such forms as untrue to the spirit of the New Testament and their antiquity as no guarantee of their soundness. They make a cardinal point of the freedom of the spirit 'which bloweth where it listeth'. Such convictions range from a resolute refusal to prepare in advance any part of corporate worship, to a more usual provision by the leader of the worship of a form of words composed with that particular service in mind, and possibly occasions too for quite spontaneous prayer. In at any rate the more traditional forms, this freedom is rigorously controlled by the knowledge of Scripture, the words and thoughts of which are the field in which freedom to move is given: there is often in each tradition a common underlying structure. Generally such traditions also make little use of ceremonial: by an association of ideas as natural as the converse which links ceremonial with liturgy, it is felt to distract from what the words say, fastening attention upon 'forms'. However, some would insist that this 'freedom' includes a freedom to use liturgies, though usually with a reluctance to standardise them or suggest their general adoption.

B

(1) *Eucharist-centred worship.* This scriptural synonym for the Lord's Supper is appropriate here because it is as a giving-of-thanks that Orthodoxy is supremely centred upon this Sacrament as the norm and fount of all worship. Whatever the tradition, whether the service be thought of primarily as sacrifice or communion, to be Eucharist-centred is to think of all other worship as preparation for, thanksgiving after or meditation upon this central act. By a natural logic such traditions hold the Eucharist as the central and most attended service of every Sunday (and other great festivals), though many would maintain that there is no necessary connection between centrality and frequency.

(2) *Preaching-centred worship.* Others maintain that the characteristically *Christian* element in worship is that it is the proclamation of the Word of God. Just as a central affirmation of Christianity is that the eternal Word was made flesh, so the central act of Christian worship is to attend upon the proclamation of that Word as witnessed to in Scripture, as it is expounded to the

congregation of faithful men by those in whom the Church recognises the right of exposition.

The drawing together of these two emphases is one of the signs of our time in the ways of worship.

(3) *Waiting upon the Spirit.* The members of the Society of Friends are not alone, though they are the best known, among those who find the centre of worship neither in traditional liturgy nor in prepared prayers: neither in a special sacrament nor in the witness of the sermon: but in a quiet waiting on the Spirit, and in the acceptance of such utterance from within the exercise of the gathered Meeting as seems to Him good 'for the building up of the Body in love'.

II. *Current Developments*

Although in many ranges of church life there is too much readiness to accept present practices in worship without any deep searching of the spirit, yet in nearly all parts of the world there is a wave of liturgical movement observable in the member-Churches of the World Council. Not least is this the case in Churches which until recently showed little or no concern about forms of worship. We may instance the liturgical movement among Dutch Mennonites, whose Brotherhood recently published a service book; the community of Taizé-lès-Cluny within the French Reformed Church; and the liturgical reconstruction in the Berneuchen fellowship.

It is possible to discern a general trend of development which is similar in nearly all Churches—though whether this similarity is more than general and on the surface may be open to question. There is a growing sense that worship is not to be thought of as a gathering of individual pious Christians, but as a corporate act in direct relation to the Lord of the Church. Dr. Schweizer has expressed this by saying that it is the Lord who holds the service: *So hält der Herr selbst den Gottesdienst.*[1] Others would rather say that the Church holds the service in the presence of the Lord. In either case worship is not an arbitrary act of piety but a rendering of glad obedience, an expression of that fealty which underlies the whole Christian life.

Connected with this is the fact that most of the present efforts

[1] V, b, p. 125.

at liturgical renewal may be said to have started, more or less consciously, from a rediscovery of the sacramental character of worship. In some cases, though by no means all, this has led to an increasingly frequent celebration of sacraments.

There is a widespread genuine unrest, a very definite feeling that worship ought to regain its central place in life, and that it can only do this if Churches return to the primitive patterns. To this end many Churches turn away from the habits and practices of their recent past in order to regain the purity and strength of worship as it was practised in their classic periods. Often it is not clear whether this return to the past constitutes any definite theologically justified movement. There is need to discriminate between the claims of tradition and the authority of Holy Scripture, between the felt attraction of what is old or 'classic', and the need to base what is done on obedience to divine commandment. But in one way or another there is a desire to recover the 'original pattern'.

For this reason worshippers in Reformed Churches are rediscovering the liturgical principles and orders of service of the primitive Reformation, while members of all Churches, including the Roman Catholic, are studying afresh the worship of the early Church. More important still, the New Testament is being studied for the information it gives concerning worship. Arising out of all this we may discern some abatement of the ruling passion for representing the ways of worship of other people as 'degenerate'. At long last we are beginning to see that, measured by the standards of the New Testament and the early Church, none of our current ways of worship is fully adequate.

We must not overlook the fact that this movement may provoke resistance based not merely on conservative dislike of change but on deeply held convictions. In the United States this underlies a widespread and long-standing insistence on free worship. As denominations become more liturgical there spring up new divisive movements of a pentecostal character, claiming the rights of the free Spirit to lead where He will. These are utterly without set forms except in so far as they generate their own traditions.

In what follows we attempt to set down under six heads the questions for discussion which arise out of these liturgical developments.

(1) *Liturgical principles and liturgical tradition.* There are some who wish to begin by discussing liturgical principles, and then test existing forms of worship with the help of their findings. Others hold that the practice of worship comes first, and that liturgical principles can only be discussed by reflection on what is being done. This raises in the liturgical sphere the question of the relative authority of Holy Scripture and church tradition.

Here a very remarkable development is taking place. The long-standing controversy between those who accept tradition together with Holy Scripture as *regula fidei*, and those who accept Holy Scripture only is not a thing of the past. Indeed much more is likely to be heard of it in the near future. But there are hopes of discussion in a new spirit. For on the one hand there is a growing Scripture-mindedness, and on the other an increasing conscious- ness that, as Professor Benoît has put it, 'we all live on tradition more than we think we do'. The recognition that tradition was present and active in the formation of Holy Scripture is met by the acknowledgement that no development of later tradition will be true if inconsistent with Scripture, since the Holy Spirit is self-consistent in all that He reveals. Moreover, there is a growing recognition that tradition is not simply a thing of the past, but a living reality. We live in it and by it, and the tenets of the Reformation are a tradition as well as those of scholasticism. No Christian age can accept all tradition at the same time, or reject tradition as such.

Contemporary literature, and papers written for this Com- mission, show that all this is eminently true of liturgical tradition. In actual practice ways of worship are never built up in a theo- retical way by drawing liturgical consequences from dogmatic tenets. Rather is the creed born from worship. There is clearly, too, a growing conviction that liturgy is not a thing which can arbitrarily be altered or corrected according to theological opinion. It is a living organism, a tree which grows and develops offshoots of all kinds, sometimes bearing fruit, sometimes barren, not constricted but in its luxuriance and solidity living and draw- ing its sap directly from Christian faith as this is given to the Church by the Holy Spirit. This 'Christian existentialism' appears in many places, as in the understanding of liturgy as being a matter of things done. We may compare Bishop Stählin's phrase 'Liturgy as Decision' (*Liturgie als Entscheidung*).

We may quote from Father Hebert. To the question whether we should want to begin by fixing principles or to live by and from tradition he answers: 'It is not for us to devise new and clever ways of worship; we must learn what the Holy Ghost taught our fathers in the faith, first during the biblical period, and then in the period which has followed.' On the whole the evidence from the papers contributed to the Commission confirms this view, though it is not always put so clearly.

This apparent change of outlook, however, does not dispense us from the difficult task of trying to discriminate between tradition and tradition, measuring them all by the standard of Holy Writ. Here we notice both the continuance of disagreements, and some changes from traditional positions. Father Hebert suggests that a reviving emphasis on the enduring value of Old Testament tradition challenges the view, traditional in some Churches, that the ceremonies of Israel were abrogated by the New Covenant. It is in our approach to one another in the way of worship that our differences about the Virgin Mary are most clearly exposed. We may find it comparatively easy to discuss the reverence due to her, or to analyse the psychological grounds of our different practices: it is quite another thing to be put in the attitude of decision by being asked to join in prayer to the Mother of God.[1]

Our coming together in the Ecumenical Movement transfers this issue from the theoretical to the existential plane. In worship we meet the problem, nay rather the sin of the disunion of the Church in its sharpest form. It is good to meet together; it is better to pray together; but this very praying together leads many to ask what value it has if we cannot now receive together the Bread and Wine of the Upper Room. Some would answer that in spite of this we find a greater growth in mutual understanding and a better approach to unity through entering into one another's ways of worship, both private and congregational, than through discussing theological formulae. Yet essential unity can only be attained if the worshipping together is not allowed to be a devotional escape from doctrinal difficulties, if among all

---

[1] At this point we have noted a clear and needless ground of misunderstanding and painful division. Nowhere, even in the supposed 'extremes' of Catholic worship, is there any permissible thought of worship (*latreia*) being directed to the Virgin Mary. God alone may be worshipped. But cf. Note 1, p. 261.

those who worship together the doctrinal implications of the worship are understood and accepted. If it be true that worship comes first and doctrine afterwards, it is equally true that doctrine in contained in worship and that every type of worship implies a type of confession.

In worship the existential attitude comes to the fore: worship is the living form of faith. Hence often in church life a degree of doctrinal toleration may be attained while the same issues expressed in forms of worship may raise most bitter controversies. The theological study of liturgy is not a matter of purely practical, still less of purely historical interest. It is a penetrating into the heart of theology. 'Caring about orthodoxy is a liturgical matter' (Bishop Stählin).

Further, we find a growing consciousness of the truth that a man should take part in worship not only as a matter of feeling or of intellect, or even as an expression of his piety, but in his 'wholeness', body, soul and spirit. Worship is not something apart from living by faith, but is the very substance of it. Hence liturgy is not simply concerned with 'services', but spreads over the whole of life. This underlies the re-discovery in many Churches of the Christian year, and various efforts to establish a non-Roman breviary. A liturgical movement which in some Churches, only some twenty or thirty years ago, was an attempt to give its due to a certain aspect of Christian life—if not merely a preference for flowers and church lights—may now become, in the words of Dr. Asmussen, 'a struggle for the centre of church life'.

To sum up. Our study has required us to repudiate the conception, at one time common in Protestant circles, that the effect of tradition has been in large part to vitiate the scriptural position, to corrupt the biblical foundations of faith. Recent studies by theologians, not only in the Catholic tradition but of schools so widely different as Rudolf Otto, Hans Lietzmann and Oscar Cullmann, show that 'biblical' is something other than the mildly humanised conceptions which have become traditional among some of us. Catholic and Protestant scholars such as Erik Peterson and Karl Barth are helping us to see more clearly what is essentially biblical. The result may be favourable or unfavourable to this or that tradition. We cannot tell in advance. Neither can we solve such questions on theoretical lines alone:

we all of us live in and form tradition. We have to try to discriminate between tradition and tradition, trusting to the guidance of
the Holy Spirit to lead us into the truth of the Bible.

(2) *Corporate worship.* There is growing understanding of
worship as essentially corporate. Individual worship is indeed
indispensable to the worship of the Church: without it the
Church's worship would lose its devotional character. But private
worship is based on corporate worship, the worship of the
Church, the Body of the Lord. For each one of us our communion
is with God in Christ, and to be in Christ is to be in the *koinonia*
of all who are one in Him. This *koinonia* is not something added
on to our private devotion, a coming together of privately saved
souls: it is the way in which God reaches man. The realisation of
this makes some regret the loss of the Agape as an expression of it.
The same truth underlies the language which speaks of the congregation of the faithful as a family. Such language must not,
however, be thought to imply 'familiarity' or 'cosiness', for (as
Principal Robinson and Dr. Zernov have reminded us) the
koinonia includes not only the whole Church militant in all the
world, but the Church in heaven—the saints gone before, angels
and archangels and all the heavenly host. Ecumenically this is of
great importance. The *koinonia* is not of this or that church, but
of the whole Church.

Recognition of the corporate character of worship explains the
connection between the liturgical movement and concern for
church polity and church order, as this is found, for example, in
Germany and Holland. Hence the view that an official order of
worship is an essential element in a church constitution, as it was
in the Didache and in the Apostolic and Hippolytean Constitu-
tions. The conduct of worship cannot be left wholly to the arbitrary will of the minister; there should be an order which to at
least some extent is fixed. Churches differ in the extent to which
they emphasise the freedom to be allowed or the conformity to
be expected. The fixedness of the modern Roman ritual and the
Anglican Book of Common Prayer may be compared with the
freedom allowed to the bishop in early liturgies, indeed for many
centuries, to use his own discretion, his 'proper liturgy', even at
such a crucial moment as the eucharistic prayer. This comparison
shows that there need perhaps be no irreconcilable controversy:

within the agreed order of corporate worship there can be a
right freedom which is something quite different from sheer
arbitrariness.

In this connection arise questions concerning priesthood and
ministry. The thought of worship as the corporate expression of
a corporate experience underlies the view that Holy Order is an
indispensable means in the administration of God's grace. This
need not involve any denial of the general priesthood of all
members of the Body of Christ. The special ministry of those in
Holy Orders may be seen as having its basis, and its essential
significance, in the fundamental priesthood which in some
Churches is given in Baptism, in others in Baptism completed in
Confirmation or Chrismation or some corresponding rite.

This conception is widespread, and finds expression in many
different ways. In Reformed Churches the 'call' by a congregation is often an essential element in ordination. Whilst Quakers
lay great stress on the priesthood of all believers, and recognise
no special ministry, yet members having greater experience of the
Quaker way of worship will be charged with fostering the spoken
ministry, and the general conduct of worship. In the Orthodox
liturgy and Roman mass the participation of the laity is indispensable under normal conditions. In a Roman Catholic pamphlet
entitled *Priests among Men* the author says that the priesthood of
the laity is an indispensable part of the work of Christ through
the Church.

One sad result of our divisions may be remarked. In some
Churches of the Reformation the outlook and government were
duly de-clericalised in the sixteenth century, and later, in the
period of the Enlightenment, there followed a tendency to secular-
ise the ministry by assimilating it to the leadership of democratic
assemblies. In non-Reformed Churches there has been a danger of
forgetting the priesthood of the laity and confining it to those
ordained to the special ministry. It has been said epigrammatically
that 'what is lacking in the grocer is something of the priest, and
what is lacking in the priest is something of the grocer'. The whole
Church stands to gain from the movement in some Churches
which is recalling their bishops, pastors, elders and deacons from
an unhappy association with secular democratic leadership to
their ancient dignity.

This is the point at which to notice the revival of monastic discipline in non-Roman Churches, a revival of long standing in the Anglican Communion and now to be seen also among Reformed (Cluny and Iona) and Lutheran (Berneuchen). However different in form these efforts may be, they are all expressive of the feeling that 'movements', even liturgical movements, are not sufficient to reform the Church. What is needed is a rule and a life wholly devoted to bringing the Church back to its primitive sense of being the custodian of the means, of Sacrament as well as Word, entrusted to it by God for the salvation of mankind—a rule and a life which is the order of battle for the Kingdom of God. This is what monasticism has meant in all the history of the Church. Some feel that nothing short of a definite monastic order can attain this end. Others feel satisfied with obeying a rule and making 'retreats'. All try to live in real *koinonia* and thus to set an example to the whole Church.

(3) *Free or set prayers.* At first sight one might expect the growing consciousness of the Church as a living entity would favour the use of fixed forms of prayer for its corporate worship. To some extent this is so: there is, for example, a movement in that direction in the Swiss Reformed Churches, whence comes the statement that 'spontaneous prayers are at best self-deceit' because no prayer can be a real prayer if not prepared carefully in advance according to the feelings and needs of the congregation.[1] It is argued that public prayer is always 'set' prayer, the only difference being that sometimes it is 'set' by one minister a short time before the service, at other times it has been shaped out of the Church's long experience of human life.

But there are different kinds of Churches, and some hold that the use of free prayer corresponds to the nature of the 'gathered' church, where there may be a very close-knit fellowship in which minister and congregation know each other intimately. Here there is a different situation from that in many parish churches where there is need of an ordered and formal liturgical service for the whole parish community. Moreover, it does not follow that because the prayer is carefully planned, its form is therefore necessarily 'set'. We have had impressive evidence of the manner of preparation employed by an American Baptist minister. Before the service he would spend a time apart deeply sensing the needs

[1] V, b, p. 136 sup.

of his congregation as real and important in the sight of God, and taking them upon his soul. What words he used afterwards in the service were not planned, but what he said sprang from that preparation.

An argument in favour of set prayers, which is said to have some weight in Switzerland, is that it is a good thing to have the preacher's choice of subject controlled by the sequence of the liturgical year. It is urged, moreover, from Holland, that it helps a congregation to enter more freely and fully into a prayer if it knows what is coming; when the mind is put at ease by its familiarity with the verbal forms of prayer, the response of the worshipping will can become more complete.

As a matter of fact, there are not two but three types of service to be considered: (a) the use of a fixed liturgy; (b) the selection from authorised sources of prayers to suit the occasion; (c) extempore prayer, or prayer specially composed for the particular service. There need surely be no ground for perpetuating such controversies. There is room for all. The practical problem is that of deciding the appropriate place for each. When visiting the sick it is important to remember that there are some who, on hearing an extemporaneous prayer, are disappointed not to have 'the prayer of the Church'; for others the disappointment is caused by the prayer having 'nothing personal' in it. In public worship different occasions call for different types of service. A book dealing with Quaker silence and 'creative free prayer' has recently been much discussed among Anglicans in the U.S.A. A great deal of use of free devotional exercises is made in the Roman Catholic Church, especially by the monastic orders. The experience of the Church of South India, already referred to, is especially instructive. The liturgy was drawn up, and found a ready welcome in large sections of the Church which had not previously had the experience of sharing in a common prayer of the whole body. It was felt, however, that there should be left in the service a place for free expression in prayer, according to the local needs of different congregations, and this has been done.

(4) *Eucharistic worship*: *The 'Real Presence'*. It is of outstanding importance that throughout Christendom there is a reaction against the persistent error which sets the spiritual and the material in complete opposition to each other. What is being given up is

not only the idealism and modernism which preached retirement into the inner castle of the soul, devaluing all outward acts and exalting 'purely spiritual' changes. Pietism and revivalism are also involved in so far as they have laid exclusive emphasis on conversion and minimised the completeness of the rule of God over the whole life of those converted and reborn in faith. There is a growing conviction that faith implies things happening in the life of the whole man, body, soul and spirit, and that the practice of worship matters above all other things. It is not that the importance of the inner life is diminished, but it is set in the context of the human situation in which nothing can have its full importance which is not human all round, physical as well as spiritual. For God did not create merely spirits, He created men. He does not merely regenerate our souls, He regenerates us.

The mode of the Real Presence of Christ in eucharistic worship is the main question in debate in those Churches which are striving for a liturgical reformation. To quote Bishop Stählin: *Die Realpräsenz Christi ist das Grundgesetz aller Liturgie* ('The Real Presence of Christ is the foundation of all liturgy'.) Evidence coming from different parts of Christendom reflects two discoveries. (i) The ministry of the Word is no greater guarantee of spirituality than the ministry of sacraments. Its true character is lost sight of whenever 'word' is taken to refer to human efforts on the part of a preacher to offer his own thoughts as a means of edification. In the true administration of the Word God Himself imparts His gifts in a quasi-sacramental way, addressing man as a person, comprising body, soul and spirit. The work of the Holy Ghost, *Creator Spiritus*, is not confined to what we are pleased to call spiritual. (ii) The words 'magic' and 'magical' have in the past been used all too loosely and too irresponsibly as terms of reproach. The sin of magic does not lie in the association of divine power with matter, but in the attempt by man to control that power by material means in an ungodly and quasi-independent way. God the Creator alone in His creative activity calls the things which are not into being through His Spirit, and in His redemptive activity, His so-called 'new creation', restores them.

We are gripped by the faith which comes to us through our different traditions. We are familiar with the fact that by our differences we are prevented from participating together in the Body of Christ at the Holy Table of His Sacrament. Do we realise that the compulsive power of this same faith often prevents us from really hearing one another's sermons, from grasping what the preacher means us to understand? Here again there is a parallelism. Both modes of intercommunion are involved in real unity.

In spite of this widespread growth of a more favourable attitude towards sacramentalism, there still remains in some Churches acute controversy over the relative priority of Word and Sacrament. There are Churches in which this controversy is symbolised by the arrangement of the furnishings of the church building, the priority given to one or other being held to be indicated by the central position of pulpit or altar respectively. Speaking generally we can distinguish three views: (a) the substance of the worship is to be found in the sermon to which the Sacrament is an addition, a confirmation of the promise given in the proclamation of the Word; indeed there are many for whom a Eucharist without a sermon is a torso, an illegitimate divorcing of the ministry of the Sacrament from the ministry of the Word; (b) the Sacrament is the substantial act of worship: the reading and preaching of the Gospel as part of the whole liturgy heralds the coming presence of the Lord, and brings the challenge of that presence to the world; (c) sermon and Sacrament are complementary. The Sacrament is upheld by, and is the bringing to life of, our Lord's words of institution; the sermon, in which God Himself addresses the congregation, though through frail human channels, is an action by means of which God's grace reaches man.

We have become familiar with all three views, together with many variants of them. Here we note especially the point made by those who speak of the sacramental value of the preached Word, a value which is not exhausted by its pedagogic worth but involves a mystery, as do Baptism and the Eucharist. In these circles it is possible to count the preached Word among the sacraments, and we find this thesis so far apart as in the works of Karl Barth and of the Roman Catholic Dr. F. van der Meer. On the other hand there are those for whom the sacraments of Baptism and the Eucharist, at least, are unique in their significance for the life of faith, and those who find in the Eucharist the beginning and essence of all Christian worship. Thus Professor van der Leeuw has written: 'Holy Communion can never be the acme of worship, since it is itself worship.'[1] The Orthodox, while not

[1] XIV, p. 226 sup.

denying God's use of the sermon as a means of grace, agree with classical Reformed doctrine in defining sacraments in a way which makes the term inapplicable to preaching. As Dr. Zernov puts it: 'The sacraments are the corporate actions of the Church which actualise the Kingdom of the Holy Trinity by uniting in Christ and regenerating their participants. They achieve this object by sanctifying the matter with the Grace of the Holy Ghost (water, bread, wine, oil, chrism) and by charging with the redeeming power social relations (community and individual, husband and wife, ruler and ruled).'

It seems clear to us that the opposition of the Word to the Table is not biblical and, where it exists, must have arisen from some misunderstanding. It is, for example, a misunderstanding to think of an original simple and straightforward evangelical message having degenerated into sacramentalism. There was just as simple and just as straightforward an injunction of our Lord to break the bread and drink the wine. Perhaps the origin of the misunderstanding is to be found in the application of modern, humanist norms to the interpretation of ancient, biblical matter. That idealist conception of the Word as belonging entirely to an immaterial realm of pure spirit endangers not only the whole conception of sacraments but such essential Christian doctrines as creation and the Incarnation.

Whether or not preaching is regarded as sacramental, a broad outlook and profound insight are attained when the preached Word is regarded as sacramental in the sense of a channel of divine grace, the voicing of the uncreated Word of God by the created word of man, a real *kerygma*. This brings us to the point that all worship as such is sacramental in character: God makes use of human words and actions for the dispensation of His grace. We are reminded that the Orthodox Church thinks of all earthly worship as part of the continual worship of the whole Church led by saints and angels. And even where the sermon occupies a central place, as in the Swedish and Scottish Churches, it is designated an 'act' by Archbishop Brilioth, and as an 'essential and integral part of any solemn act of worship' by Dr. Maxwell.[1]

In many Churches, when for practical reasons the celebration of Holy Communion is omitted, the Sunday morning service

[1] V, a, p. 112 sup.

is called an Ante-communion service. Dr. Reed (American Lutheran) and Dr. Micklem (English Congregationalist) both suggest that the use of this word expresses the truth that the service is only a torso and that weekly Communion at the least should be the normative practice. On the other hand in some Scandinavian Lutheran churches this service is called High Mass. Elsewhere the use of the title ante-communion is objected to on two grounds. Historically it is said to mean the 'Mass of the Catechumens', which was followed by the 'Mass of the Faithful', celebrated after the catechumens had left: it should not be used for what has come to be a service complete in itself, substituted for the whole. And where there is no celebration of the Lord's Supper there may be a fellowship of prayer and thanksgiving and oblation which, though an insufficient substitute for sacramental action, makes the service more than ante-communion. In this connection mention must be made of the worship characteristic of the Friends, who have no liturgy and no outward sacrament, but remind us of the place that *charismata* occupied in the New Testament. Such a saying as 'true worship consists neither in words nor in silence, but in a humble dependence of the mind upon God'[1] deserves to be meditated upon by all of us. From more than one source we have had testimony to the effect that in the silence of a Quaker Meeting worshippers have experienced the presence of the Spirit of our Lord Jesus Christ as a real presence, corporately present in His earthly body the Church.

We must not, however, shut our eyes to the fact that in liberal circles there is still opposition to the liturgical movement just because it concentrates attention on the conception of worship as giving glory to God through man's self-offering and eucharistic adoration. It is maintained that man's primary purpose in worshipping should be to seek from God that which he needs to make him a better man. On this view, a church service should be a 'pentecostal meeting' in the sense of a gathering of the faithful assembled, like those in the Upper Room on the day of Pentecost, to receive the gift of the Spirit.

There is a danger that some advocates of the liturgical movement might so emphasise the aspect of oblation that all concern for the edification of the worshipper would disappear. Were this

[1] IX, p. 170 sup.

ever the case, protest would be justified. But not to the extent of denying first place to the glory of God. God must come first, or man's edification will not follow. 'Man's chief end is to glorify God and enjoy Him for ever.'

In technical liturgical discussions the centre of interest at the moment is the eucharistic prayer, and developments in practice are expected arising out of the illuminating historical studies of Dom Gregory Dix and Dom Eligius Dekkers, O.S.B. In particular we notice the attention given to the *epiklesis* in the eucharistic prayer. This may be due to the growing influence of the Eastern Orthodox Church on western liturgical studies. However that may be, discussion is rife concerning such questions as whether the *epiklesis* is distinct from or part of the actual consecration, and whether the Holy Spirit is invoked upon the elements or the worshippers or the whole sacramental act including the elements, the worshippers and the action itself.

Finally we have to observe that in the Eucharist we commemorate not only the Lord's death but the whole of His blessed appearance on earth, His resurrection, ascension and eternal glory. This, which has always been traditional in Orthodox worship, is made especially clear in the theology of Maria Laach, theology in which Dom Odo Casel and others speak of a mystery not repeated but re-presented. This theology contains great possibilities for future development, and perhaps opens up the most promising approach to some understanding between the Roman Catholic and non-Roman Churches. The papal encyclical *Mediator Dei* has at any rate not closed this door from the Roman side.

(5) *Eucharistic worship: sacrifice.* Another live issue is the sense, if any, in which eucharistic worship may rightly be regarded as sacrificial. It is well known that both Luther and Calvin rejected this conception on the ground that the sacrifice of Calvary had been offered once for all and was not to be repeated. But recent studies of both the New Testament and the patristic evidence have led to a re-opening of the question, and it is asked whether sacrificial language does not appear in a new light when the idea of re-presentation replaces that of repetition, and when communion and offering are seen as two sides of the same thing. The paper contributed by Bishop Hicks of Lincoln to the Edinburgh

B

Conference[1] suggests that one cannot receive the sacrifice of Christ without participating in it by offering oneself. This suggests the further thought that the Church, by offering itself, is offering the Body of Christ. In the Eucharist the celebrant is the risen Lord, uniting the members of His earthly Body to Himself in His offering of Himself to the Father.

Many post-Reformation liturgies contain little, if any, trace of this conception, and it is being asked whether this should not be remedied, and the sacrificial character of the service of Holy Communion receive a stronger emphasis. Doubt is cast upon the interpretation of the Epistle to the Hebrews traditional in Calvinist Churches, according to which the sacrifice at the heavenly altar is held to imply the abolition of sacrificial practice on earth. The Epistle is interpreted as justifying the idea, traditional in Orthodox liturgical worship, that in the Eucharist the crucified, risen and ascended Lord unites His worshippers with Himself in His eternal self-offering to the Father. In this connection we recall what was said earlier about recent questioning of the view that the fulfilment of the prophecies in Jesus Christ involved the abolition of the rites and ceremonies of the Old Covenant.

The sacrificial aspect of the Eucharist, interpreted along these lines, has a prominent place in the Report of the Edinburgh Conference.[2] We have called it a live issue, because strong objection to it is still to be found within the Reformed Churches, and also among evangelical elements in the Church of England. There are those who maintain that the only sense in which the word sacrifice can rightly be used of eucharistic worship is to denote our offering of praise and thanksgiving in gratitude for the blessings received from the one sacrifice of Christ on Calvary: in no sense whatever, according to this view, should we think of there being involved any offering of Christ to the Father, and nothing in either the words or actions of our liturgical practice should be suggestive of that idea. Here, undoubtedly, is a point at which the Lund Conference will have to discuss the doctrinal differences underlying differences in ways of worship.

In recent years attention has been called to the eschatological significance of the Eucharist, and here there is less ground for

[1] See *The Second World Conference on Faith and Order* (London, 1938, p. 325) and this volume, XII, c.
[2] op. cit., V, vi.

disagreement. The service not only carries back our minds in thankful remembrance of the Lord's death and resurrection, but also points us forward in confident anticipation of His future coming in glory. In St. Luke 14. 15 ff. He spoke of the age to come in terms of a heavenly banquet; the Last Supper He had with His disciples on earth was a foretaste of the eternal life of the Kingdom of God. So for the Church every celebration of the Eucharist is a realisation in the present of that eternal life.

This eschatological significance receives clear expression in the Eastern liturgies; and the following points are to be noticed in services of Reformed Churches in the West: (i) when the Words of Institution are read, the verse 'For as often as ye eat this bread, and drink this cup, ye do shew the Lord's death till he come' (I Cor. 11. 26) is often included; (ii) in the Order for the Lord's Supper used by the Reformed Church of France the Prayer of Intercession closes with a quotation from the *Didache* praying for the final in-gathering of the Church and ends with the words 'Come, Lord Jesus'; (iii) in the Church of Scotland Book of Common Order and the English Congregational Book of Public Worship the eucharistic Consecration Prayer includes a remembrance of the promise of the Lord's return in glory. In the words of Professor C. H. Dodd: 'Past, present and future are indissolubly united in the Sacrament. It may be regarded as a dramatization of the advent of the Lord, which is *at once* His remembered coming in humiliation and His desired coming in glory, both realised in His true presence in the Sacrament.'[1]

(6) *Baptism.* A clear understanding of the *sacramentum initii* should surely underlie any fundamental reconsideration of worship. We are reminded by Von Rabenau that all instruction in faith, the sermon as well as the catechism, is at bottom baptismal education, *traditio et redditio symboli.*

We have been informed that in the Protestant Churches of the United States, while the question of the sacrificial aspect of the Eucharist has hardly as yet become a live issue, questions concerning Baptism have long been matters of acute controversy, and are likely long to remain so. These same controversies are also very much alive in India. There are two points of dispute: (i) infant Baptism, and (ii) Baptism otherwise than by immersion.

[1] *The Apostolic Preaching*, p. 234.

Here it is clear that different liturgical practices reflect underlying doctrinal differences. We have to take into account the recent rejection of infant Baptism by Karl Barth, and the discussion going on in the Church of England on the relation of Baptism to Confirmation. It is the duty of this Commission to expose these doctrinal differences revealed by divergent liturgical practice; it must be left to others to examine them. We note that the Anglican Book of Common Prayer and many other forms provide services both for adult and infant Baptism, and sanction Baptism by pouring water as an alternative to immersion; that in the Reformed Church of France two services are being drawn up for adult and infant Baptism respectively. In Ceylon, where Baptists are taking part in the negotiations for a united Church, the proposal of a similar recognition of both practices is inevitably leading to consideration of its doctrinal implications.

III. *Agenda for Lund*

If the study of Ways of Worship is to contribute to the main purpose of the Conference on Faith and Order, it must lead us to focus attention on the extent to which it enables us more clearly to see the points at which differences provide obstacles to unity.

Our different habits of worship have their histories behind them. In some ways they express distinctive doctrinal positions; in others they are the product of cultural, psychological or temperamental factors. We need to distinguish two classes of difference:

(*a*) Different ways of worship which are compatible with one another in one Church.

(*b*) Different ways of worship based on incompatible doctrinal positions which prevent their co-existence in the same Church.

(*a*) It seems to us probable that where differences have their origin in cultural, psychological or temperamental factors, the various ways of worship which result need not be regarded as incompatible. Too often this is forgotten. It has been remarked in the course of our studies that where a church which has been accustomed to 'free worship' has come under the influence of the liturgical movement and changed over to the practice of using 'fixed forms' one result has often been the separating off of sections of the congregation who feel that the new habit has a cramping effect on their worship. These churches themselves have in the past often originated in such a feeling about the way of worship in churches from which they have come out. We wish to raise the question why it should be necessary for groups of Christians to be separated into different Churches in order to be able to attend either one or other of these types of service.

Evidence from the Younger Churches is to the effect that for them this is a vital issue. In lands where conversion from heathenism finds expression in ecstatic behaviour and utterance there is a tendency for sects to arise from the desire for such ecstatic worship, if it is discouraged in the existing Churches. We have been assured that it would be a great help to many of the Younger Churches if their converts could be told that in the judgment of the World Conference on Faith and Order they need not be required to choose between one of these ways of worship or the other.

We suggest, therefore, that where different ways of worship can be accounted for on cultural, psychological or temperamental grounds, there is no reason why they should be kept apart in separate Churches. Indeed, it may be that many Churches would find their life enriched by the inclusion of practices at present characteristic of others. The Church has to provide in its ways of worship for the evangelising of unbelievers as well as for the nurture of the faithful, and we are reminded of Anglo-Catholic parishes where the worship of the High Mass in the morning has been effectively supplemented in the evening by mission-preaching almost of a revivalist type. One good outcome of our work might be a self-examination by Churches of how they stand in this respect.

It is also possible that some different practices which at first sight seem incompatible because implying incompatible doctrines may turn out to be less irreconcilable than appears. We may instance rites and ceremonies which express a sacrificial element in worship, and are on that account regarded by some as incompatible with true Christian faith. When some who worship in this way explain what they mean by sacrifice, the doctrinal implications of the practice appear to be other than has usually been assumed by those who object to the practice. The points at issue being doctrinal rather than liturgical, we have not thought it right to enter into a discussion of them in our Commission.

Our part is to point out that in some cases diversities in liturgical practice may be assumed to imply doctrinal incompatibilities which are non-existent. Here again we suggest that the delegates of the Churches assembled at Lund might well give some consideration to the question how far differences in ways of worship are mistakenly taken to be adequate grounds for disunity on doctrinal grounds.

(b) There are, however, some differences in ways of worship which undoubtedly reflect doctrinal positions that appear to be stubbornly incompatible. In the Eastern Orthodox Church, for example, there are devotions connected with the Mother of our Lord and the saints which most Protestants are convinced should have no place in any true Church of God. From the Protestant side, again, there are in some forms of Catholic worship devotions connected with the sacrament of the Eucharist which they hold to imply doctrines so false that union with any Church which tolerates them is impossible. On the other hand, Catholic and Orthodox Christians would find it difficult, if not impossible, to seek union with Churches which allow the use of unfermented grape juice in the celebration of Holy Communion, or are careless about the disposal of elements consecrated but not consumed in that service. Doctrinal differences on the subject of Baptism are also extremely serious, as has been mentioned already.

Lack of time has prevented us from giving the attention to these problems which they deserve. We have not been able to compile a list of the points at which such obstacles to unity arise, and (as already observed) the discussion of the possibility of reconciling the doctrinal disagreements involved would not be the work of this commission. We suggest that those who read this report might well spend some time between now and 1952 in noting where these differences lie, for they provide precisely the kind of problem which the Conference on Faith and Order will be assembled to discuss.

Liturgy, it may be remarked in closing, is not something prepared and made by man, as a scientific text book, or even as a novel or a poem is made. The Church is a living body and its liturgical forms are the expression of its life. Liturgical renewal is neither emendation nor creation, but an attempt to enter or re-enter the liturgy which has been alive ever since the first liturgy of the Upper Room, from which springs all our sacramental worship, and the synagogue services which are the origin of our preaching-centred worship. Such an entry or re-entry has to be made in very different conditions. Decisions have to be taken which are not only doctrinal but existential. Liturgical experiments are attempts to decide where we stand in the Church of God, and what, being where we are, we have to do.

(Signed)
> G. VAN DER LEEUW, *Chairman*[1]
> HANS ASMUSSEN, *Vice-Chairman*
> WIEBE VOS, *Secretary*

[1] This report had the approval of Professor Van der Leeuw at the last meeting of the Commission: he had died before the final version was circulated to the members for their signatures.

Part One

THE ELEMENTS OF LITURGY

PREFACE

*

The main section of the Commission's study material is printed in this Part. The terms of reference to writers, set out below, were originally drafted in 1939-1940 in a preparatory Programme of Work for the Commission. When its work was finally taken up corporately in 1947, the programme was carefully revised at a preliminary meeting.

As a result of the common study the following section attained obvious prominence. It is designed to elicit a comparative study of what may be called the 'elements of liturgy'—the parts which together make up the structure of Christian worship.

The papers forming Part One were written with this part of the programme in mind. Certain writers, for reasons stated, found it necessary to vary their approach to the subject on theological grounds. Others have, in fact, indicated their answers to the main questions without direct reference to the syllabus, though some papers will be found to have followed it closely. In one case, that of the final chapter in this Part, it was mutually agreed that the terms of reference were not relevant to the principles of worship practised by the Religious Society of Friends.

TERMS OF REFERENCE
TO WRITERS IN PART ONE

I. *How far are the following expressive of Means and Ends in worship?*

    (A) THE WORD OF GOD
        (i) Reading of the Bible
        (ii) The sermon
        (iii) Instruction
        (iv) Liturgical forms

    (B) SACRAMENTAL WORSHIP
        (i) The Eucharist
        (ii) Baptism
        (iii) Other Sacraments

    (C) WHAT IS THE RELATION BETWEEN THESE TWO ELEMENTS?

II. *How far should worship provide for:*
        (i) Thanksgiving
        (ii) Penitence and Absolution
        (iii) Adoration
        (iv) Petition and Intercession for living and dead
        (v) Oblation or offering

III. *How far should worship make use of free prayer as well as of set forms of prayer?*

IV. *What is the relation between*

        (i) The worship of the local congregation
        (ii) The worship of the Church Universal
        (iii) The worship of the Church in Heaven?

V. *Are there other elements which should be included?*

VI. *How are these elements provided in the customary worship of the writer's Church?*

VII. *Are they held to be of equal importance, or should some be given special emphasis?*

VIII. *Is there any right sequence in which they should occur in a complete act of worship?*

I

ROMAN CATHOLIC

*

F. G. Van der Meer
(Holland)

Preliminary Remarks

1. This paper is confined to a statement of facts about the traditional practice of the Catholic Church. It cannot make proposals about how things ought to be. There certainly exists a very radical movement aiming at greater simplicity, plasticity and directness of liturgical forms; and drastic reformations may be expected before long from Rome. Some forms of worship may have become too complicated and others too rudimentary; but in its essentials worship can never be considered as being vitiated or in need of elementary reforms. Liturgy is not only by far the most *impressive* creation of Christian life, but also in a most eminent way *expressive* of tradition, and as such guaranteed, as a whole, by the Spirit.

Yet the essential core might appear to be relatively small; the saying, *lex orandi, lex credendi*, refers to dogmatic content and not to formal aspects. There is no question of absolute formal values (the strictly sacramental *formæ* excepted).

2. The following answers are an attempt to condense the ordinary view and give the *status quo*. But as neither the questions themselves nor the order in which they are put, nor the preoccupations that have inspired them, are familiar to the Catholic mind; they are given without any authority as a personal view.

3. I think I have to understand 'worship' as public worship. In the strict sense it implies the liturgy as contained in the official books and performed in public holy places; in a wider sense also some approved and publicly performed devotions.

4. The 'end' of worship is the service of honour of God, *latreia*. Its indirect end is the sanctifying of the faithful in Christ Jesus; in other words, the perpetuation in time and space of the mysteries

45

of Incarnation and Redemption, during the era of the Spirit, from the Ascension until the *Parousia*. In consequence its fundamental reality depends on the theandric personality of Christ and the *admirabile commercium*, in Jesus Christ, of the Church and the Father; its formal character can be defined as sacramental and eschatological. The indirect end is in its turn a means to *latreia*.

I. How far are the following expressive of means and ends of worship:

A. The WORD OF GOD, being the first source of Revelation, is the chief object of preaching, and also the almost exclusive source of the liturgical forms of praise and worship (especially the Book of Psalms: psalms of the Office, and nearly all the Introits, Graduals, Verses, Responsories, Anthems in the Office and during the Eucharist).

(i) *Reading of the Bible*. The reading of the lessons during the former part of the synaxis is not merely a didactic preliminary to the Eucharist, but fulfils the *prædicate omni creaturæ* and gives an authorised voice to the Word of God. The choice of the portions of Scripture appointed for any day emphasises certain parts of Scripture; and their immemorial arrangement, combined with the *Proprium de Tempore*, suggests the analogy of the Testaments and the headlines of spiritual exegesis. The whole actual utilisation of holy Scripture in worship has thus the value of an authorised interpretation. That does not imply that the lectionary cannot be modified; but the general emphasis, and the sense of proportion of which the actual system gives evidence, constitute definite values.

(ii) *Sermon*. The sermon has mostly been considered as a traditional commentary on Scripture, especially on the portion just read, and in harmony with the mystery recorded on the same day. Outside the Paschal cycle and the other annual festivals the sermon ought to touch the whole of Christian doctrine.

Only the bishops from their Cathedrae (and eminently the bishop of Rome from the first Cathedra) actually exercise the *magisterium ordinarium* when preaching; priests and deacons exercise it only as delegates.

It would be difficult to define exactly the objective element within the ministry of the Word; but certainly it fulfils the prophetic mission of the Church, and here as elsewhere the Spirit blometh where it listeth, and 'the Word of God is not bound'.

(iii) *Instruction*. Traditionally the catechetical instruction of candidates for Baptism is separated from the sermon for the initiated, and today is mostly given in private.

(iv) *Liturgical forms*. The public reading of Scripture implies some practices expressive of the veneration of the Church for the inspired writings: recitation in the languages of the early Church, lights, incense, kissing of the book, solemn entry, acclamations before and after the reading. Today the Latin lessons, a venerable and suggestive remnant of antiquity, are certainly an obstacle; the translations printed in the popular missals and even the reading of a translation afterwards from the pulpit (very rare in Latin countries) seem to be insufficient remedies. Some big dioceses in France (Paris, Bordeaux) have obtained licence to read simply in French, at least for catechumens. (See also sub (i) above.)

B. SACRAMENTAL WORSHIP is the *latreia par excellence*.

Sacraments in the strict sense are the tokens and instruments of sanctifying grace. As tokens, they are 'like a visible Word' (St. Augustine); as instruments, they effect grace *ex opere operato* when certain conditions are fulfilled (personal disposition, conformity to the Church, above all personal faith); some of them edify the Church, others sanctify the individual, one of them constitutes and informs the whole of public worship:

(i) *The Eucharist* is the centre of worship. It is the daily representation, under the sacramental veils, of the Passion, Resurrection and Ascension of the Lord. As an anamnesis it renders the mystery of redemption present. As a sacrifice, it is identical with the sacrifice of the cross. As a sacrament, it unites the faithful with Christ and with each other, and, by participation in His Body and Blood, edifies and informs the mystical Body of the Church. As a token, it signifies the unity of peace and charity of the Church, resulting in the communion of each and all with one Lord in one undivided Church (*Vinculum unitatis, signum caritatis*). It is a token of Passion and Resurrection both in Christ and in the members of His Body. It is the chief *latreia* on earth—a *sacrificium laudis*, and the *gratiarum actio par excellence*. The Eucharist perpetuates the *opus redemptionis: quoties hujus hostiae commemoratio celebratur, opus nostrae redemptionis exercetur;* at the same time it points to the consummation of this age, being a pledge of immortality and of the resurrection of the body. (Even the cosmic aspect, so stressed in the Eastern Church, cannot be neglected: the cosmos by the *nova creatio* being the setting of the final resurrection.) On the other hand, the Eucharist realises the worship in spirit and truth: it is the gift by which *venit ut tibi a fidelibus tuis digne et laudabiliter serviatur*. And so the two moments, taken together, result in a supreme *latreia*. The Church in the unity of the Spirit offers, through her Lord, her thanksgiving to the Father, *donec veniat*. It is in the Eucharist that the restoration of all things to Christ is effected.

(ii) *Baptism* makes the individual a member of the Church; in water and Spirit, through faith, he is justified and baptised into Christ, dies to his old self and rises to a Christ-like life. This initial participation in the redemption has been officially linked to the Easter celebration of the Redemption. In practice, children are regularly baptised soon after birth in the presence of their god-fathers and family only. The other sacraments of initiation— confirmation and communion—are now postponed. The first, confirmation, finishes the initial regeneration by making the reborn partake in Christ's anointing by the Spirit. (Penance is a private and second 'emergency-baptism'.)

In brief mention of the remaining sacraments, Order is the instrument for the perpetuation of priesthood and of the apostolic succession. Matrimony elevates the state of marriage to a reality expressing the supreme *agape* between Christ and His Bride. Extreme Unction is a sacramental aid to the dying. As compared with the Eucharist, the relation of these other sacraments to worship seems remote; it varies with their more or less social character. The *sacramentalia* instituted by the Church borrow their value only from the mighty intercessory prayer of the Church. Notwithstanding their great differentiation, sacraments and sacramentals both tend to the sanctification of the elect, and thus to the glory of God.

C. THE RELATION BETWEEN WORD AND SACRAMENT

Sacraments being effective symbolical actions and word-tokens alike, they reconcile the polarity between word and action, good

tidings and grace, prophecy and redemption. They actualise the
realities announced in the Word. In the ministry of the Word
the revelation remains actual (especially when the Word is read
during service); in the sacraments the Incarnation and the
Redemption become actually present, under sacramental veils.
Typical worship centres in the latter; yet Word and Sacrament
are never completely separated from each other. Worship emphasises the sacramental efficacy of revelation: preaching lays
stress on its content. Yet the Word becomes visible in sacramental
worship; as expressed in human language, the Word itself can
be called, with Augustine, a lesser sacrament.

II. How far ought worship to provide for:

(i) *Thanksgiving*. See sub-section B (i): Eucharist. Actually
worship is focused in the Great Thanksgiving (from *Sursum corda*
to the Amen after the Doxology). The Office can be conceived
as a very elaborate framing of thanksgiving, inasmuch as its
chief note is *officium laudis*.

(ii) *Penitence and Absolution*. Sacramental absolution follows
individual confession. Only in cases of extreme necessity, as for
example during actual warfare, is it given in public and in common. Deprecatory absolutions are often pronounced in the name
of the Church, during the office, and before the distribution of
Holy Communion. Penitence in the sense of mortification has
always been part of Christian life; it has informed great parts of
the ecclesiastical year. Public reconciliation of sinners is a ceremony yet to be found in the *Pontificale*; penitential admonitions
are a regular part of monastic observance. The practice of fasting
has diminished considerably. The same cannot be said about
mortification in other forms; but the Catholic conception of the
value of the ascetic life has no direct relation to worship.

(iii) *Adoration* is the chief end of Eucharist and Office alike: also
of many non-liturgical and semi-public devotions such as the
adoration of the Blessed Sacrament.

(iv) *Petition and Intercession for living and dead*. Prayers for living
and dead have a traditional place in the eucharistic prayer, together with the commemoration of the holy martyrs and other
saints, which must be separated from prayers for them. The
Council of Trent has declared that the eucharistic sacrifice is

offered 'also as a propitiation for the quick and the dead'. Prayers
for living and dead are a substantial part of the Office, and a
prominent feature in semi-public devotions.

Intercession being a privilege of every member of the Body of
Christ, and a consequence of the communion of saints, the Church
intercedes herself in Christ's name for living and dead; she demands the intercession of her saints, above all that of the Blessed
Virgin, who is her own prototype.

(v) *Oblation or offering*. In the Eucharist all the members of the
Church, present or absent, partake in the sacrifice of their Lord.
The collective 'amen' after the Canon expresses their participation. The offering of material gifts may have been a means of
expressing a sacrificial attitude. Very rightly the people prefer to
concentrate on the spiritual side, and to give their material alms
in secret.

III. How far ought worship to make use of free prayers as well
as set forms?

Since Hippolytus (*circa* 218) established a preference for set forms,
these have been in use throughout East and West, and almost
exclusively since the beginning of the fifth century (parts of
Africa excepted). New formulas have been constantly added,
mostly in strict consonance with the classical palæo-Christian
prototypes of the older sacramentaries, but one may say that the
devotional additions made after the Council of Trent are far from
generally admired.

As for extempore prayer, since time immemorial it has been
thoroughly alien to the traditional cult. In practice, free prayers
publicly said are very rare (poetic outbursts such as the '*saetas*'
during processions in Spain, and the rhetorical prayers from
Italian pulpits, can hardly be considered as parts of worship). Free
prayer among Catholics is personal, fervent, and silent. Among
our people there is no demand whatsoever for loud extempore
praying by the priest; on the contrary, rather an outspoken horror,
attributable perhaps to custom, to temperament, or to instinctive
taste. The question is one which may stand open for discussion.
Devotional prayers can be read publicly when officially approved.
But these and others, especially in old-fashioned popular prayer
books, are often very far from the decency and austerity of the
official Missals and Breviaries. Today in the northern countries

the translations of the latter are in many hands; those of southern Europe prefer personal silent praying or just assisting at Mass. Even the Russians follow far more of their old liturgy than is generally supposed.

(iv) What is held to be the relation of the worship of the local congregation, the Church Universal, and the Church in Heaven?

In the Holy Eucharist, according to the sacramental modality, the identity of sacrifice unites the terrestrial and the Heavenly Altar with Golgotha. The local synaxis is the visible realisation of the Church Universal; it communicates with all its sister-churches on earth, with the Church as a whole on earth, and with the expectant and the heavenly Churches (communion of saints). Worship on earth is a modest image of the heavenly liturgy, and both are connected through the one Lord on heavenly and earthly altars. Hence the preface says: *et ideo cum angelis et archangelis . . . hymnum gloriae tuae concinent; cum quibus [celestibus spiritibus] et nostras voces ut admitti jubeas deprecamur, sine fine dicentes: sanctus;* compare the *Cheroubicon* in the Greek liturgy: *Hoi ta cheroubim mustikōs eikonizontes.*

(v) Are there any other elements of worship that must be considered?

Among minor aspects the following may be noted: supplication and propitiation; veneration and invocation of saints; penitential discipline as a whole.

(vi) Are these elements of equal importance?

The Eucharist stands above all else. Pure *latreia* must outweigh supplication and intercession; hence the '*gloria laudis*' gives character to the whole of divine worship, most especially in the Office.

(vii) Is there any right sequence in which these elements should follow one another in a service?

The traditional order of a Dominical Service can be considered as a definite and classical value.

(a) *Ministry of the Word*, and Prayer

    Introit
    Kyrie
    Gloria in Excelsis
    Collect

> Lessons from Old and New Testaments (Prophet and Apostle)
> Sung Psalm with Alleluia
> Homily or Sermon (which cannot be too biblical)

(b) *Sacrifice*

> Disposition of the Elements
> The Eucharistic Prayer, comprising:
>> Anaphora
>> Anamnesis of our Lord's mysteries
>> Epiclesis of the Holy Spirit
>> Intercession for living and dead
>> Commemoration of the Virgin, and of the Saints
>> Doxology
>> Amen
> Communion (with Pater Noster)
> Thanksgiving
> Dismissio

The Office frames the Eucharist, and follows the pattern of the daily hours, the Christian week, the Year of Grace. In practice it will be the privilege of a limited number of communities, though secular priests say the Office privately. The people rarely assist in it. Yet great parts of the actual treasure may prove to be of temporal value only, and the Church may pour the old wine into new bottles. *Deus providebit.*

II

ORTHODOX

*

Georges Florovsky
(United States of America)

1. Introductory

Christianity is a liturgical religion. The Church is first of all a worshipping community. Worship comes first, doctrine and discipline second. The *lex orandi* has a privileged priority in the life of the Christian Church. The *lex credendi* depends upon the devotional experience and vision of the Church. On the other hand, Christian worship is itself to a large extent dogmatic—a worshipping witness to the truth of Revelation. The lyrical element in the worship has a subordinate place. This liturgical emphasis of Christianity is especially conspicuous in the Eastern Orthodox tradition. In this respect the Eastern Church is, however, but a faithful heir of Christian antiquity. In fact, most of the liturgical structures and devotional habits of the Christian East were stabilised at an early date, and have been loyally preserved and continually handed down through generations. It is a plausible hypothesis that the word 'Orthodoxy' in the Eastern use means primarily not 'right opinion' (as it is usually interpreted in the West), but rather 'right glory', i.e. precisely, right worship. In any case, in Eastern tradition, the unity of doctrine and worship is strongly stressed. The doctrine itself is here not so much a doctrine taught in the class, as a doctrine proclaimed in the temple —theology speaks more from the pulpit than from the desk. It assumes therefore a more existential character. Worship, on the other hand, is free from emotionalism. Sobriety of the heart is its first requirement. The fulness of the theological thought of the Church is thrown into the worship. This is possibly the most notable distinctive mark of the Eastern tradition.

2. Public and Private Worship

There are, in the Gospel, two passages concerning prayer which seem to guide us in opposite directions. On one hand, in the Sermon on the Mount, our Lord was teaching the multitudes to pray 'in secret'. It had to be a solitary prayer, 'when thou hast shut thy door'—man alone with his Heavenly Father (Matt. 6. 5 ff.). Yet, on the other hand, on another occasion our Lord was stressing the strength of a joint and corporate prayer, 'if two of you shall agree on earth as touching any thing that they shall ask' (Matt. 18. 19-20). Is there any conflict or contradiction between these two different praying attitudes? Or, rather, do they belong together and are possible only together? Paradoxically, they presuppose each other. One has to learn to pray alone, bringing all his needs and infirmities before the Father, in an intimate and personal intercourse. Only those who are trained by thus praying this solitary prayer can really meet each other spiritually and join together in what they are going to ask for each other from their common Father in heaven. Common prayer obviously presupposes personal training. Yet, personal prayer is possible only in the context of the community. Nobody is Christian by himself but only as a member of the Body. Even in the solitude, 'in the chamber', a Christian prays as a member of the Church. And, of course, it is in the Church that he learns his devotional practice and rules. Both forms of prayer are more than complementary, they are organically linked together, as two inseparable aspects of the same devotional action. Each without the other may be even dangerous and misleading: solitary prayer can degenerate into individualistic pietism and emotionalism, ecstatic and disruptive; and when those who have had no previous private training try 'to join' with others the result may be not a true community prayer, but rather a crowd prayer (or a sect prayer), not a prayer of a community of persons, but of an impersonal multitude—or else, mere formality and hypocrisy. It is therefore the rule of the Church that the faithful should prepare themselves for the corporate prayer by their personal devotions in the chamber.

One begins to pray at home and then goes to the church. There praying persons meet and discover each other, and can join spontaneously in the act of common adoration or humble petition. Strictly speaking, the phrase 'private devotion' is a misleading and unfortunate term—it may give an impression that it is, as it were, a private affair left to the human individual's discretion. On the contrary, it is an obligatory preparation, imposed upon the indi-

viduals by the strict law of the ecclesiastical discipline. There are
definite rules for these 'private devotions', and very little room is
left to improvisation. Again, obviously it is much more than mere
preparation. Even 'in the chamber' a Christian is expected to pray
not only for himself: he is never alone on his knees before the
Father, and the Heavenly Father is not only his Father but the
Father 'of us all'; a Christian must be aware of the fact that many
others are also on their knees at the same time before the same
Heavenly Father, and each must bring before God not only his
private or personal needs, or requests, or sorrows. Personal prayer
itself should be 'catholic', i.e. inclusive and universal. The praying
heart is to be enlarged in order to embrace all needs and sorrows
of the whole suffering humanity. And only in this spirit can individuals truly meet each other as 'brethren', i.e. as living members
of the Church, and truly 'agree' concerning things they are about
to ask in common from the Lord. On the other hand, it can be
said that corporate worship is also a personal obligation, a personal
responsibility of everyone who shares in the common treasury of
redemption.

Accordingly, in the Orthodox Church there are definite ordered
forms of morning and evening prayers which every member of
the community is supposed to use regularly. They are collected
in a book called *Canonicon*: it is a book of rules and patterns. Of
course, it is only an elementary guide, to be supplemented by
spontaneous expansion. The main emphasis is, however, not on
the recitation of ordered formularies as such, but on the spiritual
concentration of the believer. 'When you awake, before you
begin the day, stand with reverence before the all-seeing God.
Make the sign of the Cross and say: In the name of the Father,
and of the Son, and of the Holy Spirit. Amen. Having invoked
the Holy Trinity, keep silence for a little, so that your thoughts
and feelings may be freed from worldly cares. Then recite the
following prayers without haste, and with your whole heart . . .'
This is the preamble of the morning rule. Two features can be
observed at once. First, spiritual detachment and concentration.
Second, a definite dogmatic emphasis from the outset: Invocation
of the Trinity, the sign of the Cross, pointing to the mystery of
redemption. On the whole, no rapture or emotion. Rather, stand
still. Prayers which follow are selected rather in order to remind
one of those topics which should naturally be considered at every

action of devotion or at least are not to be neglected in the daily meditation. The rule may be abridged if necessary. The rubric at the close of the morning rule reads as follows: 'It is preferable to say only a few of the suggested prayers, with attention and zeal, rather than to recite them all in haste and without due concentration.' One can select a rule suitable to his particular conditions, even a very short one, but then this rule should be kept rigidly, never be abolished or abridged by licence. It is a point of obedience and self-discipline. Spontaneous prayer comes only after training. This training is a safeguard against subjectivism in devotion.

Prayer is not just a recitation of settled formulas, but first of all a conversation with the living God. It may be even silent. Here are some typical advices concerning prayer, formulated by a saintly Russian bishop, Theophanes (1815-1894), who is regarded as a competent and expert writer on the problems of spiritual and devotional life. From the outset he suggests that in order to pray to God truly and efficiently, one should prepare or *rehearse* the prayers in advance. One has to study the text of the prayer book and to be sure that he 'understands' and 'feels' every word and every turn of the phrase, to meditate over every word and to grasp their full meaning. And only then should one begin to pray. The problem of prayer is, how to keep attention, i.e. to realise the presence of God and not to be distracted by external impressions and worldly cares. For prayer is essentially contemplation. The words of the prayer must be so recited that they may speak to the soul. It may happen that a particular word catches attention, then one has to stop and listen, and not to rush further through the rest of the text. Yet all this is but a first step. Prayer books are indispensable in the early stages, but they are meant only for beginners; they are just primers of devotion. No progress can be ever made if the first step be taken in a wrong direction; but one should not be satisfied with the one step. We begin to learn a language by memorising phrases and responses, often from the book. Yet, sooner or later, we begin simply to speak. It applies to the prayer also. We learn first some pattern-formulas, some phrases and turns. But sooner or later we have to begin to speak to God spontaneously. The purpose of training is to enable a person to enter into a conversation with God. Therefore prayer cannot be restricted to certain hours or some particular occasions.

It should become a habit or an attitude. In other words, the
Christian has to feel himself permanently in the presence of God.
This is the goal of devotional training. The goal of prayer is precisely to be with God always. Then the Spirit starts speaking in
the heart, joyful and burning. How far is all this from dead
formalism and 'ritualism', so often imputed to the Eastern tradition. Yet there is no room for an arbitrary 'improvisation'. It is
the Spirit that improvises. But it only happens in the soul prepared
and trained by a long and steady devotional exercise. As St.
Seraphim of Sarov (1759-1833) puts it: 'We must pray only until
God the Holy Spirit descends . . . when He comes to visit us, we
must cease to pray . . .'

There is no 'quietism' in this devotional practice. The 'search
after Spirit' is to be combined with a hard work. Prayer is to be
a spiritual formation of the new man within the old Adam.
Spiritual detachment from 'this world' does not necessarily presuppose physical separation or retirement. 'This world' is rather
'the world of passions'. And the purpose of devotional training
is precisely to overcome one's dependence upon impersonal
'passions' and to secure freedom of the 'spiritual' personality.
Idleness is an ultimate vice and sin. Nor is there any taint of
Pelagianism: 'good works' are not means of salvation, they are
rather fruits of obedience; they are a bounden duty, not a merit.
Prayer itself is a 'work', it requires the whole activity of man. Yet
the goal is to disappear in one's selfish human personality and to
be reborn as a vehicle of the Spirit. Prayer means one's dedication
to God alone. In the Eastern tradition the term 'prayer' is given a
very large and inclusive meaning. 'Teach me how to pray. Pray
Thou Thyself in me' (from the private devotions of Philaret,
Metropolitan of Moscow, 1782-1867).

Prayer should not be identified with petition or supplication.
To pray does not mean 'to ask', although it means always 'to
seek'. There are levels and degrees. One begins with supplication
and intercession, by articulating his needs and deficiencies before
God. Again, it is a prayer of beginners. Thanksgiving comes next.
It is a higher level, but not the highest. It leads ultimately to the
disinterested praise and adoration of God. When one comes face
to face with His unfathomable splendour and glory and praises
Him for His majesty, without even mentioning the benefits He
bestows upon the world—then the chorus of men joins that of

the angels, who do not ask or even thank at all, but continually praise Him: 'Holy, Holy, Holy.' Thus, in the Eastern tradition, prayer is ultimately theocentric. Eastern tradition admits no ultimate discrimination: it assumes an ultimate equality of all believers, clerical and lay; there is but one identical goal for all and everyone —the personal communion with God, through Jesus Christ, in the power of the Holy Spirit. The rule of prayers is the same for all. In fact, *Canonicon* was originally a monastic book. The only difference is the difference in stages of a spiritual ascent. Prayer itself belongs to the process of salvation: the main benefit of our redemption is assessed and appropriated precisely in a praying communion with God. The forms may vary, but the purpose is ever the same.

3. Sacraments and Corporate Worship

Personal prayer is an initiation into the mystery of the Church. This mystery is disclosed in the corporate and sacramental worship of the Church. The centre of the corporate worship is the Eucharist. It is *the* Sacrament, or (to use the authentic Eastern term) *the Holy Mystery*. It is a double mystery, or a mystery of the 'Whole Christ', the Head and the Body—the mystery of the Lord and the mystery of the congregation (the term is used e.g. by Nicolas Cabasilas in his remarkable 'commentary' of the Holy Rite). The early custom of daily celebration (attested e.g. by St. Basil the Great) has been still kept in many parish churches and monasteries, even in the period of a temporary spiritual decay (in the age of Enlightenment during the eighteenth century and till the later decades of the nineteenth). Yet Communion was rather infrequent, possibly not more than three times a year. Nevertheless, Sunday attendance was regarded as almost obligatory. Of course the non-communicating attendance does not allow for an adequate comprehension of the meaning of the Sacrament. It would not be an exaggeration to state that in the personal practice of believers the Eucharist lost to some extent its central place. This was a result of an increasing secularisation of the laity. 'Personal' was degenerating into 'private'. The corporate approach to public worship was lost, or replaced by a sort of pietistic and even aesthetic individualism. Of course the clergy was also guilty of neglect. Too often it simply complied with the changed attitude and did not, as it should, enforce a more adequate conception of

sacramental worship. There was an obvious divorce between dogmatic teaching and devotional practice, a kind of devotional
'psychologism'. Yet, already in the course of the nineteenth century (at least in Russia), a new move began towards a restoration
of the centrality of the Eucharist, not only in the practice of the
Church but also in personal practice. This is to say Communion
was gradually becoming more frequent. In Russia it was connected with the vigorous teaching and practice of Father John
Sergieff, known as 'Father John of Crönstadt' (1829-1908). Later
on, in this century, a similar movement was initiated in Greece
(usually connected with the 'Zoë Movement', a brotherhood of
lay-theologians). Both movements were connected with a more
adequate and accentuated teaching of the Eucharist and the
Church. The true 'sacramentalism' in the Church depends ultimately upon a 'doctrinal' orientation of the devotional life.
'Sacraments' lose their appeal when 'piety' is dissociated from
'dogma'. In fact, sacraments are a part and an article of the dogma.
A growth of emotionalism ('pietism' or psychologism) is always
detrimental to a true sacramental balance in the Church.

The Eucharist is a true revelation of Christ, an 'image' of His
redeeming life and work. It sets before the congregation in symbolic utterances and gestures the whole life of the Lord, from the
Bethlehem manger to the Mount of Olives and Calvary, including
also His Resurrection and Ascension, and 'pre-figuring' or antici-
pating His second and glorious coming. This 'symbolic' representation is not merely an impressionistic reminder of the remote
events, but a true 're-presentation'—a 'making present' again. This
has been a traditional teaching in the East, at least since St. John
Chrysostom. There is no repetition, for no repetition of the Last
Supper and Calvary is possible. But the Eucharist of Christ is
more comprehensive than the 'historic' Last Supper. Mystically it
till continues and is open to new generations of believers, in
the unbroken unity of the one Body of Christ which is the
Church. The sacrifice of Christ was universal and all-inclusive.
At every celebration believers are, as it were, taken back to the
Upper Room, precisely at the moment of the Last Supper. It is
to say that essentially every celebration is the Last Supper itself.
The mystery (i.e. the 'sacrament') is one and ever the same, even
as the sacrifice is one, and the table ever one. Christ Jesus is
present, both as the Minister of the Sacrament, and as the Victim

—'who offers and is offered'. He is the ultimate and perennial Minister of the Church, the true High-Priest of the New Testament, 'in His blood'. This 'sacramental realism' explains that august place which is given to the Sacrament in the life of the Church. It is the spring and the root of her spiritual existence.

The complementary aspect of the mystery must, however, be recognised at the same time. The Eucharist is also the great Christian witness, a witness of the Church to the new fellowship in the redeemed community and in the Redeemer. The Church is not passive, even while receiving the gift of redemption. The mystery of the Church is precisely in that Christ dwells and abides in the faithful and they, by faith, dwell and abide in Him. The Church carries on and continues the ministry of redemption, or rather Christ is carrying on and continuing it through and in the Church. To 'follow Christ' is not an ethical commandment only. It implies a mystical identification of the members with the Head. As the mystery of the Church, the Eucharist is, in a sense, the realisation of the Church. The Church is the growing 'fulness' of Christ. It grows precisely through the sacraments. The unity of the Church is constituted by the unity of the Spirit, and faith is but a recipient of the grace. The Church's unity is the gift of God, not a human achievement—yet it implies also an active response of the redeemed. As a sacred rite, the Eucharist is an act of 'common worship', a true 'agreement' of many to stay and to pray 'together'. The name 'liturgy' (which in the Eastern use is restricted to the eucharistic service) itself suggests precisely *a common action*. It *is* an 'action', and not just a word. It is most significant that all eucharistic prayers are composed in the plural, including the prayer of consecration (*anaphora*), which is recited by the celebrant alone, but obviously in the name and on behalf of the faithful. For indeed the whole congregation is supposed 'to con-celebrate' with its pastor (or with the bishop). This fact is considerably obscured in the contemporary practice by the secret recitation of the *anaphora*. This practice is of comparatively late origin (in any case after the age of Justinian, under whom it was formally prohibited both by the canon and secular law, as definitely impious). It does not conform with the rite itself, because the congregation (or the choir) is still singing aloud certain parts of the continuous prayer which are incomprehensible outside of their context. Even the exclamations (*ekphoneseis*) of the celebrants are obscured by this manner of recitation. Yet the rite itself is still unchanged, and it clearly implies the corporate character of the prayer. It is in the name of the whole Church that the celebrant says persistently: *We pray*. This *we* in the liturgical use has a double meaning: (1) It betokens the unity of the assembled Church, the undivided fellowship of all those who pray. 'Thou, who hast given us grace at this time with one accord to make our common supplication unto Thee' . . . And this 'accord' is not a mere mixture of many private and separate prayers. The true accord presupposes some mutual identification of those who join and 'agree'. One is expected to pray not as a self-centred individual, but as a member of the Body, of the mystical fellowship in Christ . . . (2) The liturgical plural has another and deeper significance and connotation: it points to the universal fulness and unity of the Church. For every liturgy is celebrated in communion with the whole Church catholic and universal, and in the name of the whole Church. And spiritually in every celebration the whole Church takes an invisible yet very real part—'the whole company of heaven'. This unity extends not only to all space, but to all time also, i.e. it includes all generations and ages. Therefore the departed are commemorated at every celebration. It is not only a remembrance, not only a witness of our human sympathy and love, but rather an insight into the mystical fellowship of all believers, living and departed, in Christ, the common Risen Lord. In this sense the Eucharist is the mystery of the Church, or, to be quite accurate, the mystery of the whole Christ. The Eucharist is not only an expression of a human brotherhood, but above all of the divine mystery of redemption. It is primarily an image of the divine deed. The Eucharist is thus essentially a doctrinal witness, and therefore an acknowledgment of the grace of God. The whole rite has a Godward orientation.

All sacraments and sacramental actions in the Church are ultimately related to the eucharistic office. Originally, all of them were performed within the framework of the divine liturgy. All of them are concerned with the membership in the Church. It is strongly emphasised in the undivided rite of Baptism and Chrism. The mystery of marriage is related to the mystery of the Church ('in Christ and the Church'). The sacrament of penance has a special importance in the devotional rule of the Church. It implies two different features. On one hand, there is a continuous spiritual guidance given by a Father Confessor to his 'spiritual children'. On the other, there is a special rite of confession (and spiritual examination of particular cases) and absolution. In present practice, when Communion is very infrequent, absolution (at least in the Russian Church) is regarded as an indispensable prerequisite for Communion. But in principle the sacrament of penance is not directly connected with the Eucharist. Yet, it is concerned directly with the membership in the Body, and this is clearly stated in the concluding prayer of the Russian rite: 'Reconcile and unite him unto thy Holy Church, through Jesus Christ, our Lord' . . . It is presumed that a disorderly life and any violation of the Christian rule of life does somehow compromise and reduce the spiritual status of believers, and therefore should be remedied by a solemn action of the Church. Both elements in the rite are of importance: *confession* itself, i.e. a self-examination of the penitent, his repentance and contrition, or his 'change of mind' (*metanoia*), and *absolution* by the minister. The penitent must be inwardly 'prepared' for absolution, 'lest, having come to a physician, he departs unhealed'. For the sacramental absolution is not only a declaration of forgiveness but primarily a spiritual cure.

4. *Christian Instruction and the Preaching of the Word*

The Orthodox Church is commonly supposed to be, as it were, over-liturgical and to have underestimated the importance of the preaching of the Word. This is an obvious misunderstanding. First, the rite itself is basically the preaching of the Word, an emphatic proclamation of the Good News. The main emphasis is on divine action. The Eucharist is the centre of the corporate or community worship. It is framed in a set of 'offices', which are supposed to be said by all members of the Church regularly, although the order itself grew originally in monastic communities. In old days these offices were very often said daily by the devout laymen as well, since they do not necessarily require the participation of a priest. In actual practice all of them belong, however, to the order of public worship, conducted openly in the church by ordained ministers. Yet, in principle, they can be said by lay people too, and usually are said privately by monks (who are not in holy orders). There is a special book, ordering daily offices throughout the liturgical year. It is called *Typicon*, i.e. literally a 'book of patterns'. The *Typicon* used in the Russian

Church goes back to the rule of the monastery of St. Sabbas in Palestine (and is called therefore the Jerusalem *Typicon*). In actual practice this order is variously abridged and adapted to local conditions, and only in monasteries is kept almost in full. The principle seems to be the same as with the 'private devotions'—it is better to say with zeal and attention some parts of the office than to go through the entire rite negligently. What is of primary importance is that all offices are primarily a proclamation of the Good News. They have an emphatically didactic and doctrinal character. The skeleton of the order is scriptural, and most of the hymns and collects are biblical in their inspiration and content. Biblical events are largely quoted or referred to. On the whole, there is much more of a solemn epic than of subjective lyricism, in spite of a definite poetical exaltation. The text of the hymns and collects and the symbolism of the ritual gestures and actions concurrently point to the biblical story of salvation—creation and fall, the Old Testament training and preparation, prophetic typologies, the incarnation and the whole life of Christ, and Pentecost. The amount of instruction is possibly excessive. Prayers, in the strict sense, are not the most conspicuous element of the rite. The main emphasis is on the mighty deeds of God . . . Secondly, readings from the Scripture are incorporated into all offices. The Psalter is naturally regularly recited. It is to be read in full during the week (in Lent twice, the readings being longer). The New Testament is given more space than the Old. In the *Typicon* it is ordered that every day after Vespers a portion of the New Testament should be read to the congregation, and the whole of the New Testament is to be covered in the course of the liturgical year. This is obviously a kind of preaching. At Mattins an exegetical sermon of St. John Chrysostom or some other Father is to be read. All this is in addition to the regular lessons at the Liturgy. Unfortunately these rubrics are very seldom followed, except in the monasteries. But the mind and intention of the Church are expressed in the rule and not in the fact of its neglect. The reading of Patristic writings belongs to the structure of the offices. It is a kind of preaching, 'preaching from the book'. In old days the rubrics were more rigidly kept and the amount of instruction was very considerable. There is a growing tendency to restore this ancient practice and to combine it with the oral preaching.

The sermon, in the technical sense of the word, is regarded as an integral part of corporate worship, especially on Sundays or on special occasions. In the mediaeval churches the pulpit (or the *cathedra*) was one of the most conspicuous parts of the church building (it is still the same in modern churches in Greece and in the Balkans). Yet preaching in modern times has lost something of its early importance. There was no doctrinal reason behind the change. The chief reason was rather negligence on the part of the congregation. There was an obvious revival of preaching in Russia in the nineteenth century, and many prominent preachers can be mentioned by name. There is a vigorous revival of preaching in Greece at the present time where the laity seem to take more interest in preaching. Unfortunately there is a tendency to develop preaching along non-liturgical lines. Sermons very often have little connection with the rite itself, and usually it is done deliberately in order to make the sermon more actual and to bear on contemporary topics and interests. At the Liturgy the sermon is, most unfortunately, shifted towards the end of the service, and becomes rather an addition to the service, instead of being its integral part, closely related to the scriptural lessons. Still, there is a notable improvement in this matter also. In many churches the sermon is restored to its normal and traditional place, following immediately upon the lessons and becoming more exegetical. There is also extra-liturgical preaching.

On the whole, corporate worship in the Eastern Church is meant to be above all a faithful witness to the mighty deeds of God, and not an expression or exhibition of pious emotions. There is much serenity and solemnity about the whole rite and order. The ultimate purpose is to put man before God and to impress upon him all that God had done for him. In a sense, the worship itself is included in the continuous story of salvation.

5. *Summary*

The main distinctive mark of the Eastern Orthodox worship is its traditional character. Devotional forms and manners of the Early Church are preserved, or rather have been continuously used for centuries, without any major changes. For an outsider they may seem obsolete and archaic, and the whole system of worship can be mistaken for a lifeless piece of antiquity. None the less, in the process of its continuous use the rite was kept alive, and is still a natural means of a spontaneous expression of the religious life. It is felt, within the tradition, to be the most adequate vehicle of the spiritual experience.

The whole rite is basically scriptural. Biblical idiom was persistently used in the liturgical creation. Most of the hymns and collects are simply variations on biblical *motifs* (e.g. the *Canon* at Matins). Everything is oriented towards the redeeming events of the past, in which the reality of the Church is existentially rooted. Again, the whole structure of worship is corporate in its inspiration and objective. 'Private devotions' are used to prepare the individual to share in the fellowship of the whole fellowship of believers, the Church.

The ultimate aim of the whole worship is to establish and to perpetuate an intimate communion with God, in Christ Jesus, and in the community of His Church. The ultimate emphasis is spiritual: the aim of Christian life is the acquisition of the Holy Spirit, the Comforter, by whom believers are established in the fellowship of the Church. There is no tension between the rite and the 'spirit', the rite itself being inspired.

III

ANGLICAN

*

A. G. Hebert
(Great Britain)

1. Limited and Partial Views

When a question is answered, the answer which is given provides a bearing not only on the thing which has been observed but also on the point of view of the observer. The judgments that we make on history are conditioned by the fact that we are not outside observers pronouncing a fully objective verdict, but are ourselves part of the whole movement of history, some particular episode of which is the immediate matter of our study. So it is with all study of Christian worship; the judgments which any observer makes will inevitably reflect the position in which he himself stands, within a Christendom that is broken and divided. Those divisions are most significantly reflected in the diverse traditions and practices of worship which exist today; and we, whoever 'we' are, have ourselves been formed by those traditions in which we have severally grown up, and the judgments we make will reflect our own point of view.

None of us is, therefore, in a position to pronounce magisterial judgments, or to draw up ideal forms of worship,[1] or to decide finally what is right. As the Christian faith did not begin with us, so Christian worship has had a very long history before the particular habits of worship to which we are accustomed came into being. On the other hand, as it is possible for the historian, once he is fully aware that he views the events from a particular point of view, to allow for other points of view and to try to envisage the historical process as a whole, so in the matter of worship it is possible for us to escape in some measure from our limitations by seeing our own particular tradition against the background of

[1] Cf. *Syllabus*, Sec. VIII. The question raised here is to be answered, as it seems to me, on the lines laid down on p. 74 below.

the Great Tradition of the worship of the Church of God, out of which it sprang.

There has been a Great Tradition, and it has had a very long history. There was the worship of Israel in the wilderness in the days of Moses, and later the worship of Israel in Canaan at the many local shrines, and at the central sanctuary where was the Ark of the Covenant, and the splendid worship of Solomon's Temple. Of the details of the worship of those early days we know very little, and no liturgical forms are extant, unless it be true that some Psalms were composed for sacrificial use in that period. Israel in exile was deprived of all sacrificial liturgy; but it is probable that the new liturgical form of the synagogue worship then began, with its fourfold reading of the sacred books, the exposition of them, praise, and prayer. In time the sacrifices began again in the restored Temple according to the Priestly Code, and there were many synagogues both in Palestine and in the Dispersion. The worship of the Apostolic Age continued the synagogue tradition, and added to it the rite which our Lord performed at the Last Supper; this developed into the liturgies of the Word and of the Sacrament—the Offices on the one hand, and, on the other, the eucharistic liturgies, of which the Roman Mass and the Liturgy of St. Chrysostom are in constant use today.

The Great Schism, in which East and West fell apart, left the liturgical practices of both halves of Christendom unaltered. But the Reformation brought great liturgical changes. While Latin Christendom kept its worship mainly unaltered, preserving the outward forms which enshrined the Great Tradition, Lutherans, Reformed and Anglicans all made great changes; but in each case the aim was to recover what was conceived to be the right form and the right inner spirit of Christian worship, and thus to re-create its true pattern. Thus, however many mistakes have been made, both then and since, the intention in each case was not to repudiate but to restore the Great Tradition. Somewhere within this broken and diversified inheritance we all stand—we the writers and the readers of these essays.

Somehow we are all heirs of the Great Tradition, and the chaotic spectacle which our diverse ways of worship present reflects very accurately the central problem of Christian reunion. Schism has resulted in a certain dismemberment of the Great Tradition, and it is not possible to point to any of the existing types of practice as including in itself the wholeness of Christian worship.[1] At the same time it is not possible to put the clock back and to return to the practice of the period before the schism took place. For the schisms happened because the tradition of worship had become distorted and degraded. Nevertheless, it is true that the reunion to which we look forward must bring with it a re-integration of the Great Tradition of Christian worship. If in worship above all the Church is seen to be what it is, and knows itself to be what it is—the Israel of God—then the re-integration of Christian worship is a very central element in a true reunion.

Such considerations as these appear to be the necessary basis for any right study of the Ways of Worship. We who belong to a divided Christendom must approach this study by acknowledging the incompleteness of all the traditions, including our own, and seeking to learn those insights which others have had and we have not. But while we know that our position within Christendom, whatever it be, renders our judgment partial, we have nevertheless a standard of judgment in the fact that there is one Christian faith, as there is one Lord, one Spirit, one God and Father of all. Because there is one Christian faith, there exists something of a common pattern underlying the various Ways of Worship which exist; and the aim of this essay is to try to present this pattern in a schematic form. It is submitted as an Anglican contribution to the discussion, and therefore all that has been said about partial and limited points of view applies to it and to its writer; those of other traditions will be conscious that the judgments it makes have an Anglican flavour. Yet it is written with the Great Tradition always in mind, and it aims at setting both the Anglican and other Ways of Worship in their place within that tradition.

2. The Elements of Worship

The essential elements of worship[2] are all derived from the fundamental relation of man to God; and all authentic Christian worship must give expression to them all.

Adoration. St. Ignatius Loyola and the Westminster Catechism speak with one voice when they say, 'Man was created to praise, reverence and serve God our Lord, and by this means to save his

---

[1] Cf. *Catholicity* (Dacre Press, 1947), pp. 9, 10, 17.   [2] *Syllabus*, Sec. II.

soul', and, 'Man's chief end is to glorify God and to enjoy Him for ever.' Adoration expresses man's fundamental duty to God. The opposite of it is idolatry, which is the setting up of some created object of worship in place of God, whether it be deified forces of nature (such as the sun), or natural lust (Aphrodite), or love of money and the power that it gives (Mammon), or some national-ism. But behind all these is the worship of the self, in which the fall of man consists: 'Ye shall be as God' (Gen. 3. 5). Adoration demands, but does not consist in, a right intellectual belief in God as transcendent. It consists in the self-abasement of the self before the God who is the very basis of man's existence—the ground on which he stands. In adoring God, man confesses himself to be a creature, a small rational being in a universe which God has created for His own glory, and acknowledges that his life has relevance and meaning only as directed towards God as his true God. Adoration of God thus includes holy fear.[1]

Hence the adoration of God finds expression not only in liturgy and prayer but also in life. As the Old Testament prophets taught, no outward worship is of value apart from the obedience to God's will, both in personal moral behaviour, and in the right ordering of social and economic relations. Worship in the former sense is the chief business of the Church: worship in the latter sense is the whole business of the Church.

Thanksgiving is akin to adoration, but differs from it in that man is now thinking of himself as a personal entity, a recipient of good things from God the Giver. As such, we thank God 'for our creation, preservation and all the blessings of this life; but above all for thine inestimable love in the redemption of the world by our Lord Jesus Christ, for the means of grace, and for the hope of glory'. Thus the central act of Christian worship is called the Eucharist, the Thanksgiving, and its central prayer is called the eucharistic prayer. In the old Greek liturgies, thanks-

[1] 'One of the most obvious and disturbing phenomena in the religious life of Christendom during the past seventy or eighty years has been the dis-appearance of the awe or dread or holy fear of God. We of the present older generation are not afraid, as our parents and grandparents always were afraid. It is not a marked feature of religious life to-day that we work out our own salvation with fear and trembling (Phil. 2. 12) or that we offer service well-pleasing to God with godly fear and awe (Heb. 12. 28).'

R. H. Lightfoot: *The Gospel Message of St. Mark* (Oxford, 1950), p. 97.

giving is made for God's glory as it is seen expressed in the whole created order, and in all God's dealings with men from the beginning of history, culminating in His saving acts in the incarnation, and in the death, resurrection and ascension of His son. Here, therefore, man's thanksgiving to God for benefits received passes into adoration of Him in whom is man's whole hope of salvation.

Penitence, again, lies close to adoration and thanksgiving, when in the light of God's abounding mercy man sees his own sin—not only his many sins of thought, word and deed, and of omission, but also the sin of unfaithfulness and of rebellion. Hence penitence is not self-centred regret at failure to realise a moral ideal, or shame at having been personally at fault. It is directed Godwards, and sees the sins and the sin in the light of God's purpose for man, which he has failed to carry out, and of God's love, which he has despised. But penitence is not only individual: it is also corporate. We have to confess with shame and sorrow the corporate guilt of our civilisation; and the sin of the divisions of Christ's Body—the Church; and the manifold failure of Christians to worship and serve God aright, and to bear witness to Christ as the Saviour of mankind. Every paragraph of this section can suggest matter for penitence on the part of every group of Christians with regard to its Ways of Worship.

Supplication is the act of man expressing to God his needs— 'Give us this day our daily bread'. In our Lord's model prayer this is in the plural number. Selfish man will always pray to God in times of danger or crisis, for the things which he thinks he needs. Redeemed man is taught not only to pray for the needs of others as well as himself, but also to pray 'through Jesus Christ our Lord'—that is, in union with the prayer which Christ Himself makes for the accomplishment of God's will in all for whom He died.

It seems to be right to say that in these four headings, with the various subdivisions that can be made within them (e.g. prayer for the living and the departed,[1] the analysis of the elements of worship is complete. If so, the fifth heading of the Syllabus— oblation or offering—adds only a verb to each of the four nouns. But, even so, something important is thereby added; for they really are verbs rather than nouns, since they denote the activity

---

[1] *Syllabus*, II, iv.

of those who worship. Hence the word 'offering' connects up with the worship of the Church, which is dealt with in the fourth section of this essay, and in particular with eucharistic offering. Further, the word 'offering' reminds us of the point which was mentioned under the heading of adoration—that worship is offered to God not only in liturgy but also in the whole of life. The morning prayer of the Christian must include the offering up to God in advance of all that he is to do and to suffer in the course of the day. His liturgical worship and private prayer are alike vain if he is not endeavouring to live his whole life to God's glory.

3. Christian Initiation and Various Ministries to the Individual

We pass now from considering the principles of worship to their expression in liturgy. But before we consider the regular worship of the Christian community, it is plainly necessary first to say something about the admission of a person to that community. We must deal with Christian initiation, with Baptism, and with the instruction of children in the faith, as well as the instruction of adult converts. With this is associated evangelistic preaching to those without the faith, in the mission-field abroad, and at home. While we are dealing with the individual Christian, it will be convenient to mention other ministries to the individual in the various crises of life and death.[1]

A Jew became a member of God's Israel by right of birth: a Christian so becomes by repentance unto life, and by the sacrament of new birth. Baptism must be considered in relation to the thing signified by the outward sign—namely the new creation in Christ, and the acceptance of it by faith and repentance.

Adult Baptism, at home or abroad, is always preceded by instruction in the faith. In the early Church the latter part of this was associated with the season of Lent: Baptism was administered in the night service of Easter Eve, with Confirmation and first Communion at the Easter Eucharist. Everywhere in the 'mission-field' adult Baptism is an occasion of great solemnity, and is truly what the Baptists call 'believers' baptism'. The things that the New Testament says of Baptism come alive. The sacrament is received, as the nature of a sacrament demands, with living faith.

---

[1] *Syllabus*, I B, ii and iii. But Baptism cannot rightly be discussed after the Eucharist, as indicated in the order of the *Syllabus*.

Yet infant Baptism, where there can be no active faith in the recipient, has been practised in the Church from early times—perhaps even from the Apostolic Age itself; and it is the practice of the vast majority of Christians today. It is to be defended on the ground that the children of Christian parents ought to be acknowledged members of the Christian community, and as a witness to the fact that the beginnings of faith and love in the Christian child are the work of God's grace. This demands that there shall be worthy and sufficient provision for the child to be taught, both at home and in the Church, to believe in God and to pray: and also that when he grows to maturity he shall personally accept the adult responsibilities of a Christian. This is the meaning of the scheme in the Book of Common Prayer, where the baptismal rite is followed by the Catechism, and then by the rite of Confirmation. It is coming to be widely held among us that, in reality, Confirmation and first Communion are the conclusion of the Christian initiation begun in Baptism, when the response of personal repentance and faith, which every sacrament demands, is made.[1] The right correlation of Confirmation, so understood, with the renewal of the baptismal vows, constitutes a pastoral problem which is continually present to every parish priest.

The most acute difficulty arises over 'indiscriminate Baptism', that is, the Baptism of children whose parents wish them to be baptised, while they themselves attend church very rarely, and have no conception of how a child is to be brought up in Christian ways. Some sort of baptismal discipline is needed; but it is plain that the problem can never be solved by any mere application of rules, but only by pastoral methods. Perhaps the nearest approach to a solution is that which is made by clergy who do not refuse Baptism, but devote great pains to baptismal interviews with the parents, and administer Baptism only on fixed days, perhaps six or even four times only in the year, when a baptismal festival is held and the rite administered in the presence of a large con-

---

[1] It is claimed that this is a return to the conjunction of Confirmation with Baptism in the early Church: but the mediaeval view was that Baptism by itself constitutes Christian initiation, and that Confirmation is a sacrament bestowing spiritual strength. The discussion continues. (Cf. *Baptism To-day* (Press and Publications Board, 1949) where reference to the copious recent literature will be found.)

gregation. But isolated action by individual clergy is not of great avail; there needs to be common action by all the clergy of a district, and also some common understanding of principle among the ministers of all the denominations. In some places action is being taken on these lines. Thus the baptismal problem involves the whole problem of the existence of the Church among a population which has very largely ceased to be in any real sense Christian. This brings us to the Church's evangelistic task, the aim of which is to bring those who do not worship back into the Ways of Worship. No discussion of this is possible here. Let it be said, however, that evangelistic preaching is a very different thing from the regular ministry of preaching in the worshipping community and needs a different technique.

Finally there are the various ministries of the Church to the individual Christian, which here can only be mentioned. There is the rite of Holy Marriage, for the founding of a new family. There is the constant pastoral care of souls in health and in sickness: the sacrament of Absolution, for which provision is made in the Anglican Visitation of the Sick, is in its ordinary use one form of that pastoral care of souls which is a primary duty of the Christian ministry. There is, in particular, the ministry to the sick, including prayer for bodily healing, often with laying on of hands and anointing; there is the ministry to those in mortal sickness and in the hour of death; and finally the rites of Christian burial.

4. *The Regular Worship of the Christian Community*[1]

Finally, we come to the regular worship of the Christian community, of which the outstanding feature is the observance of the Lord's Day. In Old Testament times one day in seven was kept holy, by abstinence from work, and as a ritual anticipation of the blessings of the looked-for Messianic Age. The Christian Church, for which that Age had already dawned, regarded every day as holy. At the same time it appears that, from the very first, Christians kept the 'first day of the week' as the weekly festival of the Lord's resurrection. In our own day, now that the old Sabbatarianism has gone, a new study of the Christian meaning of Sunday is demanded; of the nature of the solemn assembly of the

[1] *Syllabus*, Secs. I, III, IV.

People of God for the worship of God, at 'The Service' rather than at 'a service'; of subsidiary religious meetings; and of the way in which the rest of the day should be spent for the refreshment of body and soul. The conditions of modern life raise many difficulties.

Our problem (and it is one of the chief problems of this Commission) is to learn what is the true pattern of the Sunday worship of the Christian community. It falls under the two headings of the liturgy of the Word, and the liturgy of the Sacrament. What is the true pattern here? Is the Eucharist 'a service'; Morning Prayer another sort of 'service'; and Reformed Worship another sort; and is the worshipper to attend whatever type of service seems to him to be most helpful? Or is there in the Great Tradition a real liturgical pattern? In Catholic worship, whether in East or West, the eucharistic liturgy is regarded as the central action, to which the rest of the Sunday liturgy is subsidiary. This involves in principle a correlation of the liturgies of the Word and of the Sacrament as complementary the one to the other. Luther, Calvin and the Anglican Reformers all intended that the Eucharist, with Communion, should be the central act of each Sunday's worship; and where, as in most Protestant churches, it is celebrated less frequently, yet the fact that it is acknowledged to be the central act of Christian worship must mean in principle that all other acts of worship are really subsidiary to it.

The Liturgy of the Word had its origin in the synagogue service, of which mention has already been made, with its four elements of praise (psalmody), prayer, the reading of Scripture, and the exposition of it in the sermon. This has remained as a permanent feature of the Great Tradition and is represented in the ordinary Sunday service of our churches and chapels.

While the direct inheritance of the old synagogue service was preserved in the first part of the Eucharist, down to the offertory, a parallel development of the same scheme arose in the Offices, later codified in the breviary, from which the Anglican Matins and Evensong are descended. The Prayer Book orders all clergy to recite these daily—publicly in church if possible and, if not, then privately. Since the whole Psalter is thus recited once a month, and the greater part of the Bible is read once a year at least, this rule provides an exceedingly valuable framework of Scriptural devotion. The structure of the Offices is based mainly on the alternation of chants and lessons—a valuable principle[1] which has received a modern adaptation in the Service of Nine Lessons which we hear at Christmas, in which lessons alternate with carols.

The liturgy of the Word presents a variety of problems to-day. *As regards praise:* the psalms, which expressed the devotion of the old Israel, represent in their Christian use the prayer of Christ and of the members of His Body, a fact which needs to be explained and understood. But to-day the psalms are supplemented or even replaced by modern hymns, some of which are good and some are not. The selection of hymns is one of the chief liturgical problems of every minister. Another problem is that of the choir, which too often treats music as an end and not as a means, and robs the congregation of its opportunity to praise God in song. *As regards the prayers:* the traditional forms of prayer, which by their familiarity help the worshipper to fit his own devotion into them, and by their high quality instruct him to pray aright, seem to us Anglicans altogether preferable to prayers composed by the minister. But 'free prayer', in which any of the worshippers are free to engage, can be a most valuable practice, which we Anglicans have used very little. We have made rather more use of another very valuable thing—periods of corporate silence alternating with utterance. *As regards the lessons:* a fixed lectionary, if well arranged, covers the whole ground, and saves the congregation from the frequent repetition of the minister's favourite texts. But there are occasions when a free choice is indispensable. *As regards preaching:* the function of the sermon is that the word of the Scripture should be so expounded by this means that it becomes a living word re-expressed through the Spirit by a living voice, speaking to these people here and now. Preachers such as St. Augustine and St. Chrysostom in ancient times, or F. D. Maurice in the last century, expounded whole books of the Bible in courses of sermons, interpreting Scripture by Scripture. Such

[1] This principle is very remarkably illustrated in the very ancient Propers in the Roman Missal for the four Ember seasons, particularly those for the third Saturday in Advent, the second Saturday in Lent, the Saturday after Pentecost, and the Ember Saturday in September. In each case there is a sequence of seven Scripture lessons, alternating with chants which were originally the whole psalm, though now one verse only. The selection of texts, dating from a time when the Bible was well known and loved, will repay study. Cf. Hebert: *The Authority of the Old Testament*, pp. 287 f.

preaching is a very different thing from a discourse on some subject connected with religion, hung on some text as a peg. It is also very different from the type of instruction of which we spoke in connection with Baptism. Another question which arises is the place of the sermon in the service. Custom, in many places so fixed as to be almost irreformable, places it at the end. But the Prayer Book places the sermon at the Eucharist in the middle, and at an ordination at the very beginning. There is great value in this also in the liturgy of the Word, when the sermon is used not to remind people of things which they should have noticed when the Scriptures were read, but, instead, to prepare them for meditation upon the Scriptures which they are going to hear.

The Liturgy of the Sacrament, which is the supreme symbol and means of Christian unity, has, alas, been the chief battle-ground of controversy among us, where we have been involved in seemingly hopeless disagreement.[1] Let us then here consider it from the point of view of our agreements, actual or potential. For the various liturgical movements all over Christendom converge in a wonderful way upon certain main points.

(*a*) In the Great Tradition the Eucharist has been seen as properly the act of the local assembly of the People of God, met together to confess its faith, to offer its worship, and to find in the Communion the seal of its unity. So it was in the early Church; and such is the aim to-day of the *messe de communauté* among French Catholics, of the Anglican Parish Communion or Family Communion, and of the Protestant Communion services, at which—even if they are celebrated in some instances as rarely as once a quarter—the whole congregation is found assembled.

(*b*) It is characteristic of the liturgical movements that in every way possible the congregation is led to take an active part; in the singing and the responses; in common meditation on the Word (where the sermon finds its truest context when it is designed to lead the people to their meeting with the Lord in His Sacrament); and in the Communion itself. In the early Church the common priesthood of all believers found active expression in the action of the offertory, when the people brought to church their gifts of

---

[1] Cf. the Translator's Preface to Brilioth: *Eucharistic Faith and Practice* (SPCK, 1929). The material for this preface was mainly provided by the late Fr. Herbert Kelly, S.S.M.

bread and wine as the symbol of the offering of themselves, and presented these at the altar, that from them might be taken the bread and wine for the Sacrament. In many places to-day attempts are made to find out how this can be revived.

(*c*) The eucharistic Sacrifice, that storm-centre of controversy, is finding in our day a truly evangelical expression from the 'catholic' side, when it is insisted that the sacrificial action is not any sort of re-immolation of Christ, nor a sacrifice additional to His one Sacrifice, but a participation in it. The true celebrant is Christ the High-Priest, and the Christian people are assembled as members of His Body to present before God His Sacrifice, and to be themselves offered up in sacrifice through their union with Him. This, however, involves a repudiation of certain mediaeval developments, notably the habitual celebration of the Eucharist without the Communion of the people; or the notion that the offering of the Eucharist is the concern of the individual priest rather than of the assembled church; and, above all, any idea that in the Eucharist we offer a sacrifice to propitiate God. We offer it only because He has offered the one Sacrifice, once for all, in which we need to participate.[1]

(*d*) Once again, the adoration rendered to God and to His Christ in the Eucharist is the sign and the efficacious means to the worship of God in the whole of life. The New Testament writers had a very keen perception that the whole of their life was a sacrificial oblation.

Finally there is the question of the relation of the worship of the local worshipping community, the Church Universal, and the Church in Heaven.[2] First, the local community is a unit of the whole Church, in which the reality of the whole is present. This is what St. Paul means when he writes to 'the Church of God which is at Corinth'—the whole is present in the part. Christ is the celebrant at the Eucharist; the worship of 'the Church' is offered there; Christian unity is actualised in the *koinonia* of its members. Second, each of the great denominations exhibits a world-wide unity, and its members of all nations and races share one tradition, one confession of faith, and one communion at the

[1] Cf. the late Rt. Rev. F. N. C. Hicks: Chap. XII, c, below. Cf. Hebert: Essay in the volume issued by the Theological Commission on Intercommunion.

[2] *Syllabus*, Sec. IV.

Lord's Table. Third, there is the heavenly worship in which the earthly Church has a share, in virtue of its eschatological character as existing in the interim period between the Lord's two advents. Here is a unity which is not subject to any possibility of schism, though it is still possible for us to drop away from it through sin. Because of this unity there can be fellowship in the Spirit between the members of separated Churches. The earthly Church, being composed of imperfect men, is subject to sin and therefore to schism; and yet, because of its 'citizenship in Heaven' it is in living contact with the world of Heaven, and with the perfected Church in which the victory over sin is complete. (Heb. 12. 22-24.)

IV

LUTHERAN

*

(a) Herbert Goltzen
(Germany)

I. Some Pre-suppositions for the Reform of the Lutheran Church Services in Germany

The Protestant churches in Germany were characterised after the Reformation by a territorial development. The shape of the church services and the use of hymn books varied from one territory to another. During the periods of Pietism and Enlightenment moreover, the traditional orders frequently underwent abbreviations and alterations, or even took an altogether new form according to the type of piety or the intellectual attitude represented by the local pastors. Such isolated and independent alteration resulted in a very great variety in the shape of the church service and in hymnology by the end of the eighteenth century.

From the beginning of the nineteenth century a return to the order and authority of the church service was beginning, due to the neo-pietistic revival which (in opposition to a state-sponsored unity movement) called for a reconsideration of the heritage to which the Lutheran Church was pledged. This development has been carried on into the present century by various factors: the overcoming of religious subjectivism through a renewed attention to the Scriptures as God's Revelation; the demand for a sound ordering of life related to the Church which arose particularly in the Evangelical Youth Movement; the longing for a unity of faith and witness beyond the now meaningless boundaries of the former territories; and the experience gained from the defensive struggle against the claims of the totalitarian state, which taught the Church that the sole responsibility in all her order and life is to the One Lord, to whom the listening congregation bears witness. During this century all these factors have

79

caused the earlier romantic impulse of restoration to develop into a fundamental reconsideration of the nature of the church service, as it has been experienced from the time of the Early Church: namely as the meeting place with the crucified and risen Lord, and as the only true response to the gospel of redemption through Jesus Christ, witnessed by the Scriptures and by the confessional statements of the Reformation.

There is great willingness nowadays, therefore, to learn from the experiences of the Church as a whole, to search together for an objective and authoritative order of service, and to renounce in its favour any customs which have arisen from territorial usage or from subjective, arbitrary action. While the Liturgical Movement in its early phase still looked for a 'richer and more beautiful' church service, it is now generally agreed that there is a vital link between church service and witness. 'Liturgy is prayed doctrine'; the order of the church service should therefore be appropriately shaped so that it can express something which happens when the Lord meets His congregation. The development of Martin Luther's Reformation shows that the shape of the service is not to be reconstructed anew by each specific generation whether from a doctrinal principle or from an assumed loyalty to the Scriptures. For the Lutheran Church the Scriptures are not a principle for constructing the service, but a criterion. Luther did not interrupt the Western tradition in any revolutionary way; he took over the church service in its fundamental form and 'cleansed' it by eliminating what was opposed to the central understanding of faith, and so might darken the saving grace which seeks us alike in Word and Sacrament. By translating the service into the vernacular, he gave the congregation access to the action which takes place in the service and laid it open, in order to evoke and strengthen their faith. His church anniversary sermon at Torgau in 1544 has become the classical definition of the Evangelical Church Service:' . . . that we . . . may come together, to act and to hear God's word, . . . that our dear Lord Himself may speak to us through His Holy Word . . . That we in our turn may speak to Him through prayer and songs of praise.' This receiving and answering takes place in the parish church service in the fundamental forms which Luther took over from the tradition of the Church as a whole and wrote into the new shape of the church service.

We can see to-day that the liturgical work of the past generation has brought about a new theological understanding of these
fundamental forms, and has revived them in the consciousness of
the congregation. The study groups, and the groups within the
Church which have been working for a renewal of the church
service, have started from different points of view. The 'High
Church Union' (*Hochkirchliche Vereinigung*) tried to renew association with the Catholic tradition, whereas the liturgical work of
the *Berneuchener* circle and the Evangelical Brotherhood of St.
Michael arose out of the impulse of the Youth movement to
search for real and appropriate forms of everyday life related to
the Church, and so to learn more seriously the whole contents of
the church service. The work of the *Alpisbacher* circle is connected
with dialectical theology. The liturgical conference in Lower
Saxony has been particularly interested in liturgical values rediscovered during the Reformation, and has worked out models
based on them, which have since become significant for liturgical
work as a whole. The territorial Churches of Hamburg and
Oldenburg have followed this road for several years by editing
liturgical services and testing them amongst their congregations.
The liturgical commission of the Church in Schleswig-Holstein
has recently joined the movement. During the struggle of the
Confessional Church, theologians in the Rhineland and in West-
phalia have learnt to investigate the Reformed order of church
service from natural affinity with its Scriptural doctrine and confessional writings. This work has found its expression in the joint
edition, by Peter Brunner, Beckmann, Kulp and Reindell, of
Church Agenda. Theologians and church administrations of the
Confessional Lutheran Churches have collected the liturgical
heritage (e.g. in the *Handbook of German Evangelical Church Music*,
part I, the Chant before the Altar, Göttingen 1941), and have
revived what was still valid in the territorial Churches. With the
exception of the High Church Union these and similar movements have formed a common body in the Lutheran Liturgical
Conference in Germany and the Liturgical Commission of the
General Synod of the United Evangelical Lutheran Churches in
Germany. For several years the collection of a comprehensive
Lutheran church-book (equivalent to the Anglican Prayerbook)
has been going on, which will include the orders, the Scriptural
passages, the hymns and chants for the church services and related

action. This church-book will eventually become authoritative for the practice of church services in the various territorial Churches even beyond the United Evangelical Lutheran Churches.

II. *Original Forms of Divine Service*

In the Early Church the original form of the Divine service on Sundays was the celebration of the Holy Supper, during which the Word was also preached. According to the statement of the New Testament scholar Cullmann, of Basel (*The Early Church and Her Divine Service*), there was never a mere 'sermon service' for the congregation of baptised and full members of the Church. (The missionary sermon amongst the Jews and Gentiles is, of course, another matter.)

This service of the 'Breaking of the Bread', or the Eucharist, contained in its first part the proclamation of the Word in the lessons from the Scriptures and the sermon, and in its second part the *anamnesis* of the sacrifice on the cross (I Cor. 11. 26) and the Holy Supper, which not only fulfilled Christ's bequest of Maundy Thursday, but continued the communion at table of the disciples with their Risen Master. This service which was 'received' from the Lord has become the tradition of the Eastern and Western Churches alike (I Cor. 11. 23a). Luther, too, retained it in the *formula missae* as well as in the German Mass, and all Lutheran orders contain it.

This shape of the Divine service for Sundays and church festivals, which includes the celebration of the Holy Supper, has been pre-supposed as a valid order by the present territorial Churches, as it was for the Evangelical 'Land-Church' (of the former Old-Prussian Union) of 1895. When it came into use in the churches, however, the central part of this service was split up. The earlier part, including the Sermon (the ancient *missa catechumenorum*) is still maintained. The sacramental part is left out, save for a few pieces torn from their context to form the 'concluding liturgy' of this mutilated rite. The Holy Supper is celebrated only as a rare appendix, combined with a kind of general confession, for those few who stay behind 'after the church service'.

All church circles which are seriously interested in liturgical problems are agreed that this widespread practice is a distortion of ecumenical worship, and that, on the authority of the New Testament and the confessional statements, the restoration of the unity between sermon-service and the celebration of the Holy Supper is essential. The Confessional Synod of the Old-Prussian Church made this demand in October 1940, and a number of Lutheran territorial Churches have adopted new orders of an Evangelical or Lutheran Mass.

Apart from the Evangelical Mass and the Hours, some Lutheran Churches have developed a simple and devotional sermon-service. This should not be mistaken for the fragment of the Mass without the Holy Supper, which is widespread. There are no liturgical responses and less visible influence from the Church's Year than is seen in the Mass. It consists only of a short prayer, a lesson, a sermon, a concluding prayer, the Lord's Prayer, and the Blessing. The congregation participates merely with hymns. Such a service offers a rich chance to preach an edifying or instructive sermon, which need not necessarily be limited to the *pericopes*. It had its origin in the medieval services held by the Preaching Orders, which dealt with the problem of popular evangelism, as distinct from the ordered service of the Mass. This is the service on which the Swiss Reformers based their reconstruction of church order. In South Germany it was generally introduced into the Lutheran Church in Würtemberg, and during the nineteenth century even into the Church in Oldenburg, which had been largely influenced by the Enlightenment. There is without any doubt a need for this very simple and, in itself, clearly defined order of service. The teaching function of the sermon which Luther strongly emphasised can be fully realised within its framework, as it is not only outsiders who are in need of a missionary sermon, but the very members of the congregation, as those who 'are to be called and spurred to faith'. This missionary-teaching form of service, however, should not have a monopoly within a living Church, lest the Church should be mistaken for the mission-field.

Another original form of service is that of the Hours. Wilhelm Löhe has already revived Mattins and Vespers in his parish. But beyond a few areas of revival, these services have not become popular. Only the Liturgical Revival has fundamentally broken with the use of arbitrarily composed services and devotions, and has re-instated the Hours of the Early Church as the legitimate, original form for daily services during the week. The distinctive note is a listening, an act of praise to God, and prayer, supplementing the sacramental Sunday service. Its elements are psalms, a lesson from the Scriptures (chosen in accordance with the Church's Year) in continuation of the Gospel for the previous Sunday, or with a separate continuity; an Anthem (or evangelical hymn), New Testament canticles, Preces (Intercessions), and general prayers varying with the time of the day and the period of the Church's Year.

From the cycle of the eight Hours, which can only be appropriately kept in a monastic community, only four have been retained for use in Evangelical congregations: (1) Morning Prayer (*Mette*, i.e. Mattins) and (2) Evening Prayers (Vespers), which are similar in their structure and have as their central part the lesson for the day. (3) The Midday Prayer (corresponding with the ancient 'Sext') with only a short lesson for the corresponding period of the Church's Year. (4) The Late Evening Service (*Komplet*, i.e. Compline) unchanged throughout the year. This late Evening Service in particular has become widely popular, and is part of the ecumenical heritage which has come to life again beyond denominational boundaries.

It might well help congregational understanding of the church service if all orders of services were reduced to these three original forms: *The Mass*, as the main service for Sundays; *The Hour Services*, as the order of church services for weekdays apart from the Celebration of the Holy Supper; and the *Sermon Service* (devotional service), as a medium for missions and instruction. All other meetings of the congregation, in so far as they have the character of church services, could be arranged within the frame of the two latter forms. The publication of a new common Evangelical hymn-book will offer an opportunity to make those original orders available to the congregations in a liturgical appendix, as was decided by the Synod of the Evangelical Lutheran Church at Oldenburg in November 1950.

III. *Elements of the Lutheran Church Service*

A. THE PRESENTATION OF THE WORD OF GOD

(*a*) *The lesson*. We may assume that officially all Lutheran churches still follow the *pericopes*. The 'Reformed' parishes reject the fixing of the *pericopes* for the lessons and sermons as a restriction in the presentation of the Word, and as a tradition of Roman Catholic origin. On the other hand, according to the pamphlet

Epistles and Gospels according to the Time of the Year, as we have hitherto been used to them, Luther held that 'We find no particular fault in such a method.' Although the present selection of *pericopes* in Roman Catholic usage differs, on one or two Sundays, from the ancient Franco-Roman order of lessons, the Gospel readings in the Roman Catholic Mass on Sundays correspond with those read according to the accepted order of the Lutheran Church. We still have both chains of lessons in the form laid down by the Church Conference at Eisenach in 1896.

This order has, however, not prevented the practice of pastors choosing their own texts for the services in many places, and almost everywhere the lesson has been restricted to one Bible passage. During the period of theological liberalism the 'compulsion of the *pericopes*' was heavily attacked, and the principle of 'unity' for church services was proclaimed: namely, that the theme chosen by the pastor should dictate the liturgical unity of the service, and that all lessons, sentences and prayers of the liturgy, should conform to it. The *Private Agenda* by Aper and Zillessen, which was widely used and had a new edition as late as 1940, carried this principle to an absurd extreme: here models could be found to suit all religious needs and conceptions. The *pericopes* of this book are even patched together with quotations from the Bible, which have been torn from their contexts and often came from several different books.

The time for this 'subject-liturgy' has passed. The authority of the old order of *pericopes* has been generally restored. It has been a wonderful experience for many that Sundays are characterised by the Gospel of the day, and that the understanding of its subject in connection with the set periods of the Church's Year promotes a closer link with the Church's life throughout the year. As the order of *pericopes* returns with each new year, it serves effectively to impress the regular customs of the Church. The newly aroused appreciation of the Church's Year is a sign of the return from religious individualism to corporate life.

The *pericopes* of the ancient Church were texts for the liturgical lesson during the Mass. They were also favourite texts for sermons, though this was not their main purpose. The sermon may be based on a greater variety of texts than those of the two cycles alone. Nevertheless, the 'old' Epistles and Gospels should be read in the liturgy even when texts are chosen elsewhere for the sermon.

The revision of the order of the *pericopes* as used by the ancient Church has occasionally proved rather unfortunate. The selection and limitation of the lessons has been carefully compared with the old lectionaries and church orders and sermon collections dating from the Reformation. Dr. Peter Brunner has presented the results in his research into *Church Agenda I, 1, part III* (*Gütersloh*, 1949). The lectionary of the Lutheran Liturgical Commission has been based on these investigations.

The daily services of Mattins and Evensong also have the lesson as their nucleus. It may be taken from the Lessons for the Church's Year which continue the theme of the lessons for Sundays, or, corresponding to the ancient Matutin, the *lectio continua* of complete books of the Bible may be read during Mattins.

(*b*) *The sermon in the setting of the church service.* Luther said, in his *Order of the Church Service for the Congregation*, 'Where God's Word is not preached, it would be better that no one should sing, read or come together.'

This statement should not be understood to imply that every meeting of the congregation for worship must include a sermon. The 'Word of God' should not so be equated with the sermon. The Proclamation of the Word of God, the witness to Jesus Christ, the Incarnate Word, is carried out in the whole existence of the Church, which is called to life through the Holy Spirit in the world. Christ is proclaimed in her doctrine, in her witness and suffering, in the continuing love amongst the brethren and towards their neighbours, and above all, in the distribution of 'the means of Grace' through Word and Sacrament. The witness to Christ appears particularly in the sermon, but not exclusively. All actions of the Church carry out this 'proclamation of the Lord's death until He come' (I Cor. 11. 26) and not only that part of the action which is called the Sermon. Mattins, Evensong or Compline, a Celebration of the Holy Supper, or even a Baptismal Service can be held without a free exegesis of Scripture, and can nevertheless be a lawful 'service' in a parish where sermons are preached regularly and instruction is given.

The sermon is not free opinion, but a witness to the Gospel as it is contained in the Scriptures. The link with the Scriptures generally appears in the fact that the sermon is an exposition of a certain 'text'. Although there is no compulsion regarding the *peri-*

copes for the sermon in most of the territorial Churches, a willing-ness has grown in the Evangelical Church in Germany during the last ten years to keep to definite texts for sermons, which have been suggested by the Church Administration, and for which valuable 'helps' (*Handreichungen*) are being offered from various quarters. The series of lessons suggested by the Church Conference at Eisenach planned a cycle of five years: a series of Epistles and Gospels from the ancient Church, with a further 'new' series of Epistles and Gospels respectively, and a series of lessons from the Old Testament. But since some other Churches, such as Würtem-berg, have other series of their own, the Bishops' Conference of the United Evangelical Lutheran Churches in Germany has asked the Lutheran Liturgical Commission to work out a new series for sermon texts. For these a cycle of ten years will have to be planned so that they would appear twice during this period, while six other series for the Epistles, Gospels, and the Old Testament would appear once in the cycle. These 'new' series of lessons, however, maintain the connection with the *pericopes* of the ancient Church by their common theme. It may well be possible, how-ever, that a sermon is an introduction to the whole Proclamation of the Word for a particular Sunday, or that the sermon deals with some action during the service, or with a liturgical part, or even with a doctrinal subject—provided that such a sermon re-mains within the context of the Christian Faith, being 'concerned with Christ'.

In services such as the Mass, the sermon is usually preached after the Creed, from which it is separated by a hymn. Some Lutheran Churches have developed the custom of transferring the Creed into the sacramental part of the church service, as was done in the Early Church, i.e. into the *missa fidelium*. In such a case the sermon can be placed directly after the lessons. Thereby the neces-sary connection between read and interpreted Word is presented even better.

Apart from regular church services, other activities are both necessary and customary, during which an evangelistic or apolo-getic sermon is preached. Texts for such services are influenced by the condition of the parish, or by the intentions of the preacher. Besides the evangelistic mission to the people, or the 'tent' mission of the old pattern, to which preachers from other districts were invited to address outsiders, the new form of 'Evangelical' or

'Church' Week has emerged from the struggle of the Confessing Church against the Third Reich.

Both the style and the composition of the sermon have in fact undergone a change during the last generation. The sermon on 'subjects', which was artistically subdivided and systematically developed, has been abandoned more and more. Amongst the conservative theologians it took a biblical or doctrinal form, while amongst the liberal theologians it dealt with religious and ethical problems, and general human experience. Such sermons have been criticised for subjecting even their texts to a scheme which would no longer let these texts speak in their own right. The text-homily tries to elaborate the setting of the text, but in the composition of the sermon the preacher is guided more by the structure of the text itself and renounces schematic methods of subdivision.

(c) *The teaching character of the church service*. It has been realised to-day that a onesided teaching-motive for the church service is insufficient. To uphold the authority of 'the pure doctrine' is the only justification for the office of the minister as servant of the Church. He is bound by his ordination vow 'to preach the Gospel clearly and purely'. The church service, however, is not exclusively an occasion for instructing the congregation. And it is not the only or most important opportunity for teaching. It was characteristic that in many churches the pastor retained a position facing the congregation throughout the service; he was always in the attitude of the teacher in front of his pupils. Many Lutheran churches have now returned to the custom that the pastor turns towards the altar during all acts of prayer and adoration, and during the Creed. His attitude thus illustrates that the church service is not directed unilaterally to the mind of the people who are to be instructed, but that it also has a God-ward reference.

In the Children's Services particularly, it would be easy to shift the main emphasis to that of teaching. This happened during the last century after the model of the Anglo-Saxon Sunday School. Apart from the Free Churches the Children's Church Service has now overcome the atmosphere of the school. The Children's Services' Association formerly demanded that the Children's Service should have 'a childlike', simplified order following the pattern of the main service.

To-day it is realised more and more that the church service for children must have a valid order of its own and should not be a mere watered-down repetition of the service for the adults. The Pattern of the Mass is held to be unsuitable for a children's service. Several Lutheran churches, as in Hanover and Oldenburg, have now introduced the order of Mattins for their children's service.

There are also special Youth Services in several parishes in order to give specific addresses to young people, which cannot always be done during the sermon for adults.

B. THE SACRAMENTS

(a) *The Celebration of the Eucharist.* From Apostolic times the main service of the Church has been that which unites the proclamation of the Word in lessons and sermon with the Celebration of the Holy Supper. The Lutheran Church is at present proceeding to regain this complete service after neglecting it for generations. There is still no agreed name for it. The term 'Eucharist', which was used by the Early Church, is unknown to parishes in Germany. The term 'Main Service' applies to all types of services in the local tradition, where the 'Holy Supper' is frequently celebrated in a mutilated form as an appendix to the sermon-service. The term 'Mass' which had been traditional for the West, and which was taken over by Luther for his 'purified' service, is considered to be 'Roman Catholic' amongst church folk and is therefore disliked. Nevertheless, Mass is the only term that cannot be misunderstood and which, at the same time, corresponds with Lutheran tradition. Several territorial Churches have therefore begun to call this service the 'Lutheran' or the 'Evangelical Mass'. The next generation in the parishes will probably become accustomed to using it.

The first part of this complete service has been essentially maintained:

Introit—Kyrie—Gloria in excelsis—Salutation—Prayer (Collect)—Epistle—Gradual Psalm or Hymn—Gospel—Creed—Sermon.

A preparatory act may precede the actual service: in the confession of sins the pastor and the congregation, or all officiants in the vestry, prepare themselves 'to enter the Holy of Holies'.

A certain difficulty arose at first in Bavaria and later in Prussia during the nineteenth century due to the coupling of this preparation with the Kyrie, in the following manner: Introit—Confession

of Sins and Kyrie (the Kyrie here was misunderstood as a
confession of sins)—Absolution (*Gnadenspruch*), followed by the
Gloria. Apparently this created a psychologically effective procedure: i.e. the humiliation and comfort of the soul. It has been
realised now that this psychological misunderstanding in the
Preparation (*Eingangsliturgie*) must be overcome. The immediate
succession of Kyrie and Gloria is being restored. In this case the
confiteor must once again precede the service.

On the other hand, the composition of the sacramental part of
the service raised a series of questions, with which theological
discussions and the Liturgical Reform Movement in the Lutheran
Church are at present occupied. In a careful and objective research
into the shape of the church service (*Untersuchungen der Ordnung
des Gottesdienstes, Gütersloh*, 1949, page 70 ff.), Dr. Peter Brunner
writes: 'It was not granted to the Lutheran churches during the
sixteenth century to carry out the "Reformation" of the Canon
in such a way that the link with the worship of the Early Church
could be maintained.' With the elimination from the Communion
Service of those prayers which were associated with the Roman
Catholic idea of a meritorious sacrifice, 'the remaining structure
of the service fell into pieces'. It would thus be impossible to
reintroduce a Lutheran liturgy for the Holy Supper from the
sixteenth century.

This clearly shows the difficulties which arise in the appropriate
reconstruction of the customary practice of the neglected Communion Service. It may be said, however, that far-reaching agreement on a new order of the Holy Supper is apparent in the
Lutheran churches in Germany. The following parts definitely
belong to the Communion Service:

> The *oratio fidelium* (Intercession)
> The Sacrifice of Love (Heb. 13. 16)
> The Main Prayers of the Eucharist (*Hochgebet*):
> > *Praefatio, Sanctus* and *Benedictus*, followed by:
> > The Lord's Prayer
> > Consecration Prayer (or vice versa).
>
> *Agnus Dei*
> The Communion (Holy Supper)
> The Thanksgiving: Concluding Prayer

The *missio* (the sending into the world, whence the name Mass) and The Blessing.

Apart from the position of the Lord's Prayer, which in the Lutheran church orders sometimes precedes and sometimes follows the Consecration Prayer, it is generally agreed that these parts belong to the Communion Service. Discussions are still going on as to whether the break in the sequence of the eucharistic prayers could be bridged again with prayers expressing the old *anamnesis* and the *epiclesis* in a way acceptable to the evangelical understanding of Christ's death upon the cross and His Presence at the Communion.

At the same time parallel theological and liturgical discussions on the eucharistic prayers in the North American Lutheran churches show that we are confronting new problems in the doctrine and practice of the Holy Supper which have not yet found a generally acknowledged answer.

(*b*) *Holy Baptism*. On account of Karl Barth's attack on Infant Baptism (*Die kirchliche Lehre von der Taufe*, München, 1947), the custom of baptising infants, which had so far been unconsciously preserved, has become a problem for congregations. Barth considers the action of the Church to represent only an 'image' of the spiritual event through which man enters into communion with Christ's death and resurrection. The action of Baptism itself is, in his opinion, not connected with this event, but has a merely 'cognitive importance'. Apart from God's promise, he maintains that 'the willingness and readiness of the candidate for Baptism to receive this promise' is essential.

The centuries-old battle of Calvinism and rationalism against exorcism (which in fact rejected the belief alike in the reality of freedom from the domination of darkness offered in Baptism, and in the real acceptance of the baptised person into the Covenant of Grace), has been carried a step further in the attack of this eminent modern theologian. For the past two centuries, wide circles of the Lutheran Church have in fact carried out the Baptismal Service in such a way that the emphasis is no longer on an objective action upon the child, who, being born in Original Sin, could be saved from this deadly power and put under the protection and reign of the Lord only through the authoritative spiritual action of the Church following the command of Christ. The emphasis has rather been on the impression made on the parents and relations by the baptismal sermon, which is intended to make them willing 'to educate their child in the Christian way'. A result of such a shift of emphasis is, for example, the fact that the decisive questions of the Baptismal Service are no longer addressed to the candidate, but to the godparents or parents. The formulas for Baptism according to Luther's tract on the subject are still authoritative in the territorial Churches, but there are parallel formulas in use, not only omitting exorcism and *abrenuntiatio*, but even with questions which demand a promise from the relations: these psychological alternatives are undoubtedly used by most of the pastors.

Against such facts we can only express a few considerations at this point. Was it just thoughtlessness that led the Early Church to see no reason for essential changes in the rite of Baptism of adults, when the missionary situation came to an end and infant Baptism became the rule? Were there not the same psychological difficulties during the second as during the sixteenth and twentieth centuries, namely, that in Baptism infants were addressed and placed under the 'decision' which was brought about by Christ's death upon the cross, although conscious 'willingness and readiness' on their part must have been out of the question? Does not Mark 10. 13-16, as well as Luther's *theologumenon* on 'The Faith of Children', show that from the very beginning the Church was under criticism from an anthropology to which consciousness was more important than God's objective action defining and changing the being of man—an anthropology which considered it more important that man reached a knowledge of God rather than 'being known' by God first and foremost? Is not the background for the modern Protestant changes of the rite of Baptism, from which all trends of negative action against the devil have been eliminated, and where belief in the reality of the saving Grace, expressed in and with the action, has thus been weakened, more than a mere pastoral concern for the mentality of modern man? Does it not reveal a non-biblical, optimistic anthropology—an underestimation of the spiritual powers which the Lord administers through the medium of His Church, and an overestimation of the possibilities of achieving impressive reactions in human understanding through our words? The philosophical climate and the structure of society has changed. Since the *corpus Christianum* of the Middle Ages was destroyed, the modern national state developed from a period of parity with the Confession (or church) into philosophical neutrality, and eventually became more and more secular and anti-Christian. Did this development change the nature of man, his position before God, and his access to Salvation so greatly that it has become urgent to abandon the Western and Lutheran Order of Baptism? The abbreviations and alterations of the Order of Baptism have been undertaken partly under the pressure of the State, partly and imperceptibly, under the influence of contemporary thought, through the arbitrary action of individual pastors. But the Churches of the Augsburg Confession have never taken a Confessional decision which would justify or sanction these changes in the administration of a basic sacrament by reference to the Scriptures. Only the attack of Barth, which surpasses all former Baptist and sectarian negations of the Church's doctrine of Baptism, has forced the Lutheran Church to reconsider its legitimate Order of Baptism from a theological point of view, and to bring it back out of decay into a living recognition. The section of the *Church Agenda* by Beckmann and Brunner which is to deal with the 'Actions of Initiation' will have to take up this task.

(c) *Confession and Absolution*. The Augsburg Confession maintained confession and private absolution for the Church (*Confessio Augustana* XI and XII). What the sermon proclaims to everyone about the justification of the sinner, becomes the property of the repentant and believing sinner in the action of confession and absolution. Here again, no binding decision going beyond the confessional statements has been attained; but through an act of revolutionary high-handedness the personal confession which was given by the Lord was rejected, and replaced by a 'general confession', during the early phase of Pietism. This general confession, which cannot replace the personal and secret confession, or the personal absolution and advice of the confessor, has further been coupled with the celebration of the Holy Communion, which had been torn from its context in the main service. Such lawless amalgamation of the two actions concealed the joyful character of the Eucharist and deprived the believer of the pastoral help which secret and individual confession is meant to offer.

It will be the task of the Liturgical Movement to disentangle this habitual confusion. The *confession of the congregation* must become a service in its own right. Such an independent service of confession will contain the reading of the Ten Commandments, of the New Testament Commandment of Love, a successive and mutual confession of sins by the pastor and the congregation, the confessional questions and a word of promise (*votum*) from Rev. 1. 18, and Eph. 5. 25b-27. After this the members of the congregation will come to the altar, and be given a word from the Bible followed by the Blessing from I Thess. 5. 23, with the laying-on of hands.

This confession-service would intentionally avoid formal absolution, which must be left to the individual confession. This individual confession, which has officially never been abolished in the Lutheran Church, but has rarely been demanded in practice, has already been revived by Wilhelm Löhe in his parish. The demand for this well-ordered pastoral help which cannot be replaced by any individual pastoral encounter, is growing again. There are set forms for the confessional conversation, although the usual *agenda* offer little assistance for it. Where the 'general confession' in connection with the Holy Supper, containing an explicit absolution, is still in use, a reservation should be added for truth's sake, warning those who do not repent that the absolution does not apply to them, and moreover, that their sins have not been forgiven according to the Word of the Lord.

(*d*) *The Occasional Services and the Blessing (Sacramental) Actions of the Church.* The Lutheran Church only recognises three sacraments properly so-called—Baptism, Absolution, and the Holy Supper. All other church actions are liturgically ordered services of witness for certain conditions of human life, or sacramental blessings for a certain 'state'.

The natural outcome of the Catechumenate in Confirmation generally takes place after an instruction for two years with a public examination; the actual confirmation (*Einsegnung*) is in the presence of the congregation. The confirmation is set within the framework of the parochial worship. Most of the orders for confirmation contain a link with 'the Baptismal promise'. The candidates join the congregation in the Creed (corresponding to the *redditio symboli* in the Early Church), they answer the questions of promise with 'Yes, so help me God,' and are blessed at the altar by the laying-on of hands. They are then admitted to the Holy Supper, and may become godparents.

For about a century the practice of confirmation has caused pastors a good deal of concern. Can young people during their period of development be expected to take a conscious decision, and to make such a promise? This concern has caused frequent changes in the form of words used for the questions or even by their omission. A satisfactory solution for the Church, which could only be found by making sub-divisions of the rather complex action of confirmation (taking the various steps of the catechumenate into consideration) has nowhere been found, although theological discussions on the subject have been going on for years. The action itself has been maintained less for its biblical and dogmatic basis than for its great popularity.

The ordination of the clergy is held during a public service, preferably in the parish where the ordinand will hold his office. It is a rule that the ordination is performed by the bishop or a superintendent authorised by him such as the Dean, or Rural Dean (*Kreispfarrer*). Two further pastors assist, and the ordination is carried out by the laying-on of hands. The ordinand must take his vow first. The appeal to this ordination vow was a strong support of conscience for the pastors during the struggle of the Church against the Third Reich. During that time the obligation of the Church to witness in its church service to the whole Church, and the blessing and commission (*missio*) received therein have proved an untold comfort and protection.

The consecration of deacons, deaconesses, organists, and other officials in the Church's service, as well as the inductions into a new parish, or the consecration of a bishop, are similarly constructed. A common *agenda* for all these acts of consecration is being prepared for the United Lutheran churches in Germany.

The church service of marriage is a blessing by which the marriage (after the public and legal proclamation at the registrar's office) is placed under God's Word and the Promise of the Lord. It is then consecrated to the Holy Estate of Matrimony. Biblical lessons on the institution and the purpose of the Estate of Matrimony, marriage questions directed to the partners, the exchange of rings, as well as the act of blessing by the imposition of hands upon the joined hands of the couple, are provided in all orders for marriage services.

The last service which the Church renders to its deceased members is the church burial. A service in the home, or in a church or chapel, with lessons, address, intercession for the deceased and the bereaved, and the blessing over the coffin are generally held before the actual burial. After the coffin has been lowered into the grave a word of blessing is spoken over both coffin and grave, accompanied by the throwing of three handfuls of earth. Then follows the Lord's Prayer.

The name of the deceased is mentioned during the main service and intercessions for him (or her) and for the relations either follow directly, or are included in the prayer of the church. Questions as to whether it is right and proper to pray for the deceased at all; whether intercession and blessing are directed to the dead person himself, and thus whether the making of the sign of the cross over the coffin or the open grave is permissible; or whether there should be only an intercession in general terms for God's mercy on the dying and the dead—all these questions are answered in different ways by contemporary theology. There is a certain tendency to consider the possibility and the value of such an immediate intercession and blessing with more confidence than would have been possible a generation ago. The respective attitudes to this question find expression in the different burial formulas.

Since Wilhelm Löhe presented an order for the visitation of the sick, the inclination not to leave such pastoral visiting merely to individual skill, but to offer a set order, is at present increasing. An *Agenda for the Visitation of the Sick and the Pastoral Care of the Infirm and Dying* (Kassel, 1948) therefore suggests an order for the unction of the sick based on James 5. 14, and the Apol. XIII. The readiness and confidence in using a set form for ministry to the brother in the state of ill-health—a form based on a biblical documentation and suggested by the Scriptures—will grow in the same proportion as the Lutheran Church overcomes the after-effects of frustration caused by rationalism, restriction by the theology of intellectual consciousness and the tendency to think merely in abstracts.

C. CHRIST'S ACTION IN THE CHURCH'S WORSHIP

All action of the Church during its services proclaims the gospel of the Grace of God in Jesus Christ. All witness draws its life from the effective Presence of the Lord. The insoluble link between the preached Word and the liturgical action on the one hand, and the liturgical completion of the read, preached and prayed Word on the other hand, witness to the fact that the whole worship of the Church draws its life from the Presence of the Lord. It is a witness to the Presence of the Lord, who in His full power speaks the effective Word of the Creator, and who acts in His Church 'in Word and Sacrament through the Holy Spirit as the Present Lord' (*Theological Declaration of Barmen*, III).

It is the One Word, in which Jesus Christ the Incarnate Word of the Father comes to us; and which is simultaneously presented and distributed in the oral witness as well as in the liturgical actions during the service.

The Lutheran understanding of God's condescension will have to guard against any separation of spiritual event and visible church action. Worship will be deprived of its comforting strength, if it is so misunderstood that all that happens in it is seen to represent merely the memorial of an event in the past. This would interpose between the original event and the present congregation the distance of history. The congregation would be merely induced to think itself into the 'History of the Religion of Israel', or into the 'Theology of the Early Church'—and Christ would remain in the grave of the past. Yet another deprivation can arise when the gulf of transcendence is opened between the risen Lord and His visible Church. This would imply so much emphasis upon the absolute freedom and sovereignty of the Divine Will and the raising of the Lord to sit at God's right hand, that it would remain uncertain whether according to His Promise Christ really and physically does give His Saving Presence in, with, and under the action of the Church. This attitude sees in the church service merely a symbol, sign, or image of the redemption. The redemption itself, however, is not involved in the action of the Church. The action only expresses some hope for the transcendence or the *eschaton*. Again, the service may become only a theoretical instruction. The religious act itself is realised in terms of Christian ethics 'in life', where the suggestions of the sermon will have to be put into practice. Here again worship has been emptied of its content. It is not even the exercise of faith and obedience; the practical sphere, the actual encounter, is somewhere else.

The Church is opposed to any such transfer of the real encounter into history, into transcendence, or into ethics. She firmly

D

maintains that, according to His promise, the Lord Himself gives His effective presence in the proclamation of the active Word, and in the sacramental activities of the Church, for the salvation of the believer and the judgment of the wicked.

D. 'ENTHUSIASM' OR LITURGICAL ORDER

The tension between the improvised or free prayer which flows out of the spiritual life of the individual, and the ordered and set prayer of the supra-individual liturgy is as old as the Church herself. An example of this is given in I Cor. 14, and the directions of the Apostle are still significant to-day.

It is true that every believer remains the same, unchangeable, even while he prays. A congregation would be without flesh and blood if it did not possess many individual people who prayed outside the church service, having the welfare of the kingdom of God at heart; or if it did not leave room for a manifold and living piety in the families and among groups of neighbours; or if it did not grant voluntary organisations permission to lead a common life and prayer life of their own.

All special gifts, however, are administered by the Church and serve her 'for the benefit of all'. The worship of the parish brings them all together. What happens there is not what has been called 'edifying' in a weakened meaning; it is the veritable building of the Body of Christ. The ordered action of the congregation, however, is possible only in set forms which will survive the present generation. Only those things which have been received and handed on through generations will have authority. A congregation can only pray together when the prayers of the pastor can be accepted by the members and answered by their Amen (I Cor. 14. 16). The structure of the church service, therefore, must be laid down, and should not be improvised according to the religious mood of the individual. Even the texts which will be heard within the framework of the set service must have a greater authority than that of the local congregation. The demand of the Schleswig-Holstein teacher of liturgy, Roger von Liliencron, for 'the same liturgy for village and cathedral' did express the legitimate desire of the congregation to find the same elements in the church service in different places, thus making it independent of the particular type of piety found in any particular preacher. The prayer of the pastor, again, will have to be composed in an imaginative way in order to enable the congregation to join without intellectual difficulties and to seal it with their Amen. The composition of a collect or intercession will become known through repeated use. The prayer of the preacher is not meant to express his own religious feelings, and it is not meant to give him a chance to include in a prayer what he did not like to say in his sermon. The prayer is meant to express those things which the Church as a whole, going back to the Apostles, must bring before God, its adoration and confession, intercession for its members and for the world. A model for a prayer in which the congregation can join is, for example, the Deacon's Litany which in a special bidding names the objects for intercession, which are then presented by the pastor and answered by the congregation with interceding response. The intercessions which arise from special needs and situations will have to be added spontaneously. Thus an intercession for the oppressed members and congregations during times of persecution should be included at the appropriate place in the Church's intercession. During catastrophes, and special emergencies in the parish, or on occasions for special thanksgiving, such additions would be appropriate in the section of the prayer where we pray for the whole state of the Kingdom of God, for the Church, for the nation and its government, and for different vocations, for the parish, for the deceased, etc. The pastor should, however, think about these additions beforehand so that nothing will be omitted, nothing be voiced, that might be disordered and open to misunderstanding. In the Mass and the Hour Services some time for silent prayer during the intercessions is desirable, where each member may remember those whom he loves and for whom he has to pray. In cases where intercessions for persons are requested the names should be announced beforehand.

Apart from such occasions extempore prayer does not belong to the ordered church service. It should be reserved for private devotions, for the free meetings of smaller circles, and for extraordinary missionary meetings.

E. THE SERVICE OF THE CHURCH AS A WHOLE

The church service held in a single parish is at the same time a service of the whole Church. Only the technical means of its practice differ. Where several pastors can conduct the service, where a trained choir is available, where institutional communities or keen parish groups can support the service, it will be much easier to carry out the musical side of the service, the antiphonal work of the choirs and the singing of the psalms, than in the ordinary parish service where the pastor virtually stands alone. All these variations in the technical perfection of the service, however, do not really cause a difference in its content. The lessons, prayers, psalms, and set hymns, which belong to the order of the service, should be maintained unabridged even in the smallest congregation. The aim which the Liturgical Movement tries to reach is to give an assurance to the congregation that what happens in our own church service now, will be carried out on the same day in all other congregations. Innumerable members are united with us at the same hour in the same act of hearing and adoration.

We are thankful that essential parts of our church service here on earth are taken from the celestial liturgy. Such knowledge gives new strength to the conviction of the congregation that here in her pilgrimage, as it were, she can already join in the eternal songs of praise in the service of the heavenly Church of the angels and the congregation of the saints.

Our witness to the Catholic and Apostolic Church is not only a statement about time and place. As the Early Church built her basilicas on cemeteries, and over the tombs of martyrs, so we likewise know ourselves surrounded during our acts of worship by a 'cloud of witnesses'. Yet we must renounce any interference with the judgment of the Lord and His almighty authority, such as the Roman Church has committed by its acts of canonisation, which anticipate God's judgment on certain deceased persons, and assume that it is possible to make definite statements on their functions in the heavenly hierarchy.

Yet the pre-supposition of all actions of worship in church services is the fact that the service is not only a human festival (*Feiergestaltung*), but that it unites the *whole* Church, those who are already perfected, and those who are still struggling and wandering here on earth.

IV

LUTHERAN

*

(b) Pehr Edwall
(Sweden)

Swedish theology has given less consideration to questions of principle in connection with worship, than to the historical development of worship. In this paper we shall, of course, try to take account of works in which these problems are discussed, as well as of the confessional documents of the Swedish Church in so far as they are relevant to the subject. But our main source will have to be the actual forms and practice of worship in the Swedish Church, since these reflect, either by statement or implication, the attitude of that Church to the matters under discussion here.

To begin with, it must be observed that sections A and B of the syllabus (concerning the Word and the Sacraments) cannot be regarded by a Swedish theologian and churchman as distinct and separate. In the Swedish Lutheran view, all acts of worship are governed by the Word. The Word is found in the spoken words of the service—in lessons and prayers, in hymns and sermon. The Word takes flesh and becomes action in the sacraments, especially the Lord's Supper. From a Swedish Lutheran point of view, it is impossible and absurd to play off the Sermon and the Sacrament against one another, treating them as separate from one another and assessing their relative value. The essential unity of the divine Service is based on the Word; and the two manifestations of the Word—spoken and visible—are complementary in God's dealing with men.

Historically, however, practical considerations have in some measure modified the principles. The Swedish Church after its reformation was faced with a heavy educational task in seeking to develop an active communicant membership. In reaction against the prevailing Roman practice, it became the custom in the reformed Church of Sweden as elsewhere, not to celebrate the

Eucharist without the participation of the congregation in the Communion. This resulted in a reduction of the number of celebrations, which in turn led to the development of a Sunday Service without the Sacrament. Provision is made in the *Kyrkoordning* of 1571 for just such a Service—a Preaching service of a very simple nature. The seventeenth century *Handbooks* embellished this service with a number of liturgical elements, but stopped short of turning it into an abbreviated High Mass. The *Handbook* of 1811 developed it into a kind of ante-Communion; that of 1894 gave it the name of High Mass, which has been officially applied to it ever since. Both the last-named and subsequent *Handbooks*, however, make it plain that High Mass with Communion is the main service of the Church.

In this connection it should be remarked that a eucharistic renaissance has been taking place for some time in the Swedish Church, beginning with the so-called Young Church Movement (*ungkyrkorörelsen*) at the turn of the present century. Present-day developments probably owe most (*a*) to Brilioth's scholarly studies of eucharistic problems; (*b*) to the movement known as Churchly renewal (*Kyrklig förnyelse*) which, drawing its inspiration partly from Anglican sources, has devoted much attention both to the theory and practice of eucharistic worship; and (*c*) to the influence of the Student Christian Movement. Naturally, it is among 'high-church' groups that this concern for eucharistic revival is chiefly felt, for in 'low-church' pietistic circles more fundamental importance is attached to the sermon than to any sacrament, not excluding the Lord's Supper. Yet it would be wrong and misleading to associate the desire for a richer eucharistic life exclusively with a 'high-church' outlook. It would be truer on the whole to regard it as the natural expression of churchmanship without any particular prefix.

The view of the Eucharist expressed in theology and preaching is marked by the Lutheran doctrine of the Real Presence—the sacramental presence of Christ 'in, with and under' the Bread and Wine. This leaves room, however, for a variety of interpretations —from the purely symbolical to the romanising. The official position of the Swedish Church may be said to lie between these two extremes. A characteristic idea, which goes back to the Swedish reformers, is that the Real Presence is to be found only *in usu*, not *extra usum*.

The main elements in the Swedish eucharistic rite are: Remembrance (the Words of Institution), Thanksgiving (*Sursum corda*, Proper Preface, *Sanctus*), Adoration (*Agnus Dei*), Communion (the partaking of the Elements), and the thought of Sacrifice (the Words of Institution, the Preface, *Agnus Dei*). In the communion hymns and the introductory address these elements are often included in whole or in part.

The celebration of the Lord's Supper in the Swedish Church used quite generally to be, and to some extent still is, especially in pietistic circles, marked by a strong emphasis on the Passion, an emphasis exaggerated by a one-sided understanding of the Sacrament in terms of sin and grace, which often resulted in a deeper sense of sin and penitence than of a childlike joy in forgiveness. The conception of the Sacrament as the forgiveness of sins can be traced back to the Swedish reformers; it is also reminiscent of the distribution formula of the Greek liturgies, where the thought of forgiveness is predominant.

The eucharistic note in the celebration has been strengthened, however, by the *Handbook* of 1942. The *Sanctus*, for instance, has been restored to its traditional position in direct connection with the Preface, after having stood in various places ever since Olaus Petri's time. This change strengthens the introductory note of praise, to which an alteration of the latter part of the Preface also contributes in the words: 'Therefore with Thy faithful and with all the heavenly host will we praise Thy name and sing in adoration.' In the current hymnbook (1937) the eucharistic note is sounded more frequently and more strongly than before in the hymns for the Lord's Supper. Finally, the exposition of the Sacrament in sermons and communion addresses in recent years has given much more prominence to the element of praise and the living presence of the Lord in His Church.

Celebrations of the Sacrament independently of High Mass received official sanction in 1861, though they had occurred much earlier. The Order of Service laid down in 1894 for use on such occasions is: Address, Confession and Absolution, Collects, and then the usual order of the Mass from the Offertory Hymn onwards. This form is in frequent use.

The *Handbook* of 1942 also provides for a sacramental service which consists, broadly speaking, of a complete High Mass, though without a sermon and as a rule with only one reading from Scripture. This form of service is, however, but little used.

Returning now to the section on *The Word of God*, the writings of the Swedish Reformers and the Confessional documents of the Swedish Church reveal a deep concern for preaching and a great reverence for God's Word. Ever since the Reformation the sermon has been regarded as an indispensable part of the High Mass. A number of other services centre entirely round the sermon— e.g. matins, evensong, mid-week services, Holy Week services. In all these services the sermon is the main thing, though it is accompanied by a brief Altar-service (as it is called) of which the main elements are a Prayer for the Church Universal, the Lord's Prayer and the Blessing.

The sermon is conceived in the Swedish Church, not as a religious address or a lecture on philosophical, ethical or religious topics, but as a part of the indivisible Work of Christ, continued in His Church on earth. Christ is not only our High Priest, but also our Prophet; and as High Priest and Prophet He is King in the coming Kingdom of God. It is therefore the duty of the Church, through the ministry instituted by Christ, rightly to administer the sacraments and rightly to proclaim God's Word, in loyalty to her Lord and Master. The Church can as little cease to preach the Gospel as she can cease to celebrate the Eucharist.

Two recently published theological works deal with the essential significance of preaching as seen in the light of the Swedish tradition. Archbishop Brilioth in his History of Preaching (*Predikans historia*) analyses the liturgical, prophetic and exegetical elements in preaching through the ages. Prof. Wingren of Lund, in his *Predikan*, emphasises the character of preaching as the *kerygma* of God's work of salvation through Christ.

The importance attached to the sermon is a characteristic feature of Swedish worship. The form of the sermon varies from the traditional style, with its exordium, the silent praying of the Lord's Prayer, the announcement of the subject, and the development of the theme, to a freer construction; but theme-preaching is much more common. In content, the sermon naturally varies with different types of piety. 'Low-church' preaching emphasises the preacher's personal experience of the Gospel, the need for conversion, and the aspect of personal testimony in preaching. The 'old-church' tradition of pietism strongly stresses the *ordo salutis* and the pastoral function of preaching. 'High-church' preaching

is of a less homogeneous nature, and though more nearly akin
to the 'old-church' than the 'low-church' type, it gives greater
weight to the sacraments and the Church.

The view taken of the Bible naturally has its effect on preaching. A thoroughgoing modernist view, such as that represented
by the Religious Reform Union of Sweden (*Sveriges religiösa re-
formförbund*), is rare. Fundamentalism still persists in some quarters,
but for the most part a position between the two extremes prevails. A historical view of the Scriptures is combined with a sense
of their authoritative character, and there is an increasing measure
of agreement on this subject. The old conflict between modernism
and fundamentalism can be regarded as belonging to the past.

A clear distinction is maintained between Word and Sacraments. The sermon is not in the Swedish view a sacrament,
though we might perhaps speak of a 'mysticism of the Word' in
this connection. The Word operates through its own indwelling
power, for in the Word is Christ and His Spirit.

The chief service of the Swedish Church, the High Mass, is
dominated throughout by the Word. It includes two Scripture
readings, the Epistle and the Gospel, taken from the traditional
series, which has largely been preserved intact. There is a three-
year cycle of preaching-texts, so arranged that the Gospel together
with the so-called Second and Third Year's High Mass texts are
treated in due order—all of them being prescribed in the *Evangeliebok*. But from other points of view also, the Swedish High
Mass is a Service of the Word. The Introits for the Festivals of the
Church Year are taken from Scripture; the introductory Trisagion
echoes Isa. 6. 3; one of the Confessions is Ps. 51. 2-6, 12-13; the
versicles of the Litany come from Ps. 103. 10; 51. 13, and
28. 9; in the *Sanctus* and the *Agnus Dei* there are reminiscences of
Ps. 118. 26, and Matt. 21. 9, or John 1. 36. The language of the
liturgical prayers is very close to that of the Bible. Last but not
least, the Swedish hymns are closely dependent on the Bible,
especially the Psalter. No less than 96 of the 600 hymns in the
hymnbook are Scripture paraphrases, 38 of them from the Psalter.

Baptism occupies an important place in the life and preaching
of the Swedish Church. Baptism is regarded as the foundation of
the Christian life and the washing of regeneration. As a rule it is
administered in church and in connection with the High Mass,
so that its character as a churchly occasion is emphasised. In some

churches it is administered immediately after the opening hymn of the High Mass.

Penance (which is not strictly counted as a sacrament in the Church of Sweden) has been given to some extent a liturgical form, but as it belongs rather to the individual cure of souls than to public worship, it does not come within the scope of this paper.

With regard to other ecclesiastical ceremonies, the Swedish Church follows the Lutheran tradition in not considering them to be sacraments.

II

The liturgical motifs mentioned in Section II, (i) to (v), should in the Swedish view all have a place in worship. In the Swedish High Mass they are to be found as follows:

(a) Thanksgiving: The *Laudamus* (or on other than Feast days, hymn 24 in the *Psalmbok*: *Allena Gud i himmelrik*—'To God alone in heaven be glory') in gratitude for the forgiveness imparted through the Absolution; the concluding words of the Preface, quoted above, together with the *Sanctus*; the concluding *Benedicamus*; and hymns of praise sung during the service.

(b) Confession and Absolution open every High Mass, the former usually in the words of Olaus Petri's prayer: 'I, poor sinful man . . .' The *Kyrie* which follows may be regarded as the response of the congregation to the Confession read by the minister, just as the *Laudamus* can be regarded as a response to the Absolution pronounced by him. A similar order with introductory Confession and Absolution is found in the other services named above, and also in the so-called 'Short High Mass' (a simpler preaching service on the lines of the High Mass) and in children's services. In the two last-mentioned types, however, somewhat different forms of words are used.

(c) The element of adoration is less well provided for in the Swedish High Mass. There is, of course, something of it in the point mentioned under sub-section (a) above, and also in the Collects, which are mainly of mediaeval origin and express direct adoration. But there is little of adoration in the more precise sense, though it may be said to occur in the Silent Prayer which, according to the Handbook, can be introduced after the Confession at High Mass or after the Lord's Prayer (and immediately before the

Pax and the *Agnus Dei*) when the Lord's Supper is celebrated. In the form provided in the *Handbook* for liturgical Evensong—the fuller form—there is a similar Silent Prayer before the Lord's Prayer. After the Lord's Prayer at High Mass such silent worship can be said to have a sacramental content as connected with the Lord's Supper, though in the other two cases there is nothing so specific about it. Adoration of the eucharistic Elements *extra usum* is foreign to the tradition of the Church of Sweden.

(*d*) Intercession for the living is made at High Mass and at all the other services listed in the Handbook, both in the prayers for the Church Universal and in the Litany. Special intercessions for the sick are sometimes read at High Mass from the pulpit after the sermon, and in some churches are followed by a special hymn of intercession. But the practice of praying for the sick by name in the public services of the Church is not general. Nor are any prayers offered for the dead, unless the so-called Thanksgiving for the Dead be counted as such. This is also offered from the pulpit and is often accompanied by the tolling of a bell. There is, however, nothing that can really be called intercession for the souls of the departed; it is rather a form of commemoration, which includes an exhortation to those present at the service. The Burial Service is of a similar character. Although Luther did not altogether reject prayer for the dead, such prayer soon fell into disuse in the reformed Swedish Church; and, if it occurs to-day, it is undoubtedly regarded by the congregation as a romanising practice.

(*e*) The Oblation in kind can be said to survive in the Church of Sweden in the form of a collection taken during the hymn after the sermon. In some places, however, collections—especially the major ones—are still taken in such a way that the congregation go up to the altar or the communion rail during the Offertory Hymn (or the last hymn) and place their offering either on the altar or on a table near it, or on the communion rail. The custom of making a money offering at the communion rail at the Lord's Supper survived until recently, but has now practically disappeared. It cannot be said that the idea of the Christian's oblation or sacrifice is often present in the preaching of the Swedish Church. There may sometimes be a reference to it in the sermon, especially in connection with the Lord's Supper, but it cannot be claimed that the thought is prominent. Fear of Romanising notions and of anything that could be conceived as 'works-religion' is no doubt the reason why this idea, which in itself is one of the central ideas of the Bible, has not received justice in the doctrine and worship of the Swedish Church.

III

Only set prayers are used in a Swedish service—with the possible exception of the prayer that accompanies the sermon. The *Evangeliebok* preserves (as was noted above, Section II, subsection (c)) the traditional Collects, and includes besides for every Sunday and Feast Day a special Collect, taken as a rule from Veit Dietrich's Children's Sermons. In addition, the *Handbook* contains a series of prayers for festivals and special occasions. Such prayers can also be issued by the Bishop for a particular diocese or by the Archbishop for the whole Church. Extempore prayer has its place, according to the Swedish view, in the private devotion of individuals or the prayer-fellowship of smaller groups, but not in the corporate liturgical prayer of the Church.

IV

There cannot be said to be any developed theory or clearly formulated view on this point, though we may recall that the Preface has reference to the fellowship of the Church as both in and above space and time ('all Thy faithful', 'all the heavenly host'). It is significant that it is in connection with the Lord's Supper that this communion across all barriers is recognised. The same point of view is represented in the Introit and prayers for All Saints' Day, and also in some of the hymns in the hymnbook. These often give expression to a stronger sense of Christian unity than one would expect simply from a study of the liturgy. And in preaching to-day it is quite often emphasised that the worship of the local congregation is a part of the Communion of Saints, which embraces both earth and heaven.

V

1. *Congregational singing*. This is so characteristic a feature of worship in the Church of Sweden, that it ought not to go unnoticed. Hymn-singing and joining in the choral portions of the

Mass form an essential part of the liturgical responsibility of the congregation, which is thereby actively engaged in the aspects of worship discussed in section II above. Where the choir sings, it is not regarded as a substitute for the congregation, but as its representative.

2. *Church music.* The musical aspect of the service as a whole deserves special attention. The present *Mass-book I* (1942) is so arranged that it is possible to have, from the musical point of view, a pure Gregorian Mass, from the Introit to the Benedicamus. The melodies are taken from Swedish manuscripts dating from the time of the Reformation. The austere tone of this ecclesiastical music imparts to the Swedish Mass a special character of objectivity and sacredness. Besides the Gregorian, however, there are a series of newer melodies, all of a thoroughly ecclesiastical type and arranged in a musically perfect form, without any secular elements. The music for the purely liturgical services of Morning and Evening Prayer and for the more solemn form of Holy Week Service, is wholly Gregorian and is taken from Swedish Manuscript material of the sixteenth century. It is to be found in what is incorrectly called *Mass-book II* (1944). The Swedish *Chorale-book* (1939), which is similarly governed by the strict principles of ecclesiastical music, contains chorales from the Early Church and the Middle Ages as well as from later times, all of which are harmonised in correct ecclesiastical style. The Anglo-Saxon 'revival hymns' which were introduced to a limited extent into the Hymnbook Supplement of 1921 and the Hymnbook of 1937, have for the most part been set to new tunes, and where the old melodies have been retained (generally as alternatives) they have been re-harmonised on stricter lines. Hence the Swedish chorale has a character all its own, and the whole Service of Worship is from a musical point of view chaste, unsentimental and objective in style.

It should also be remarked that other forms of church music (preludes and postludes, etc.) are becoming more and more definitely ecclesiastical in style, and that the principles of the so-called 'Organ Movement' are governing the restoration of old, and the installation of new organs in churches.

3. *The Canonical Hours.* Notice should also be taken of the restoration of the Canonical Hours in the Swedish Church. After the Reformation these were preserved in an evangelical form in

Sweden. With the disappearance of the Choir-priests about the middle of the sixteenth century, the singing at the Hour-services in cathedrals was entrusted to a much larger extent than previously to the pupils of the cathedral schools. This resulted in a reduction of the number of Hours observed; but some observance persisted into the seventeenth century, until the catechetical and homiletical interests of the time transformed them into the non-liturgical Matins and Evensong which we have to-day. Around the end of the nineteenth and beginning of the twentieth centuries, liturgical material from the time of the Swedish reformation was discovered and made the subject of scholarly investigation. This has had practical results both for the music used in worship generally, and for a direct restoration of the Swedish observance of the Hours. The Swedish Church has no officially authorised form of the Hours, but the ritual prescribed by the *Handbook* for solemn Morning and Evening Prayer reflects the principles of the Hours, and it is noted in the *Handbook* that Matins and Evensong may, if due permission is obtained, be exchanged for Lauds and Vespers. Private initiative has, however, produced a Swedish evangelical Book of Hours based on material from the time of the Swedish Reformation, in the shape of Adell-Peters' *Den svenska tidegärden* (1944), which has been followed by a complete *Antiphonal* (1950). Some use has been made of the former, chiefly in 'high-church' circles, though the services have been more read than sung. In these circles it has been felt to meet a need of regularity in the devotional life. The fact that the Hours are based on the Word is also regarded as an asset: 'to pray the service is to pray God's Word'. It has also been maintained that observance of the Hours answers a felt need for liturgical devotion, and accentuates fellowship with the Church Universal in its service of prayer.

VIII

The Order of High Mass in the Swedish Church is an example of the traditional Western Mass in harmony with the fundamental principles of the Reformation and in conscious fidelity to *la grande tradition*. Strictly speaking, this provides the answer to the question raised here. The Swedish Church has difficulty in envisaging any more fundamental changes in this historically developed order of Divine Service.

V

REFORMED

*

(a) William D. Maxwell
(Scotland)

This paper is written unofficially to express briefly the doctrine
and practice of the Church of Scotland in worship. While not
conforming strictly to the 'Lines of Enquiry' first suggested by
the Commission on Ways of Worship, or to the revised Syllabus,
it does attempt to cover most of the points raised by them.

A. *The Word of God*

The phrase is used in this paper not of Christ the Incarnate
Word, but of the living disclosure of God 'contained in the Scriptures of the Old and New Testaments'. Christ, the Incarnate
Word, is at once source and goal of all Christian worship and this
is firmly believed in the Church of Scotland. It is this that makes
worship to be offered 'in spirit and in truth', which does not
mean merely 'spiritually and truly'. It is informed by the truth
that is in Christ, and imbued by His Spirit. But the Word contained in Holy Scripture is also integral to Scottish worship and
dominates it throughout. Such worship is both a means and an
end: as a means of grace it edifies, builds up men in the Christian
religion; but it is primarily an end, indeed 'man's chief end' which
is 'to glorify God and to enjoy Him for ever'.

The Word of God finds expression in the Scripture Readings
which are present in all acts of Scottish worship. Though not
universally followed, the practice authorised by the Church is,
on Sunday mornings and at the Lord's Supper, that 'A lesson
from the Old Testament shall be read, then a lesson or lessons
from the New Testament, of which one shall be taken from the
Gospels,' and at the evening service, lessons from the Old and
New Testament are read. A lectionary is available in the *Book of
Common Order*, expressing these principles and following the

Christian Year. In this way, the central passages of the Bible, chosen for their evangelical emphasis, are read in the churches week by week.

The Psalter also plays a large part in Scottish worship. A metrical version, in use for three hundred years, set to strong, virile tunes, is generally preferred for congregational use, and from it selections suitable to the day are made; but prose psalms (A.V.) are also sung, set to Anglican chants, in many of the larger churches. Anthems, using or based upon the words of Holy Scripture, are in wide use; and metrical paraphrases of passages from the Scriptures, set to psalm tunes, are in general use. The New Testament canticles take their place with the prose psalms. Sentences from Holy Scripture comprise the Call to Prayer, and the prayers themselves are rich in Scriptural content. Scottish worship is impregnated through and through by the Word of God.

The sermon is considered to be an essential and integral part of any solemn act of worship in the Scottish Church. It is an invariable custom to include a sermon in morning and evening worship, at the celebration of the Eucharist and in services of ordination and induction of ministers.

A high doctrine of the sermon predominates. It is regarded as an extension of the Word of God, an exposition of Holy Scripture and Christian doctrine, and an exhortation to dedication and obedience to God. Ministers before their ordination are subjected to a long course of study. They must first qualify as Masters of Arts, after which they proceed to three years' study in Divinity, also at the university. Except in very unusual circumstances, Divinity students must be able to read the Scriptures in the original tongues, in addition to having undergone thorough instruction in Divinity, ecclesiastical history and cognate subjects. The reason for the strictness of this discipline is to ensure as far as is humanly possible that ministers be adequately trained to interpret the Holy Scriptures in their preaching. Care and study are also devoted to homiletics; and in parish work a high priority is given to biblical study and preparation of sermons.

Although the Reformers themselves did not teach this doctrine, some later non-Scottish apologists of the Reformed tradition have said that the sermon in the Reformed Churches is a substitute for the elevation of the Host in the Mass. This in fact is not so—

the Reformers were drawn into no such false antithesis between Word and Sacrament—but it is an interesting indication of the high regard in which the sermon is held in the Reformed Church, including the Church of Scotland. It is considered to be indeed the showing forth of Jesus Christ crucified and the power of His resurrection, that He may be worshipped, adored and served. In this sense it has an almost sacramental significance, but is better described as truly prophetic. The sermon has never been understood in Scotland as being in any sense a substitute for the Sacrament of Holy Communion, or as in itself sufficient.

In the early Reformed Church, great emphasis was laid also upon catechetical instruction, both in the church and in the home. That emphasis predominated in Scotland up till the Edwardian period, and the *Shorter Catechism*, compiled by the Westminster Fathers in the mid-seventeenth century was the manual used.

Now, however, that has ceased. But although no longer catechetical in method (as a method of instruction it is now seen by many to have been too lightly departed from), instruction still retains an important place in the Church of Scotland. There are Sunday schools for the young, and recently also a vigorous effort has been made to teach religion more adequately in the day schools by the appointment of school chaplains in many places. Bible classes exist in large numbers for those of 'teen age and beyond it. Extensive Confirmation classes are held to prepare young communicants, the ordinary age for Confirmation being from sixteen to nineteen in the Church of Scotland. This means that the final preparatory instruction is given on an adult level.

Thus emphasis is continually placed upon the Holy Scriptures as containing 'the whole counsel of God, concerning all things necessary for His own glory, man's salvation, faith and life'. And, as 'man's chief end is to glorify God, and to enjoy Him for ever', so 'the Word of God', it is steadfastly believed, 'which is contained in the Scriptures is the only rule to direct us how we may glorify and enjoy Him'.

B. *Liturgical Forms*

In the Church of Scotland the *Book of Common Order*, 1940, (which represents the mind of the united Church of Scotland after the union in 1929) published by the Oxford University Press, is the standard of worship, but its use is not compulsory.

The preface states the position clearly: the General Assembly in authorising this book 'recognised that the provision of such forms implies no desire to supersede free prayer. Liberty in the conduct of worship is a possession which the Church of Scotland will not surrender. But a service-book is necessary to express the mind of the Church with regard to its offices of worship in orders and forms which, while not fettering individual judgment in particulars, will set the norm for the reverent and orderly conduct of the various public services in which ministers have to lead their people . . . In preparing this book, the Committee has been careful to keep in mind the doctrinal basis of the Church as stated in the first Article of her constitution. The Church of Scotland is "part of the Holy Catholic or Universal Church". As such, it has the same roots as those from which has sprung the life of every Christian Communion ancient or modern, throughout the world; it therefore claims the right to avail itself freely of the precious heritage of devotional literature which . . . has proved its fitness to survive. Further, the Church of Scotland, adhering to the Scottish Reformation, and receiving "the Word of God which is contained in the Scriptures of the Old and New Testaments as its supreme rule of faith and life", bases all its worship on Holy Scripture. Without reservation of any kind it may be asserted that everything contained in this book receives its warrant from that source.'

Thus, liturgical forms in the Church of Scotland are not only dominated by the Word of God but, by virtue of that fact, they also reflect and proclaim it. This, however, is not to say that they are subjective and didactic—they come from God and are offered to God; and their purpose is to give adoration, make oblation and remember the faithful before God. They are an end, and primarily so; yet they are also a means of grace.

C. *Sacramental Worship*

A brief but profound definition of a sacrament is given in the *Shorter Catechism*: 'A sacrament is an holy ordinance instituted by Christ; wherein by sensible signs, Christ, and the benefits of the new covenant, are represented, sealed and applied to believers.' Some, without knowledge of the historical meaning of these terms have supposed that this is mere memorialism; for their benefit it is well, therefore, to recall the words of the First Scots

Confession of 1560, the background against which the Church of
Scotland accepted this definition and which still remains a standard of the Church: 'We utterlie dampne (condemn) the vanitie
of those that affirme Sacramentis to be nothing ells but naked and
bair signes.'[1] Sacramental doctrine in the Church of Scotland is
the high Calvinian doctrine without taint of 'Zwinglianism'.

(a) *The Eucharist*. This is seen in the Eucharist, where the Confession of Faith asserts that 'the body and blood of Christ are as
really, but spiritually, present to the faith of believers in that
ordinance as the elements themselves are to their outward senses'.
The Scots Confession is even more explicit: 'We confess and
undoubtedly believe that the faithful, in the right use of the Lord's
Table, do so eat the body, and drink the blood of the Lord Jesus,
that He remaineth in them, and they in Him; yea, they are so
made flesh of His flesh, and bone of His bone, that as the eternal
Godhead hath given to the flesh of Christ Jesus life and immortality, so doth Christ Jesus, by His flesh and blood, eaten and
drunken by us, give unto us the same prerogatives.'

It may be added that, when the word 'symbol' is used, it is
not used in the easy-going popular sense of a mere sign, but in the
theological sense of a point of contact between the divine and the
human. A symbol is a symbol of 'things present' not 'things
absent', to use Calvin's phrase. This definition is decisive and it
will be seen from the quotations above what its implications are.

What now, we may ask, is the doctrine of sacrifice in the
Eucharist? This is not mentioned in our standards, but is implicit
in the words of the consecration prayer contained in the *Book of
Common Order*. The determinative words are 'pleading His eternal
sacrifice, we thy servants do set forth this memorial'. The Scottish
rite lays emphasis not upon 'the oblation once offered', though
this, of course, is there in recollection and theology, but specifically
upon the eternal quality of our Lord's sacrifice: it happened once
for all in time, but it belongs to eternity where He continually
presents Himself before the Father. Similarly, the Eucharist is of
eternity, and when we plead 'His eternal sacrifice', we desire Him to
unite our offering and prayers with His, which is eternal, and 'this
memorial' in time and space is a part of that eternal memorial.
His sacrifice is not repeatable, but it is continually renewed; the

[1] Knox's *Works*, ed. Laing, II, 114.

'remembering' is not mere recollection in the psychological sense (which, in fact, is never the biblical sense), but a real uniting, possible by grace and through faith, faith which is not mere intellectual assent, but a committal of the whole person to Him. It is, thus, as Calvin declares, a *vera communicatio* with Him.

The familiar Scottish paraphrase nearly always sung at Scottish Communion services as the elements of bread and wine are brought in solemn procession to the Holy Table echoes this doctrine:

> '*And oft the sacred rite renew*
> *That brings my wondrous love to view* . . . . .
> *In this the Covenant is sealed*
> *And Heaven's eternal grace revealed.*'

The note of bringing what is eternal into time and linking what is in time with eternity is unmistakable here. And 'renew' has a special significance: it is not 'repeat' or 're-enact', but what is eternal is 'renewed' in time and 'wondrous love' is 'brought to view', 'the Covenant is sealed' and 'Heaven's eternal grace revealed'.

One may add that Holy Communion in the Church of Scotland may be celebrated only by ordained presbyters, ministers of the Word and Sacraments. They are ordained by the presbyters of a presbytery, acting together and constitutionally and by authority of the whole Church. And the Succession has not been broken.

Celebrations of the Eucharist, however, in the Church of Scotland are, generally speaking, infrequent. Although it was the expressed wish of Calvin to have the Lord's Supper celebrated each week as the chief Sunday service of the Reformed Church, he was not successful in giving this effect, owing to ignorance and prejudice (as he himself said). After prolonged controversy, some of it extremely bitter, practice in Geneva became quarterly celebrations—at Christmas, Easter, Pentecost and Harvest-tide. The first edition of the *Book of Common Order*, 1562, issued in Scotland, directed that Holy Communion be celebrated monthly; but this in fact was never done owing partly, if indeed not chiefly, to the great shortage of ministers (there were only two hundred and eighty-nine ordained ministers in the Church of Scotland in 1567) during the first forty or fifty years of the Reformation

in Scotland. Thus Holy Communion was, of necessity, celebrated infrequently, from once to four times a year, depending
upon the circumstances; and ministers had to travel about to
different parishes to celebrate Holy Communion, while people
from parishes adjoining those where celebrations were made available came to the celebrations there. The custom of infrequent
Communion thus became established, and it was, moreover, con-
genial to the people, since before the Reformation they had been
in the habit of communicating but once a year. The ideal of more
frequent celebrations was not, however, forgotten, and in 1644
the Westminster *Directory* directed that Holy Communion be
'frequently celebrated'; but it is doubtful if this injunction was
ever obeyed.

During the last seventy-five years, however, efforts have been
made in many parishes to establish the custom of more frequent
celebrations. Weekly celebrations are now not unknown; there
are monthly celebrations in a few parishes; in others, in addition
to the statutory quarterly celebrations, there are celebrations at
Christmas, Easter and Whitsun. The practice is growing, but
progress is slow. It is not, however, a sign that the Sacrament is
held in low esteem. The precise contrary is the fact. Opposition
to frequent Communion is no doubt mistaken, but it derives
from a high view of the Sacrament as an action so holy as not to
be frequently repeated. When celebrations do occur, very large
numbers attend; and probably the great majority of the membership receives Communion several times in the year.

The content of the service may be briefly described, as set out
in the *Book of Common Order*. It begins with a Psalm or Hymn of
praise, traditionally Ps. 43. 3-5, in metre, followed by a Call to
Prayer in words of Holy Scripture, suitable to the season of the
Christian Year. Then follow the collect for purity, a confession of
sins, prayer for pardon and a collect. A canticle, psalm or hymn is
then sung, and the Lessons (O.T., Epistle and Gospel) follow,
which may be interspersed by singings. The Nicene Creed may
then be said after the Gospel; General Intercessions and the Commemoration of the Departed follow; and after a psalm or hymn
the sermon is preached, preceded by a prayer for illumination and
followed by an ascription of praise. The Offertory, consisting of
the collection of the people's gifts, their presentation at the Holy
Table, Scriptural words of invitation, a psalm or hymn (tradi-

tionally Ps. 24. 7-10, or Paraphrase 35) during which the offerings are taken to the vestry and the elements of bread and wine are brought to the Holy Table in solemn procession; the Creed, if not used before, is then recited by all, and the minister unveils the elements saying the prayer of the veil and an offertory prayer. He then reads the words of institution and proceeds to the prayer of consecration. It is preceded by the salutation and *sursum corda* and in content is as follows: preface (including thanksgiving for creation and providence), proper preface, *Sanctus, Benedictus qui venit* with *Hosanna, Vere Sanctus* (thanksgiving for redemption), amamnesis, epiclesis, oblation and self-oblation, communion of saints and doxology. The Lord's Prayer follows, after which comes the Fraction, when the words of institution are said and the manual acts performed. After the *Agnus Dei*, the minister receives in both kinds and delivers the bread and the cup to the people. After all have received, the *Pax* is given; and the service concludes with a post-Communion thanksgiving, a psalm or hymn (traditionally Ps. 103. 1-5) and the Benediction; after which the elements are removed from the church and meanwhile *Nunc dimittis* may be sung. The basilican posture is normally used by the minister, and elders serve the people at Communion, who receive sitting. The consecrated elements have been traditionally taken to the sick after the service, and an order for this is provided in the *Book of Common Order*.

(b) *Holy Baptism.* The *Shorter Catechism* defines Baptism thus: 'Baptism is a sacrament, wherein the washing with water in the Name of the Father, and of the Son, and of the Holy Ghost, doth signify and seal our ingrafting into Christ, and partaking of the benefits of the covenant of grace, and our engagement to be the Lord's' (Ans. 94). According to the law of the Church of Scotland, Baptism is to be ministered only by a minister, and (except for urgent reasons) before the congregation. For centuries, however, private Baptism was customary, introduced in the early seventeenth century, but public Baptism is now general and normally takes place after sermon on Sunday mornings.

The order may be briefly described, as containing all that is essential to this sacrament. It opens with a sentence from Holy Scripture, the invocation in Ps. 124. 8; then the words of institution (Matt. 28. 18-20) are read with a brief exposition, and if infants are to be baptised, Mark 10. 13-16, is also read. Confession of faith is then made by the parents or sponsors in the words of the Apostles' Creed, and the vows are taken. After consecration of the water, Baptism is ministered by affusion while the baptismal formula is recited. Then the minister blesses the baptised person, and declares him to be 'now received into the membership of the holy Catholic Church'. The service then concludes with prayers for the baptised person, and for all present that they may more truly live in Christ.

(c) *Other Sacraments*. The Church of Scotland accepts as sacraments the two alone which were ordained by our Lord. But other acts of a sacramental nature have their place in her rites: e.g. confirmation of baptised persons, solemnisation of matrimony and ordination of ministers.

In Calvinian theology it is held that the sacraments cannot be separated from the Word without losing their nature—*Rectam sacramenti administrationem verbo contineri*.[1] This also was doctrine and practice in the early Church. The Word and Sacraments are not to be set in opposition; they are complementary, each fulfilling the other. This view governs the doctrine and practice of the Church of Scotland, representing the Christian tradition in its fulness.

D. *In view of the syllabus, some other matters fall briefly to be mentioned.*

(a) *Adoration*. Adoration must transfuse all worship. 'Le premier poinct de la chrestienté est d'adorer Dieu droictement,' said Calvin;[2] and again he declares that worship in its purpose and nature exists for the glory of God rather than the consolation of man: *In gloriam Dei petimus . . . Antequam ullam pro nobis precem concipimus, praefamur ut eius voluntas fiat*.[3] This is a cardinal principle of Reformed worship; it received its strongest expression from Calvin.

Adoration therefore receives due emphasis in Scottish worship. It is not only an act in itself at the very beginning of worship in psalm and prayer, but it pervades the whole worship of the day. This is seen in the choice of psalms, hymns and anthems, which

---

[1] *Inst.* IV, xvii, 39; see also *Tracts*, ii, 344.   [2] *Op.* vi, 485.
[3] See *Op.* i, 9-7, 917, 936.

traditionally have always been chiefly in praise of God rather than
sentimental and subjective. The metrical psalms are set to fine
strong tunes, expressing the glory and grandeur of Almighty God;
and their use is an act in which all can join. The metrical psalms
are often rugged, and sometimes crude; but they are always
strong, never weak or sentimental, in contrast to many modern
hymns which are preferred by some communions. Such hymns
are not easily admitted to Scottish worship because of the conscious bias towards objective worship.

(b) *Petition and Intercession for the living and dead.* Intercession
has always occupied a conspicuous place in Scottish worship, but
until recent years—the change was effected perhaps chiefly by
the war of 1914-18 with its roll of the dead—following the teaching of the Reformation, prayer was offered for the living only.
The dead, however, were always commemorated with thanksgiving before God, for the Church of Scotland has always been
deeply conscious of its unity with the Church invisible in heaven.
In modern Scottish practice, although there has been no controversy, the practice of praying specifically for the dead that God's
will and purpose may be perfected in them is becoming gradually
more widespread; and support is given to this practice by some
prayers in the *Book of Common Order.*

(c) *Oblation or Offering.* For Christians *the* oblation or offering
is the Eucharist, and reference to this has been made earlier in this
paper.

In a lesser degree, all Christian acts of worship are an oblation,
for worship in the true sense is something offered to God; it is
not a manipulation of Him. We speak, perhaps too readily, of the
gifts we bring as the 'offerings' (some, indeed, grotesquely, speak
of them as 'the offering'); but it is not to be supposed that they
are the only or indeed the principal offerings made in worship.
Worship is grievously and fundamentally misunderstood if it is
not seen throughout to be an offering to Almighty God.

Certain consequences of this doctrine emerge. If throughout
worship we render back to God all that we have and are, it is
indispensable that we bring to Him in our worship our best
resources of goodness, beauty and truth. These values derive
ultimately from God, and in worship they are offered back to
Him. Consequently, the speech and words of prayer must be

direct and simple, preserving the rhythm and structure of good prose; the ceremonial must be ordered and reverent; and the music must be strong and pure. The church building itself must be well designed and kept clean and comely. All that contributes to worship, while of necessity it may not be elaborate or expensive where resources are limited, must still be good—the best that we can offer within the limits of our resources. Nothing must be shoddy, slipshod, ugly, careless or false; for to offer such to God is to profane His holy Name and to cast opprobrium upon Him before men.

(*d*) *How far ought worship to provide for free prayers as well as set forms?* Here again a quantitative answer is hardly possible; but where worship is to be a common action in which all actively and physically share, it must take place through set forms. Worshippers cannot be left free to compose their own hymns—they must have a set form of words, if they are to sing together. This principle applies throughout worship.

On the other hand, free prayer has also its place in common worship; and when it is used the many must be led by one.

Much misunderstanding has been generated by setting free prayer and fixed forms in opposition to each other. They should be recognised as complementary, not antithetical. Both have their rightful place in common worship.

Calvin's words on the subject of set forms are well known: 'Concerning a form of prayer and ecclesiastical rites,' he wrote to Somerset, 'I highly approve of it that there should be a certain form from which ministers be not allowed to vary. That first, some provision be made to help the unskilfulness and simplicity of some; secondly, that the consent and harmony of the Churches one with another may appear; and lastly, that the capricious giddiness and levity of such as effect innovations may be prevented . . . Therefore, there ought to be a stated form of prayer and administration of the sacraments.'[1]

At the same time, it was recognised from the beginning, in the Reformed Churches, that opportunity ought to be given for free or extemporaneous prayer to express the mood and needs of the moment and to give liberty to the impulsion of the Holy Spirit. Thus provision was made for free prayer, usually in the prayer

[1] *Op.* XIII, 70.

before sermon. Later, controversy arose between the out-and-out advocates of free prayer and those who defended set forms. It was a mistaken controversy, which can never be usefully revived: for both have a place. Provision should be made for each in any truly ecumenical Church; with set forms and a fixed structure predominating, for the same reasons (although additional reasons might be adduced) as those laid down by Calvin, whose argument is still valid.

(e) *What is held to be the relation of the worship of the local worshipping company, the Church universal and the Church in heaven?* This question has been already answered by implication. In spite of the divided state of Christendom, the Church of Scotland considers herself a part of the Church Universal, and that her ministry and worship are valid, catholic and in agreement with Holy Scripture. It is unnecessary here to argue the grounds for this belief, as that belongs to another Commission; but it is necessary unequivocally to state it. Therefore, in its worship the Church of Scotland believes that the local worshipping company is united with the whole Church in heaven and earth, and the worshippers are deeply conscious of this unity. This fact has been repeated in all her standards and it is evident in her practice. At Holy Communion, her table is open to all Christians. Moreover, it is interesting to observe that the Church of Scotland has never used the description 'Protestant' but always 'Reformed'. The Church of Scotland is not a new protesting Church formed at the Reformation, but she is the ancient Church of Scotland, Catholic and Reformed.

(f) *Are there any other elements of worship that must be considered?* In common with all other Reformed Churches, the Church of Scotland has neglected the use of silence in its worship. It is true that there is one outstanding point when silence is observed, namely, at the Eucharist during Communion. But this is insufficient. When worship came to be guided by ritual and the spoken word, and ceremonial fell into a secondary place, the ministry of silence almost disappeared from worship. It should be restored. How and where will require careful study, and the elucidation of guiding principles.

(g) *Sunday morning worship.* Sunday morning worship in the Church of Scotland is derived from and modelled upon the

Eucharist, even when the Eucharist is not celebrated. The order therefore is traditional and provision is made for all these elements in so far as it can be made in a non-sacramental service. There is not, however, even within the Church of Scotland, complete agreement upon a 'right' order. Consequently, two orders are given in the *Book of Common Order*, the second of which represents the main stream of Scottish tradition while the first shows the influence of Anglican Morning Prayer at one or two points. Of these two orders, in the writer's opinion the second is to be preferred as more nearly related to a 'right' sequence, and it is also the traditional sequence. They may be briefly set out as follows:

I. *Book of Common Order, pp.* 11-17

Psalm, paraphrase or hymn of praise
Call to prayer in words of Holy Scripture
Prayers of Adoration, confession of sins, prayer for pardon and supplication
Psalm, paraphrase, hymn or canticle
Old Testament lesson
Prose or metrical psalm
Epistle and Gospel
Apostles' Creed
Prayers of Thanksgiving, Intercession and Commemoration of Departed
The Lord's Prayer
Psalm, paraphrase or hymn
Prayer for Illumination
Sermon
Ascription of Praise
Collection of offerings
Prayer of dedication and oblation
Psalm, paraphrase or hymn
Benediction

II. *Book of Common Order, pp.* 42-45

The order agrees with that above until the conclusion of the Apostles' Creed, and then proceeds as follows:
Prayers of Intercession and Commemoration of the Departed
Psalm, paraphrase or hymn
Prayer of Illumination

Sermon
Ascription of Praise
Collection of Offerings
Great Prayer of Thanksgiving, Dedication and Oblation,
 Intercession (brief) and Communion of Saints, Doxology
The Lord's Prayer
Psalm, paraphrase or hymn
Benediction

V

REFORMED

*

(b) Julius Schweizer
(Switzerland)

The common aims of the Commission will be best served if as far as possible views are here represented and wording used such as would be approved by the majority of the Reformed membership in German Switzerland. Too subjective a statement might not be appropriate.

I. *What do the Reformed Churches of German-speaking Switzerland understand to-day by Divine Service?*

Divine Service is based solely upon God's gracious gift to sinful man made manifest in Jesus Christ. The Lord alone, therefore, is the subject of every service, and not the devout individual or the worshipping congregation. As the heavenly High Priest He has, through His sacrifice on Calvary, completed once for all the perfect Service, to which nothing can be added and from which nothing can be taken away. The congregation therefore have nothing else to do but to go to their Lord, who stands as their Mediator before God and makes intercession for them, and to accept what He gives them. Thus the Lord Himself holds the true Service with His Church, giving her that which He has accomplished for her through His incarnation, His life, death and resurrection.

In the gathering of the Church for worship the appropriation of the sacrifice of Jesus by those who are His own is continually happening. In her worship the Church appropriates to herself the merit of the One High Priest Jesus Christ; this is the work of the Holy Spirit, who awakens the Church to life and keeps her close to her Lord.

It is the Lord's will to come to His Church in Word and Sacrament. There He stands before her as her Lord. But He proves

Himself Lord of the Church by addressing her. Through His Word directed to her He claims her as His own, and thereby the Church becomes what she otherwise would not be, the congregation of servants called by God and so serving Him. It is this fact alone which gives reality to the divine service of the Church.

The actual worship of the Christian Church consists therefore in just this going forth of the Word to her, because in His Word God Himself enters the field and ever anew offers and promises to His people what our Lord has done for them in His sacrifice once for all. This Word going forth from God therefore makes possible and real again and again through the power of the Holy Spirit true and genuine worship, and anything further that can be rightly said about a legitimate Divine Service can only be a development of this proposition. This is the test of everything which has its place in our orders of service.

A. *The Word of God:*

> (i) Reading of the Bible
> (ii) Sermon
> (iii) Instruction

Before every service of the Church something decisive has happened. In boundless mercy Almighty God has turned to sinful man and asserts the claim of His grace on him. This act of divine love is fully made known in the Holy Scriptures of the Old and New Testaments, in which God witnesses to Himself and calls on apostles and prophets of the Church to testify what the Risen Christ has done for her, and what else she may hope for. To hear this and by the help of the Holy Spirit to believe it, and then to respond to it in word and deed, is a matter for the congregation, who are gathered and called by the impact of the Word: to lead them where the revelation of divine mercy is testified and imparted—that is a matter for the ministry of the Church, to which the preaching of the Word (*Verbi divini ministri*) is entrusted.

This work of the Church is based upon the Bible, which she strives to expound. She can do this by choosing texts with a bearing on particular circumstances, or she can do it *expressis verbis*. Between these alternatives there is a whole gamut of liturgical possibilities, for which the promise is valid that belief cometh of preaching and preaching by the word of Christ. Wherever His

Word is preached, there the Lord Himself wishes to be with His Spirit, and if only two or three are gathered in His Name, He Himself seeks to make His Word a present reality to the hearers, and to grant them a true faith and a true response. True preaching therefore can only come by constant prayer, beseeching the Lord Himself to witness to His promise and by the power of His Spirit to make the weak words of men the living Word of God. Thus the reading of the Scriptures and the art of preaching are not left covered by the dust of centuries; nor does their life depend on human understanding, but wherever the Word of the Bible is proclaimed, there is an act of God: thus preaching becomes Sacrament. No Church has the right in any circumstances to hinder this divine act; no Christian divine service is legitimate unless the Word be proclaimed, heard and with God's help believed.

It must be noted that there are two sides to all the Church's preaching; on the one hand it points men to the Scriptures (Lesson and Sermon) and on the other hand its ultimate aim is a coming to life of the Word which depends neither on the behaviour of the congregation, nor on that of the minister, but only on the work of the Spirit. The former is a duty of the Church, the latter is a matter for prayer, but it will seldom be given to the congregation to recognise when or how its prayer has been heard.

There are a variety of possible methods for introducing people to the Scriptures, which may begin with the imparting of elementary knowledge and impressions, and should culminate in witness to the great promises of God. The reading of the Scriptures without explicit exposition always assumes all that. In this connection it must not be overlooked that the preacher, even when he comes to his congregation as a witness to the mercy of God in deed and truth, does no more than give instruction in regard to judgment and mercy. His teaching remains abstract even when he speaks most graphically and awakens in his hearers religious insights and emotion of all kinds. It yet remains mere talk of mercy and mere listening to such talk on a human footing. Mercy only becomes real when God opens hearts by His Spirit and makes His Word alive, present and effective. That is why from the human point of view the speech of the Church will to a large extent consist of instruction. Where, however, instruction springs from the Word, she may be confident that even in its barest form in-

struction is still a preaching of the Word and in the Spirit is able
to lead to faith. It is therefore not inadmissible if in liturgical usage
the Confession, prayer, and even the singing of the congregation
becomes instruction and proclamation: that also is covered by the
promise of the Lord.

Finally, we must be clear about the point of contact with the
hearer on which the speaking, exposition, reading and teaching
of the Church may reckon. Every secular attempt to develop into
the maturity of a full personality the spiritual and religious possibilities given to man is founded on the expectation of some existing point of contact. The goal may then be reached by way of a
harmonious development. It matters little whether it is religious
understanding which is emphasised, or the presentation and perception of values, or religious feeling and experience. The Church
knows that all these possibilities and developments occur in a
humanity fallen by its own fault away from God and under the
condemnation of death. She cannot therefore believe that from
within this place of death new life could arise, and rejects the
Pelagian view, which seeks to secure in some form or other a
point of contact with a humanity still accessible—one in which
corruption has not yet set in. The Church is comforted by the
knowledge that, before man had committed deeds condemning
him under the Law, God had provided for salvation, which
through the Spirit is always renewed and made actual. Only from
this act of God can preaching take its start, not from any form of
human understanding. Only where God through Word and
Sacrament does something new, can the end be not death, but
the call to life. God Himself in the service of His Church starts
from that which He Himself has done for her. This is true of every
possible type of service.

The proclamation of the Word of God, through which the
Lord speaks to His people, gathers them and keeps them close to
Him, cannot be replaced in the Service by anything else. There
is no true divine service, nor is there any true celebration of the
Sacrament without the proclamation of the Word. The Reformers are agreed in this, that the exposition of the Word is a
constitutive part of divine service: a worshipping congregation
first comes into being through being addressed by the Word.
The catechisms of Reformation times, which count as the confessional documents of the Reformed Churches, agree in this,

that the Spirit of the Lord does His work where the Word is read, taught and preached, and where the Sacrament is ritually administered. And when Calvin describes the preaching of the Word (*Doctrina*) as the *Mater, ex qua nos Deus generat* and stands by it (*Il y a nulle édification, sinon où il y a doctrine*) this conviction has become so deeply rooted in the consciousness of our church-going Swiss, that our churches would rather abolish the last traces of a liturgy than remove the sermon from its predominant position. For our Church divine service consists of the right hearing of the Word in the reading of the Scriptures and the sermon. So reading of the Bible, sermon and instruction stand—with surprising onesidedness—in the centre of all services. This is so much so that even short morning or evening prayers would be unthinkable without a Scripture exposition. And we believe that so it must be.

(iv) Liturgical forms

Beside the constituent parts of a preaching service already mentioned, in the Swiss Reformed Churches (in the German-speaking East more than in West Switzerland) the liturgical forms proper to the Christian Church are coming back into use. Our Reformed Churches firmly hold that God and man can only meet in His Word, which has gone forth and still to-day goes forth to us. To attempt to find God in any other way, or approach Him in any other place, must be renounced as presumption and idolatry, however much the devout soul may seem to profit by it and although it may seem easier to conform to the laws of aesthetics. The *Confessio Helvetica Posterior* sums this up in the words: 'The preaching of the Word of God is itself God's Word. If therefore to-day this Word of God is preached in the Church by preachers whose calling is valid, we believe that the Word of God Himself is preached and heard by the believers.' But then liturgy can be nothing else than prayer for right hearing of the Word and a response from the congregation to the Word heard and believed.

For the Reformed Churches of Switzerland to-day there is a difficulty in the way of a liturgy so understood—a misunderstanding arising from the widely held opinion that the sermon is meant to give guidance for right living and that the response must be seen outside the church walls in *Praxis Pietatis* in everyday life. It is one of the present tasks of liturgical circles in Switzerland

E

to make it understood that, even in a Reformed Church which claims the name of Zwingli, the Word is not spoken at random, but requires a response consisting of singing and praying, praising and extolling, thanksgiving and adoration, petition and intercession, true Christian communion and Christian almsgiving, and not least a trustful and joyful approach to the Lord's Table. About the details of such a response to the salvation imparted through the preaching of the Word, there will be more to say below.[1]

B. *Sacramental Worship:*

(i)   Eucharist

(ii) Baptism

C. *The relation between* A *and* B

Christendom of old only knew two forms of congregational worship—apart from a missionary service: the Communion of the Lord's Supper with the preaching of the Word included; and Baptism. It is the great predicament of the Reformed Churches (it is not for us to speak of other Churches) that for them the normal service consists of preaching taken out of the Communion setting, the Communion having become a rare and, for the members, an unfamiliar occasion. But the association of the two seems to a great extent to be for the Reformed Churches a cause of unavowed uneasiness.

This false position would seem to be especially acute in the Reformed Churches of Switzerland. The explanation of this is to be found in the peculiar historical development of these Churches at the time of the Reformation. In the course of the fifteenth century a special preaching service can be traced in the cities of South Germany and of Switzerland, which appeared alongside the chief service (Mass) and showed certain peculiarities. Beside the Mass it indeed possessed only complementary significance, but it was upheld by circles in the South German cities which were full of the new thought-forms of religious humanism. Because of this the preaching service found its place in the churches which were under the City Councils. In consequence, where the Council was concerned to carry out the Reformation, existing forms of simple preaching services could be made the basis for the development of a Reformed liturgy. This

[1] Cf. p. 134 f.

has been of fundamental significance for the choice of the liturgical elements which are important for the chief Sunday service.

It proved, however, to be very significant that the late mediaeval preaching service lost all connection with the sacramental part of the chief Sunday service, for the Communion remained indissolubly bound up with the celebration of the Mass. This situation could well be tolerated so long as the way to the Sacrament was open daily in the celebration of the Mass in the parish. The Fathers of the Reformed Church in Switzerland took over without scruple this order of things, which certainly afforded the Word and its preaching the desired scope, but permitted no introduction of the Sacrament into the general structure of the chief Sunday service. In this way there came about in the Churches of Reformed Switzerland an unintentional separation between the service of the Word and the sacramental service, in consequence of which the way to the Lord's Table was barred to the Reformed Christian nearly every Sunday, while the service of the Word came to be stamped, quite improperly, as the service which is the only normal one and fully sufficient to the Christian. No change has been effected by well-meaning attempts to have a celebration of the Lord's Supper, at least in the towns, in different churches by turns each Sunday. This solution still leaves untouched the real problem, the question of the spiritual connection of the two proper forms of the Reformed Service.

To this has to be added a further aggravation. Public confession of guilt (*Offene Schuld*), Kyrie, the comfortable words, Absolution, the remains of a form of excommunication—all of which would be more in place in a service of preparation—bring into the celebration the deepest note of repentance, which is echoed in the singing and in the tones of the organ, and reflected on the faces of those present. One has the impression of standing at the open grave of the Lord and of all our hopes, rather than at the Lord's Table in the company of the saints and the redeemed.

Correspondingly, the suffering and death of our Lord is spoken of so seriously that there is little space left for the message of His resurrection, His return in glory and His presence in the midst of the congregation assembled round His Table. As a natural result this good tidings is difficult to believe. In Switzerland to-day the attempt is being made to provide forms of celebration in which the Lord's death is thought of as the foundation for His resurrec-

tion, while the latter is emphasised and the mood of the congregation is guided rather into joy than into gloomy gravity. But even
these efforts, which are motivated by pointing to the character of
the sacrificial supper, not identical with the blood sacrifice itself,
do not silence questions as to the correct combination of the two
distinct aspects. The churches of our country have not found a
solution, but they have been led in recent times to an earnest
consideration of the orders of service of the Early Christian congregations.

The following appear to be the findings:

(*a*) The service of the Word and the service of the Lord's
Supper are originally identical. Both find their life in their certainty of the presence of the Risen Lord, which depends neither
on the Bible as a book, nor on the sacramental elements, but on
His own promise. Word and Sacrament have their place within
the same celebration, in which the old prayer, *Maranatha*, finds
fulfilment. Where the assembled congregation offers this prayer,
the Lord wills to be there in the Spirit.

(*b*) The eucharistic Supper of the Church stands between the
Resurrection Supper of the Lord with His disciples and the
eschatological Supper of the Lamb—being in fact a meal with the
Risen Lord and an anticipation of the messianic Supper of the
returning Lord. In this the emphasis is first of all on the glad
knowledge of those meals which the Risen Lord celebrated with
His disciples after Easter; interpretation based on Christ's death
plays only a minor part. It is possible that at first even the drinking
of wine was not associated with the breaking of bread. In his
fight against abuses in Corinth (I Cor. 11), St. Paul was the first
to call attention to the institution of the Supper on the evening
before the Lord's death, and to bring into the foreground the
thought of the Lord's death as a vicarious sacrifice, which in the
Early Church seems to have been little emphasised. Following on
this development, the 'Blood of Christ' became predominant in
the Communion of the Lord's Supper, through which the congregation enters into the experience of Good Friday. In reality,
however, the Eucharist is celebrated after Easter and in the sight
of the Kingdom of God soon to dawn. Certainly the event on
Calvary is always presupposed, but on the occasion of the Lord's
Supper the Risen Lord, ascended into heaven and to return in

the clouds of heaven, enters into the midst of His congregation. It is therefore worth considering whether it would not be better to allow for the influence of the *Didache* on the liturgy, and so to avoid further one-sided development along the lines of the Roman tradition.

It is certain that a Christian Church is a worshipping Church only when the Risen Lord tarries in her midst and imparts to her His joy. For this she has to pray, for this she may gain courage through the preaching of the Word and to this she should respond in her liturgy. This our Church is in danger of forgetting, in the service of the Word alone, when the sermon is put in the central place as a 'lecture', and the presence of the Lord is forgotten owing to the prominence of the preacher. On the other hand, where interpretation through the Word is missing from the Eucharist and the promise is not proclaimed, the presence of the Lord may be expected and experienced in a sense which is false. Even the Reformed Churches of German-speaking Switzerland, aware of the presence of the Lord in Word and Sacrament, are beginning to make attempts at celebrating the Supper in such a way that the Risen Lord Himself speaks through His Apostles. Owing to the warping of tradition even in the early Church, but still more in the Swiss Reformation, this is made so difficult that as yet we can only speak of good intentions and not of achievements already reached.

Beside the missionary sermon and the church service as a service combining Word and Sacrament, the Early Church knew *Baptism* as a normal act of worship, which certainly took place outside congregational worship, since it occurred once only, and thus was the presupposition for admission to the Church's full communion of the Word and Sacrament. If to-day in the Swiss churches the public character of Baptism is more emphasised, and greater importance is attached to the holding of Baptism within the church service, the reasons for this derive from the nature of our time. Through special emphasis on the character of Baptism as decision, the problem of infant Baptism has become more and more a burning question and it is not without anxiety that the Swiss Church awaits its further development. This at least makes for unrest in the congregations. As increasing the difficulty it is to be noted that an attempt to base infant Baptism on the *Gratia praeveniens* meets with opposition throughout as not being in accordance with the teaching of Scripture, and the conviction prevails generally that the maintenance of infant Baptism originates from the historical and unscriptural fight of Zwingli and Calvin against the Baptists. This view is noted as a matter of fact, but is not that of the present writer.

Apart from Baptism and the Lord's Supper, the Reformed Church in Switzerland knows no sacraments and recognises no 'sacramentals'. She does not regard Confirmation or church marriage as in any sense sacramental. Indeed, exception is taken even to the ordination of ministers, on the ground that a Reformed Church only knows an induction by the Church to a particular office, but not an ordination undertaken *per se*. Here is reflected the strong Congregational trend of our churches, which have little use for an office as such. But in this connection also reconsideration is going on, and it is not unthinkable that Bucer's sacramental laying on of hands, as well as the question of standing within an apostolic tradition of preaching, may come under discussion. It is impossible, however, to count on the slightest understanding of the office of bishop, or the least desire for an Apostolic Succession, finding its way into the Swiss churches. In particular, the German-speaking Church in Switzerland is in this respect compelled by the Zwinglian Reformation to take up a fixed position, in which it is kept firm by an emphatic, and in no sense church-ridden, democracy.

II. *How far should worship provide for:*

        (i) Thanksgiving

      (ii) Penitence and Absolution

    (iii) Adoration

    (iv) Petition and Intercession for living and dead

     (v) Oblation or Offering

If regular divine service consists of the true exposition of the Word, which the congregation through the power of the Holy Spirit may rightly hear and believe; and if they dare to go to the Lord's Table and take the Sacrament full of joy in the presence of their living Lord, they cannot do other than respond. According to the testimony of the Scriptures right hearing manifests itself through the mouth of the believer, speaking out of the fulness of his heart. God, graciously addressing His people through Word and Sacrament, does not speak at random, but expects the response of the congregation in obedience and trust. Where the Word awakens faith, that faith will become articulate, for there is no real faith without the confession of the lips. Where the message of the boundless mercy of God is heard, there comes conviction of sin and confession of guilt, a turning to the Lord and to the immediate promise of forgiveness. Where through the Word the forgiveness of God has become effective, thanksgiving is inevitable. Where God's glory has broken forth from His Word, worship and praise will find expression. Where the Word relates to one's neighbour, if the message is rightly heard the result will be that the congregation will go to her Lord in intercession for the neighbour in need. The Church's almsgiving will reveal whether the Word has been rightly heard and rightly understood; whether in fact the congregation is willing to obey her Lord. From this interweaving of hearing and response results the peculiar character of a Reformed Liturgy and when Calvin says of prayer, *orare nisi praeeunte Verbo non possumus*, this applies fully to all other liturgical forms. The congregation can respond only when she knows herself so called of God, and even when the *Affectus animi*, the spiritual joy or affliction, forces utterance, the Church, as with the individual, can only speak rightly when she speaks in the form of a humble, trustful, joyful reply to the words of God. With the liturgical elements therefore it can never be a matter of religious exercises, leading to a climax of glorifying God, or of methodically putting the congregation in a devout mood. Still less is there any attempt in one's own strength to force the way to God. Only where God's presence is manifest, namely, in His Word and Sacrament, is there true liturgy. What God offers in His revelation of Himself, the worshipper appropriates to himself and asserts before God. Nothing therefore has its place in the Christian liturgy but that which reveals God. And the reverse is true—everything which reveals God has its place, in principle, in the liturgy of the Church. And if we are clearly told in Scripture that the Church may appear before her Lord with praise and thanksgiving, with petition and adoration, these elements must find expression in divine service.

The liturgical forms which since the Reformation have been at the disposal of our Reformed Churches in Switzerland should on the whole come up to these requirements; the fact that in the more recent liturgies they should be placed more plentifully at the service of the Church, seems to accord with the present development of our churches. On the other hand much remains to be desired as regards pure adoration, which takes only a second place after all attempts at instructing and educating. This may be connected with the particular type of our church membership, and only by degrees shall we succeed in bringing about a change.

It should here be added that the liturgies of our Church certainly allow ample scope for 'Petition and Intercession for the living', but that in accordance with the doctrine of the Reformed Churches prayer for the departed does not occur. Zwinglian congregations know only a 'commemoration of the departed'.

III. *Free Prayers*

Spontaneous prayers are at best a self-deception: either they are carefully thought out beforehand and perhaps even written—when they are no longer free prayers; or else there lies in them the danger that they give less scope to the Holy Spirit than affording an opportunity to the preacher to expand his sermon in the form of prayer, and perhaps also to upset the congregation by inept faltering. Free prayer on special occasions should not be excluded, but it should not be a rule.

IV. *Relation between the worship of the local worshipping company, the Church Universal, and the Church in Heaven*

In the services of a Christian congregation there should be some room for recognition that there is one Lord, one Spirit and one hope, expressed in all gatherings for worship all over the world, and that there is only one Lord's Table for all Christians. A full understanding of this has at all times been shown in the forms of service of our Reformed Churches in Switzerland. It may be that the constant link with the needy Reformed Churches of Europe has contributed to this attitude. In petition and intercession, in prayers of praise and thanksgiving, also in the hymns of the Church, there is expressed again and again a desire for fellowship with the whole people of God and the prayer that the flock may be one, and this large-mindedness should work out in a far-reaching readiness for intercommunion.

On the other hand our churches are very far from seeing any connection between the worshipping congregation and the Church triumphant. Certainly there are in some forms indications that the congregation may join in the celestial Liturgy of the Angels and the Redeemed, but they are only occasional notes, which are quite in the background in relation to the acts of worship in the visible congregation. Yet there are to-day in Switzerland church circles whose concern it is to make it understood that the visible Church stands with the assembly of angels and saints before the same Lord; that her adoration and praise before the throne of God may harmonise with the Sanctus and the Gloria of all Redeemed; and that in celebrating the Eucharist she stands at the table of her heavenly Lord Himself and takes part in faith in the Supper of the Returning Lord. But it must not be overlooked that this happens by faith and not yet by sight, at the end of time and not yet at the consummation of the Kingdom. Of necessity, therefore, the prayer and singing of the Church on earth will sound differently from that of the Redeemed.

VIII. *Is there any right sequence in which these elements should occur?*

The Fathers of the Reformed Churches in Switzerland deliberately refrained from making of their Service a Drama following a fixed sequence; nor do they wish to see in it the reflection of that worship which in Heaven angels and saints bring to the Lord; nor do they claim that their orders are based on a divine ordinance found in Scripture and Tradition. It was sufficient for them if through the liturgy the preaching of the Word and the administration of the sacraments were guaranteed to be in 'decency and order'. Thus the Fathers resist the temptation to set up an order which would be in keeping with the event of divine service. For if in the worship God Himself renders us the service of standing in our midst and turning towards us in mercy, He would Himself have to provide an order which corresponds to His act. That is how the Roman Church understands it, when it imagines it possesses in the Mass the form willed by God for the mystery of His presence. The Holy Scriptures, however, do not lay in our hands any sacred liturgy to match the glory of God.

There have therefore been again and again attempts from other directions, on religio-psychological grounds, or from other considerations, to create a form adequate to the event of divine service. We cannot approve such intrusion into a sphere reserved for the action of God and we decline to allot a particular place to each portion of a form of service. We have to be content to indicate the acceptability of an order, but not its necessity as a means of salvation or as having psychological efficacy. Within the wide framework allowed, tradition may, however, assign to certain parts their rightful place in the course of the service, provided that thereby the proclamation of the Word and the response of the congregation are not distorted.

VI

BAPTIST

*

R. Claibourne Johnson
(United States of America)

How to provide in worship for the needs of those whose experience and training have been in other Communions without violating Baptist principles and traditions is the challenge that confronts any Baptist church which is identified with and is a part of the Ecumenical Movement. To meet this challenge adequately there must be understanding and appreciation, understanding of the distinctive Baptist witness and appreciation of the work of the Holy Spirit in the forms and practices of other Communions.

In many Baptist churches this is not an academic problem but a practical task. The writer has in mind a Baptist church which includes in its congregation worshippers from some twenty-two Communions, of which thirty-eight per cent are Baptists, about twenty-five per cent Methodists, about twenty per cent Presbyterians and lesser percentages of Episcopalians, Lutherans, Roman Catholics, Congregationalists, Friends, and others. While this particular church may have a larger percentage of people from Communions other than Baptist than most Baptist churches, due to its location in a residential area, and because of its sense of mission to the community of which it is a part, this is more or less true of most churches. Christians are becoming ecumenically minded and an increasing number choose their church affiliation on the basis of considerations other than denominational loyalty, such as the convenient location of the church, the appeal of its programme, social ties and such like.

This admixture of people from various Communions has been accelerated by the shifts of population which have assumed major proportions in recent years. There has been a mass-shift of population within the city itself, from the centre to the residential area, and then to the suburb. The machine age, which has facilitated reasonably easy transport, the organisation of business in larger units covering vast territories, and the changing social scene due to wars and national mobilisation, have combined to cause millions of people to move from one section of a country to another.

Regardless of how an individual may have been received into the local church, or whatever the requirements of entrance into membership may have been, the fact remains that the experience of worship is a part of the emotional framework of one's being. In order, therefore, to meet the needs of worshippers, account must be taken of the experience and background of people from other Communions.

It is the conviction of the writer that a Baptist church can be true to its distinctive principles and heritage and provide in its services and forms and practices of worship patterns, helps and experiences which will satisfy the deepest needs of all of whatever denominational 'name or sign'. In fact, many Baptist churches are actually so doing.

For those who do not understand the distinctive Baptist witness and heritage, a concise review is permissible. With this in mind as a frame of reference, a consideration of the various elements of the programme of worship indicated above will be listed, and to some measure interpreted, in the light of the demands of the increasing ecumenical interest and participation on the part of contemporary Christians.

To locate and define the distinctive witness of a religious fellowship is not an easy task, especially when that fellowship has no single authoritarian head, and recognises the autonomy of the local church. Certainly the name Baptist is misleading and confusing. While Baptists get their name from the form of Baptism which they now almost universally practise, as a matter of fact they share the practice of immersion with several other groups of churches: notably with the Disciples, who constitute a denomination of considerable size and strength. An eminent Baptist historian tells us, on the basis of detailed evidence, that our early English forebears, both General and Particular Baptists alike, did not give up affusion and begin to practise immersion as their specific form of Baptism until the second generation of their continuous history as organised Baptists.[1] He reminds us that one of the most famous

[1] 'Principles of the Early Baptists of England and America', R. E. E. Harkness, *Crozer Quarterly*, October, 1928.

Baptists in all history, John Bunyan, 'the immortal tinker of Bedford Jail, who was himself immersed in a creek by the River Ouse in 1653, was pleading twenty years later that differences about the mode of Baptism should never be made a test of fellowship with other Christians. On his release from prison in 1672 he wrote three articles on 'The Terms of Communion and Fellowship of Christians'. Dr. Harkness quotes from one of these articles by John Bunyan: 'I plead for communion with men, godly and faithful, I plead that they may be received, that God hath shewed us He hath received, and commanded we should receive them. . . . I count it so far off from being any act of friendship, to press baptism in our notion on those that cannot bear it; that it is a great abuse of the peace of my brother, the law of love, the law of Christ, or the society of the faithful. Love suffereth long, and is kind, is not easily provoked; let us therefore follow after the things that make for peace, and things wherewith one may edify another.' In this article Dr. Harkness summarises the evidence gathered by many historians which shows that it is doubtful whether the earliest Baptist churches in America or in England practised immersion at all; indeed, that it is more doubtful whether Roger Williams and his fellow Baptists in America were themselves ever immersed. Immersion seems to have replaced affusion during the second generation of Baptist history in sequence to the original protest against infant Baptism, and as a result of a more careful study of the New Testament as it was realised to be of primary importance in Baptist faith and practice.

Historical evidence and contemporary practice seem to show that the distinctive principles of Baptists were, and are, the following:

1. *The Right of Church Covenant: but the refusal to make any covenant, statement of faith, particular interpretation of the Scripture, or creed a test of fellowship between Baptists*

Because of this, some have felt that, having no creed, Baptists do not believe anything. It is because they believe so much that no creed is sufficient, for no creed is flexible enough to contain a growing Christian experience. Through the years they have accepted the whole New Testament as an all-sufficient rule of faith and practice. They believe that Baptists should never be hesitant about formulating confessions of faith, and should be vigilant concerning doctrinal matters. However, they have always been reluctant to erect a confession of faith into a standard or test of doctrine. In his *History of British Baptists* W. T. Whitley writes: 'Baptists have never been backward to explain what they believe; they have always been reluctant to erect a confession into a standard, or test of doctrine. If a later generation finds that it does not agree with its predecessors, whether in content or in emphasis, it has openly revised and restated what it does believe, or it has discarded the old confession and framed another. Therefore Baptists are always restive when they are asked to signify their adhesion to any confession as though it were a standard.'

While Baptists appreciate and profit by the study and use of the creeds of others, and recognise the right of others to make confessions of faith a test of fellowship, they humbly hold for themselves that to formulate a creed which is authoritative and binding would be to usurp the place of God, and to impose in His name a man-made instrument, thus binding and delimiting the mind of God with fallible human constructions.

As an illustration of the characteristic Baptist attitude toward creeds, Whitley quotes a statement of spiritual humility and intellectual open-mindedness from the Confession of the Particular Baptists in London in 1646 which had been twice revised from its original form in 1596: 'Also we confesse that we know but in part, and that we are ignorant of many things which we desire and seek to know; and if any shall doe us that friendly part to show us from the word of God that we see not, we shall have cause to be thankful to God and them.'

2. *Salvation by Personal Faith in Jesus Christ rather than by the exercise of sacramental rites or religious observances*

To Baptists, ordinances are not sacraments, that is, specially endowed vehicles of grace. Although some Baptists might state the matter differently, most Baptists hold to the essential truth of a statement made in 1940 by Ellis A. Fuller, the President of the Southern Baptist Theological Seminary: 'We suffer at the hands of those who pass us by with a flippant gesture saying: "Baptists believe that people have to be immersed to be saved." When will this delusion be lifted from the minds of people, in the churches and out of them? The fact is that there is no group of Christians anywhere to whom the ordinances are as utterly destitute of meaning from the standpoint of saving efficacy as they are in the thinking of Baptists. To us the ordinances are not sacraments; that is, they are not vehicles of grace. They are teaching ordinances and valuable only because they symbolise the two truths which constitute the eternal gospel of grace; namely, our Lord's death and His resurrection; and they are accepted only by people whose experience of saving grace, which was made available by our Lord's death and resurrection, leads them to seek, in obedience to the Master's command, to proclaim their faith in the efficacy of His death and resurrection in realising God's eternal purpose to redeem from the fallen race a family unto himself.'

3. Believers' Baptism and the consequent rejection of Infant Baptism

Baptists insist that believers' Baptism is a necessary safeguard for a regenerate church membership. Therefore, from the beginning of their history they have been primarily concerned with the fact of conversion rather than with the mode of Baptism, although immersion came, in fact, to be the mode practised. This was due largely to the fact that it symbolises the death and resurrection of Christ. Early Baptists, seeing the abuses that were in the Roman Church of their day, and even in the Reformation Churches of Luther and Calvin, owing to the inclusion of entire populations in the Church through the rite of infant Baptism, were absolutely convinced that a regenerate membership could never be possible as long as this rite was practised. They therefore rejected the practice of infant Baptism, re-baptising new believers and baptising only those who were at such an age as to be able and who did actually show evidences of regeneration.

There has arisen an intense and searching debate about Baptism in recent times. It is particularly vigorous in the Reformed Churches, in the wider circles influenced by Professors Brunner and Barth, and in the Church of England. Brunner declares that wherever in the New Testament Baptism is enjoined it is regarded as a 'two-sided happening', involving what he calls 'personal correspondence'. 'Baptism', he says—in words which well express what Baptists have always believed—'is not merely a gift to man, but also an active receiving and confession on the part of man.' And it is a man's own faith that is involved. To declare with Luther that even infants possess incipient faith (that is, knowledge of the Word, assent and trust) or to assert, as did Zwingli and

Calvin, that faith is that of the family or the Church is to obscure the true nature of both faith and the Church. 'The contemporary practice of infant baptism,' says Brunner, 'can hardly be regarded as being anything short of scandalous.'

Karl Barth is no less trenchant. He is ready to condemn as fundamentally unsatisfactory any Baptism of children, even if they have Christian parents. He declares that 'the baptismal practice found in use on the basis of the teaching prevalent to-day is arbitrary and despotic. Neither by exegesis nor from the nature of the case can it be established that the baptised person can be merely a passive instrument or recipient. Rather it can be shown, by exegesis and from the nature of the case, that in this rite the baptised must be an active partner . . . Plainly,' says Barth, 'no infant can be such a person.'

No less surprising and significant is what has recently been said by Dom Gregory Dix, O.S.B., one of the ablest and most influential of Anglo-Catholic protagonists. He has come to the view that Baptism without Confirmation is only half a sacrament. Infant Baptism, he says, should be regarded 'always as an abnormality, wholly incomplete by itself and absolutely needing completion by the gift of the Spirit and the conscious response of faith'.

4. *Freedom of Conscience*

Baptists' trust in the competence of the individual soul to interpret Scripture according to the free dictates of conscience as led by the Holy Spirit demands that they recognise the sovereign right of the individual even in the local church, that is, the right of the individual to follow his own conscience in matters moral and spiritual.

This respect for the rights of the individual forbids the administration of ordinances to any person against his will or without the full consent of his will.

Out of this insistence on freedom of conscience and soul liberty, which Baptists hold not for themselves alone but for all 'by whatever name or sign', comes their consistent refusal to recognise any union of State and Church whereby the State is given power to dictate directly or indirectly to the conscience of men pertaining to moral and spiritual matters. For the same reason, ecclesiastical authority has been denied. It is not dislike for civil authority or ecclesiastical authority that causes Baptists to take this position. It is because they tolerate nothing civil or religious which presumes to interfere with the conscience of men in their search for and service of God.

*   *   *

Without violating these principles, what can a local Baptist church provide to meet the needs of those who worship therein? Let us look at the actual worship of the specific church referred to above.

This church makes an extensive and effective use of symbols. The Communion Table, located at the rear of the chancel, takes the form of an altar. On it is a large open Bible brought into sharp focus by a special beam of light, flanked by lighted candles and flowers in brass vases. Behind and just above the Bible is a Celtic wooden cross against the background of contrasting colour. Over and above is a beautiful and lighted window, with the figure of the Christ with outstretched hands. Beneath that figure, unobtrusive and yet plain to see, are the words 'Come unto Me.' The ministers and choir are robed so as not to draw attention to themselves. The ministers wear Geneva gowns or academic robes which indicate a teaching and preaching rather than a priestly function. Pictorial glass and the use of symbols in appropriate recesses remind the worshipper of the great truths of the Christian gospel and of the facts of Christian history. The most liturgically-minded seem to feel at home, and yet those whose background of religious experience has been largely void of such things quickly appreciate the beauty and value of such a setting even for quiet meditation.

Major emphasis is placed upon the use and reading of the Bible. Because of the limited knowledge of the average congregation concerning the content of the Bible itself, the minister does three things in an attempt to overcome this deficiency. First, whenever it is felt necessary and appropriate, the reading of the Scripture is prefaced by a few words of explanation. This is more than identi-fication of the portion to be read: it is an attempt to help the congregation to understand what is being read by putting it in its larger setting. Second, the minister memorises the Scripture lesson so as to give the reading of it intelligent and effective inter-pretation. Third, the technique of the expository sermon is em-ployed so that those who come to worship may leave with an understanding of the meaning and relevance of the teachings of the Bible for their lives.

The two ordinances that are administered are Baptism and the Lord's Supper. The mode of Baptism is immersion, although the church practises the policy of open membership and recognises the validity of any form of Baptism. The Baptism itself is preceded and followed by recitation of appropriate Scripture. The candidate makes a public confession of faith before being baptised, and after the minister has received this confession of faith, he baptises in the name of the Father, the Son and the Holy Spirit. The baptistry is so arranged that curtains are drawn only during the act of confession and Baptism, and are closed quickly thereafter so as to make the procedure one of dignity and impressiveness. The ordinance is always administered during one of the regular services of worship, so as to make it an act of worship both for the one baptised as well as for the congregation.

Although infant Baptism is not practised, for the reasons already made clear, the service of dedication of infants is not only universally accepted but warmly welcomed. This service is primarily a service of reconsecration on the part of the parents. They covenant with God to provide a Christian atmosphere in the home, to co-operate with the church, and to strive by teaching and exemplary lives to bring the child up in the nurture and admonition of the Lord. The minister, as a part of the service, takes the child into his arms and, in the exercise of his faith in intercessory prayer, pleads for God's tender care and keeping in the name of the Father and the Son and the Holy Spirit.

Special attention is given to the ordinance of Communion, to administer it in such a way that there is time for meditation, remembrance, personal confession of sin directly to God, acceptance of His grace, reconsecration of life and surrender of the will. The minister's invitation is 'All ye that do truly and earnestly repent of your sins and intend to lead a new life, following after the commandments of God and walking henceforth in His holy ways, partake of this ordinance to the strengthening of your faith.'

The order of worship is so designed as to lead the worshipper through the following experiences in the following order: Adoration, confession, thanksgiving, supplication (including intercessory prayers for others), and surrender. Hymns, anthems, Scripture selections, written prayers and incidental sentences in the service are chosen so that there is unity of theme and progress of thought and experience, which leads to intelligent commitment of energy and life.

Finally, by design and by unconscious direction, the worshipper is made to feel that he is a part of the whole family of God, that in worship he is in unity with all who are a part of the Christian fellowship now, and all who have been in times past.

To fail to meet the vital needs of worshippers who represent a wide variety of religious background is to fail in the most crucial part of the Church's programme. Conscious of this responsibility, with some measure of understanding of our Baptist witness and heritage, and with genuine and sincere appreciation for the work of the Holy Spirit in ways which sometimes seem strange, this Church confidently faces the future in the conviction that it can maintain its essential distinctiveness and yet be a vital unit in the 'whole household of God.'

VII

CONGREGATIONALIST

*

John Marsh

(Great Britain)

The fact that one of the basic principles of Congregationalism is that of the spiritual independence of the local church has meant that all through its history it has included within itself considerable variety of opinion, belief and practice, and yet, at the same time, has exhibited and itself recognised some substantial form of common life. This paradoxical fact about the life of Congregational churches is due in large measure to three significant emphases that are sometimes overlooked by Congregationalists and their critics alike.

First, Congregationalism is essentially a *church* polity. The rugged individualism of the nineteenth century which flourished in it, as in other Communions, is not native to it. Neither is the strict 'independence' of the local congregation, in any sense that would detract from the entire dependence of the local church on Christ as its head, or from its vital need to articulate that dependence in fellowship with other such churches. That has been made clear again and again, from the writings of Robert Browne down to our own day. But with this combination of spiritual independence and spiritual fellowship or communion of churches, variety within a recognisable identity becomes much more understandable.

Second, the Scriptures were regarded as providing the norm for all aspects of the Church's life; and while nowadays, in common with others, Congregationalists may prefer to substitute 'the Gospel' for 'the Scriptures', there is still an acknowledgment that what God has done in Christ is the source of all the forms and the substance of all the content of the Church's life.

Third, worship, like every other particular aspect of the Church's life, is but one part of what is, in all its essentials, a whole.

The theological expression of this consists in maintaining the Gospel (or the Scriptures) as the authoritative norm for every part of the life of the Church; the practical expression is found for Congregationalists in their being members of a 'gathered' and 'covenanted' church. To be in the Church for them is more than to attend on her worship (to hear the Word rightly preached and to share in the Sacraments duly administered): it is to share in her mutual exercise of godly discipline as well. Worship is thus seen as one part of a whole way of life of God's people, gathered together in covenanted committal to Him and to one another, and it is this conception of churchmanship which still enables Congregationalists to live in one gospel fellowship with its (to them) normal and healthy tensions of diversity in unity, and unity in diversity.

A modern Congregationalist can thus regard himself as the true heir both of those who in Elizabeth's reign would meet in private houses for worship, which was characterised at the time as 'prophesyings', and which almost exalted the 'sermon' (though it was an expository sermon) to become the whole of worship; and of those who, like Barrowe and Greenwood, would undergo sacramental starvation rather than accept sacraments which, in their view, were not duly administered. But what needs to be noted about the many varieties of Congregationalist worship is that, at its best, and where it has been theologically aware of itself, it has been concerned to establish for itself and to enjoy with all Christians, the fulness of Christian worship. If at times the preaching of the Word has been over-emphasised, that has been to redress a balance: it would be unjust to conclude from a thirsty man's copious and quick consumption of water that he was not concerned to have a balanced diet !

There is another point about which the modern Congregationalist, like many of his predecessors, finds much misunderstanding—that of fixed forms of prayer. Their sense of the integrity and spiritual responsibility of the local church led them to object to the Elizabethan Act of Uniformity, which sought to make the Book of Common Prayer the one legal form of worship; and to that of 1662 which restored the Prayer Book to this place. The events preceding the second Act show that there was no objection to the provision of some form of common prayer; Baxter's 'Reformed Liturgy' is eloquent testimony to that. What was objected to, and what would still meet with resistance, was the imposition by magisterial authority of an inflexible liturgical standard. It is interesting to note that in the present century British Congregationalists have officially and unofficially been responsible for the publication of a number of directories of public worship, thus showing that still there is no objection in principle to the use of 'set prayers', and indicating that the freedom for which Congregationalists have striven is not simply freedom from such printed or traditional forms.

Throughout their history Congregationalists have used 'free' and 'extempore' prayer in their worship. The freedom of free prayer consists in its independence of set or liturgical formulas, and its growth out of the living needs of the contemporary congregation as it seeks to bring its life to the touchstone of the Gospel. Free prayer thus demands, as the best writers about it have known, much preparation by the minister, not only in the compilation of prayers, or of notes for prayers, but in the pastoral knowledge of his people. Extempore prayer comes, as its name implies, out of the needs of a particular moment; though this does not of necessity rule out all preparation of form and content beforehand. But Congregationalists would generally hold that however much traditional forms may help worship and the worshippers, something vital would be lost were these two forms of prayer to disappear from their practice of public worship. To the consideration of that practice let us now turn.

Congregationalism stands in the liturgical tradition of the Reformation, and on the Calvinist wing. Its worship therefore shares with that of other Reformed Communions in being an attempt to renew the fulness of worship in the life of the Church. It is well known that Calvin intended to do this, as Luther also desired, by arranging for the full service of the Lord's Supper, Word and Sacrament together, to be celebrated every Lord's Day. It is even more universally recognised that neither Calvin nor Calvinism achieved this. But it is important to remember that the form of Reformed worship is related to the 'eucharistic' worship of the Church. It is thus parallel to the Service of Holy Communion in the Book of Common Prayer (the only place in the Prayer Book where a sermon is required by the rubrics!) rather than to the 'Choir Offices' of Morning or Evening Prayer.

Modern Congregationalists differ considerably about the frequency of Communion Services, as their ancestors did before them. There are some congregations which have a weekly Communion, though they are the very rare exceptions. Most churches celebrate the Sacrament of Holy Communion once a month, though a growing number, to meet the needs of what are practically two separate congregations, celebrate it fortnightly, once in the morning and once in the evening. But the important point, which has been acknowledged in a report of a Commission on the Sacraments, which reported to the Assembly of the Congregational Union of England and Wales in 1936, is that Word and Sacrament, Sermon and Supper, constitute the real unity of Christian and evangelical worship. This monthly or fortnightly Communion must therefore be taken as the norm of Congregationalist worship, and the apocopated forms in use on other occasions must be interpreted in their terms, and not *vice versa*. How, then, can we interpret Congregationalist worship?

First, as to its form. This, it is believed, is something which flows from the Gospel, as that has been given us in the Scriptures. There we learn that God created the world for His own purposes; there we learn, what we know also in our own hearts, that we have rebelled against His purposes for us and sought, wilfully and in sin, to have our own way with our life; there we learn that 'even while we were yet sinners' God redeemed us in Christ. There we learn that what God did through Christ is available to every man until the very end of the world. This is the setting and this provides the form of Congregationalist worship. The Bible drama is the 'control', and if it does not persuade Congregationalists to any one fixed form of words, it does constrain them to a definite liturgical pattern. They are concerned with liturgy, if not with *a* liturgy.

One of the chief factors in the life of Reformed Churches, especially those of the Calvinist tradition, is the emphasis given to the need for Scripture to be and to provide the norm for all the Church's life. It is very easy to see how Scripture provides the form of Congregationalist worship, and gives substance to the form. The public worship of God opens, normally, with the recital of sentences from Scripture, which are meant to articulate the basic relationship in which man stands to God. The traditional form in the Calvinist Directories was in the words of

Psalm 124: 'Our help is in the name of the Lord, who made heaven and earth.' Herewith each believer is brought at the beginning of each service to the point at which the whole Biblical story begins, viz., to that point at which God had created man, and set him upon earth, to live his life of dependence upon God, and communion with Him. Like Adam, each Christian man is a divine creation, dependent upon God alike for his life and for his continuance in life. When the words of Scripture have made this starting-point clear, the praise of the Creator is often sung in a hymn. Then the next step in the Biblical progression of worship is taken: in prayer confession of sin is made to God, and His grace is sought to give the worshippers such strength as they need to withstand the enticements of evil. This brings the members of the congregation to the point at which Adam stood when he was ejected from Eden, a man made in God's image, but who had rebelled against God, and become a servant of evil powers, and who could not be restored to his first dignity unless God were to effect the restoration. But at this point in the service, as at this point in the Bible story, there begins the story of what God has done in our human history to effect man's full restoration.

The readings from the Old and New Testament follow the prayers of confession and petition, bringing to sinful man the news that is good news—that God has met man's need in Jesus Christ His Son. But for all this impressive setting out in liturgical form of the great historic drama of the Bible, Christian faith might appear to the worshipper as little more than an antiquarian interest, unless those great events of the past reach out into our present. That is why the sermon follows the lessons; for the sermon is meant to 'contemporise' the Gospel, to bring the redeeming acts that God has wrought in Christ into the milieu of our modern world—or rather, to let us see that those redeeming acts of God are ingredient in and determinative of the course of events of the contemporary world, public and private alike. After the sermon follows the 'long prayer', i.e. the Church joins in making intercession for the world at large. It is very significant to see what conception of intercession this position of the long prayer implies; it means that we cannot know what to ask of God, for ourselves or for the world, unless and until we know what sort of a God He is, and what kind of gifts He offers to us in His Son. After this prayer the congregation joins in saying the

Lord's Prayer, and then, after a final hymn, it is dismissed with the benediction. So the believer, who came from a world in which he is committed to a ceaseless struggle with sin, is sent back to it and to its warfare having been confronted with the picture of himself as God sees him, with the story of what God has done to save him, and with the assurance, in sermon and benediction, that the God who promises His succour will not fail to provide it.

At this point the opportunity is taken to dismiss with the benediction those who are not remaining to partake of the Sacrament of the Lord's Supper. As we have seen, this may mean that in many Congregational churches there is no Sacrament of the Lord's Supper on three Sundays out of four, and then the whole congregation is dismissed. But the unit and the unity of Congregational worship is the Word and Sacrament together, and as such an unity we must consider and expound them.

In original intention the Sacrament of the Lord's Supper was meant to remind us every Sunday that the centre of God's self-revelation to us, the centre of His redemption of us, the centre of our knowledge of Him, of our faith and trust and hope in Him, is the life and death and resurrection of Jesus Christ our Lord. And just as the reading of the Scriptures is meant to bring before us now the things that God has done in the past to achieve our redemption, so the various parts of the Sacrament of the Lord's Supper are meant to bring before us in word and action the central things of our faith and of God's gift.

At the close of the liturgy of the Word (often during the singing of the last hymn) the minister and deacons take their places at the Lord's Table, and after the benediction the elements are uncovered. Then the words of institution are generally recited (if not here, then later in the service) as a warrant for what is to be done. Then prayer is offered, a prayer of thanksgiving, of consecration, of petition that in and through what is done, the elements that are used, God will so grant the gift of His Spirit that we may truly feed upon Christ, and have our communion in Him. Then the actions of the Upper Room are repeated. The thanksgiving has been made, but now the bread is broken, and the wine is poured out, and minister, deacons and people all partake, the elements being taken to the people by the deacons. When all have partaken, there is a post-Communion prayer, an offertory for the poor, a final hymn, and the dismissal of the faithful with a benediction.

It is important here to consider the relation of Word and Sacrament as Congregationalists understand it. We may say that Christian worship, like any other religious activity of men, takes hold of some sort of 'natural' trait in the character of man. But what the form of Christian worship does with that natural trait is to direct it, not to some god made in man's image, but to the living and true and only God who has in fact acted in human history to redeem mankind. The importance of the reading of Scripture as over against any sort of 'edifying' literature is to be understood in these terms, and the preaching of sermons as distinct from the offering of pious and moral reflections enjoys something of the same character. But about both these activities which bring the 'Word' to the congregation more must be said, and it is best said, in the first place, about the sermon. For Christian faith is not exhausted by affirming that God has acted in the past; it is the potency of His past actions in the present that constitutes the news of the Bible as the good news of the Gospel. God has spoken His Word to man in certain actions, and that Word, those actions, have been enshrined in the words of Scripture. Those words of Scripture are the basis of the sermon, in which the Word which God spoke in His historic actions is intended to come to contemporaneous effectiveness. 'Is intended to come'; we cannot say more, for 'the wind bloweth where it listeth, and thou hearest the voice thereof, but knowest not whence it cometh, and whither it goeth; so is every one that is born of the Spirit.' The quickening word is not at the disposal of the preacher, as if God delivered Himself to His ministers for congregational distribution. The preacher has a very responsible office to perform, viz. to be or to become the servant of the Word, so that in the abiding faithfulness and the contemporary relevance of what he says, he may offer to the Spirit a vehicle fit for His coming. But with that said, it must be added that neither preacher nor congregation come to church as to some house of magic, wondering whether the great conjuror will perform his trick on this occasion. Rather do minister and people alike live in the assurance that God is a faithful God, who keeps His promises, and so uses the words that men speak to convey His own word to the heart. Like the ancient Thessalonians, modern Congregationalists receive the message that they hear 'not as the word of men, but, as it is in truth, the Word of God, which also worketh in (them) that believe'. In this sense the sermon is sometimes spoken of as a 'sacrament'; like the sacraments of Baptism and the Lord's Supper as described in the Book of Common Prayer, the sermon is 'an outward and visible sign' (the words of the preacher) 'of an inward and spiritual grace' (the Word of God to the heart). It is of no small importance to add that the responsibility for the word that is spoken in the sermons that are preached is not confined to the minister, but shared by the whole congregation. That is the reason for the demand that the calling of a new minister to a church must be preceded by at least two visits to it by the candidate for the pastorate, so that the congregation may make its own responsible judgment whether the message that the new minister will bring is likely to be what Paul called 'the word of God'. So the emphasis on the centrality of the sermon is not an attempt to magnify the human wisdom or virtue of the preacher; on the contrary, it arises from a concern to take God at His word, and believe that when minister and people together covenant to live in dependence upon God's promises, He will not fail to fulfil them. It is because it is thus believed that in the sermon God has promised to speak, that it is given a place and function that some Christian traditions have forgotten. At their best, Congregationalists are not sermon-tasters; they wait upon the speaking of the Word with that awe and expectancy that properly belongs to the sinner returning to the redeeming Father of justice and love.

The sermon, then, contemporises the Gospel. But the Sacrament displays it before our eyes, in such a way that we are taken out of the successiveness of this temporal world, and transcend it in some foretaste of eternity. In terms of the Scripture story, by the time that the liturgy of the Upper Room begins, the believer has been reminded of the creation (the opening sentences), the fall (the prayers of confession and supplication) and of the whole drama of our redemption from its beginning until its consummation (the reading of selected passages from Scripture). He has also been helped to see, in the preaching of the sermon, both that the story is about his own contemporary world, and that he has an effective part to play in its drama. So much has the liturgy of the Word done for him. But what the liturgy of the Upper Room does is to make the whole Church aware that the participation of

Moses and Abraham and the prophets, as well as his own sharing in the story, depends upon one central act in the great drama, that of the ministry, passion, death and resurrection of Jesus Christ. Here each believer and here the whole Church is fed on that which is its true life—Jesus Christ Himself, the Jesus who lived and died and rose again. Together with the whole Church, Congregationalists know that when bread is broken and eaten, when wine is poured out and consumed, then we are confronted with much more than 'signs' that stand for something they are not: we are confronted with the presence of Christ Himself. But to say that He is present in His dying and rising love is to say that our time with its successiveness is transcended, as it has been transcended and will be transcended by each successive generation of believers. As we repeat the actions of the Upper Room we know that they are not actions that are just past and done with, any more than the death upon the cross or the rising from the tomb is an act of history that is past and done with; rather are these the points at which we live not only at the moment of our own sacramental actions, but also at the 'moment' of their fulfilment in the death and resurrection of our Lord. Here we know in our experience, so far as it is possible for us to know, that in Christ we are joined with men of all times, and with the spirits from the eternities, at the day of His victory, the everlasting day of His reign. So that as the sermon brings the once spoken Word into our contemporary world, so the Sacrament takes us, and in some sense our world, into the eternal world of the Word; and both those things are possible, and are mediated, through the things that God wrought in Christ. The spoken Word claims the present for itself: the 'acted' Word makes manifest that all times belong to God in Christ.

If, then, one were to ask a modern Congregationalist what were the realities of his Church's worship, he would not reply in terms of orders of service alone. For he sees these as the media in and through which the eternal Word is given to man, and in which man holds communion with the eternal God, and is thus bound together with all the saints into one people of God.

Congregational church polity has another important consequence for the experience and understanding of its worship in its insistence upon the church as the organ of action and authority. Congregationalists believe that the gifts of ministry and the orders and offices in the church are given not to individuals to exercise in the church, but to the church to be exercised by individuals. Thus while the ordained minister is almost invariably what in other church orders would be called the 'celebrant', in Congregationalism it is the whole church which celebrates the sacraments, and offers worship. It is at this point that the words of I Peter are applied to the life of the Church, that we are 'a holy priesthood'. The priesthood of all believers does not mean that there is no distinction between ministers and laity; but it does mean that both laity and ministers are necessary to the true worship of the Church, and especially to her sacramental life. For this reason Congregationalists have consistently refused to practise private Baptisms or private Communions, but have always insisted that these always take place as part of the public worship of the people of God.

These considerations lead modern Congregationalists to speak much of 'fellowship' as a characteristic note in their tradition of worship. The word is a rich if dangerous one; but in the context of Congregationalist church life it draws attention to the fact that the basic thing about us human beings in the Church is not our individuality, but our being made a 'people for God's own possession'. If Congregationalism still needs, with other traditions, to purge itself fully of that false individualism which infiltrated into its life and thought about a century ago, it can find no more finished nor handy an agent than those traditions of worship which properly belong to it.

VIII

METHODIST

*

Harris Franklin Rall
(United States of America)

This paper is intended to set forth the place of worship, the meaning of worship, and the ways of worship in the Methodist Church. The task is not an easy one because here, as elsewhere, Methodism takes the way of freedom as to form, in contrast with any rigid control of authority or tradition. There is, however, a definite quality or character of Methodism which appears clearly in its worship. Though written by a member of the Methodist Church of America, this paper seeks to represent Methodism as a whole. Methodist ecumenical conferences have made plain the essential unity of its different branches.

Let us inquire first as to the meaning of Christian worship in itself. Religion has a double root: the reality of God as He speaks to man; the need of man as he turns to God. Always there is in religion a double movement, and first that of God toward man. God is the beginning and the end in religion: God as the power that rules, as the holiness that stands above us in demand and judgment, as the love that seeks to save and gives itself in fellowship to those who turn to Him. The first function of worship is to bring God to man: to show God forth, to make God real, to let God speak.

The second movement in religion is that of man to God. Religion is man's response to the Eternal. That response comes to conscious expression in worship. So it is a function of worship to help men to come to God. In worship man looks up to God in adoration, brings his whole life in devotion, and seeks God's blessing and help for all that life.

In such worship there is a deep simplicity, simplicity like that seen in the Lord's Prayer. But there is a richness and inclusiveness as well. It brings God in all His fulness: God far above us in holi-

ness and wisdom and might, near us in love and help, within us
as indwelling Spirit, God in His will for our lives. Hymn and
prayer, Scripture and sermon, the offering in which we bring
ourselves and our gifts, speech and silence, all should serve this
end. The inclusiveness of worship is quite as clear when we see
it as man's approach to God. Adoration and praise as we look
up to God, confession and repentance as we bare our life to Him
with all its sin and failure, devotion as we offer ourselves anew
to Him, thanksgiving for all that God gives, petition and intercession as we pray for ourselves and for all men, and through it
all the trust in the God of might and love.

In our consideration of the practice of worship we must always
keep in mind these two great aspects and inquire how far it brings
to the worshipper the living God with all His meaning for our
life, and how far it serves to help men to come to this God, to
worship Him and receive His help for all the needs of life.

The worship of a Church is the expression of its total faith and
life, of its faith in the God whom it adores and of the life which
it has from this God. True worship is thus something organic
and unitary, not a compound of traditional or adopted forms and
acts. Rightly to understand the worship of a given Church, therefore, one needs to look at it against this broader background of
its conception and practice of Christianity. This is especially true
of Methodism. It can be done, of course, only in bare outline.
What is here proposed is to consider first the main influences
which have entered in historically to shape the Methodist movement, in order better to understand the character of its worship
alike in its freedom and diversity, and in the common spirit which
animates it.

In considering the Church and its worship we commonly use
certain contrasts to describe the varying conceptions. Thus the
church concept is set against the group concept, the priestly
sacramentarian position against the evangelical, and free worship
against the liturgical. To understand Methodism and its worship
we need to see the varied influences which entered into her making
and how often she drew from both sides of the contrasted positions.

From the beginning Methodism was under the positive influence
of the church concept, which came to it through Anglicanism.
Methodism began as a movement in this Church, not as a departure from it. Wesley considered himself a good Anglican to the

end of his life, and sought to maintain the tie between the growing movement and the mother Church. Strong forces, at work from the beginning, finally changed this situation, the dominant attitude of the Anglican leaders and elements in the movement itself both working to this end. But the influence of the Anglican tradition remained even in America where the development of the new movement was freest and the contact with the Anglican Church much slighter. More important still was Methodism's conviction that it was an integral part of the historical Church, the one Church of Christ, sharing its heritage of faith and doctrine, owning the same Lord, having the same Scriptures, free to use its forms of worship.

Within this historical heritage, however, it was the Reformation influence that was decisive. The central fact for Methodism has not been the Church as an institution, nor a system of doctrine, nor a theory of the ministry and the sacraments. It has been the gospel of God's free grace in Christ. What marked Methodism was the way in which it accepted and carried out the implications of that gospel which the Reformation had reasserted. The gospel was for all men, therefore it was the Christian obligation to carry it to all: hence the stress upon preaching and an aggressive evangelism. God with His grace is directly accessible to all; but the priesthood of all believers meant not simply privilege but obligation, the obligation of all to witness to the gospel and to carry it to others. There was not simply a new stress on lay activity, but the development of a lay ministry. This began as leadership in group meetings, with a real pastoral supervision of class members, and moved on to lay preaching in public gatherings and finally to a system of lay preachers carrying on the work of the ministry either as a full-time vocation or in addition to their daily work.

The third element which entered in is not so easy to define, though it was deeply important. One may speak of it as mysticism. Wesley, having in mind some of its more extreme forms, strongly rejected the term. But if we think of mysticism in its broader sense as the soul's personal awareness of God and personal communion with Him, keeping in mind Methodism's emphasis on the doctrine of the Holy Spirit as personally and consciously received, then the mystical element is clearly present. Thus, despite certain marked differences, there is an interesting kinship of spirit between Quakers and Methodists.

A better term would be pietism, having in mind the Moravian brethren and the pietists of Halle. Better still, one may speak of the 'group movement' which these German pietists so well exemplified. Throughout its history the Church has revealed two contrasted tendencies. The first is the concern with what may be called the objective or the institutional. In its developed form it meant a faith given in defined doctrine; the Church as an institution with priesthood, authority, and organisation; a worship with prescribed forms. The contrasted emphasis was on religion as a conscious personal experience of saving fellowship with God and on a direct, personal fellowship with others in common worship and service, as well as in mutual aid.

The second emphasis is clearly seen in the primitive Church. The first, in rightful form and measure, was a necessary development, but the constant tendency of the institutional was to become dominant, with a loss of this second vital element. As a result, there have always been in the Church what might be called group movements. Some of these were separatist, but many simply worked within the Church to supply a deeply felt need. This was Wesley's attitude. Wesley was acquainted with the Moravians and the Halle pietists, and felt their influence, but his own groups ('classes', 'bands', 'societies') arose through needs which he discerned by personal experience and in his work. Their activity in common worship, mutual aid, common effort, and personal supervision was much that of the pietist groups. Though their meetings were never thought of as taking the place of public worship, their influence was seen in that worship when the movement became a Church, especially in its freedom, its spontaneity, and the place given to congregational singing.

Methodist worship in its earlier period, especially in America, was affected by the conditions under which it worked and by its sense of mission. It felt strongly the call to take the gospel to the unchurched and unsaved. In America that meant reaching those large and sparsely settled sections where there were no church privileges. Hence the itinerant preacher, who not merely sought out individuals, but called people together for worship in school houses, private homes, or wherever small groups could gather. Services under such conditions were necessarily simple, with the singing of familiar hymns, prayer, sermon, and evangelistic appeal. The camp meetings grew out of these conditions, and

F

these still further promoted free and spontaneous worship.

The purpose of this survey is not to suggest that Methodism was simply a resultant of the play of these various influences: Anglicanism, the Reformation, pietism, and the environment in which it worked. Its vigorous individuality, beginning with its founder, is manifest in the way in which it brought these varied elements of the Christian tradition into unity. Nor is it intended to suggest that it was indifferent to the basic questions as to the nature of the Christian faith and what constitutes a Christian Church and Christian worship.

There is a certain likeness here between early Methodism and the beginnings of Christianity. The Christian Church did not begin with an organisation or a system of doctrine. It was a fellowship, united by a common faith and experience, following a new way of life, holding a common hope for this life and for the world to come, charged with the proclaiming of Christ and His salvation. With the growth of this movement—and very early—there came the problems of leadership and authority, of declaring the meaning of this faith in doctrine and creed, of forming organisation and directing work and worship. We may hold that God's presence and guidance were in this development without thinking of the guidance as compulsive or the results as infallible.

Something of the same process was repeated in Methodism. It began as a fellowship of faith and experience, not as an organised Church. Wesley saw the needs of these early converts and gathered them together for counsel and common worship and mutual help under the guidance of selected leaders, commonly laymen. That this resulted ultimately in an independent church body was almost inevitable, and with this came the problems of organisation and administration, of the ministry, forms of worship, and doctrinal statement.

What is important to note, however, is not simply the order of this development: it is the relative emphasis that came with it. In those first years the Methodists had found the vital elements of Christianity: faith in the one God who had come to men in Jesus Christ; the gospel of God's grace for sinners; religion as conscious personal experience and assurance of salvation; the Christian life as one of holiness in love through the work of God's Spirit; the rich meaning of the Christian fellowship in common worship and mutual aid; the work of evangelism and teaching and care for its members to which the fellowship was called.

In this distinctive character of Methodism a marked element is the spirit of freedom. It followed, as with St. Paul, from this emphasis on grace and faith and love as central. It saw this freedom, as did St. Paul, in relation to the individual life. That meant no lessening of moral demands: on the contrary there was a renewal of the Christian demand for holiness as entire consecration and a life wholly ruled by the spirit of love. The same freedom obtained in the matter of credal statement and systems of doctrine. Doctrine was important, for the crucial matter in gospel preaching and in personal life was a clear and definite faith. But the object of faith was not a system of doctrine; it was the God who had come to men in Christ. In formulating all that was involved in this faith the individual church, under the rule of the gospel and with the guidance of the Spirit, acted in freedom. And the same freedom was assumed in matters of organisation and orders. In America the episcopal form was adopted: in Great Britain it was more presbyteral. In both countries, the organisation was close and effective. Here Methodism followed Wesley's spirit and shared some of his genius, but in that spirit it felt free to modify and adapt and at times to depart from Wesley's position.

This freedom appears clearly in relation to the use of liturgical forms in worship. Wesley was deeply devoted to the Book of Common Prayer. He sent a somewhat abridged form to the newly organised Church in America, calling it the Sunday Service for the Methodists in North America. It was adopted by the organising conference in 1784. The forms of public worship never came into general use, though the Anglican Church was the home Church of most Methodists at that time. The customary order for public services was constituted by song, prayer, Scripture readings, and preaching, to which were gradually added the Lord's Prayer, the doxology, and the apostolic benediction. The book itself was but once reprinted, but important parts were taken over into the Methodist *Discipline* and have remained, with some change, to this day, including the Articles of Religion, orders for the administration of the Lord's Supper and Baptism, the ritual for marriage and burial, and forms for the ordination of deacons and elders (using Wesley's terms).

The general trend in Methodism is now toward a larger use of ritual forms in public worship. Orders of worship are provided but are not prescribed. Their use is left to the minister and the local congregation, so that a rather wide variety in worship still obtains. There is a growing appreciation, however, of order and beauty in worship and of the value of forms which provide larger opportunity for common participation, the use of responsive readings having been an earlier step in this direction.

The Sacrament of the Lord's Supper has a recognised place in Methodist worship. Its uniqueness is recognised, though not as conferring a special and necessary 'sacramental grace'. In it the great elements of worship all come to moving and effective expression. It uses the language of symbol, setting forth central truths of our faith, truths which the words of rational discourse cannot adequately express. It preaches the gospel. It calls back the great deed of our Lord's saving love. It summons to confession, repentance, faith, re-dedication, and voices the joyous assurance of forgiveness. It is not the act of a priest for the people, but a shared celebration of Christ's followers gathered around His Table. It offers the same salvation as that which is proclaimed from the pulpit: the free grace of God forgiving sinful men who come in repentance and faith, and bestowing on them the Spirit and the new life in Christ. Something happens in this celebration of the Sacrament. God is here, God in action. But His action is not mechanical or magical. Here, as always, grace is mediated by the Word that God speaks, a Word that comes in Scripture and in symbol; and the gifts wait, as always, upon the penitent and believing response.

Central in worship, as in faith, is God's Word to man. The creative source of our religion is not man's search for God, but God's Word to man. It is this truth, the truth of God and from God, that makes us free. The Word comes to the worshipper in many ways. The Scriptures of the Old and New Testament come first, the record of God's revealing and redeeming work consummated in Christ, and in turn the means by which He speaks to us today.

The reading of the Scriptures, therefore, is viewed by Methodism as an essential part of every service of worship, including the Communion service, Baptism, and the service of burial. Methodist ministers are enjoined to read from both Old Testament and New in the services of public worship. A lectionary is provided for the minister, and responsive readings for the use of the congregation.

While this represents the ideal of the Church, the practice varies. The traditional freedom still obtains at this point, perhaps more in America. It is seen in a frequent tendency to neglect the Old Testament and to choose the Scripture reading in connection with the sermon, with the result that often only limited parts of the Bible are brought to the people—a real loss in a day when, with many people, there is so little reading of the Bible.

The sermon is the second way in which the Word is brought to men. The preacher is a speaker for God. He is not an individual bringing his wisdom on religious and social problems in lecture or address. The sermon should be a real part of worship. Not the preacher, but God should stand forth. Reverence, humility, and faith should inform the spirit alike of preacher and people.

Such preaching will always have the twofold reference that belongs to all worship. It will be a Word from God. As such it will be rooted in the revelation of God and of His gospel recorded in the Scriptures. One form of it would be expository preaching, but it would not be limited to that. Always it will be directed and determined by that final act of our faith, that God in Christ has revealed Himself in His love, His saving purpose and way, and His will for our life. But ours is a living God, working in the world today, guiding and illuminating by His Spirit, revealing new meanings of His truth.

This wider scope is seen clearly when we note the second reference of preaching, that which concerns man and his needs and the conditions of life. The true preaching of the Word must bring these two together: the eternal Word and the human condition, our time and the Eternal. As the Church considers the world of today, the sin and need of the peoples of today, it must proclaim the will of God for the world's life, and the way of God for its salvation. Here again, bringing God to the world and the world into the presence of God, we have a preaching which should form a part of real worship. The evangelistic note is still present in Methodist preaching. The abiding problems of the individual still receive primary emphasis. But it is increasingly realised that the Church, facing crucial social conditions, must interpret God's Word in its meaning for the associated life of man. And this is not merely moral demand. It is a proclamation of the gospel, of the God of redeeming love at work in the world and of the way by which this world may be saved. Methodism has co-operated with other church bodies as well as setting forth its own statements as to what the gospel demands for the associated life of men.

In common with other Churches, Methodism is recognising the need of a teaching pulpit in the stricter sense of that term. An effective religion, whether individual or social, must be intelligent and informed. The Church needs to set herself systematically to the task of informing and training her people. The teaching of youth in Sunday School and catechetical instruction is not enough; the work must be carried on with adults. The printed page is important, and Methodism from the beginning has made large use of tracts, pamphlets, books, and journals.

A special responsibility, however, rests upon the pulpit: hence the need of a teaching ministry. There is a vast deal of religious illiteracy, within the Church as well as without. The teaching of the Bible comes first. Our people need both right understanding and personal acquaintance. They should know how the Bible came to be, where its treasures lie and how to use them, and the centrality and supremacy of Christ and His gospel in interpreting the Bible. Above all, they need encouragement and guidance in the reading of the Bible. Further, the pulpit needs to teach the great doctrines of the Church. That means more than a casual reference which assumes a knowledge that does not exist. Only so can we expect victory in present-day conflicts of faiths, in which the enemies of Christianity are carrying on a constant work of indoctrination. Our people need instruction as to the Church, their own branch of the Church, the ecumenical Church, great events in church history and the great spirits of the past, the varied work of the Church, especially in its missions, as well as the great movements looking toward Christian unity.

There is the need of systematic education as to the great problems already referred to connected with man's social life. That does not mean that the Church should identify herself with particular ideologies, political or economic, in the conflicts of today. It does mean that our people should know the great evils that obtain: pride and prejudice of class and race, national selfishness and isolation, international exploitation and oppression, economic injustice and war. And they should be taught the great principles which are inherent in the Christian faith: good will, justice, freedom, the worth of men as men, the solidarity of human life, the way of co-operation, the confidence in the forces of truth and right and love in which we see the power of God at work.

The place of congregational singing needs special mention here. From the first it had a large place in Methodism. It made possible the sharing of the whole company in worship. The warm personal religious experience here found rich expression. The Wesleys, Charles in particular, rendered great service by the hymns which they wrote and by other hymns made available by their translations. The itinerant preacher could enrich his free and simple service by song. Adoration, praise, penitence, confession, dedication, the assurance of salvation, all found expression here. A study of the Methodist hymnal, and especially of the hymns of the Wesleys, will show that the great doctrines of the Church all came to expression here. The hymns brought the Word of God to men and helped them to understand its truths.

II

The essential elements of worship for which provision should be made have been indicated in connection with the preceding statement. They may be briefly summarised in conclusion.

There is first the worship that is called forth by the vision of God. We see the Lord, high and lifted up, the transcendent God of holiness and power and wisdom. We meet the God of infinite love who has come to men in Christ, who draws near to us in mercy, who gives Himself to us by His Spirit. Before this God we see ourselves as sinful men, standing under His judgment. We know ourselves as creatures, finite, wholly dependent, having nothing except what comes from Him. Yet we hear His voice calling to us: Son of man, stand upon thy feet. He offers us reconciliation and receives us as His children.

There is a worship that goes with this vision and for which the Church must provide. It is the worship of adoration, awe, and humble reverence, whose one thought is the glory of this our God and the wonder of His love. It is a worship of praise and thanksgiving, owning the goodness of God, mindful of His mercies. But it will always be the worship of the sinner, confessing sin and failure, coming in penitence, making the offering of self-devotion, receiving the assurance of forgiveness.

The means for such worship will be varied: Scripture, the hymns of the congregation, free prayer, forms of prayer in which the people may unite, the preaching of the Word, and especially the Communion Service. There will be no absolution through priestly word and authority. The forgiveness will be from God, given to the penitent and believing. The assurance will come through the gospel of grace and the witness of God's Spirit.

Petition and intercession belong to this worship. We bring to God all our needs, of body and spirit. We remember before God all who are dear to us. We pray for all sorts and conditions of men. Our prayer is for the nations, for the coming of peace and righteousness, the coming of God's kingdom. But always two elements enter in: the desire before all other desires that God's will may be done; the confidence that enables us to ask with joy and to leave all our needs and petitions with Him. There is inter-cessory prayer here: not the intercession of priest or saint with special access to God, but that of the children of God, praying in the spirit of the Son, gladly heard by the Father.

The offering belongs to Christian worship as truly as it did to that of the Jewish people. It is not an oblation of sacramental elements: we believe in Him who made the one offering of Him-self for the sins of the world. It is, first of all, the worshipper's offering of himself, of soul and body, 'a living sacrifice, holy and acceptable unto God'. It is the consecration of possessions, recog-nising God's ownership and our stewardship. It is the presentation of gifts for the work of the Church and the aid of men.

Earlier reference has been made to the important aspect of corporate worship. It remains to be noted that Methodist worship has room for the thought that the body of this corporate worship includes the Church of all the earth and the Church in heaven. We join in the *Tersanctus*: 'With angels and archangels, and with all the company of heaven, we laud and magnify thy glorious name.' We sing with Charles Wesley: 'Let saints on earth unite to sing with those to glory gone.' 'One family we dwell in Him, One Church above, beneath.'

IX

THE RELIGIOUS SOCIETY OF FRIENDS

*

*The following statement has been prepared by the
Committee on Christian Relationships of the Religious
Society of Friends in Great Britain*

*

For members of the Society of Friends the meeting for worship
is the central fact of their corporate religious life and the basis of
their common service. As the Quaker meeting has a character of
its own, differentiating it markedly from other forms of Christian
worship, some contribution is required from Friends if a discussion
of ways of worship is to be complete. But just because the Society
has no liturgy or ritual, administers no outward sacrament,
ordains no priest, does not recite a creed, and refuses to consecrate
any building, what it may have to offer is hardly likely to provide
direct answers to a questionnaire appropriately addressed to other
parts of the Christian Church. Nevertheless, if a freer form of
answer is admissible something perhaps may usefully be said in a
short memorandum about a tradition of worship, now three
hundred years old, in which groups of men and women have
regularly met in holy communion with God and with one
another and in a deep sense of the real presence of Christ, coming
to 'know one another in that which is eternal, which was before
the world was',[1] and are knit into a unity 'treating one another
as those that believed and felt God present'.[2]

The Meeting for Worship

Meeting for worship from Sunday to Sunday, and frequently
on other days too, Friends have regularly spent a considerable
part of their time together in silence, but have always felt free also
to minister to one another in the spoken word of exhortation and

[1] Fox: *Epistles*, p. 115.
[2] Penn: Preface of Fox's Journal, Bi-Cent. edition, Vol. I, p. 11.

in uttered prayer, under what they have felt to be the constraining and restraining influence of the Holy Spirit. It is misleading to say that Quaker meetings are silent; their true basis is attentive and expectant waiting on God in worship with full opportunity for ministry. Nor is the silence to be regarded as a rite. In the early days of Friends, Robert Barclay[1] wrote: 'True worship consists neither in words nor in silence, as silence, but in a humble dependence of the mind upon God.'

Worship is man's response to God and the fixing of attention on Him as He has revealed Himself to us in history. It is to a God who not only 'is love' but who 'so loved the world' that we lift our hearts in an act of adoration and thanksgiving, self-giving and penitence.

Meetings for worship held after the manner of Friends vary considerably in content, cultural level and religious quality and experience. They have often been, and still are, attended by quite small numbers; indeed large gatherings have sometimes been found difficult. Nobody would claim that the form and method of the Quaker meeting for worship was one to be imposed on others: even for Friends it often falls short of the ideal. Yet others besides Friends have come to recognise the worth of a time spent in quiet waiting on God, with complete freedom of responsible utterance for all, old and young, man and woman, cultivated and uninstructed; and this practice has undoubtedly influenced and helped other branches of the Christian Church.

The meeting for worship is a venture of faith; and every one involves risk not only at the hands of the insensitive and those who do not fully understand, but equally because of unfaithfulness to the Light on the part of others. The following queries which are read aloud in our meetings from time to time are intended to remind Friends of their personal responsibility: Do you maintain a steadfast loyalty to our Lord Jesus Christ as the Head of the Church and the Shepherd of souls? Do you look to His Holy Spirit to give the true call and qualification for the ministry? Are you faithful in your witness to the freeness and spirituality of the Gospel of Christ? Are you obedient to the Divine Call whether your service be through words or in silence?

[1] Robert Barclay of Ury in Aberdeenshire, the first systematic theologian produced by Friends, was born in 1648 and died in 1690. He published in Latin *The True Christian Divinity*.

While rejecting outward forms, Friends do, of course, for ordinary convenience, appoint a time and a place for meeting; and the fact that this mode of worship is recognisable and that examples of it may be criticised shows that after all it tends to a certain form. Yet the successful use of Friends' mode of worship depends first on the practice of communion in silence, an expectant silence in which the worshippers wait on God, are listening and attending and responding to the guidance of the Spirit; and on the emergence from this silent communion of a responsible spoken ministry.

To the non-Friend, who too often has gained the impression that a Friends' meeting offers nothing but empty silence, the whole idea may at first be repellent and intolerable; nevertheless, it is certain that many a stranger has found rest and comfort and healing of soul in the quiet of a Friends' meeting, and has come to know something of the presence of God there. It is equally certain that many who have turned away unsatisfied from liturgical forms of worship and official ministries have found freedom of spiritual exercise and a message to their own hearts either in the silence or in some simple word spoken out of it in the name of Christ.

The Ministry

Addresses and lectures for religious instruction are in place in gatherings arranged for that purpose; but a prepared address or sermon is felt to be out of keeping with the spirit of meeting for worship. Worshippers are indeed urged to attend 'with hearts and minds prepared'; and those who from time to time feel called to speak will often, but not always, be able to render the greater help to those who listen if they speak out of well-stored minds and rich experience; but in this case it is the person—not the sermon—that has been prepared. Friends believe that true ministry arises out of the exercise of the meeting and is given of the Holy Spirit. The group becomes fused into an organic whole through the empowering and enlightening action of the Spirit. In the language of another seventeenth-century Friend, Isaac Penington (1616-1679), 'The life flows from the vessel of life in one to the vessel of life in another.' In consequence the ministry speaks to the heart and 'condition' of all those present. It will relate to what the speaker knows to be true in his (or her) own experience. Yet, it grows out of the experience not of one person only but of the whole company of worshippers, who themselves have been given a deeper insight into the meaning of life as they have waited together in the presence of God. It has expressed and has responded to the search of the human heart for the heart of God.

This true ministry, according to Friends' understanding, is characterised by a deep sense of responsibility alike to God and to fellow men; none may claim exemption from the call when it comes. The vehicle of the message may just as well be an uninstructed and hitherto tongue-tied worshipper as one capable of polished and accomplished utterance. A few words 'from the Lord' may have as much value as a longer address. 'We bring our varying gifts to Thee and Thou rejectest none'[1]; 'They that have the spirit are ministers of the spirit and they minister to the raising up of the spirit in others' (James Nayler).

The Fellowship

Worship has a twofold reference; vertically to God, horizontally to man. The meeting is not a collection of individuals but a religious community joined in a common purpose. Friends agree with other Christians in feeling that individual communion with God is no substitute for corporate worship; each has its place. Something is given to the gathered group that can never be known in isolation. Again Robert Barclay writes: 'As everyone is inwardly gathered to the measure of life in himself, there is a secret unity and fellowship enjoyed, which the devil and all his instruments can never break or hinder.'

Friends' sense of fellowship and of mutual responsibility is, of course, not confined to the time actually spent in common worship: but, generated and centred there, it extends through all the dimensions of the common life, and gives foundation, quality and strength to the wider sense of Christian responsibility towards all sorts and conditions of men, of no matter what colour, class or creed, that expresses itself in social and international service.

The Bible

Friends place a high value on the Scriptures. On the one hand they are the record of God's disclosure of Himself to men through

[1] 'Our Master', J. G. Whittier. The spirit of a Friends' meeting is well expressed both in this poem and in 'The Meeting'.

the Hebrew people, culminating in the unique personality of Jesus Christ (in His life, death and resurrection), and, on the other hand, they tell the story of man's discovery of the nature and purpose of God as conditioned by his response and obedience to the Light leading to growth in insight and knowledge of truth.

Our members are advised ' to be constant in the private reading of the Bible' (General Advices), 'to be diligent in reading and meditating upon the Scriptures' and 'to seek to come into the living experience from which the Scriptures sprang, and to find words to express it simply and worthily' (Advices on Ministry). At least once a year the following Query is read in every meeting for worship, 'Do you gather daily in your families for worship, and for reading from the Bible?' and Friends are reminded that 'great care should be used in the choice of passages of Scripture for family reading'. We regret that the practice of family worship is not now so generally followed as it should be and used to be.

The debt we owe to modern scholars for their reverent study and unfolding of the Scriptures is thankfully recognised. Friends are urged to take full advantage of these resources now so abundantly available. It is laid upon our Elders to provide opportunities for instruction in the study and interpretation of the Bible.

At the same time the reading of the Bible in meetings for worship may form a valuable contribution to that worship, and the devotional use of the Bible throughout the week and familiarity with its contents are regarded as a vital and essential part of that preparation of heart and mind for worship which is enjoined upon all our members.

The Sacraments

Friends, as is well known, affirm that the outward and visible forms of sacraments of Baptism and the Lord's Supper are not necessary. This does not mean that they are indifferent to those deep spiritual values which the observance of these sacraments have for most other Christians. Friends emphasise the necessity both of being baptised of the Spirit and of inward communion with Christ, and these experiences they feel are not conditioned by the use of any outward forms.

The following passages taken from a statement prepared for the World Conference on Faith and Order in 1920 clearly represent the Quaker point of view:

'The main difference between ourselves and most other bodies of Christians arises from the *emphasis* we place on the light of God's Holy Spirit in the human soul . . . This direct contact between the Spirit of Christ and the human spirit we are prepared to trust to, as the basis of our individual and corporate life. . . . The Light of Christ in the soul may be experienced by all: no form of the Divine Grace is the monopoly of a priestly caste, through whom alone it can be ministered to others. . . . We do not make use of the outward rites of Baptism and the Lord's Supper, but we do believe in the inward experiences they symbolise. Our testimony is to the actuality of this experience even without the external rite.'

There is no altar in the Friends' meeting house, but in the meeting for worship the experience of the presence of Christ in the midst is the means of grace and the source of life. 'The sacrifices of God are a broken spirit.' God, the Father of Jesus Christ, is our loving heavenly Father to be approached directly and not by way of oblation; and prayerful thought is naturally turned to the meeting place with God found both in the individual heart and in the communion of the worshipping fellowship. The fact that many others find the forms of outward ritual helpful to them or even an indispensable expression of their worship is fully recognised. But Friends feel that the outward form tends to draw attention to itself and to blur the true vision of God. Relying on the promise of Christ they pray for a fresh outpouring of the Holy Spirit which brings the assurance of grace and power.

Part Two

THE INNER MEANINGS OF
WORD AND SACRAMENT

PREFACE

*

It became clear after the meetings at Clarens in August–September 1947 *that certain central problems were recurring in the foregoing studies, and were presenting the sharpest differences of view. The issues treated in Part Two are, to some extent, all latent in Part One, but were actually brought into focus by some passages in a paper by Dr. Robert Will of Strasbourg, which was read at Clarens, and is summarised as an introductory chapter to this Part.*

As a result, members of the Commission were invited, in October 1947, '*to send in a statement on the following subjects:*

(a) The relation between Word and Sacrament

(b) Sacrament and Symbol

(c) Offering and Priesthood.'

The responses, together with certain papers written subsequently, are here collected to form Part Two.

X

INTRODUCTORY

*

R. Will

(Alsace)

In a paper dealing ostensibly with the state of public worship in the Lutheran Church of Alsace, Dr. Will raised issues of great importance which are discussed in the papers which form Part Two. On the question of the relation of Word and Sacrament, in which he saw the whole issue between the two main concepts of worship, he contributed another paper which is printed in full below. His initial paper, however, may first be briefly summarised.

There have been conflicting tendencies since the Reformation, culminating in a tension between a liturgical revival of classical modes of worship and the accepted 'immanentist pietism' which fears departure from the freedom and purity of the worship which, it believes, was gained in the Reformation. On the one hand, the national temperament craves for liberty, finding support in Luther, Calvin and Bucer. The quest for ecclesiastical order, however, led the same authorities to 'rise up against the iconoclastic enterprise of "spiritualisers"'. The sentiment of to-day continues to reject the 'legalism of a liturgical uniformity such as holds sway in Catholicism', but on the other hand 'to refuse to admit innovations introduced as a result of individual insights or confessional fashions'.

'At the present time there is a movement which is realistic, objective, and theocentric, as against the immanentist tendencies of pietist subjectivism.' This has brought 'a new intuitive grasp of the profound nature of the Church'—a transcendental element and a mysterious power. However the Church may grow in a human sense, she is also the object of her faith—an incarnation of God. This sense brings a like objectivity to worship. It is not a

vague sense of divinity, but a living dialogue—a creative act of
God and a filial response to that act. 'This is what happens in the
House of God,' wrote Luther; 'Our dear Lord Himself speaks to
us through His Holy Word. On our side we speak to Him in our
prayers and hymns of praise.' Dr. Will comments thus: 'A circuit
of divine grace is set up. Divine life pours itself into the eternal
Word. The Word is made flesh in Jesus Christ. Christ transfuses
it into the gospel and the sacraments. By the action of the Holy
Spirit those means awaken human faith, which turns into prayer
and so ascends again to God. He is alike subject and object of all
worship.'[1]

Sacrifice and Priesthood[2]

God opens the way to the life of worship and blesses the following of His way. The human worshipper responds to the initiative
of God. His response becomes his Sacrifice—a purely spiritual
sacrifice (I Pet. 2. 5)—the fruit of the lips (Heb. 13. 10) as it is
found in prayer, in singing, and to some extent in the sermon.

All sacrifice requires a priesthood. Sacrifice and priesthood, in
the Christian Church, have their foundation in Christ, who is at

---

[1] In this and following papers, writers both from French- and German-
speaking Churches frequently use the terms *Spiritualisme* or *Spiritualismus* to
indicate tendencies which have had a marked effect upon the matters under
consideration. A mere transliteration would completely distort the meaning,
since the English term *spiritualism* has a totally different connotation.

The theological sense is the same both in French and German. The reference
is to an ancient heresy, originally Gnostic and Manichaean, which supposes that
any contact with the material and the outward is opposed to true 'spirituality'.
This view persisted, and indeed gave rise to various Catharist sects, and was held
by groups of 'Illuminati'. From the evidence here collected, it also had its effect
in long-established Christian Communions. As is pointed out especially in
Chapter XIII (*a*) below, the heresy is common where a supposed mysticism is
exaggerated out of relation to Christian doctrine, and thus gives rise to the
modern Protestant distrust of mystical theology. (Cf. also footnote 2 to Chapter
XVII.) In present-day forms, as Bishop Stählin further points out, the view
leads to a total disuse of sacramental worship, which is held to be the 'shadow'
of the Old Covenant, superseded by the 'substance' of the New Covenant.

Since there is no single English equivalent, the terms 'spiritualisers' and
'spiritualising' have been used, together with the above note, to indicate the
sense—cf. Report: pp. 28 f.—ED.

[2] The relation of Word and Sacrament is fully discussed by the author in
Chapter XIII and is thus omitted in this summary.—ED.

once sacred victim and sovereign High Priest (Heb. 2. 7; 4. 14; 10. 21). The Church, being the Body of Christ, is called upon to re-enact her sacrifice, i.e. to renew spiritually the work which has been accomplished by her Head once and for all on the Cross. Now the Church is the community of the members of Christ, and not merely a hierarchy of the *élite*. Should such an *élite* claim to incorporate the transcendent substance of the Church, they would be arrogating to themselves the exclusive right of mediation between man and God through ritual sacrifice. There is a universal priesthood taught by the New Testament (I Pet. 2. 5; Rev. 1. 6; 5. 10) which was adopted completely by the Reformers. Each member of the Church can approach God as spirit to Spirit, to offer for himself and his fellows the spiritual sacrifice of prayer and praise 'unto the work of ministry, to the building up of the Body of Christ'.

To ensure that things are done decently and in order (I Cor. 14. 40) the ministry of the Word and the service of the Altar are entrusted to a representative of the congregation, i.e. to an individual qualified by inner vocation, prepared by solid religious training and called as pastor by the congregation, in accordance with the Church's laws. (*Rite vocatus:* Augsburg Confession: XIV.) Some consider that the laying on of hands (I Tim. 4. 14; II Tim. 1. 6), by which the pastor is ordained, confers a priestly character marking him out from other believers, who know themselves to be members of the Body and who feel the inspiration of the Holy Spirit. Others consider that the laying on of hands symbolises intercession and the invocation of the Holy Spirit, but that it gives no supernatural power conferred by the intervention of another person himself so endowed with a supernatural gift.

The sacramentalism current to-day would seem to require the enhancing of priestly dignity. The service of the Altar is felt to be the centre of worship, as the Altar is the centre of the sanctuary. If we adhere to biblical principles, the Elders may also be called to perform other priestly offices, such as the admission of catechumens, assisting at the Holy Table, bringing forward the people's offerings, and private confession. In special circumstances our Church would not only call upon the ministry of women, but laymen also would be invested with authority to preach the Word and administer the sacraments for the service of a parish which was in need. This auxiliary ministry, of course, requires vigilance and direction, to prevent sectarian fancies, or the introduction of untrained people to a task which needs knowledge of the Bible and a delicate sense of responsibility.

Symbolism in Worship

The question of the symbol is an acid test between followers of the old tradition and Lutheran innovators, and yet it is the point at which realism and 'spiritualising' might come together to merge their inherent values in the interests of reunion.

By symbolism we do not mean signs chosen arbitrarily to illustrate some idea—just as scales are a symbol of justice—but something which, by facilitating intercourse between the Spirit of God and the spirit of man, takes on a special character of transcendent value. Now each form of worship allows words, actions, and objects to be used for the purpose of sustaining the worship in spirit and in truth (John 4. 24). These outward signs are not in themselves sacred, but they may become vehicles for that encounter in which the Word of God is truly received in faith. The human word will not be a formula stripped of meaning, nor will the human act be merely a mechanical practice, nor again will the object be a substance credited with supernatural virtue in itself. Such things lead to blasphemy. But this need not imply that the Word, which is certainly the most appropriate symbol for the spirit, is the symbol *par excellence* of Protestant worship, for even the word might be debased with vain repetition (Matt. 4. 17).

There are other symbols which help spiritual worship, quite apart from hearing and speech. By neglecting these an exaggerated 'spiritualising' risks the loss of very real religious values. Those concrete symbols which appeal to the senses of sight, touch and taste, may also be channels through which the Holy Spirit may reach a faithful soul, or through which the soul may go out to the Spirit. Thus the bread and the wine of Communion are not allegorical forms chosen by chance. There is no thought of transubstantiation in calling them symbols which the love of the Saviour has endowed with a fulness of reality for those who believe in the power of His Sacrifice. By the suggestive effect of the symbol consecrated by the Spirit of Christ, our spirit may reach to 'things which are not seen, and which are eternal' (II Cor.

4. 18) and may gather the divine graces which are there to be found.

Without becoming an object of worship, a crucifix can be a symbol of powerful reality by revealing to those who gaze upon it that love of God which inspired the sacrifice of Calvary. If lighted candles in a dim sanctuary arouse only a sterile sentimentalism, the symbol will have failed to help a truly spiritual worship: but the saying *In serviendo consumor* will suggest in this symbol the real force of the words in Matt. 20. 28, and will constrain us to burn ourselves up—we members of Christ—in the service of our brethren. Even the least noticed acts—standing, sitting, joining hands—carry a symbolic interpretation. The very place in which we worship may be used merely for pious assembly, or it may be the very House of God where He will vouchsafe to visit the faithful gathered in the name of Christ. We do not suppose that He dwells in temples made with hands when we say that a church beautifully adorned may become an offering to the source of all Beauty, and thus a symbol of worship.

The Christian Year is not merely a calendar. It is the symbol of a reality which adds spiritual value to the thoughts and the conduct proper to each season. God the Eternal steps into time, and brings its ceaseless flux into line with the divine permanence and stability. Thus the moving sequence of the Christian Year invites the worshippers to seek eternity in a world beyond time. Thus, through the channel of the divine Word, and the sequence of its Holy Days, the Church uses the cycle of her canticles and Scripture readings to bring together the two currents of the spiritual life—the flowing down to men and the flowing up to God. Through an ever-renewed Christian worship it accomplishes its object; and, taken as a whole, it represents the miracle of salvation from the beginning to the end of time.[1]

Sacrifice and Priesthood

In principle the 'ritualists' and the 'spiritualisers' are in agreement in attributing a spiritual character to these two aspects, and in rejecting any hierarchical or supernatural priesthood. It may seem paradoxical that the liturgical wing, who give an almost mystic value to personal priesthood, will still ask from the universal

[1] (In his closing section Dr. Will relates these themes to the possible future development of worship in his church.—ED.)

priesthood of the congregation an increasing share in worship through responses and chants. But the 'spiritualisers' who chiefly stress the universal priesthood will reduce the congregational part in worship to a minimum. There is surely room here for mutual appreciation and common practice. One can welcome the way in which a priestly function is accorded to the congregation, provided that the pastor realises that the priestly and ministerial sides of his work complement one another, so that the administration of sacraments and the service of the Word are bound into one; and realises that his dignity is owing to the same grace of God which confers the universal priesthood, and not to mere ritual consecration. The 'spiritualisers', on the other hand, might well call for the sacrifice of the lips from those whose priesthood they so clearly recognise. God is at the heart of worship, and should be able to count on the oblation of all His servants.

Symbolism in Worship

The 'spiritualising' Protestants should recognise that many symbols which they label 'Catholic' are not thereby un-evangelical. Forms which are addressed to sight and touch can still assist a worship in spirit and in truth. God may speak to souls by many means other than speech itself. As to the 'ritualists', they must show that the symbols they value are indeed the means to a fully spiritual reality. They must not overlook the danger of a return through an artificial piety to certain forms of Catholic worship, however venerable, without asking whether this compromise with the actions and the formulas of the Mass is really adding evangelical values to our worship. They must be sure that it is the Lord Himself who seeks to speak through these symbols, for to worship also we must apply the test that 'of him and through him and unto him are all things' (Rom. 11. 36). It would indeed be sad if Christians were to be led astray into formalism or magic by using what they had not learned to understand. This continual initiation of Protestant congregations into the meaning of symbols is an imperative duty laid on those who take the grave responsibility of formative changes in established worship. The very safety of uninstructed believers may be at stake. There is a work of education to be done if the Churches are to understand that only when the Spirit of God joins with the spirit of man will concrete symbols truly serve a worship in spirit and in truth.

In the various branches of religious life and thought and practice in worship there are promising signs of a coming agreement. These promises will bear fruit if those who love the Church of Alsace, and wish to see peace and order reigning in it, strive with heart and mind and soul to find in God the ground and the life of the Church, and to open their eyes as they worship to the radiance of the mystery of Christ.   *

XI

ORTHODOX

*

Lev Gillet
(Great Britain)

I. *The Sacramental Teaching of the Orthodox Church: Sources and References*

(i) Neither the Nicaean Creed nor the seven ecumenical Councils have formulated a developed doctrine of sacraments. Therefore the Orthodox Church has no *official* systematic teaching on the topics: Word and Sacrament, Sacrament and Symbol, Offering and Priesthood.

(ii) All the Orthodox faithful agree nevertheless on some fundamental points related to those topics. The basis of this agreement is the tradition of the Church as expressed in the Holy Scripture, in the acts of local Councils, in the writings of the Church Fathers and of recognised theologians, and in the liturgical life of the Church.

(iii) In order to give an accurate view of the Orthodox *consensus* on the three topics mentioned above, we shall quote some passages of the Edinburgh Conference report (1937) adopted by the Orthodox delegation, which Archbishop Germanos of Thyateira was leading.[1] We shall add passages from eminent modern Orthodox theologians. We shall strictly avoid all originality, all personal or school *theologumena*, confining ourselves to some sober and objective notions generally accepted.

II. *Word and Sacrament*

(i) 'We concur in affirming that the Word of God is ever living . . . A testimony in *words* is by divine ordering provided

---

[1] *Second World Conference on Faith and Order, Edinburgh,* 1937, SCM Press (quoted as E.).

for the revelation uttered by the *Word*. This testimony is given in Holy Scripture, which thus affords the primary norm for the Church's teaching, worship and life . . . We all agree that the Christian Church is constituted by the eternal Word of God made man in Christ and is always vitalised by His Holy Spirit.'[1]

(ii) 'We are agreed that in all sacramental doctrine and practice the supreme authority is our Lord Jesus Christ Himself . . . The Holy Spirit enables the Church, walking by faith in its risen Lord, to interpret Holy Scripture as expressing the living Word of God to every age and to exercise a stewardship of its tradition concerning the sacraments . . . All church tradition regarding the sacraments ought to be controlled and tested by Scripture.'[2] Orthodox rider: 'All the sacraments can be founded upon Holy Scripture as completed, explained, interpreted, and understood in the Holy Tradition by the guidance of the Holy Spirit residing in the Church.'[3]

(iii) 'God's gracious action is not limited by His sacraments.'[4] Orthodox rider: 'Orthodox delegates . . . desire to exclude from the reference of this proposition cases in which failure to receive the sacraments is due to contempt or culpable negligence, since sacraments are divinely instituted means of grace generally necessary for salvation.'[5] The word *generally* is here very important.

(iv) Besides the general relationship of the sacraments to the Word, there is an inclusion of the Word in each sacrament under the form of certain *words* which are part and condition of the sacrament (formulas used in the administration of Baptism, of the Lord's Supper, of Penance, etc.). According to Dyobounotes, the sacramental signs are not only certain actions, but also 'those . . . words . . . which are absolutely necessary for the accomplishment of the sacrament and for the communication through it of divine grace'.[6]

III. *Sacrament and Symbol*

(i) The Orthodox Church prefers the word 'mystery' ($\mu \nu \sigma \tau \acute{\eta} \rho \iota o \nu$) to the word 'sacrament'. The first one, says Mesolora, 'expresses

---

[1] E, chap. III.   [2] E, chap. V.   [3] *Ibid.*, footnote.
[4] E, chap. V.   [5] *Ibid.*, note.
[6] Constantine Dyobounotes, Tὰ $\mu \nu \sigma \tau \acute{\eta} \rho \iota a$, Athens, 1913, pp. 13-14.

more deeply and amply the mysterious character of the power and concurrence of divine Grace in the believer'.[1]

(ii) Orthodox theologians nowadays avoid using as synonymous the words 'mystery' and 'symbol'.

The mystery is much more than the symbol. 'The sacraments are given by Christ to the Church as outward and visible signs of His invisible grace. They are not bare symbols, but pledges and seals of grace, and means whereby it is received.'[2] The symbol is the outward sign. The mystery is the outward sign and the grace. According to Androutsos, the grace is not merely symbolised or promised, but actually given to the believer; any conception of the mysteries as mere signs or symbols is utterly contrary to the Orthodox teaching.[3]

(iii) Between the outward signs or symbols (either acts or words, differing in every mystery) and the grace given; between the physical and visible part of the mystery and its invisible and spiritual part, there is a relationship that eludes our speculations. It is well known, for instance, that the Orthodox generally disavow any attempt to explain the manner of the presence of Christ in the Lord's Supper. While the way whereby grace is conveyed in the sacraments has been for centuries, and remains, a subject of theological discussion in the West, such questions, as Androutsos says,[4] are without importance for the Orthodox faith.

IV. *Offering and Priesthood*

(i) 'It is our Lord Jesus Christ who through the Holy Spirit accomplishes every sacrament, and the action of the minister of the Church is only instrumental.'[5] This is well in line with the liturgy of St. John Chrysostom where Christ is addressed as: '. . . thou that offerest and art offered'.

(ii) 'The sacraments are celebrated by the minister, not in virtue of any personal right of his own, but as minister of the Church.'[6] 'We believe that every sacrament should be so ordered that all may recognise in it an act performed on behalf of the universal Church.'[7] 'To this end there is need of an ordained ministry

---

[1] T. E. Mesolora, Συμβολικὴ, IV, p. 149.   [2] E, chap. V.
[3] Chrestos Androutsos, Δογματική, Athens, 1907, p. 299.
[4] *Ibid.*, p. 299.   [5] E, chap. V.   [6] E, chap. V.   [7] E, chap. V.

recognised by all to act on behalf of the universal Church in the administration of the sacraments.'[1] Orthodox rider: *Validity*. As regards the validity of sacraments the Orthodox delegates would like to confine themselves only to the following statement: according to Orthodox doctrine valid sacraments are only those which are (i) administered by a canonically ordained and instituted minister, and (ii) rightly performed according to the sacramental order of the Church.'[2] One notices that this statement defines the conditions of validity, but does not say what validity essentially is. The Orthodox Church lays more emphasis on the spiritual than on the canonical or legal aspects of Christian life; hence her exercise of 'economy', of which Androutsos writes: '. . . this notion . . . is founded on the practice of the Church, in which the same sacrament in different circumstances has been pronounced at one time valid and at another invalid'.[3]

(iii) As regards the offering of Christ made in the Eucharist, Androutsos writes: 'The Eucharist is not a new act of immolation of Jesus Christ different from the immolation of Golgotha as to its content and its power, but a new representation before God of that sacrifice made once for all and a new mystical reiteration of it.'[4] The sacrifice of the Eucharist and that of Golgotha coincide 'inasmuch as both have the same Offerer and the same Thing offered, the same Sacrificer and the same Victim, our Lord Jesus Christ'.[5] And again: 'It is not a new act of immolation of Christ, but a new presentation of the sole and final sacrifice.'[6]

(iv) The ministry officially delegated by the Orthodox Church by no means eliminates or diminishes this universal and invisible offering priesthood of which the Apostle Peter speaks: 'Ye also, as lively stones, are built up a spiritual house, an holy priesthood, to offer up spiritual sacrifices, acceptable to God by Jesus Christ.'[7]

---

[1] E, chap. V.
[2] *Ibid.*, note.
[3] Δογματική, p. 308.
[4] Δογματικαί μελέται Α'.
[5] Δογματική, p. 371.
[6] *Ibid.*, p. 374.
[7] I Pet. 2. 5.

XII

ANGLICAN

*

(a) A. H. Couratin
(Great Britain)

It is very difficult for an Anglican to explain to a non-Anglican the Anglican situation in connection with the Eucharist. The Church of England, so far as the present writer understands the matter, has never claimed to bear witness to any particular aspect of the Gospel, nor does it stand by any particular confession. It possesses a liturgy and a set of Articles; but the Articles are only Articles of Agreement, and the liturgy was only imposed to secure peace and quietness. It claims rather to teach the Apostolic Faith, and to minister the sacraments of the Gospel and other traditional rites of the Church, by means of a ministry inherited from the Apostles, to the people of England. It denies that either it or any other Church is or can be infallible. If it were to make any claim for itself, it would declare that it endeavoured to present undifferentiated Christianity, and had always tried to avoid the systems of Rome on the one hand and of Geneva on the other, on the ground that systematisation is normally effected only at the expense of part of the truth. No such thing as an Anglicanism, comparable to Lutheranism or Calvinism, is therefore desirable or even possible; and any attempt to establish as Anglicanism any one of the theological traditions within the Church of England has always been strenuously resisted. Insofar as a Court of Appeal in matters of doctrine is required, it is generally thought to be found in the Scriptures as interpreted by the Catholic Fathers and right reason; and the various theological traditions in the Church of England stress the various ingredients differently, as might be expected. To the outsider such a position seems intolerable; but to the born Anglican it seems preferable to any of the present alternatives.

The various eucharistic traditions in the Church of England

depend inevitably upon its history during the four hundred years of its separation from the rest of Western Christendom, Catholic and Protestant. Inevitably, then, they must be looked at historically. Cranmer, the leader of the sixteenth-century Reformers, in reaction from the corruptions of the later mediaeval teaching and practice, regarded the doctrines of the Real Presence of Christ's Flesh and Blood and of the Sacrifice and Oblation of Christ made by the priest as the two chief weeds to be plucked up. He maintained—mistakenly in the opinion of the present writer—that such doctrines were unknown in the Christian Church for a thousand years, and therefore on Anglican principles rightly rejected them. In consequence he equipped the Church of England with a liturgy, which it has used ever since, explicitly designed to exclude any association of the elements with the Lord's Body and Blood, and any oblation other than the praises and the self-offering of the communicants, together with their alms.

But the Church of England was never satisfied with a Zwinglian doctrine of the Presence and a *nuda commemoratio* view of the Sacrifice. Within a generation of Cranmer's death, teachers like Jewel and Hooker were reasserting some notion of Consecration, and their successors a generation later were playing with a fuller doctrine of Sacrifice. When, therefore, the Revisers were producing the present edition of the liturgy in 1661, a number of changes were made or proposed which mark a heightening of eucharistic doctrine. In the matter of the Presence, Cranmer's prayer for the communicants before reception is labelled the Prayer of Consecration; the elements must now be reverently disposed of and not treated as common food, and if more bread or wine is needed for communion, a second consecration is demanded. But the attempt to introduce a higher doctrine of Sacrifice failed. The phrases proposed, however—'by the merits and death of thy Son Jesus Christ, now represented unto thee, and through faith in his blood, who maketh intercession for us at thy right hand'—show the lines on which the Revisers of the seventeenth century were thinking. It was the reading of the Fathers which led to this reinterpretation of the Anglican eucharistic tradition. But, as Professor Ratcliff writes, 'for all their patristic interest the Anglican divines of the seventeenth century never abandoned a reformed position with regard to the effects of consecration. Their eucharistic doctrine was mostly Calvinist'. Their sacrificial doctrine was correspondingly limited. They regarded the representation of the Lord's death effected through the Eucharist as symbolical in the modern sense of the word; and they restricted any objective offering in the Eucharist to the Church's material gifts of bread and wine.

With the Tractarian Revival of the nineteenth century a further development took place in the Anglican eucharistic thinking. Again, the appeal was made to the Fathers of the Church, and on their authority those who came under the influence of the Tractarians claimed to teach still higher doctrines of Presence and Sacrifice. The notion of Consecration, reintroduced by theologians like Jewel and finally expressed in the rubrics of the Prayer Book of 1661, was now expanded under cover of these rubrics into a doctrine of an Objective Real Presence, which barely stopped short of Conversion; and this was expressed in a ceremonial which departed wholly from the reformed tradition, and was in fact mainly borrowed from the contemporary Church of Rome. The seventeenth-century notion of Representative Sacrifice was similarly expanded into a doctrine of Real Sacrifice, which bore a striking resemblance to that of the Council of Trent. But since Cranmer had specially designed the Anglican liturgy to exclude any doctrine of eucharistic Sacrifice in the traditional sense of that term, and since the seventeenth-century Revisers had failed in their attempt to readjust the liturgy to their doctrine of Representative Sacrifice, it proved impossible for the Tractarians and their Anglo-Catholic successors to express a still higher sacrificial doctrine through that liturgy. Many therefore have taken the law into their own hands and attempted to turn the Prayer of Consecration into a sacrificial prayer, either by attaching to it the Prayer of Oblation on the lines of the rejected proposal of 1661, or by inserting it between the two halves of the Roman *Canon Missae*.

Such action received a certain justification from the statements on Anglican eucharistic doctrine made to the Pope by the Archbishops of Canterbury and York in 1897, and repeated to the Patriarchs of Eastern Christendom by the Lambeth Conference in 1930, which form the nearest approach to an official exposition of modern Anglican teaching on the subject. It was here maintained that we do not believe the Eucharist to be a nude commemoration of the Sacrifice of the Cross; but that in the Prayer

Book liturgy, besides offering the sacrifice of praise and thanksgiving, and the sacrifice of ourselves, our souls and bodies, we also offer a material oblation of bread and wine, and *Sacrificium Crucis Patri proponimus et repraesentamus*. A minimising interpretation of this phrase seems to require at least a doctrine of Representative Sacrifice; a maximising interpretation seems to allow of a doctrine of Real Sacrifice.

Taking into consideration the history of the Church of England, one is not surprised to find three main traditions of eucharistic teaching.

(1) The first stands by the sixteenth-century Reformers and teaches a Presence of Christ in the ordinance as a whole, but denies any particular Presence in connection with the act of Consecration or the act of Communion, and any Sacrifice other than the self-oblation of the communicants.

(2) The second stands by the seventeenth-century Revisers and teaches a Real Presence of Christ in the act of Communion, but denies any objective doctrine of Consecration and therefore any possibility of the worship of Christ in the consecrated Sacrament. In the matter of Sacrifice this second tradition is a little less eager to follow the lead of the seventeenth-century theologians; and there is little emphasis upon the material oblation of the elements or upon the Representative Sacrifice among the followers of this tradition.

(3) The third stands by the nineteenth-century Revivalists and teaches an Objective Real Presence of Christ in the Sacrament and a Real Sacrifice propitiatory for the living and the dead.

Since the Church of England makes her appeal to the Scriptures as interpreted by the Fathers and right reason, it may be that the Anglican contribution to modern eucharistic thinking is to withdraw from the post-mediaeval disputes of the Catholic and Protestant theologians, to refuse to be conditioned by her own post-mediaeval formularies, and to make some attempt to understand what the patristic theologians really thought about the Eucharist. This is the method suggested by such teachers as Professor Ratcliff, Dom Gregory Dix and Fr. Hebert; and it is the method which will be followed in the remainder of this paper.

A convenient starting-point will be found in the versicle which immediately precedes the eucharistic Preface in the Prayer Book Communion Service—one of the few elements in that service which goes back into the patristic period—'Let us give thanks unto the Lord our God (= our Lord God)'. The eucharistic action is primarily a thanksgiving; it is a thanksgiving offered to the God of the Bible (Lord = Kyrios = Adonai = Jehovah); and He is declared to be our God, because as members of the Church we are His peculiar people, the new Israel of God.

This eucharistic thanksgiving is the *Anamnesis*, the Memorial, of the Lord Christ. It is not merely a memorial of His death, or of His death and resurrection; it is a memorial of all that He has done and suffered for us. That is why the eucharistic thanksgiving must thank God for the creation of the world and of men through the Son-Word; for the incarnation of the same Son-Word by the Holy Ghost of the Virgin Mary; for the overthrow of the powers of evil and the deliverance of men by His passion and resurrection; and for His acquiring of the People of God for His own possession, as the true worshippers of His Father.

But the People of God must not come before the Lord empty-handed. God, of course, does not stand in need of anything from us; and indeed we can only give Him of His own. But to come before Him empty-handed would be to show ourselves unthankful. Besides, the People of God is a royal priesthood, and a priest must have somewhat to offer. We therefore offer not only our praises and thanksgivings, but also bread and wine, as an expression of our thankfulness, in fact as a thankoffering.

This thankoffering is not something which we have thought out for ourselves, nor something to which we have been led by the Spirit of God in the life of the Church. It is something which Jesus Christ, the night before He suffered, commanded us to offer. When He took bread and wine and gave thanks and said 'This is my Body', 'This is my Blood', He was teaching the new oblation of the New Covenant. The sacrifices of the Old Covenant have been rejected by God; and only the pure offering, which is offered in every place among the Gentiles, is now accepted. For it alone is offered by the People of the New Covenant; and they alone have been constituted the Priests of the most High God.

What is the purpose of this dominically appointed thank-

offering? It is to enable the People of God to gain admittance
to the heavenly worship. It is the new and living way into the
heavenly places, where we have a High Priest who ever lives to
make intercession for us. It is through the veil which is His *Flesh*,
and it is consecrated in His *Blood*. By means of it we come boldly
to the throne of grace, primarily , no doubt, to give thanks and
to worship, but also to obtain mercy and to find grace in time
of need. So we fulfil the end for which we were made at the
creation, the end to which we have been restored by the redemption. For we enter into heaven itself, we stand before the face
of God with angels and archangels, and we minister to Him by
offering with them the sacrifice of praise and confessing to the
adorable Name of Jehovah Sabaoth.

We are now in a position to appreciate the other versicle which
precedes the eucharistic Preface, 'Lift up your hearts'. Originally
peculiar to the Eucharist, it proclaims the fact that the scene of
eucharistic worship is laid in heaven. Christians have an altar; but
that altar is in the heavens; and it is thither that our prayers and
oblations are directed. For our Great High Priest has passed into
the heavens, and is at once the Priest and Sacrifice of the Heavenly
Altar. But He is also the High Priest of our offerings, the Angel
of the New Covenant, by whose hands our oblations are carried
up to the Altar on high. As He offers our sacrifice, so we are
enabled to offer His; and the Passion is the *Lord's* Sacrifice which
we offer in the heavenly places, where it abides for ever in the
glory of the divine acceptance.

The Holy Thing which we receive when we partake of the
Sacrifice is the glorified humanity of Jesus. Our earthly bread
and wine becomes His heavenly Body and Blood, so that there
is in the consecrated gifts an earthly thing and a heavenly. This
consecration is effected when the Holy People constitute the
thankoffering by uttering as the Lord's *Anamnesis* the thanksgiving over the gifts. He said: 'Do this as my *Anamnesis*'. Therefore the Church offers the gifts with thanksgiving. He said: 'This
is my Body', 'This is my Blood'. Therefore the Church believes
that the gifts so offered become what He has promised. If a
moment of consecration is looked for, it is naturally found in the
recitation of the institution narrative. For this at once rehearses
the divine command and the divine promise before God, and
identifies the Church's Eucharist with the Lord's. But we are here

G

moving in a different and perhaps more spacious world as compared with the disputes of the Reformation period over Presence and Sacrifice. For we and our gifts are taken out of this present age into the heavenlies; and so we taste of the powers of the world to come.

How, then, is the eucharistic action accomplished by the People of God? Everyone must make the Eucharist to God in his own order. The laity must produce their individual gifts or sacrifices of bread and wine, as the outward sign of their own self-oblation. The deacons must carry the gifts of the people up to the altar. The bishop must then offer the gifts, by uttering the thanksgiving which constitutes them as the thankoffering, the new oblation of the New Covenant. The deacons must then take the gifts and distribute them to the whole People of God, whether they are present in church or not. For all are members of the royal priesthood, and all must therefore partake of the Covenant Sacrifice. There is no question here of a priest offering sacrifice instead of the people or instead of Christ. It is rather that Christ, embodied in people, deacon and bishop alike, performs the various actions of the eucharistic rite.

This is the way in which the Catholic Fathers and the Ancient Bishops, Cyprian and Tertullian, Hippolytus and Irenaeus and Justin, Ignatius and Clement, and the authors of Apocalypse and Hebrews, thought about the Eucharist and carried it out. Perhaps the Church of England can best serve Christendom by setting her own eucharistic house in order in accordance with the standard to which she professes to appeal.

XII

ANGLICAN

*

(b) G. W. H. Lampe

(Great Britain)

'The genius who succeeded in writing a history of prayer,' it has
been well remarked, 'would by that very fact furnish us with a
history of all religion.' We might go further and assert that a
history of man's worship, its objects, and the methods by which
he has from time to time sought to express his reverence for them,
would involve a commentary upon the entire range of his activity;
for man is a worshipping animal, and has been such from the
most remote antiquity of which we have any knowledge. His
worship has assumed an extraordinary variety of forms, almost as
varied as those of his social and political life, which itself has been
profoundly affected by the character of his religious devotion.

Certain elements in worship have, however, remained constant
and are to be found in all genuine worship, however widely their
expression may have varied from age to age and from one place
to another. From man's first experience of contact with the
'numinous' and the sense of awe and fear which this mysterious
quality evokes, or at least from the moment when the 'other' is
recognised as possessing some degree of kinship with himself,
adoration, wonder and aspiration have taken their place in man's
response to the sacred along with the primitive emotions of awe
and terror. There is thus, even in the simplest religious emotion,
an element of attraction and exaltation. Man feels the impact of
some mysterious power external to himself, which lifts him above
his normal environment and his normal self to seek after it and
to offer to it the reverence which he feels to be due to the sacred,
to that which is holy because, while in one aspect it is awful and
indeed dangerous, it is also of supreme worth and desirability.

All worship expresses something of this twofold reaction to the
holy. It is the medium at once of abasement before the *mysterium*

tremendum and of response to the attraction of that which is perceived to be of the highest worth. It therefore necessarily comprises awe and reverence, adoration and (as the object of worship
comes to be recognised as personal) praise and sacrificial offering,
which reaches its culminating point in self-dedication and devotion. Christian worship contains all these elements; yet it is at the
same time fundamentally different from all other worship. It is
true that Christianity is in no way unique in its experience of
prayer as being, according to the famous definition of *Evagrius
Ponticus*, 'the elevation of the mind to God'. What is, however,
distinctive of Christian worship is that it is offered to God through
Christ. In the express image of the person of the Almighty the
true object of man's worship has been made known and the worship of the unknown God of paganism, or of the partially revealed
Jehovah of Hebrew religion, has been transmuted into that of our
Father in heaven. Through the atoning work of the High Priest a
way of access to Him has been opened and the barrier between
the transcendent God and mankind has been broken through by
the efficacy of the self-offering of Himself as the victim pre-
figured in a shadow by the ancient sacrifices. Christian worship is
grounded upon the foundation of the reconciliation effected by
Christ, which alone makes possible our free access to God. At the
same time it is the response of redeemed man to the love of God
shown forth in the saving act of Christ, by which, as it is accepted
in faith and confidence, the sinner is placed in a new relationship
to God and given the status of a son.

The New Testament doctrine of justification by faith is the
ground of our worship. Justification is more than that almost
purely forensic act of God which some traditional teaching,
especially among the Reformers, has represented it to be. It is the
'making righteous' of the sinner; but 'righteous' is a theological
rather than an ethical term when we thus use it. It denotes not the
moral character of righteousness in its commonly accepted sense,
but the status of acceptance with God in and through Christ, and
the possession through the unmerited grace of God of an adoptive
sonship which is a participation, in our own degree, in the eternal
and natural sonship of Christ. As sons we are enabled to draw near
to the Father in worship with the distinctively Christian quality
of *parrhesia*, the freedom of sons as opposed to the attitude of
slaves; for we approach Him through Christ as members incor-

porate in His Body. Justification directly implies our membership of the Church. The grace of God sets us in the spiritual temple not made with hands which is the house of prayer for all nations. The uplifting of our minds to God in worship is the response to God's approach to us through Christ in the Spirit; and our response as sons is, in its turn, made to our Father through the Son in the Spirit.

The pattern of worship is thus determined by its character as the expression and renewal of the movement of the justifying and sanctifying grace of God towards us through Christ, imparted to us by the Holy Spirit, and of the reciprocal Godward movement of our response of faith to the Father through Christ in the power of the Spirit. Though in the teaching of St. Paul the effective symbol of the justifying grace of God and the expression of the believer's response of faith is primarily the sacrament of Baptism, all worship reproduces in a sense something of the character of that sacrament. The essence of worship is a double movement of the Holy Spirit. The initiative is, as always, on the side of God. His gracious approach to us through Christ is mediated to the believers by the Spirit declaring, effecting and renewing their status as free sons of God. In their response of faith there is a movement of the Spirit back, as it were, from the human side to the Father, taking up into itself the penitence, adoration and self-offering of the worshippers. Christian worship is the means by which the believer is in a measure caught up through the divine initiative into the life of the Trinity, being enabled through Christ to rejoice with Him in the Holy Spirit and say: 'I thank thee, O Father, Lord of heaven and earth.' It is the point at which the eternal order breaks directly into the temporal, and ultimate reality is shown forth in the world of space and time.

It is in the process and pattern of worship that God is in fact experienced as the Trinity. The concrete reality of the adoration of the Father through the Son in the Spirit necessitates the credal dogma, and it is out of such experience that the Church has proceeded to rationalise and make intelligible its realisation of the Trinity in the metaphysical terms of doctrinal formulations. In this fundamental instance, at any rate, the sometimes dangerous statement that the *lex orandi* is prior to the *lex credendi* is entirely true. It may be observed in passing that, since the peculiar characteristic of Christian worship lies in the fact that it is offered to

God in the Spirit as a response to the approach of the Spirit to ourselves, the common supposition is likely to be untrue that the way towards a deeper and more vital Christianity lies in a more frequent use of devotions addressed to the Third Person of the Trinity. This notion probably rests upon a certain misunderstanding of His work in Christian worship.

It is this twofold movement of the Spirit which it is the purpose of liturgical worship to embody and express. It therefore consists on the one hand of the proclamation and commemoration of the saving acts of God in Christ, the setting forth in Word and Sacrament of the supernatural gospel. On the other hand it expresses the carrying up of the response of human worship to the Father through Christ in the Godward movement of the Spirit. This response comprises many varied expressions of faith and its consequences. It embraces penitence and self-abasement in face of the perfection of the Father's love, and thus carries over into Christian worship, though with a far more profound significance, that basic element in primitive man's worship, the sense of awe and fear, and the realisation of personal unworthiness to approach what is recognised as holy. It finds expression in adoration and the sacrifice of praise and thanksgiving, and it reaches its climax in the 'reasonable service' in which the worshipper makes his sacrificial presentation of himself to God in devotion and self-offering, made possible by his incorporation into Christ, the one acceptable sacrifice, and taken up to the Father through Him as the sacrificing Priest. By virtue of these movements of the Spirit we are also enabled to offer prayer and intercession, the Spirit interceding for us.

This pattern of worship is discernible in all liturgical worship soundly based on the New Testament. It is to be seen in the Prayer Book Offices of Morning and Evening Prayer. It is true that the summary there set out in the preface of the objects of worship (an otherwise admirable statement which, if more usually read in full, would dispel much popular ignorance about the purpose of church-going) does not sufficiently clarify the relationship between the hearing of the Word and the offering to God of our penitence, praise and prayer. It is, however, well exemplified in the sequence of alternate Lessons and Canticles and in the place assigned to prayer in the context of the proclamation of the gospel and the response of praise.

It is, as we should expect, in eucharistic worship that the man-ward and Godward aspects of worship receive their clearest expression. In all the liturgical forms of orthodox Christendom the Eucharist affords, in the first place, a medium for the approach of the Spirit to the worshippers in the reading of the Word as contained in Scripture and in the preaching of the gospel. This is the preparation for the sacramental imparting of Himself by Christ to the faithful in the bread and wine which He makes, through the action of the Spirit, the effectual symbols of His Body and Blood.

By a 'symbol', of course, we do not mean a bare sign. 'Symbol' does not connote the absence of the thing signified. Rather it is to be interpreted as, together with such related terms as 'type', 'antitype' and 'figure', it was understood in the early Church. During the first four centuries at least, and in some quarters until much later, these words denoted not the absence but in some sense the actual presence of the reality signified; the symbol was regarded as expressing the actuality of that which it represented. Similarly, a 'type' was in fact so called because in some sense it actually was that which it typified. Thus when the marking of the Israelites' doorposts with the Passover blood, or the sacrifice of Isaac, are described as types of Christ's redemptive work in various aspects, they are not mere pictorial illustrations of that reality; although they do not possess in themselves the full force of their antitype, yet the reality of the latter is already present in them, though not yet fully revealed. When the same term is applied to a sacramental sign it is clear that the type participates in the reality of its antitype and possesses its power.

As symbols or types or figures, the eucharistic elements are not static pictorial illustrations of the absent Body and Blood of Christ. They are dynamic, conveying to the believer the full *dynamis* of the reality which they signify. The ancient simile of a ring or crozier, by the bestowal of which the recipient was in actual fact invested with dignities and possessions, is a favourite illustration among the older Anglican writers of the nature of the eucharistic elements as effectual signs (see, for example, Daniel Waterland's *Doctrine of the Eucharist*). They are the means by which Christ acts. Their status depends upon His Word—not upon the subjective attitude to them of the recipient, though their efficacy for salvation is of course conditioned by the worshipper's faith.

We speak in terms of activity rather than of presence. Not that there can be any ultimate distinction between these terms; for Christ is not active *in absentia*, nor is He present but inactive. We prefer, however, to think in terms of *energeia* and *dynamis* rather than of 'presence' in order to safeguard the theory (characteristic of the main stream of traditional Anglican doctrine and strongly maintained by many Anglicans to-day) that it is in the eucharistic action that Christ imparts Himself to us through the medium of the consecrated elements, and that, outside the context of the Communion, adoration of Him as present under the forms of bread and wine is impermissible. At the same time we wish to emphasise our belief in the Real Presence (or Activity) of our Lord in the eucharistic elements as He uses them as the means of His self-giving to us in the Communion.

As we consider this manward aspect of the Eucharist we must strongly emphasise the truth that in this service there is most strikingly demonstrated the direct and intimate connection of Word and Sacrament. In both alike the gospel is proclaimed. The one is complementary to the other. Christ is presented to the faithful in the ministry of the Word, and the presence of Christ in power and action is mediated to them in the Sacrament. The gospel of Christ is not only in word but in power, and, as word and power are inseparable, so also are Word and Sacrament. The ministration and reception of the scriptural and preached Word and of the Sacrament are parallel, and cannot properly be separated, since through both *media* Christ is made present to the believer and imparts to him His life. If a sacramentalism divorced from the evangelical proclamation of the Word degenerates into superstition, it is no less true that to exalt the ministry of the Word at the expense of sacramentalism quickly causes the Word itself to degenerate into a word without power—the acts of power by which Christ incorporates us into Himself and sanctifies us.

In its Godward aspect the Eucharist is the pre-eminent expression of the Spirit's movement from the human side to the Father, taking up the adoration and self-oblation of the worshippers. Christian worship, in the sense of the public worship of the Church which is the subject of our consideration, is essentially corporate. By the indwelling presence of the Holy Spirit the congregation of the faithful is in all its worship constituted and renewed as the Body of Christ and the temple of the Spirit. In the

Eucharist the community is renewed as the Body of Christ through its reception of His sacramental Body, so that it is in this supreme act of worship that the Holy Catholic Church is manifested and its true character realised in every congregation of faithful men. There may be said to be two consecrations in the eucharistic action. There is the consecration of the elements to be received as the Body and Blood of the Lord, and there is a second consecration as Christ, when He is sacramentally received by the worshippers, renews their consecration as the Body of Christ. They are transformed from a random collection of individuals into a single corporate whole which embodies and manifests the Catholic Church in a single place and at a given moment of time. The Church is, in fact, renewed and realised afresh in each Eucharist. It is with something approaching this thought that the eucharistic language of the *Didache* draws out the analogy between the union of the scattered grains of wheat in the one loaf and the ultimate union of Christ's Church in its in-gathering into His Kingdom. St. Augustine gives more precise expression to the truth of the reconstitution in each Eucharist of the Church as the Body when he bids his congregation see in the Communion elements the mystery of themselves. The elements, as brought forward and laid upon the altar at the offertory, may be said to represent the community of the faithful in their daily life, secular pursuits and ordinary social relationships. As consecrated and made the vehicle of Christ's Presence, they symbolise the community as consecrated and made Christ's Body by the Presence which they are at the same time the means of imparting to that community. The Church expresses and realises its own true nature most fully in its eucharistic worship.

By its sacramental reception of Christ's Body as broken and His Blood as outpoured, it is constituted a sacrificial body, sharing by grace in His priesthood and participating in His own self-oblation. In union with Him it corporately offers itself to the Father by virtue of His one sufficient sacrifice. In saying this we are laying stress upon the scriptural truth of the priesthood of all believers, which has nothing to do with any theory of a 'priesthood of the laity' which would deny the necessity to the Church of ministerial priesthood. The ordained priest is commissioned by Christ in His Church to act as the Church's representative and spokesman in the eucharistic action; whose words and acts in the eucharistic prayer the congregation seals as its own by the saying of 'the Amen at the giving of thanks'. In his peculiar and special office in sacramental worship, as well as in his task as the preacher of the Gospel, the Christian minister exercises a priesthood within the body which is one of the manifold gifts, as St. Paul teaches, of the ascended Christ which He bestows upon the Body for its edification.

We are concerned rather with the priestly character which is given to the Church as Christ's Body through its sacramental participation in Him. This union of the worshipping community with its Head is expressed in various ways in the Church's liturgies. Classically, of course, it is associated with the Prayer of Consecration. In the English rite of 1662 it is expressed in the Prayer of Oblation set after the Communion. It is at this point that the Body of Christ makes the corporate sacrifice of itself or, alternatively, expresses its renewed consciousness of itself as the mystical Body of the Son of God, ready, with the aid of God's grace, to do all such good works as He has prepared for it to walk in.

The Prayer Book's departure from the classical norm in this respect is one of the features of the 1662 rite which the liturgiologist is usually most anxious to correct. Yet it may be suggested that this alteration of the ancient form was not without theological value. If it is after and by virtue of the renewal of its life and true nature by communion with its Head that the Church is enabled as His Body to offer both its corporate prayer to God as Father and its oblation of itself in union with Christ, then we have here the supreme expression of the double movement which runs through every act of worship. It is through Christ's gift of sacramental participation in His glorified humanity that the Church is enabled to share in His priesthood and His sacrifice. Moreover, this particular liturgical pattern seems to lay special emphasis on the corporate character, not only of the Mass in the narrower sense, but of the actual Communion. When the significance of the ordering and content of the post-Communion prayers is properly understood there should be no possibility of a merely individualistic attitude to Communion. It should be difficult for the worshipper to think in terms of 'making my Communion' when the response to Christ's sacramental Presence in the Communion is the Church's corporate prayer and its offering both of the sacrifice of praise and thanksgiving and of the sacrifice of itself as the Body of Christ.

ANGLICAN

Certainly there is no place for mere individualism in eucharistic or any other Christian worship. Worship passes over into the Christian life, of which it is at once the symbol and the focus. It is worship which represents and sums up the Church's service to God in daily life, and it is through worship that that service is made possible. Similarly, it is in worship that the Christian community is constituted and finds expression. It is not too much to say that it is only the community as so constituted and expressed that is a true community, that is to say, a community of spirit. The worshipping congregation, provided that its worship is consciously corporate, is no haphazard group of individuals. It is a body bound together by the operation within it of the one Spirit. Its bond of union is the divine Person, and of the Church alone is it true that it possesses a true corporate spirit, greater than the sum of the individuals who compose it, and, one might almost say, a corporate personality. Its divine Spirit is the antithesis of the unreal corporate spirit imagined by political philosophies. Indeed, no human society, not even the family, can form a genuine spiritual unit unless it forms part of that body in which there dwells the Spirit of God. A non-worshipping society is in the last resort an artificial and unsubstantial entity.

We can here discuss only these few aspects of worship; but something must be briefly said on two points besides. First, on the impact of worship on the world outside the generally small circle of the congregation. Apart from the observable fact that worship is a most potent instrument of evangelism, we must not forget that since the worshippers are drawn to the Father in the Spirit, they are at the same time drawn to their brother men in general, and, indeed, to the whole creation. Intercession is thus rendered possible as a natural, though highly mysterious, element in all worship and one which has incalculable effects. Secondly, we must remember that the Spirit in whom we worship is the 'earnest' of the final complete redemption, so that in all worship, and explicitly in the Eucharist (especially in the earlier liturgies) our worship is the expression of the eschatological hope. It is a pledge of, as well as a means by which we look forward to, the complete realisation of all that it now symbolises and expresses imperfectly, in the full and unhindered communion with Christ promised in the day of His appearing.

ANGLICAN

*

(c) F. C. N. Hicks
(Great Britain)

The Eucharistic Sacrifice[1]

1. The Eucharist, from its institution onwards, was connected with the idea of sacrifice. Our Lord used technical sacrificial language at least when He spoke of His 'blood of the Covenant', 'the Covenant in His blood'. The language of different parts of the procedure of sacrifice is often used in the Epistles. He and His followers were Jews, brought up in the Jewish tradition. It is therefore to the Jewish system of sacrifice that we must turn to interpret this language.

2. The Church, in the liturgies and in the writings of the Fathers, continued the use of sacrificial language. The outline of pagan sacrifice was, at bottom, the same as that of the Jewish; and pagan sacrifice continued before the eyes of Christians as a working system until the Christianising of the Empire destroyed the pagan worship. The Jewish sacrifices had ceased in A.D. 70. After the end of paganism there remained no visible system of outward sacrifice. In later centuries the Christian world ceased to be aware of it; and by the tenth century, when eucharistic theology—soon to become controversy—began in the West, there was no technical knowledge available.

3. It was at that time that the western world began to assume that sacrifice consisted almost solely in the death of the victim. There was the immemorial tradition that in some sense the Eucharist at least had to do with sacrifice: from some points of view was sacrifice. It was understood that our Lord's redeeming

[1] This memorandum by the late Bishop of Lincoln was originally printed in *The Second World Conference on Faith and Order*, Edinburgh, 1937, ed. Hodgson (SCM Press, 1938), pp. 326-329.

work was a sacrifice. That, so far, was New Testament teaching and, as tradition, historically true. But when the equation 'sacrifice = death' had become established, the question came to be asked: 'What is the sacrifice which the priest makes upon the altar?' or 'What does the priest do when he offers Christ in the Mass?' The inevitable answer under the compulsion of the only existing theory of sacrifice was in the direction of the language of mystical immolation. Christ was slain—however 'mystically'—in each Mass.

4. There followed two consequences in the West, but not in the East:

(*a*) As regards the sacrifice in the Eucharist it became in some sense a repetition of Calvary. Christ's sacrifice had to be thought of simply as His death on the Cross. The representation of the sacrifice became in a sense a repetition, each time, of the death. Against this the protest of the Reformers was justified. The uniqueness of the Cross, the all-sufficiency of the One Sacrifice, was seen to be of the very essence of redemption, and had to be vindicated at all costs, even at the cost of abandoning the age-long association of the sacrifice with the Eucharist. Hence the general movement of Reformed Western Christendom away from the language of sacrifice in connection with the Eucharist, the Holy Communion, the Lord's Supper, except where, as in the Church of England and in some other quarters, it was retained somehow in loyalty to the ancient tradition.

(*b*) As regards the Presence in the Elements, if the Christ of the Mass was the Christ at the moment of death, His Body must be the Body as it suffered on the Cross, the Body of His humiliation; the Body in the state in which our bodies are in this life, the body not of the spirit but of the flesh. Whatever was the case with the theologians, there was created the popular idea of the Presence as material and carnal: an atmosphere in which it was natural that there should be 'miracles' of bleeding Hosts. Again, if this was what the Real Presence meant, the Reformers could not but, in greater or less degree, modify, explain it away or deny it.

It is surely from these consequences that the 'Protestant' denial or mistrust both of the Sacrifice and of the Presence arose. It is doubtless true that it was from popular conceptions, not from the more refined official teaching, that the reaction came. It is only fair to say that St. Thomas Aquinas' treatment of 'transubstantiation' was an honest attempt, in the philosophical language available to him, to spiritualise the doctrine of the Presence. But his teaching was not proof against popular superstitions and misunderstandings.

5. On the other hand, the mediaevalists or Western 'Catholics' were right historically. Their belief in Sacrifice and Presence as part of the primitive tradition was justified. They had a real loyalty of their own, to which they had to try to be true.

6. It was only after the researches of the nineteenth century into the history of early religion and sacrifice, and in particular of Old Testament sacrifice, that the deadlock began to be removed.

We begin to recover what our Lord and the New Testament writers, and the Christians of the earliest centuries, meant when they used sacrificial language. The central fact is that the death of the victim was only one stage, and that an early stage, of the sacrifice as a whole. This began with the sinner's solemn approach with his victim: he 'drew near', and this drawing near gives us the New Testament word *corban* for an offering. Next he pressed his hands upon the victim's head—a solemn identification of himself with it, meaning, inwardly and spiritually, that what happens to it in the rest of the action happens to himself. Thirdly, he himself kills the victim. He surrenders its blood, which is its life, now his blood, which is his own life, to God. The priest takes the surrendered life, symbolically, into the nearer presence of God (the horns of the altar or even the Holy of holies); and God and man are made at one—'at-one-ment'. Next, the substance of the victim, its slain body, representing the returned sinner himself, all that he is and has, is offered upon the altar of 'burnt offering'. It is accepted by God in the kindling upon it of the holy fire, His fire that has come down from Heaven, and it is burned. But the burning is not for destruction—the word for that sort of burning is not used. It is '*Olah*, 'that which goes up'. It is transformed, etherealised, and rises in smoke to the heaven above, where God dwells; it is no longer gross and carnal and earthly, but spiritualised and accepted into the presence of God, as all earthly effort is when offered to Him, and He transforms it in accepting it. Lastly, when, in the voluntary return to God, sin has been acknowledged, the rebel life has been surrendered and forgiven in the at-one-ment between God and man, and the carnal man has been transformed into spirit, in self-offering, God and man, and man and man, can become one in the meal on the flesh of the sacrifice.

This, and nothing less than this, is true sacrifice. There is no meaning in the Communion-meal, in the language of eating the Body and drinking the Blood, except as the last stage of sacrifice.

So our Lord, our Victim, the Lamb of God, comes with us as we draw near. He makes Himself one with us in the incarnation. We sinners kill our Victim; we crucify Him, the best of us hardly knowing what we do, prophesying only a little better than Caiaphas prophesied. He, our High Priest, takes His Blood, which is His Life—our blood, by the power of the incarnation, and our membership of His Body, and therefore our life—through the veil, His broken flesh, into the very presence of God. He atones for us. His Manhood, in which our separate manhoods are by degrees joined, is offered to God in eternal service, and as God accepts the offering by the fire of the Spirit, He transforms it. It was the Body of His humiliation, carnal and material, as ours are, mainly, still. It becomes, by His Resurrection and Ascension, wholly spiritual and heavenly. It is the same Body, of the Lamb as it had been slain, but glorified.

The motive of His eternal life, as it was, for Him, in His earthly life, is the inner motive of all true sacrifice: 'Lo! I come to do Thy will, O God!' He still obeys, while He reigns at the Father's right hand, for He is still Man. But as the Christian Church grows, He no longer obeys alone. His obedience is His offering, and we obey in Him. As we offer Him we offer ourselves—our souls and bodies, with the offerings of the elements of bread and wine, and whatever other gifts we bring. They, like ourselves, are offered; offered and, in acceptance, transformed; and the eternal Sacrifice, vindicated and secured by the all-availing death, once died, is the whole Godward movement of service, which is also worship, of worship, which is also service, towards the Throne.

That offering is what we join in, not in our worship only in the earthly sanctuary, but in the dedicated conduct of our daily life; and since our contribution to worship and to service alike is still imperfect, we can only offer it in union with the whole Body of which He is the Head. So we offer ourselves in Him, for His merits, and Him for ourselves. And in and through that offering we are received, at the earthly image of the heavenly Altar at which we make it, at what is also the earthly Table of the Lord, as children at our Father's Board, at home, already on earth, in our Father's eternal House.

So the Communion is not possible without the offering, the offering incomplete and purposeless without the Communion: and both are covered by the ever-renewed memorial and pleading of the Cross.

It follows, from this conception of the sacrifice of Christ, that (1) there can be no sort of repetition of His sacrifice in the Eucharist, no slaying of Him on the altar, no taking away from the uniqueness and all-sufficiency of the Cross; (2) there can be no idea of anything materialistic in the Presence. It is only 'true' or 'real' because it is spiritual: but spiritual not in a purely negative sense: for it is a 'mystery' in which, by the power of the Spirit, earth and heaven, earthly things and heavenly things, are joined. The whole action, indeed, takes place in the realm of things spiritual: we are, in fact, lifted up to Heaven in the earthly worship. We are admitted to the scene of the Eternal worship of which we are given a picture in Rev. 4-7. We are one with the angels and archangels and with all the company of heaven: with the whole communion of saints, on this side of the veil and that, alike in our offering, our worship and the mutual interchange of prayer, and the fellowship of service.

Both the Reformers' difficulties therefore disappear.

Further, the Jews, by our Lord's time, had learnt the secret that thanksgiving, under all circumstances, even in adversity, is the secret of effectual prayer, for such thanksgiving means real faith in the praying. So our Lord prayed, before He broke the loaves at the feeding of the multitude, and before He broke the Bread and gave the Cup at the Last Supper. He gave thanks (*eucharistēsas*) or 'blessed' (the Jewish equivalent of the idea expressed in Greek by Eucharist). Indeed we may say with confidence that, if we want to know what His 'consecration prayer' at the Last Supper was, it was the words that He used when He gave thanks; and what we call His 'words of institution' are more correctly thought of as what we should call 'words of administration'. So also the 'sacrifice of praise and thanksgiving' in the Old Testament is really a technical term for the peace-offering, the imperfect Old

Testament foreshadowing of the Communion meal which is the last stage of sacrifice.

Lastly, the whole of true sacrifice is bound up, if with thanksgiving, so also with prayer. 'He ever liveth to make intercession for us.' As He reigns, He also pleads. And it is only in the power of His prayers, by the merit of His saving work, that our imperfect prayers have any value. So we testify when we end our ordinary prayers: 'Through Jesus Christ our Lord.' It follows that it is through His supreme, eternal prayer of thanksgiving and intercession, and self-offering, that, above all, our earthly prayers will avail. That is why it has been the age-long instinct of the Church that the Eucharist or the Lord's Supper is the supreme moment, or opportunity, for our prayers, of whatever kind, in union with His. It follows also that the whole action of the Eucharist, however we describe it, and above all what has traditionally been called the consecration, is an effective prayer. There can be no magic in it. We ask for God's greatest gift, Himself, and because our Lord is the celebrant of every earthly Eucharist, it is He who asks, and to the prevailing power of, and the fulness of the inevitable answer to His thanksgiving prayer there can be no limit.

XIII

LUTHERAN

*

(a) Wilhelm Stählin
(Germany)

(a) *Word and Sacrament*

In the Confessional Writings of the Lutheran Church (*Confessio Augustana*, Article V) 'Word' and 'Sacrament' are described as the two 'means' (*tamquam instrumenta*) through which the Holy Spirit is given, 'who evokes faith in those who hear the gospel where and when He wills'. It is therefore the task of the Ministry (*ministerium ecclesiasticum*) to preach the gospel and to administer the sacraments. So the Lutheran Church has defined the terms in which she speaks of 'Word' and 'Sacrament' as the two 'means of grace'. This interacting relationship of Word and Sacrament also characterises the original shape of the Lutheran church service (the German Mass, Luther, 1526) in which 'the Word' is preached and the Sacrament is celebrated.

The question of the relationship between these two 'means of grace', these foundations of worship, has been discussed by Lutheran theologians not only in terms of the right order and understanding of liturgy; but no one can deny that from the very beginning there was a tendency even in the Lutheran Reformation to emphasise the Word rather than the Sacrament and to interpret the Sacrament in the light of the Word, i.e. as the Word in another form (*verbum visibile*). If in this process the 'Word' is no longer understood in its own right but is devalued into the sense of human conversation about God, we lose the meaning which the Reformation attached to the twin elements of Word and Sacrament; and thus whenever the Evangelical Church considers and describes herself as the 'Church of the Word' in contrast to other Churches as 'Churches of the Sacrament', the primary stress on the Word and the Sacrament as objective 'means' of grace is abandoned.

It is therefore natural that we should try to understand Word and Sacrament as a unity. The link with the Sacrament saves the Word from the danger of becoming merely an intellectual communication and, on the other hand, the link with the Word saves the Sacrament from degenerating into mere magic, in which all personal responsibility of the individual would cease. It is therefore intelligible when we occasionally speak in such terms as the 'Word-character' (*Worthaftigkeit*) of the Sacrament and the sacramental character of the Word.

Furthermore the question has been raised by some theologians whether there is any justification for the distinction between 'Word' and 'Sacrament' in the light of the words and the meaning of Scripture. The conception of *sacramentum*, which was used originally only to translate the biblical term *musterion*, has developed a definite and much narrower meaning in theological tradition during the course of many centuries. *Logos* and *musterion* in the New Testament connote the whole Revelation as well as the witness of the Church. Each proclamation and each action of the Church witnesses to the *logos* and for this very reason it is also *oikonomia tou musteriou*. With this knowledge it becomes impossible to separate Word and Sacrament from each other, or to play one off against the other.

(b) *Sacrament and Symbol*

The word 'symbol' has many meanings and there is no generally acknowledged connotation of the term even in theological literature. This fact justifies most Lutheran theologians in avoiding the word 'symbol' to prevent misunderstandings, which nearly always arise where the word is used.

The most commonly held opinion understands 'symbol' to be merely a sign, the symbolical expression of the implied spiritual reality, something unreal, something in which the matter itself implied and symbolised is not really present.

Such a conception is the inevitable expression of a 'spiritualising' way of thought[1] which looks upon physical and spiritual as two separate spheres, severs the outward appearance from its spiritual meaning, and generally recognises what it terms the 'spiritual content' as the only effective essential. This way of thinking, however, does not correspond with biblical thought. The relation-

[1] Cf. footnote to Chap. X, p. 178 *sup.*

ship between outer and inner, the physical and the spiritual realities, is inherent; the knowledge moreover evoked by the action of the Holy Spirit enables us to perceive the Divine Epiphany whether in word, action, or historical event. We can still see the original meaning of *symballein* in Luke's narration of what happened to Mary (Luke 2. 19). It is very important to realise that *symballein* literally means the direct opposite to the work of *Diabolos*. The outward appearance ('symbol') is there in order to signify a spiritual reality or a spiritual event. Thus Christ's healing acts should be understood as *sēmeia*, and St. Paul's teaching on Baptism (Rom. 6) and on the Holy Supper (I Cor. 10. 11) should be understood as realities: the same would apply, for example, to the laying on of hands as the medium of a real transfer of spiritual power (II Tim. 1. 6). The conception of the *symbolum efficax* in the early Church, i.e. of a sign which effects that which is its meaning, is more appropriate to the biblical facts than is the shallow modern conception of symbol as something 'only symbolical' and thus lacking full reality. If this simultaneity of the physical and spiritual event is lost, the 'symbolical' activity of the Church becomes empty ceremony and it is of no importance for the spiritual event whether or not it is accompanied by any symbolical practice.

There is one further question which appears in theological discussions within the Lutheran Church. It is the question whether this understanding of the 'symbol' relates to the incarnation and the biblical notion of 'seeing' as visual knowing.[1] Only in such a context can we describe the relation between Sacrament and 'symbol' in the right way. Many are compelled to judge that a spiritualising way of thought which devalues the *symbolum efficax* to a 'mere symbolical' sign implies the denial of the reality of the Sacrament.[2]

(c) Sacrifice and Priesthood

It would be wrong to maintain that the Reformation completely erased the words 'priest' and 'sacrifice' from their vocabulary. Moreover, all Lutheran confessional writings (in particular the 'Apology' of the Augsburg Confession) deal at some length with the conception of sacrifice, and state the sense in which we can understand and describe the Eucharist as a sacrifice, i.e. as a

[1] Cf. John 14. 7—ED.   [2] See footnote to Chap. X, p. 178 *sup*.

sacrifice of thanksgiving. In addition, the words *sacerdos* and *sacerdotium* are freely used both for the Ministry and its bearers without restraint. Whoever demands nowadays that these two conceptions should disappear altogether from the language of the Lutheran Church will contradict the tradition of the Reformation.

Meanwhile the fact that Luther in his 'German Mass' (1526) radically eliminated all parts of the traditional order of the Mass which contained the conception of sacrifice (offertory and *anamnesis*) has had great influence. Since then the Lutheran Church has shown an almost ineradicable suspicion concerning the very idea of sacrifice in the Eucharist, for fear that the emphasis on man's sacrificial activity might obscure the exclusiveness of the divine gift of grace which we human beings can only gratefully receive and accept.

In present discussions amongst Lutheran theologians in Germany there are not a few who demand the re-institution of sacrifice to its due place within Christian worship. This is due to a conviction (notably held by Hans Asmussen) that we cannot receive anything without offering our sacrifice of thanksgiving and surrender. Such a view aims at interpreting the conception of sacrifice in such a way that the above objections may not affect it, and to show above all that the New Testament itself (apart from the Old Testament and its sacrificial rite) makes use of the conception of sacrifice in a threefold way:

(1) for acts of charity (Heb. 13. 16);

(2) for witness as a sacrifice of praise (Heb. 13. 15);

(3) for the laying down of one's life in all its physical appearance (Rom. 12. 1).

Is it permissible to extend the necessary objection against a sub-Christian concept of sacrifice to the length of actually renouncing a term which is so strongly emphasised in biblical language?

The same applies to priesthood also. The emphasis on the 'priesthood of all believers' (in contrast to the ministry) is commonly held to be a mark of distinction between the Protestant Churches and the Roman Catholic Church, the latter being considered as a 'priest-Church' (*Priesterkirche*). The priesthood of all believers is thereby confined in popular Protestant belief to the religious independence (the 'coming-of-age') of each baptised

Christian, which abrogates all mediation through and representation by a priest. ('We do not need a priest and we do not want a priest.')

Lutheran theologians from various traditions strive in a similar way against such misrepresentation and devaluation of the 'priesthood of all believers', and try to focus primarily upon the biblical meaning:

(1) The expression 'priest' in the New Testament never appears where various offices and functions are mentioned as given by the Holy Spirit in and for the community (Eph. 4). On the contrary, the word 'priest' is only used with reference to the profession common to all Christians (I Pet. 2. 5; Rev. 1. 6; 5. 10).

(2) The profession of a Christian in the world must thus be understood and fulfilled as a priestly office. The priesthood of all believers must witness to the 'priestly office' of Jesus Christ through word and deed. There is no passive attitude towards Christ's sacrifice (i.e. 'enjoying the fruits of His sacrifice') without simultaneous participation on our part in the action of His sacrifice. If we understand it in this way, the 'priesthood of all believers' is vastly different from any quietism which has frequently been described as the specific danger of the Lutheran Church. At the same time this priesthood is a strong link between faith and charity, faith in Christ and service to the world. Such knowledge based upon the Bible is of great importance for the understanding and ordering of Christian worship.

(3) It would be a contradiction to the tradition of the Reformation to call a pastor a 'priest', not even in his liturgical activity. Yet, as a bearer of the office, he shares as a matter of course in the ministry which is given by his very existence as a Christian. In a specific sense he has to represent not only the teaching office of Christ, but also His priestly office and (in the leadership of his congregation) His kingly office. So far it is correct for the Lutheran confessional writings to refer to their pastors as *sacerdotes* and to their office as *sacerdotium*. In all these endeavours to obtain a right understanding of the ministry we begin to realise that not the sermon alone, but prayer and sacrament also, are factors contributing towards a real conception of the ministry. We shall have to understand it as a priestly office and shape the preparation for such new knowledge accordingly.

XIII

LUTHERAN

*

(b) R. Will
(Alsace)

During the meeting [at Clarens in August 1947] of the Continuation Committee of the World Conference on Faith and Order a further step was without question taken towards the *Una Sancta*. We found a decided will to meet one another in the single necessary thing. We felt ourselves to be united in Christ. It was in His name that we gathered round the Word and at the Holy Table, in prayer and at the very heart of our conversations. For the Commission on Ways of Worship it was no mere question of drawing up a liturgy which might suit all Christian denominations. Would it not have been absurd to wish to harmonise the rigidity of a Puritan service and the richness of High Church ritual or to replace by the 'German Mass' of Luther the 'Holy Liturgy' of the Eastern Churches? There can be no question of creating an ecumenical type of Christian worship. What *did* impress us, however, was the fact that, while each one remained attached to the conceptions of worship of his Church and to the observances on which ancestral tradition has set its seal, we succeeded in discerning the unchanging divine impulse beneath the confessional and liturgical variants of the different communions. Now there are in Christian worship, in all ages and all regions, two sources from which the Christian soul will always see welling up the authentic springs of the eternal love, and where he may feel the presence of the living God and know communion with Christ. These unique sources are the Word and the Sacrament. It was natural that the problem of these two fundamental elements in all worship should have evoked serious thought in the Commission. The following comments reflect not only the thought provoked, but an intimate event.

*   *   *

By reason of His absolute sovereignty, God is also the efficient and final cause of the life of worship. It is 'of Him and through Him and unto Him' that the drama of worship is enacted.

Now God appears to us in worship in two forms. He is at once the revealed God and the unknowable God. God has revealed Himself in Jesus Christ, in His person, His work, His gospel, His Cross, His Resurrection; and it is in Christ that all the prior and subsequent revelations of God in the Bible and in the Church converge. It is in worship above all that our Father in Jesus Christ opens Himself to man, seeks him, visits him, and also the assembly of the faithful, and announces to them His will to save that which is lost.

But, although He has revealed Himself once for all in Christ, God remains, in Himself, enveloped in mystery. Unfathomable, His being goes beyond all the capacities of our understanding. It even runs counter to the judgments of our reason. However, His mystery attracts the human soul enamoured of infinity; He induces the spirit haunted by the absolute to take flight. In worship He entrances those who adore Him.

Yet the revelation and the mystery of God are never to be found separated: in fact they interpenetrate one another. Although never completely unveiling itself, the mystery makes itself felt in worship as a presence. On the other hand the revelation never exhausts itself in the means which it uses. Itself transcendent, it is accompanied by factors that are beyond reason. God has revealed Himself in the observable facts of the history of salvation, yet the mystery of the incarnation and of redemption eludes our grasp even in the virgin birth of Jesus, in the scandal of His Cross, or in the miracle of His Resurrection.

Revelation and mystery—*Facies Dei revelata, Deus absconditus*[1] —this double condition of God induces in man a twofold reaction. Two types of piety correspond to it: the sheer certainty of faith, and the deep moving of mystical perception. Revelation, the emanation of saving powers, stirs up faith in God the heavenly Father, and in Christ. The soul of the believer, feeling itself carried and sustained, experiences a serene and stable joy. On the other hand the divine mystery exerts an attractive force; the restless soul, unquiet, bounds forward in order to lose itself in the 'sea

---

[1] Luther in *De servo arbitrio*.

without bottom or shore' which is God, or in order to be united
to Christ in a rapture which can overreach itself.

However, these two spiritual attitudes are themselves destined
to meet. Without the mystical values, a worship resting only on
faith may so decline that it becomes merely an abstract 'spirituality'. On the other hand the over-devout soul, with its will
unsupported by conscious faith, is in danger of trying to lift itself
by the vehemence of its own desire into the infinite, and so of
falling back in a sorrowful dryness, because, trusting only to its
own fervour, it is no longer supported by the givenness of revelation. Great religious personalities such as St. Paul, St. Augustine
and, among the great mystics, St. Teresa of Avila, bring together
in their spirituality these two stresses, the assurance of faith and
the mystical disposition of soul (cf. Phil. 3. 12). They avoid the
hidden dangers which threaten either aspect of divine communion
when they are expressed in isolation—the intellectual withering of
faith or the dangers of spiritual excess.

★   ★   ★

What are the liturgical conclusions from these facts? The two
aspects of the real presence of God in worship—revelation and
mystery—and, on man's side, pure faith and fervent desire, are
reflected in the two basic elements of Christian worship, the
Word and the Sacrament. The idea of the Sacrament needs less
comment. The real difficulty lies with the Word, because, bound
up with it, is the human word of the preacher. The Word of God
is the vital flux of the divine revelation which, incarnate in Christ
and contained in the Bible, has repercussions in the innermost
hearts of the believers assembled at worship. The human word
both interprets the scriptural truth and evokes an answer in the
human heart. Word-centred worship comprises, then, both the
divine message and the response of the worshipping soul. It will
be the Word of God that is heard in Scripture and doctrine: the
human word in the prayers, responses and songs whether of the
congregation or of its minister. The sermon is bound to be at the
same time Word and words. But who ever, in the dialogue of
worship, is the speaker, it is a fact that, taken as a whole, the use
of words in worship reflects a different attitude of soul from that
which the Sacrament brings with it by its very nature. Given the
difference of sensibility presupposed by the experience of revela-

tion and the aspiration to which the divine mystery gives rise, it
may well be asked whether it is possible as a rule to unite in a
single service two states of soul so dissimilar and, hence, two
expressions of worship at first sight so heterogeneous: the message
of the Word and the celebration of the Sacrament.

*   *   *

First of all, let us set forth their unlikeness. The history of worship proves how difficult it is to strike a balance. In the primitive
Church, Word and Sacrament co-existed without being united in
one and the same service: there was the missionary preaching and
there was the agape. A little later we see them united, but already
the sacramental tendency predominates, while the Word, intended
primarily for the catechumens, is considered only as a preface to
the *missa fidelium*, to the *musterion*. In the Greek Church, the sacred
action of the Eucharist goes on surrounded by secrecy, behind the
iconostasis; the only trace of the Word is found in the solemn
procession of the Holy Book; preaching disappears when it has
reached its zenith in St. John Chrysostom. The 'Holy Liturgy'
contains, it is true, biblical readings, but they are sometimes almost
incomprehensible. The Roman Catholic liturgy culminates in the
sacrifice of the altar. The Word has no longer any but a subsidiary
role in the readings which precede, in the psalms which accom-
pany, and in the prayers which surround the canon of the Mass.

The Reformation brings about a total reversal of worship-
values and the Word of God comes into its own. Luther still
preserves the balance between the Word and the Sacrament. His
Deutsche Messe is an ellipse with two foci. At Strasbourg Calvin
still celebrates Communion in the frame of the dominical service.
But little by little Protestantism cuts off the Sacrament from
Word-centred worship. Christian people abandon their altars and
turn towards the pulpit. It is in the Word that the presence of
God bursts forth. In the Reformed Church of Zwingli, Communion is from the beginning eliminated from the regular service.
Pietism and rationalism have still further alienated from the
Sacrament those influenced by them.[1] And now to-day a new
change of direction is occurring. In many Protestant Churches it
is becoming the practice to dethrone preaching and to revive and
intensify the mystery of sacramental life: as for example in the

[1] Cf. footnote to Chap. X, p. 178 *sup.*

Reformed Churches of France, Holland and German Switzerland, in the Evangelical Church of the Augsburg Confession in Alsace, and elsewhere. This movement of reaction coincides with the theocentric tendency which is coming to the fore in present-day Protestant theology. The sermon is reproached with having pushed into the background, by its subjectivism, not only the Sacrament but the Word of God itself. It is considered that the concrete realities of the Sacrament are a better guarantee of the real presence of God and of communion with Christ than is the spiritual fluidity of a sermon which, being a human production, causes the divine substance of the biblical Word to vanish. This alternating depreciation of the Word and the Sacrament proves how difficult it is to find a true balance and to make evident their complementary graces.

It is not only ecclesiastical traditions which break the link between the Word and the Sacrament. There are in man's very nature dispositions which react differently to revelation on the one hand and the divine mystery on the other. A sober temperament will respond rather to a call of the Word; a sensitive nature will more readily abandon itself to the powerful attraction of the Sacrament. There are even whole races or nations, whether frigid or passionate in temper, where two expressions of worship so different from one another cannot be expected to have equal value attached to them. There are, again, inherent in the Word or in the Sacrament differences of expression which correspond to two different mentalities: the Word develops a divine thought in an animated discursive rhythm (*der Rede inniges Bewegen*, Goethe); the Sacrament gathers up the mystery of the incarnation and of redemption in the immediacy of one sacred act. The Word makes known to us the facts of salvation in terms of an abstract spirituality; the Sacrament offers us the pledge of divine grace and of the presence of the living Christ in picture form.

*   *   *

If these, then, are the differences, there are, on the other hand, intimate affinities which allow the Word and the Sacrament to exchange their virtues and to blend their action. The spirituality of the Word can, by penetrating into the sacramental realm, prevent the hardening or the debasement of the material symbols in the mechanism of rites, or in the aberrations of magic. The

Sacrament seals the given facts of the revealed Word, and makes meditation easier by offering illumination to the intuitive and contemplative powers of the soul. The Word brings back the mystical glory of the historic facts of salvation: 'my body given for you'. By thus making explicit the sacramental act, the Word preserves religious feeling from the danger of dissolving into a sterile ecstasy. The immediacy of perception which the Sacrament promotes will forbid dissection in rational terms, whether liturgical or homiletic, of the transcendent facts both of the divine Word and of the eucharistic mystery. Finally, Word and Sacrament exert, each in its own way, a corporate action. The Word which unites children to their heavenly Father awakens in them the consciousness of their brotherhood in Christ; the Sacrament which invites the guests of the Holy Table to unite themselves *to* Christ impels them simultaneously to realise their unity in Christ. In short, the Word, *sacramentum audibile*, and the Sacrament, *verbum visibile*, refer back their potentialities to one another, and in the last resort mutually enrich each other.

★   ★   ★

Once the harmonious balance and the interaction of these two elements of worship is achieved, two significant attitudes of worship will also be seen to be in accord—edification and adoration.

Edification is an heightening of the religious perception which the Spirit of God releases through the Word: the Word engenders faith and so imbues the noblest faculties of the human being. The Word edifies the Christian personality. The Word then unites these believing souls; it builds up the Christian community, inviting its members to rise together into the transcendent sphere and to edify one another. Thanksgiving, hymns, prayers, preaching, the confession of faith will be the response, in worship, of the assembly that is being built up by the Word of God.

Adoration grows with mystical perception. The soul in quest of God, drawn by an inconceivable majesty and by the mystery of infinite love, bounds forward to find in the fulness of God the integration of its scattered faculties (*haplosis*) and to find perfect beatitude in union with Christ (*henosis*). The Sacrament offers us these unitive graces. In sacramental worship adoration will find adequate expression in the minor mode of the *Sanctus*; the

lament of the *Agnus,* as well as in the eucharistic joyfulness of
the Preface, *Sursum corda.*

Edification and adoration, so conceived in separation, will
merge into one another. The joyous assurance of the children of
God and the rapture of contemplative souls will be harmonised
in the wonderful consciousness of a peace which passes all understanding. Furthermore, those who, united beneath the pulpit,
know themselves to be edified by the Gospel, and those who
adore at the Lord's Table the ineffable love of the Crucified,
will be conscious of a solidarity in which Christian brotherhood
is reinforced by an intimate communion.

* * *

If it is at all possible that such disparities both in God's action
and in the response of the faithful can be brought back into one
rhythm of expression, it will be appropriate to fuse the message
of the Word and the celebration of the Holy Communion (or of
Baptism) in one and the same service. We do not, however, admit
a gradation from one to the other in either direction, as though
the Sacrament alone realised divine communion in all its depth,
or as though, on the other hand, communion was nothing but
an appendix to worship centred in the preaching of the Word.
These two acts, each by its own means, make vivid the reality of
the presence of God and the very advent of Christ. Together they
co-ordinate the revelation expressed through the Gospel and
through the sacramental mystery.

* * *

It may be asked whether the average Christian who takes part
in worship thus doubly-centred (whether his temperament requires him to rest in pure faith or in mystical apprehension) is
capable of laying equal hold upon the two modes of the divine
presence of which the Word and the Sacrament are the variants.
Will he find at once the shining certitude of faith in the first part
of the service and the mysterious communion with Christ in the
second? It may be, indeed, that a man fully assured by the Word,
of the promises of his salvation in Christ, no longer troubles to
seek for its confirmation in the Sacrament. Again, a particular
ardent or sensitive nature will consider all the verbal expressions
of the worship as no more than a kind of Gradual, leading to the

event towards which his most intimate longings carry him. It must be admitted that a worship which embraces both the Word and the Sacrament requires a sustained tension of spirit. But if the worshipping individual, and the whole congregation of which he is part, are duly initiated into the meaning of this double encounter of worship, which is in fact one and the same event: if the organic structure of the service assures the transition from edification to adoration and from the message of the Word to the sacramental act: if the biblical readings and even the sermon commute the living Word of God, and if the eucharistic symbols are the vehicles of His real presence: then we may rest assured that God, who is the initiator of the whole life of worship and who carries it to its perfection, will bless its unfolding, and each believer will be able to sense that the Word and Sacrament, if not themselves the two foci of worship, are yet the two incandescent poles which the fire of the divine love in Christ has kindled.

★   ★   ★

It is true to say that, with regard to the concurrence of the Word and the Sacrament, there is taking place at this very moment in most Christian Churches—not least in the Roman Catholic Church—a convergence of tendencies which, for centuries, seemed irreconcilable. The reports, coming from all angles of the ecclesiastical horizon, which the Commission has taken under review confirm this centripetal trend of the liturgical movement. It is true that the extreme positions are not yet abandoned, but while there are still Churches which admit only the proclamation of the Word as the unique element of divine worship, and others which still accord absolute pre-eminence to the Sacrament, a middle type of worship can now be seen in which the stress moves from one pole to the other and yet tends always to unify them. Even in certain Churches which are traditionally sacramental (in the Eastern Orthodox Church, for example) there is a real attempt to restore to the Word and to preaching a place which has been lost in the course of the centuries. We see, moreover, in a good number of Protestant Churches whose worship used to be centred in the preached Word, a marked intention to re-introduce Communion into the normal service of each Sunday. This can be seen in the Reformed Churches of France, in the Evangelical Church of the Augsburg Confession in Alsace, and in

Germany, Holland and Switzerland. Let us add that in numerous Protestant Churches liturgical chants, prayers or readings are being re-introduced which, in the Roman Mass and in the Eastern Liturgy, are associated with the Eucharist, without thereby denying the principles of the Reformation. 'It is permissible, after the passage of centuries, to think that the Calvinist Reformation was too severe, and that liturgical elements which come to us from the primitive Church could have been preserved, as the Anglican Church has done.'[1]

If this readjustment reflects more than preferences of an archaeological nature, or a slightly servile admiration of the Catholic model: if it is due to the conviction that Word and Sacrament together present us with the facts of salvation in their fullest expression, and that they realise the ends of worship by the most adequate symbols and in the most fitting rhythm: must we not see in this almost universal movement a symptom of a renascent piety, and the promise of an ever closer and surer ecumenical understanding?

[1] Jean Cadier: *Etudes théologiques et religieuses*, Montpellier, 1947, No. 1, p. 100.

XIV

REFORMED

*

(a) G. van der Leeuw[1]
(Holland)

Word and Sacrament

As in all Churches of the Reformation, especially those of the
Reformed (Genevan) type, the Dutch Reformed Church has from
its earliest beginnings stressed the necessity of the preaching and
exposition of the Gospel. Not pedagogical reasons only—and not
even those reasons in the first instance—prompted our Reformed
fathers to stress that necessity. People will certainly not be able to
believe, when there is no preaching and no clear exposition of the
contents of Holy Writ. But, though the sermon from the beginning has been in some of its essential parts a religious instruction
—and has always remained so—yet preaching has always been
felt to be in its essence something more: the proclamation of
divine grace.

Strong as the emphasis on the Word and its preaching was, it
cannot however be said that it was ever put above the sacraments.
The task of the Reformed minister has always been and is still
the preaching of the Word and the administration of the sacraments, and the sign of the true Church has always been held to
be that the Word of God is being set forth and that the sacraments
are administered according to Scripture.

However, sacramental practice deteriorated rapidly after the
classical period of the Reformation. It is well known that Calvin
himself regarded the administration of Holy Communion only a
few times yearly as a popish abuse and strove for at least weekly
communion as a rule. But his effort was in vain. Not only in his
own Geneva, but in most Reformed countries, Holy Communion was reduced to a celebration at most four times a year.

---

[1] This paper had not been revised by the author at the time of his death in
1950. It is therefore printed virtually as first written in English early in 1948.

So it was in our Church and so it has remained till our present times. The reign of the pulpit was well established and going to church is still alluded to as 'going to sermon', whereas the minister does not generally conduct a service but sets out 'to preach'.

In the forms of worship this was shown by the entire separation of the two aspects. The Catholic form of worship was thereby broken up: the principal service on Sunday morning was not an Antecommunion but a queer mixture of an Office with catechising, prayer being confined to a 'prayer for the opening of the Word' before, and the prayer of thanksgiving after sermon, whereas ritual was nearly wholly absent, except in the benediction, the Creed and the Confession of Sins. Confession was confined to a passage in the opening prayer. There was, of course, always the 'ritual' of singing.

The celebration of Holy Communion was conducted after an Order which is still in use; it is a veritable monument of deep religious feeling and conceived throughout in a spirit of true devotion; but it is mainly didactic in character (with the exception of the magnificent *Postcommunio*), and even the *Sursum corda* was transformed by Calvin into an admonition not to be fettered by the elements but to lift up the heart to heaven, the true abode of Christ.

Not all these deviations from Catholic use were derogatory to the spirit of Christian worship. The Roman Mass itself was felt to be a deviation, and though the purification of rite was somewhat drastic, yet we may be grateful that the doctrine of transubstantiation was put aside and that all stress was laid not on the miracle performed but on grace provided, not on divinisation of the elements effected but on Bread and Wine being received in Communion. The infrequency of the celebration was not without its saving grace. Holy Communion was regarded as a spiritual peak in the life of the congregation; it was prepared for by a special service of humiliation and followed by a service of thanksgiving. It was an occasion of great solemnity, just as it was in the Church of Scotland and still is in the Reformed Churches of South Africa.

But in recent years it has been felt increasingly that Christian worship has its base in the Breaking of the Bread; that the liturgy of the Upper Room is not only historically the fountain-head of all worship, but that also in a doctrinal sense the New Covenant instituted by our Lord is the foundation of all intercourse between Him and His Church.

Holy Communion can never be the acme of worship, since it is itself worship, and every gathering of the members of Christ's Body is essentially a gathering at the Table where He laid down the law of the New Covenant in His Blood. So the demand for revision of the eucharistic practice of the Church, which had remained much the same through more than three centuries, grew and became the moving force behind the so-called liturgical movement. Not only in this movement, however, but also in Barthian circles, the need of more frequent Communion is felt.

At the same time, largely by the influence of Barthian theology, there arose a conflict about the pre-eminence either of Word or of Sacrament. Whereas frequent Communion was conceded in accordance with divine commandment, some theologians in our Church wanted to stress the primacy of the Word over the Sacrament, which was thought to be only an addition to the preaching of the Word. This conflict found its outward form in a controversy about the respective places in churches of the Lord's Table and the pulpit. Since the Reformation there had not been anything like a fixed table in our churches, and the faithful took their places at Communion at a temporary table, removed after service.[1] Now in many communities the need is felt for a permanent Holy Table, and architects in building or renovating churches take this into account. The Catholic view is that the Table ought to be the centre of worship, even when there is no Communion, in order that the sacrifice of our Lord may be for ever put into the minds of the congregation, and that it may be apparent that all worship presupposes the Lord's Supper as its focus; also to remind the faithful that should the main service on the Sunday morning not contain the celebration of Holy Communion, it is only a truncated service, and only to be permitted for practical reasons. On the other hand, many people wish the pulpit to maintain its central place either behind a permanent Table, or in no connection with any Table at all.

On the 'liturgical' side the Table has often been considered too much as a beautiful ornament, only to be used at Communion,

[1] The Dutch Reformed Church has always retained the ancient custom of the congregation being seated at the Holy Table. With increasing numbers of communicants this custom seems likely to prove impracticable.

and not even implying necessarily frequent Communion, whereas it was not used during 'ordinary' services. Only in recent years a change is being effected. On the Barthian side, the significance of the term 'Word' is left largely undecided. It may be the written word of the Bible, the word as it is preached, either in the sense of simple information (catechising, evangelism), or in the deeper sense of a proclamation of grace. It may even be the Word of God made flesh, and in the customary indiscriminate use of 'Word' there is something implied of all four meanings at the same time. This does not make for clear reasoning or reasoned practice.

It has been remarked even by Barth himself, as well as in our Church, that the significance of the proclaimed Word in Lutheran and Reformed doctrine and practice has developed into its becoming itself a 'sacrament'. The proclamation of grace is certainly a sacramental act. It is performed by man, not as an arbitrary act under his own responsibility but at the behest of Christ and in the power of Christ. It is in its essence nothing but the absolution, the acquittal of sins which is commanded us expressly in the Gospel. Should sacramental doctrine develop along these lines then the four meanings of 'Word' which are now combined in a somewhat confused way would all come into their own place and right. The written Word of God as the repository of revelation preserved and transmitted by the Church; the catechising and the instruction as the necessary preparation for the reception of grace; the proclamation as the sacramental act confided to the Church, whereby the effects of the atonement are not only announced but given to the faithful ('My Word shall not return unto me void'); and the Word which was made flesh as the ground and warrant of all.

The conflict between Word and Sacrament would then appear senseless. There can be no conflict between one sacrament and another. Also it would be possible to maintain fully one of the essential tenets of the Reformation, without disparaging in any way the value of Sacrament: namely, *that no act is to be admitted in Christian worship without its significance being expounded*. Grace in the Sacrament being implicit needs to become explicit in order to be appropriated. Sacraments are mysteries certainly, but they should not remain 'mysterious'; their contents should be proclaimed and professed. Then only they are complete. The Sacrament is not without the Word and the Word not without the

Sacrament, and both are sacramental in character. It could be expressed also in these terms: he who administers the Sacrament is a priest, for his act is dependent on the Act of Christ in His sacrifice. But he is also a minister of the divine Word. There is no discrepancy between these terms; they are the expression of the same thing.

Sacrament and Symbol

According to the doctrine of Reformed Churches the sacraments are tokens and seals of divine grace. This may be understood in a superficial but also in a deeper sense. It may mean solely a kind of acted parable, an aid to our sensual nature, provided by God's mercy as a complement to the preaching of the Word. There is no denying that from the beginnings of our Churches and thence in ever-increasing measure this superficial meaning has been adopted. On the other hand, however, the Reformed Churches have always preserved a sense of the mystery in the Sacrament, i.e. of the real Presence of our Lord and of His sacrifice under the tokens of Bread and Wine. In the writings of Calvin, and also in our own Order of Service, this sense is very deep. Fear of Roman superstition may have tended to emphasise the 'spiritual'[1] in a degree which brings a real danger of heresy; on the other hand, realism has never quite deserted us. The 'bread-god' of the Roman Church was detested, but the Sacrament has never been degraded into a mere memorial service.

All depends on the term 'token' being taken in its original meaning, not of a signpost but of an act of God—in the biblical sense, as a wonder, a *sēmeion*—whereas the 'seal' is the *sphragis* of the ancient Church. Signs and seals interpreted in this sense are sacramental in the full meaning of the word, that is to say, they are not only indications or affirmations, but constitute the act of God in the Sacrament.

The word 'symbol' might be used here too, but only in its original meaning of two things coming together (*symballein*), in such a way that one may be taken for the other. Also the Reformed Churches are returning to sacramental realism. Of course they will continue to be averse from any conception of the Sacrament pointing to transubstantiation. It is to be hoped that they will also object more and more to every form of 'symbolism' in

[1] Cf. footnote to Chap. X, p. 178 *sup.*

the modern superficial sense. The position indicated for them is neither on the side of St. Thomas nor on that of Zwingli. They ought to reject both forms of rationalisation.

The idea of re-presentation as it is advocated in many circles nowadays, Roman Catholic as well as Anglican and Lutheran, seems to present some perspectives for a future development of sacramental theology for the Reformed Churches also. The central Sacrament, the Eucharist, is not a repetition of Christ's sacrifice, neither is it a making mention of it in a solemn way. But it is the re-presentation of the Act of God on Golgotha. By our humble means God is offering to us the sacrifice of His Son, presenting it to us. *Benedictus qui venit in nomine Domini* is no ornate phrase but a blissful reality: Christ suffering, Christ risen is coming ever anew to meet and to bless us.

Sacrifice and Priesthood

There is one thing in the sacramental practice of our Church in which it is sinning continually against the spirit of Scripture, though it is not alone in this sin. There is a nearly exclusive relation stated, in theology as well as in devotion, between the Eucharist and the death of the Lord, with a total neglect of the resurrection. The influence of pietism is here very apparent. The fact that resurrection is included in the sacrifice of our Lord; that the celebration of Holy Communion is not a funerary ceremony but a joyful feast, partaken of with exultation (Acts 2. 46), was nearly wholly forgotten, so far that the day *par excellence* on which to go to Communion came to be Good Friday—the only day on which the Catholic Church does not celebrate the liturgy of the Upper Room. Only recently this misconception was remarked, but it will take some time to correct it.

The repetition of Christ's sacrifice, the 'Lord being slaughtered anew by the priests of the Mass', was a kind of black rubric with our forebears. And they were right: even Roman Catholic divines are now conceding that a repetition of Golgotha is an abomination. But this does not in any way diminish or disfigure the idea of Sacrifice itself. At the Lord's Table the sacrifice of Christ is re-presented and the faithful are called upon to partake in this sacrifice. They cannot receive it and make it their own without giving themselves, without offering up their lives. At the Table of the Lord they are not only receivers of the gifts of Christ, but they officiate, they partake, they exercise the priesthood conferred upon them by Baptism and Confirmation We have already seen that the expressions 'minister of the Word' and 'priest' are no opposites, but mean the same thing. All priesthood, however, rests in the priesthood given to us all when the seal of Baptism was put on our foreheads. The representing of the sacrifice of Christ is not the affair of the administering priest only, but of all participants.

The special office of the minister, that of the elder and of the deacon, are mere specialisations of the general priesthood. To create them, ordination is sufficient. There are only very few in our Church who would ascribe any intrinsic value to Apostolic Succession. There are more (but not many) who believe that the presbyteral organisation of the Church should be modified by episcopal elements, and that an equilibrium between the congregation and the bishop would best guarantee the scriptural idea of priesthood. What is abhorred by all Reformed is the idea of a clergy as opposed to the laity. We would say, rather, that there is no such thing as a laity.

To what was said above must be added that these questions have been discussed for twenty-five years with ever-increasing interest. But since the war they have become for the first time a subject of active discussion in the Church itself, in its assemblies and councils. In this way the somewhat haphazard discussions of theologians are developing into real theology, the process of realisation by the Church of what it has been given by Christ.

XIV

REFORMED

*

(b) Artur Graf
(Switzerland)

(a) Word and Sacrament

Even before the Reformation there were non-sacramental services
in the German region, in fact preaching services, as well as celebrations of Holy Communion, though after the Reformation the
sacramental element fell into the background to a surprising
extent. The result has been that in our time the Sacrament has in
the end become just an embarrassment, and it cannot be said that
it is celebrated joyfully. Theologians of very different movements
or theological schools often speak anxiously of the *lack* of sacraments, particularly of the lack of the Lord's Supper.

But how did it happen that the preaching service, without the
Sacrament, could so take root, and that worshippers were satisfied
with *communio spiritualis*? In this matter we are inclined first of
all to assume psychological causes. It is striking that to a great
extent we must speak of a certain reserve towards the concrete
representation of the spiritual, particularly of religious things. We
should like to see in this attitude a national peculiarity—*sit venia
verbo*. We meet it, so far as I can see, in the whole German region
up to the line of the Main. The Churches of this Upper German
area are distinctly different from those of Lower Germany;
Strasbourg would then represent in a spiritual respect as well as
geographically the 'Centre'. Convictions change with the geo-
graphical latitude. Is that not expressed in architecture, and also in
the national costume? It seems to us that the north is in general
more conservative, disinclined to revolution. Things are kept in
being there, which in the south are much more easily given up.
It is well known that this is true of England to a peculiar degree.
But Scandinavia presents a similar picture. Official attire in particular is characteristic of this. In divine service vestments are still

extensively worn, while in the south they are no longer understood.

Perhaps it may also be said that there is a certain rationalism peculiar to the people of this southern area, from which springs a deep mistrust of anything which is not, so to speak, 'transparently' comprehensible and convincing to the reason and which is therefore suspect as 'magic'. The word does not necessarily imply trickery, for any happening is magical which cannot be explained on rational lines. It is not denied that there has also been, even in this part of Europe, a great deal of magic and sorcery—that superstition has flourished here too. But perhaps it should be said that these things take place 'in the dark' to a quite peculiar degree, shunning each other. The rationalising attitude mentioned would to some extent be a defence against powers moving in the dark, of which people are ashamed. In this connection we may recall a saying of Zwingli's, which emphasises the presence in Zürich of plain places of worship, the walls of which are beautifully white.

One could also speak of a matter-of-fact form of thought, which is unfavourable to all speculation. There are few metaphysicians in this school. The dreamy recluse (*Sinniere*) is an eccentric, the exception to the rule. There is a preference for the epic style, from Walter of Rheinau and Gottfried of Strasbourg to Gottfried Keller. There is a great liking for history which gives a reliable picture of the past. Sagas, and fairy-tales as well, certainly exist, but they live in the shadows. What they have to tell is somehow 'not true', because it cannot in a material sense be established as fact.

The Zürich Church historian Emil Egli spoke incidentally of the 'rationalist element in the Zürich Reformation'. Joseph Nadler, who was a professor in Freiburg, writes in his *History of the Literature of German Switzerland*: 'The pathos of this nation is the State.' That is certainly rightly judged. Quite a different attitude is taken to political decisions from that taken to anything else. In the political sphere a matter is understood, or even misunderstood, with great facility, which elsewhere would be regarded and judged differently. When again Nadler says: 'One does not expect any spiritual adventures from this nation,' he supplements the former statement. Again and again it is a matter of very concrete things, of the democratic state, in which the nation is sovereign —a matter of very concrete national rights. That involves the distinct refusal of all privileges and prerogatives not only to the nobility but also to the clergy, to the priests.

We place these considerations in the forefront. They may to some extent explain how, with the Reformation, celebrations of the Sacrament were immediately curtailed. That which could not be based on the Bible was omitted; new texts and forms were provided and the celebration was limited to four times in the year. Certainly it is very clear that here humanism played its part. *Ad fontes* ran the slogan. In this case the source was the Bible. Therefore only that which was based on the Bible was legitimate. But in the 'autumn of the Middle Ages' all sorts of things had been allowed to grow up which were not good, and those decades experienced profound changes of conviction. Celebrations must henceforth be public and accessible to all. Everything must be spoken aloud and audibly. The people must know what is said, must understand it. Everything mysterious is repressed, indeed removed. Even though the Sacrament may be taken very seriously, again and again it is emphasised that it is no longer a mystery. The Word as the means of the rational conveyance of truth, i.e. of a doctrine which must be discerned and known, stands foremost. It is gradually forgotten that there is a sort of experience which has nothing to do with knowledge. The really sacramental music, the Gregorian, is described as 'absurd' (Bullinger). There, too, something unequivocal is wanted, with a clearly recognisable end, a conclusion which cannot be in doubt. So first all music disappears out of the service. In its place verbose and learned expositions are often actually inserted into the sacramental forms. The celebration becomes almost a catechism and to a great extent has so remained until to-day. Reason carries so much weight that all mystery is on that account repressed.

Here attention must be called to what Wilhelm Dilthey has established in his *Analysis of Man* since humanism and the renaissance: in place of the biblical, trinitarian faith in God there has slowly come in, as he says, Universalist Theism, a Unitarian understanding of God. *Where, however, the Trinitarian belief fades, the ground is taken away from beneath the Sacrament.* Here pietism has altered nothing, and our people continue to live 'in the first article': *Credo in unum Deum, patrem omnipotentem.* The second Person of the Holy Trinity is 'the Lord Jesus', regarded as the 'dear Saviour'. More interest has been taken in 'Lives of Jesus' than in the presence of Christ in the Sacrament. Compare, for instance, the hymn books of our Church with the English Hymnal and notice how the former speak very clearly of Jesus the Christ, while in the latter on the other hand is expressed the Holy Trinity, the Three in One, etc., i.e. the form of experience derived from Archetypes. The Churches have held to what the Bible says about the proceedings at a celebration of the Sacrament (as if it were a Handbook of Liturgy!), so the *Credo, Sanctus, Benedictus,* and *Agnus Dei,* are gradually omitted. Only in recent times have shy attempts been made to insert into the hymn books hymns on these lines, certainly without yet knowing how they could be brought within the existing forms.

All the weight is laid on the 'Word'. The one thing that matters is preaching. Recently, it is true, the conception of 'prophecy' has been emphasised, without, however, protecting it against the possibility that what is really meant is the spoken word and the rational, abstract truth conveyed by it. So the Sacrament is generally spoken of as the *Verbum visibile.* In consequence it is not important in itself, but serves as a demonstration of that which has been set forth in abstract speech. Therefore there must be no celebration of the Lord's Supper without sermon or address, and on those the emphasis is laid. Likewise there must be no Baptism without an explanation of the Baptism, even if actual baptismal addresses are not the rule. Hence comes also the theological-rational instruction on admission to the Lord's Supper. The phrase 'explanation of the Mystery' was used as early as the sixteenth century. It seems to us that again and again 'intellectual' and 'spiritual' have been confused and so the possession of theological knowledge has been placed on an equality with spiritual experience and maturity—*Declaratio doctrinae: professio fidei.*

When, in 1940, Bishop Küry in *Statements of the Conference on Faith and Order* put the question to the representatives of the pure theology of the Word, whether it would not be consistent with their theology to give up the Sacrament, no answer was forthcoming. It is in fact a question whether the loss of the Trinitarian conception does not as a spiritual necessity lead to Quakerism,[1]

---

[1] This question could be pressed beyond the writer's intention. He refers to Quakerism merely in so far as the Religious Society of Friends does not observe sacramental rites: no further judgment is here implied. Cf. footnote to Chap. X, p. 178 *sup.*—ED.

however much that conclusion may be resisted. In the Swiss 'Preachers' Society' the question of the Lord's Supper has for decades been a perennial matter of discussion. No solution has been reached: there still lives in more orthodox as well as in modernist circles of German Switzerland so much of the modernist, 'theistic' (and therefore non-Trinitarian) thinking, and in addition so much aversion from and animosity to Catholicism and the Mass, that among us any desire for developing an Evangelical Mass would find little support, much as it may be urged by Prof. de Saussure, Frère Max Thurian and others.

At present the question of the legitimacy of Infant Baptism is under discussion; church discipline is also spoken of, with particular reference to the Sacrament. Here and there new forms for the celebration of the Sacrament are suggested. As long as the traditional interpretation of the Lord's Supper as a 'memorial' service is firmly held, without the nature of this memorial being thought out afresh, so that a new understanding of the *anamnesis* and also of the *epiklesis* may be reached, all attempts of this kind will remain unfruitful. For it is really not the case, as Prof. Farner wrote in 1945 in *Reformierte Schweiz*, that the presence of the Lord in the Sacrament and in the congregation celebrating the Sacrament is taken for granted, unless we are to think of God on the lines of Hegel and Biedermann. It is not even the last word to say that the Lord's Supper demonstrates as *verbum visibile* what happened on Calvary.

There is no evidence among us of a fresh enquiry into the relationship of Word and Sacrament. Probably it is a result of the actual division of the Churches into different 'movements' and theological schools that there is an avoidance of such investigations, which must eventually take a concrete, liturgical form. There remains, therefore, something of a deadlock.

(b) *Sacrament and Symbol*

It may be said in general that our German-Swiss Protestantism has to-day more than ever a distinct anti-Catholic bias, and very decisively dislikes anything at all reminiscent of Roman Catholic sacramentalism. Without, of course, being able to prevent in the civil sphere pseudo-sacramental acts which are at least parodies of the sacraments: (e.g. the christening of flags and ships and similar things) a strong dislike of anything symbolical can be observed.

As far as possible even the words 'sacrament' and 'symbol' are avoided and 'signs' is the term preferred when a Baptism is solemnised or the Lord's Supper celebrated. 'Signs of the Covenant' is a usage of speech already traditional. It is emphasised that in the Church reformed according to the Word of God only these two 'Signs of the Covenant' are permissible.

We cannot resist the impression that here, in a more or less nervous way, a question is being begged which in recent times has not been thoroughly thought out. It is often emphasised that the whole question was really settled long ago by the forbidding of images in the decalogue, without admitting that in the very Bible which contains the commandment forbidding images, imagery actually occurs to a large extent. Hermann Kutter wrote his *Bilderbuch Gottes*, and in it underlined the significance of the symbolical. Since then, in the psychological sphere important investigations of 'picture-thinking' have taken place, and significant works have been published. It is known to-day that the so-called visual consciousness preceded in time the present-day rational consciousness, and that in so far as rational consciousness has prevailed, visual consciousness has degenerated. But it is also known that in spite of this the picture still precedes the idea, and that visual impressions cling more strongly than aural ones. But even Calvin in his *Institutes* leaves no doubt that in the commandment forbidding images it is the worship of the images which is forbidden, and that the image is to be removed in so far as it must be reckoned among the 'other gods' which God's people must not worship and serve beside the One God. It is also forbidden to make for oneself an image of God, a thing one can well do in thought without the use of chalks or paint-brush. In fact, when hearing an address, one must be able to picture something—otherwise speaker and hearer have wasted their time.

The significance of picture and parable, of symbol and symbolic action, has been too little examined. In this connection a very careful start should have been made from Greek language usage and such connections should have been noticed as are perhaps indicated by the following words: *symballo: symbolon*, on the one hand; *diaballo: diabolos* on the other. From such an investigation the significance of genuine symbols would have become apparent. It would have been revealed how rich is this indispensable world of symbols, and how the language of man includes it, because in language not only the content, rationally understood, is important, but its sound, accent, and syntax. It would then have become clear that the mere rational meaning of words is never sufficient unless the 'Symbol' is added, as that which alone can bind together figure and spirit, and give them one meaning.

From this standpoint the symbolical significance of the Sacrament could be made comprehensible. But we are not yet ready. It is still thought sufficient to say that the Sacrament is to be understood 'only' symbolically, on no account 'magically', as if the magical were the opposite to the symbolical. If, indeed, as appears in the previous Section, the 'Word' alone carries revelation, if this Word-conception is held in a nominalistic, narrow sense, then it is understandable why all further symbolism is avoided; why in our churches there is neither on the pulpit or on the lid of the font so much as the 'dove' of the Holy Spirit; why even the sign of the cross is suspect and lighted candles can only be 'Catholic' and are therefore objectionable. On the other hand, worldly symbols, weapons of the state and city, are smuggled right into the Holy Place, symbols not of the sacred but of the profane; so that the revealed 'Word' is in a way bound up with the profane, resting not on *symballein*, but on *diaballein*. The Word alone does it, we are taught. Anything else may be permissible 'embellishment', but is to be used with great care.

It must be clearly said that in this attitude the double inheritance of humanism as well as nominalism finds expression. From both, later Protestantism has received its propensity for 'spiritualising', in which again it seems to be nearly related to Idealism. Biblical realism must unfortunately not seldom have yielded to a rationalistic 'spiritualising' in which the reality was dissipated in the idea.

A further heritage from pre-Reformation times has worked out disastrously—namely, the over-emphasis given to the elements in Baptism and the Lord's Supper, the water, bread and wine. It must, however, be pointed out that the act as a whole, including the act of sprinkling, including eating and drinking, makes up the Sacrament. The Sacrament consists of certain symbolical elements, but there are many such symbolic things—actions and proceedings. Finally, colour is symbolic. Zwingli's strong preference for light walls in places of worship was symbolically understood. Curiously enough it escapes notice that the preference for the black gown of the preacher is also a symbol, even though it points in another direction from the white surplice of the ancient Christian liturgy.

John Harvey wrote in his *Gothic England*: 'Genuine piety testifies to itself. The puritanical—religious purism—needs the icono-clastic.' Does that explain the permanent iconoclasm in Protestantism once mentioned by C. G. Jung? There is a psychological limit beyond which one cannot pass. We have already mentioned the dislike for Gregorian plainsong, and even for Psalmody itself, since the sixteenth century. There, too, the thing is no longer understood as a genuine symbol, i.e. as a form which corresponds to the 'Word' of revelation. The discussion about the hymns for the new Swiss hymn book in this connection was very illuminating.

Prof. Emil Brunner has emphasised repeatedly the 'shrinking process' which our Reformed Churches have experienced. That is justly observed. We may indeed shrink in alarm when we become aware how far we have 'expanded', i.e. how much has been lost, from Trinitarian thinking to the sense for genuine parable and symbol, as well as to meditation. Is there not, behind all that, the 'autonomous man' who wants to be simply that which he is, as represented by E. Englert Faye in his book, *Vom Mythos zur Idee der Schweiz*? Sovereign people, 'enlightened' confidence in the authority of reason, autonomous personality. Is it not there lies the key to the questions put among us in Switzerland—and elsewhere?

(c) *Sacrifice and Priesthood*

These are biblical conceptions and not only conceptions of religious history. The protest of the Reformation was directed against the abuses of the Church of that time, above all against merit on the one hand, which was actually even promised for the sacrifice of the Mass; but on the other hand against the commercialisation of religious and even of priestly conduct, from which charge Zwingli himself was not held clear. So it came to the abolition of the office of priest (however long the expression itself remained current). The offertory was cut out of the order of the Mass and the altars were broken down (again with the result that the idea of the Altar proved to be ineradicable, even though in other spheres sacrifices were still made, e.g. for national purposes). There are indeed primary facts and with them primary

ideas, which only fanaticism and theorising (which are strangers
to reality) will attempt to destroy.

Priesthood and altar were set aside. But has attention really been
given to what the Scripture has to say about both? The sacrifice
of our Lord once for all on Calvary was emphasised. As at one
time against the Gnostics, the historicity of this sacrifice has
rightly been underlined. Yet a solitary historical fact can be so
tied to its place in history that it sinks into the past with just
that place and hour. In the eighteenth century a mathema-
tician from the circle of the encyclopaedists wanted to reckon out
the point in time at which the last effects of the martyrdom which
took place on Calvary under Pontius Pilate would die out. The
sound alone dies out; the light, which dims with the ratio of
distance, is extinguished. When the Church of old conceived the
idea of the Mass as representing the sacrifice on Calvary she
intended to express something true. She knew the meaning of the
anamnesis (cf. Theol. Dictionary of the New Testament, Vol. 1).
Zwingli, too, spoke of the representation of Christ's work of
salvation fidei contemplatione, and therefore of the realisation of the
sacrifice of Christ. Unfortunately, since his time this experience
has not been made fruitful. The Church does not simply remember the death of the Lord: she 'represents' the sacrifice itself,
letting herself enter into the suffering and death of Christ, into
His obedience. In that way she proclaims His death 'until He
come'.

The same is true of the priesthood. What is the biblical priest?
Neither preacher nor teacher, but he who offers the sacrifice,
i.e. of God's love. He is there for the others, their servant for
Christ's sake. He is intercessor, too, and God's instrument in the
work of forgiveness and of redeeming love.

Modest beginnings were made among us with a view to regain-
ing the Orders of Ministry attested by the early Church. In the
end we contented ourselves with the one office, which occupies
the highest step on the ladder of the spiritual life: the Presbyter.
So we became a Church of ministers (Pfarrerkirche). Again, under
the influence of humanism the highest value was placed on learning, and the Church was delivered up to the theologians. The
minister is a theologian academically trained—that he certainly
must be. But it was too often forgotten that he must also be a
spiritual man. 'Spiritual', however, must not be misunderstood as

'moral'. Here, too, rational and democratic thinking has played its part.

To sum up: The problems set by the conceptions of Sacrifice and Priesthood are as yet by no means fully covered. Those under (a) and (b) have largely been left unresolved. Clarification of the idea of sacrifice, and a new experience of what the old *anamnesis* is and intends, will finally also answer the questions as to the relationship of Sacrament and Symbol, Sacrament and Word (i.e. prophecy and preaching). In the case of everything valuable which has been delivered into faithful hands in the Swiss German Church, that Church must be required to overcome, by a new consideration of the Holy Scriptures, that modern-democratic prejudice, the humanistic overrating of reason, the nominalistic narrowing down to the particular, and the consequent disregard of ecumenical ecclesiastical tradition.

XIV

REFORMED

*

(c) R. Paquier
(Switzerland)

It is difficult to formulate exactly the position of our churches on
the topics in question, for these churches possess no detailed confession of faith. The Apostles' Creed is the only doctrinal statement which they use even occasionally in public worship, and
which witnesses to the faith of these churches. For the rest, their
position is only that of the totality of theological professors and
pastors, who experience periodically the consequences of the flux
and reflux of European theological thought as a whole. At the
beginning of this century, and up till 1930, liberal Protestantism
reigned almost unchallenged in our churches, and if it has been
victoriously attacked since then by the neo-Calvinist and Barthian
renaissance, it must be admitted that this corrective has hardly
extended beyond the fields of doctrine concerning God, Christ
and redemption. So far as the Church, the sacraments and the
ministry are concerned, the liberal mentality has lived on, in a
weakened form, in our church life, lightly tempered by a desire,
as yet unformulated, for a richer community and sacramental life.

The Word of God is considered the unique means by which the
Lord enters into communion with His sinful creatures. This Word
reveals to man his state of sin, and manifests to him the glory, the
holiness, the justice and the love of God, and also His redemptive
purpose. This Word must be preached, that is to say, not only
read in the letter of Scripture but 'actualised' by the preacher, in
such a way that a direct call of God resounds in the heart of each
hearer. In the liberal period, it was said that the message of the
Gospel edified, meaning (in the pietist sense of the word) that it
exhorted and consoled. Now, under the Barthian influence, we
prefer to say that the Word acts, that it judges and that it saves,
that it edifies (in the sense of constructing and gathering the com-

munity), and we readily evoke the 'miracle of the Word', which operates *hic et nunc*, making the grace of God effective towards sinners.

But in any case the Word remains, from the Reformed point of view, the sole path from God to man. Hence Reformed worship is above all the place and the moment where the Word resounds and acts. People shrink from assigning to the sacraments a value *sui generis*: they are accorded only the importance of a concrete seal or sensible pledge of the grace which the Word by itself suffices to confer. There is then no difference between the Word and the sacraments, neither quantitative nor qualitative: the sacraments are the outward expression of the Word, *verbum visibile*, and they derive their value and their efficacy solely from the Word which they signify, which connotes and determines them. It is admitted that since the Word became flesh in Christ, this condescension of God in adapting Himself to our carnal weakness explains the institution of the sacraments, and justifies their place in the life of the Church. But we scarcely succeed in going beyond this theoretical concession, and in finding room for the sacraments in the ordinary round of the Church's life, with the same status as the Word.

There are two main reasons for this. To begin with, liberal idealism, which rests upon a disjunction of spirit and bodily nature, has not been completely overcome. It is not for nothing that it has been the spiritual climate of two generations of churchmen, and its traces survive tenaciously in our communities. As a result the baptismal water, like the eucharistic bread and wine, are envisaged as *symbols*, that is to say as allegorical signs of a spiritual reality which is without a real and organic relation to them. A canticle of the French Swiss Psalter (No. 359) speaks of the 'touching symbols which call to mind the bloody sacrifice of Christ', and the Lausanne liturgy twice employs the term symbol, which in current acceptation can only mean figure, allegorical image, as opposed to the real object. And the verb 'to represent' appears there too, not with the strong sense of 'to make present', but in the weakened sense of 'to picture', 'to symbolise'. A baptismal formulary exhorts the faithful not to rely upon an outward ceremony for the eternal salvation of the child. Most of the official liturgical and catechetical texts concerning Baptism and the Holy Communion tend to suggest a sort of concomitance, without any intrinsic necessity attaching, between a grace from on high and the ceremonial act.

One can go back further in the analysis of factors in this symbolic conception of the sacraments. It is known that the truly Reformed christology of Calvin and Zwingli—as opposed to that of Luther, who was more faithful to the ancient Church—has exaggeratedly separated the human and the divine natures in the unique person of Christ, following a tendency which leads ultimately to Nestorian dualism, not to mention Adoptianism. This too sharp distinction between the divine and the human, between that which is of heaven and that which is of earth, in the person of the Lord, has necessarily had its repercussion on the diverse levels of ecclesiastical dogmatics and practice. It has found its logical culmination in the theology of Barth. At the point where it would be legitimate to distinguish, in order better to discern how God unites, this theology tends to separate, and sometimes to oppose. Hence its denial of any mystical and unitive element in faith, and the suspicion which this denial arouses regarding 'sacramentalism' and 'liturgism', which are accused of being an irruption, or at least showing the influence, of the *theologia gloriae*. Thus the Barthian perspective, superimposed on the liberal perspective in the new generation of pastors, cannot but perpetuate the restricted idea of the sacraments which was inherited from the Calvinist-Zwinglian Reformation. In reality the New Testament data, notably Romans 6 for Baptism, and John 6 for the Eucharist, imply a unitive value, a grace of indwelling and, in a truly mystical sense, of assimilation, which the Scriptures nowhere attribute to the Word as such. But it goes without saying that the theologians influenced by Barthian dogmatics are no more ready to accept such considerations than are the ordinary pastors who grew up in the purely Reformed tradition, and sometimes still unconsciously draw on their liberal heritage.

It is notable that the theology of Barth has not exercised in the French Reformed Churches of Switzerland the considerable and even dominant influence which it has in German Switzerland. Its effect here has been above all that of a useful corrective of the insipidity which liberalism had inflicted on faith, and of a salutary recovery of theocentric preaching. But the result is not so one-sided as to corrupt the true faith and close the doors to all other manifestations of the Spirit as He speaks to the Churches. Thus a slight change can be seen taking shape under the influence of the liturgical movement. The new liturgy of Lausanne (1940) includes a formulary of the Holy Communion which reads: 'We pray thee, O God, thyself to bless and to consecrate this bread and this cup: that through this perishable food thy Spirit may aid us to discern thy imperishable grace, and to find in this bread the body of our Lord Jesus Christ, and in this cup the blood of our Lord Jesus Christ.' And on two occasions it speaks of the bread which *is* the body of Christ, and of the wine which *is* His blood. This is clearly going beyond anything merely symbolist or allegorical, as also beyond the idea which Calvin held of the value of the elements in the economy of the Sacrament. The new liturgy of Geneva, a little more recent in date (1945), avoids the word symbol, and employs the terms sign, mark, seal and pledge. In one of the eucharistic formularies one reads: 'Bestow upon us Thy Holy Spirit, so that in partaking of this bread and of this cup, we may, through faith, have communion with the body and blood of Thy Son.' On the other hand, one of the formularies of Baptism specifies that 'it is neither the water nor the formula which renders Baptism efficacious, but the Spirit of God', and one of the eucharistic formularies exhorts the communicants as follows: 'Without dwelling on the external signs of the Holy Communion, as though the Saviour were materially enclosed there, let us lift up our hearts on high, where He now is in the glory of God His Father'; here is a faithful echo of the teaching of Calvin. In yet another place it is said: 'May Christ give us the grace to be nourished and quickened, not by these earthly and corruptible elements, but by the living bread which comes down from heaven and which we receive through faith.' There can thus be discerned in these liturgies two distinct if not opposed currents: on the one hand the old Reformed doctrine, careful to avoid any interference between the material sign and the spiritual grace, for fear of taking from God Himself the least part of His glory; and on the other hand the new insights which a truer understanding of sacramental realism, included in the biblical doctrine of man, has more recently revealed, thanks to ecumenical contacts. But in practice it is still the old Reform which clearly prevails. It cannot in any case be otherwise until the whole problem has been reconsidered theologically. As long as one is content to be influenced by trends, and to borrow eclectically from them, without a directing principle, what one judges attractive or useful, one will not succeed in overcoming what is, at the moment, a mere hesitation—certainly not a salutary tension. Unhappily, as the Rev. H. W. Newell very rightly declared at the assembly of delegates from all the Swiss Reformed Churches in June 1947, where he represented the World Council: 'Problems of doctrine and order do not seem to interest the Swiss Churches very much.'

However, it is only in elucidating the relation of the Word to the Sacrament, and in discriminating between symbol and Sacrament, that a solid foundation will be assured for the laudable efforts made during the last few years in the Reformed Churches of French-speaking Switzerland to restore the sacraments to their proper place and value in the worship of the Church. It must be recognised that the Sacrament is not, purely and simply, the Word under another and unusual form, but that there is in it something different—which does not necessarily mean something more and better—than in the Word. The new element lies in that unitive and mystical quality, which the Word does not contain, since it has itself other and archetypal characters. With such recognition established, the sacramental and liturgical renaissance will be doctrinally and reasonably assured. Without the adoption of this truly theological view, the sacraments, and the community-making liturgy which normally accompanies them, will always appear as invaders, or as needless postscripts, in the minds of Churches which wish to be fundamentally Churches of the Word. The present state of theological ideas still sensibly falls short of such perception, and therefore there is in our Churches no decisive advance towards a restoration of Baptism, and above all of the Holy Communion, to their respective importance and stature.

Up till now the sacrificial aspect of worship has been almost completely ignored by our Reformed Churches. Sacrifice is only admitted in the sense of I Pet. 2. 5 and Heb. 13. 15. Even this has hardly more than a theoretical bearing. Since preaching constitutes the essential element in worship, prayer, the hymn of praise, and adoration have only a limited place. The Holy Communion makes room for the sacrifice only inasmuch as it is the bare commemoration of the sacrifice of Christ, unique and perfect, accomplished once for all in the historical event of nineteen centuries ago. In a general way, while it is willingly maintained that the Church has a prophetic ministry, the continuation of that of Christ, there is a refusal to recognise that a priestly sacrificial ministry could possibly also be given, as a prolongation and a delegation of the priesthood of Christ. People are pleased to accord to all the faithful one unique 'priesthood', without discrimination, called for that reason 'universal priesthood'; but this formula means nothing except a recognition that they have equal rights in the Church of God; it does not imply any specific relation to sacrifice, unless in the ethical sense to which Rom. 12. 1 witnesses. The result of this situation is that texts like I Pet. 2. 9 (royal priesthood or royal sacrificing) and Rev. 1. 6 and 20. 6 (sacrificers or priests of God and of Christ) cannot but have a strange, almost unintelligible, sound for the bulk of the Reformed. The pastoral ministry in our churches deliberately excludes any sacerdotal idea; it is the prophetic ministry of the Word, a Word essentially preached, and only incidentally illustrated in sacramental form. As to the relation between the universal priesthood of believers and the specialised pastoral ministry, it remains theologically ill defined. It is not easy to determine what the particular character of the sacred ministry really is—when it is denied that it is a priesthood, or any inspired member of the faithful should not announce the prophetic Word or administer the Sacrament, if this is only a simple pledge or visible seal. As to the 'apostolic succession' it is formally rejected, because it is totally misunderstood and underestimated.

However, a slight advance has recently been achieved towards a more concrete idea of sacrifice in worship. The new liturgies of Lausanne and Geneva have given a liturgical form to the collection of gifts for the Church. The offertory is introduced and concluded by adequate words pronounced by the officiating minister, and the liturgy of Lausanne specifies that the alms shall be placed on the Holy Table with a short prayer.

One of the new Genevan formularies for the Holy Communion, by reintroducing the traditional scheme of the eucharistic Canon, formulates the *anamnesis* as follows: 'We remember then, O our God, the sufferings and the death of Thy Son, His Resurrection and His Ascension, and while awaiting His return, we praise Thee for having regarded the sacrifice which He offered on the Cross once for all, and *accepted His perpetual intercession on our behalf in the heavens.* . . . Receive also the homage of our hearts which offer themselves to Thee and consecrate themselves to Thy service in a living and holy sacrifice.' For the first time, in a Swiss Reformed Church, the great theological idea so familiar to Catholics finds entry, though as yet in embryonic form—the idea of a mystical relation between the liturgical act of Communion and the eternal oblation which Christ the High Priest, glorified, makes of His death to God, in heaven (Heb. 9. 14). But this idea, which has here found an entry with the help of the liturgical movement (cf. the booklet No. 1 of the collection 'Eglise et Liturgie') is still far from being supported on solid theological foundations, and linked to the total economy of religion and worship.

In short, our churches, so far as sacraments and ideas connected with sacrifice and priesthood go, have remained in essentials where they have always been, still living in the controversies of the sixteenth century which unfortunately presented the problems in a false light. However it is possible to note a few modest signs of a new evolution towards a less one-sided and more complete view of these great realities of the life of the universal Church.

APPENDIX

Statements on the Nature of Sacraments
adopted by the Sub-Commission on Ecclesiastical Discipline of the
National Vaudois Church, on 11th December 1947

1. A Sacrament is a visible sign and seal of an invisible grace. Instituted by Christ, it is efficacious proportionately to our faith, yet without this efficacy being limited by the measure of our faith.

2. The Word of God alone makes the Sacrament what it is, and faith alone receives the grace which accompanies it, through the action of the Holy Spirit.

3. The material element of the Sacrament, and the grace which it signifies and presents, must be neither confounded nor separated. The link between the sign and the reality is not definable in our rational categories: it is of the order of the Spirit (pneuma).

4. (a) From one point of view, the Word of God is more than the Sacrament, for it is the Word which, before everything else, awakens faith and gathers the Church, and which, later, constitutes

the sacraments by determining the meaning and value of the material elements which the latter include. The Word can exist without the Sacrament, but the Sacrament cannot exist without the Word.

(*b*) From another point of view, there is more in the Sacrament than in the preached Word of God, in that the Sacrament synthesises, unites, and creates community.

(i) *It synthesises:* The Word only reaches the spirit of man through the sense of hearing and thus appeals primarily to the intellect; being discursive and analytic, it cannot present more than one aspect of the divine message at one time.

The Sacrament, addressing itself to the spirit equally by the senses of sight, touch and taste, reaches the whole man, in his bodily aspect (that is to say in his sensible perceptions and his imagination) as much as in his intellect. It presents simultaneously, in a concrete whole, the whole Person and work of the Lord.

(ii) *It unites:* In the worship of the Church the preached Word is addressed first of all to the community in general, in order to reach each individual in it, while the Sacrament concretely places each believer personally in a relation of covenant with the Lord in order through that very fact to constitute and to edify the community.

The Sacrament unites the believer to his Lord by a mystical and reciprocal bond, including the entire being of the believer, spirit and body. Through the Sacrament the Lord takes possession of the redeemed, and dwells in him, as he dwells in his Lord (cf. Rom. 6 and John 6).

(iii) *It creates community:* The sacraments incorporate the believer concretely in the community of the people of God, the Church. Baptism makes him a member of the Body of Christ, and the Holy Communion renews and sustains this membership.

5. The sacraments are prophetic signs of the total and final salvation in the Kingdom to come. They announce, beyond our death with Christ to the world and to sin, our final resurrection, in the 'adoption, the redemption of our body' (Rom. 8. 23). They are for the believer the first-fruits of the 'powers of the age to come' (Heb. 6. 5) and for the community of the Church an anticipation of 'new heavens and a new earth' (II Pet. 3. 13).

XV

OLD CATHOLIC

*

A. E. Rüthy
(Switzerland)

Word and Sacrament

Before anything can be stated about the relationship between Word and Sacrament, it is necessary to determine what is to be understood by 'Word' or 'Word of God'.

The 'Word of God' may mean:

(a) The direct speech of God to man, e.g. through prophetic revelation or in the preaching of Jesus;

(b) the written word of the Bible in the Old and New Testaments, in which the spoken word is contained and passed on;

(c) the content of the Church's preaching, as derived from the Holy Scriptures; indeed, sometimes even this preaching itself (the sermon);

(d) in the Johannine sense, the *Logos*, who is Christ.

As regards the 'Sacrament' it should first be said that the Old Catholic Church, in agreement with the Catholic Church of the West and the Orthodox Church of the East, adheres to the Seven Sacraments, among which, however, the two chief Sacraments, Baptism and the Eucharist, have special prominence.

Of the possible meanings of 'Word of God' which we have mentioned, the first does not arise for the present purpose. As regards the last (Word=*Logos*) it follows that the sacraments only have their power through and in Christ. This statement, wherever the Sacrament is seen as a reality (and not merely as a symbol or act of commemoration), is a matter of course and needs no further discussion here.

The second meaning raises the question of the institution of the sacraments in Holy Scripture. This is unequivocal in the case of the two chief sacraments, Baptism and the Lord's Supper. As to Confirmation, the anointing of the sick, and ordination, the institution by Christ is certainly not expressly stated, but we read of the practice in fact in the time of the apostles. The question of institution cannot here be followed up in detail; it is not only the witness of the New Testament which has to be taken into consideration, but also the tradition of the Church (particularly the liturgical documents of the ancient Church). The most urgent question is that raised by the third meaning—namely the relation of the Sacrament to the proclamation of the Word. Is the Sacrament a part of the proclamation (merely a *Verbum visibile*), or is it something in itself?

The presence of Christ in His Church is manifest in the preaching of the Word as well as in the Sacrament. As in the Gospels Christ is shown in two aspects, namely, as the teacher (e.g. in the parables) and as the doer (e.g. in the healing of the sick), so He is also present in the Church in preaching and in action. Certainly in most cases of healing the Word of Jesus also plays an important part, not however as a teaching but as an acting Word. The objection could be made that teaching itself is action; but that easily gives rise to a confusion of ideas. There is a difference between, for example, Jesus telling a parable about relationships in the Kingdom of Heaven and Jesus giving back health to a sick man. Preaching awakens and establishes faith, but the healing word assumes it ('thy faith hath made thee whole'). So in the Church both are continued: preaching and action—Sermon and Sacrament. The former (as in a missionary sermon) calls the unbeliever to faith, or (as in a congregational sermon) strengthens the believer in his faith. The Sacrament, however, is always directed to the believer, with whom Christ deals in a special sense.

The efficacy of the Sacrament is not of a magical nature, because it is always the work of the personal Christ; it is not the act itself, or the signs and forms used, which do the work. Not only so, but the faith of the communicant is a necessary hypothesis, since we are considering not a magic force but God's gift of grace to the believer. A Word, too, is bound up with every dispensation of the Sacrament, but it is not a teaching word, but rather a declaration. It confirms what Christ is doing at that moment to that particular believer. It takes the proclamation for granted and is always directed to such as have already accepted the Word of God. It is not merely as a matter of form that each administration of the Sacrament is bound up with a visible act. That is the clearest way of pointing out that the Sacrament is quite distinct from the preaching of the Word. The significance of the visible sacramental signs must now be considered.

Sacrament and Symbol

In the liturgical service symbols are plentifully used, whether material symbols or symbolic acts. To the former belong, for instance, the candles, or the colours of the liturgical vestments, to the latter, signs of the cross, genuflexions, the laying on of hands, etc. Frequently both are used together, e.g. sprinkling with water or anointing with oil. Such symbols can exercise different functions. They can be a medium of proclamation: the flame of the sanctuary lamp tells us that Christ, the Light of the World, is at all times present in His Church. They can also express the spiritual attitude of the believer: kneeling, for example, or incense rising to heaven like the prayer of the congregation: 'May our prayer, O Lord, rise to Thee like a heavenly fragrance' (*Messbuch der Christkath. Kirche der Schweiz*)—or they may bring into sight the object of the prayer, as in the sprinkling of holy water. 'As the dew of heaven, O God, may Thy blessing descend upon us' (*ibid.*). Thus symbols supplement or interpret the spoken word, whether it be the Word preached to the congregation, or the words of the congregation's prayer to God.

The administration of the sacraments is also accompanied by symbols, not only in accessory ceremonies but in the central place. Baptism can only be administered with water, the Lord's Supper only with bread and wine. Mere words would not suffice for either. Thus the two chief sacraments conform to the clear command of the Lord.

Are, then, the Sacraments also 'symbolic acts'?

A symbol can eventually be understood by anybody, even by an unbeliever. It can if necessary be explained to him. Incense can also be offered to false gods, and candles be lit on pagan altars. Symbols are something universal to man and can be used in every sphere, even in the quite profane. The sacraments, however, can only be administered and received in the Church. Only the believer understands them. Symbols are signposts and means of expression. Sacraments, however, are reality, actual happenings. The signs accompanying them are more than just signposts; they not only symbolise God's grace, they also guarantee it. Symbols can lose all meaning if they become merely an external formality. Behind the sacramental sign, however, stands always the reality which is an act of God.

Sacrifice and Priesthood

Sacrifice in a Christian sense can only mean the sacrifice of God's Son on the Cross. Beside His, no sacrifice has value in itself. The sacrifice of Christ was made once for all, and needs no completion or repetition, and it is effectual henceforth for believers throughout time. This continuous efficacy of the sacrifice on the Cross is represented in the Church by the celebration of the Holy Eucharist. By receiving Holy Communion every believer is assured that Christ died for him too. Christ gives him a share in the sacrifice of His flesh and blood. The celebration of the Eucharist is accomplished by the celebrant, who thus, as it were, represents the sacrifice of Christ before God and before the congregation. He appeals before God on our behalf to the sacrifice of His Son. He represents it before the congregation, so that they may know themselves saved by this sacrifice. In this sense the celebrant of the Eucharist stands as a mediator between God and the believer; his mediation is not his own act, but a representation of the sacrifice of Christ and an appeal to it. This places the celebrant in a special position and therefore the Church has a special office for those to whom the representation of the sacred act is entrusted.

This office is a priestly one. Even the Old Testament priest did not sacrifice in the sense that he brought his own sacrifice; he rather brought before God the sacrifices of the believers. As these sacrificial gifts, however, were but earthly, they have faded away before the sacrifice of Christ. So the Old Testament priesthood has also decayed, since the One High Priest, Christ, was not standing behind it. The priest of the Church, however, has his office from Christ. Neither does he offer his own sacrificial gift, nor those of the believers, but he represents the sacrifice of Christ alone. He does this representatively: as the representative of Christ to the congregation, and as representative of the congregation before God. It is just this double position which makes the cele-brant's office a priestly one. The sole High Priesthood of Christ is not here encroached upon. For the priest of the Church does not himself sacrifice, but only represents the bringer of the one effectual sacrifice. His representative priesthood would be untenable if the Son of God did not stand as High Priest before the Father and evermore intercede for the believer.

★　　★　　★

N.B. *The above expositions do not represent any official utterance of the Old Catholic Church. The author believes, however, that he has given the point of view of his Church in essentials.*

Part Three

LITURGY AND DEVOTION

PREFACE

It would have been insufficient for the Commission to have confined itself to corporate worship without taking into account at least the impacts of such worship upon personal life. The Report (p. 23) observes that the test both of dogmatic positions and of their liturgical expression is often an 'existential' one. The attempt to confront a given situation in actual penitence, petition, or intercession will show clearly the true attitude of the worshipper to that challenge.

I. The clearest example of this marginal field, where liturgy and devotion interact, is perhaps found in the Church's regard for the person of the Blessed Virgin Mary, the Mother of our Lord. In Chapter IV of the Report of the Second World Conference on Faith and Order it was noted that 'the way in which we should understand the words "all generations shall call me blessed" was considered. No agreement was reached, and the subject requires further study.' In 1948 the Commission agreed that this matter was primarily a liturgical question, and considerable discussion of it took place in the following year.

The question is here discussed by four writers:

(a) A brief statement from the Roman Catholic standpoint.

(b) and (c) Papers from Orthodox and Anglican standpoints, originally contributed to a symposium The Mother of God, *edited E. L. Mascall (Dacre Press, 1949), and here reprinted by kind permission.*

(d) A longer statement prepared for the Commission in 1949.

II. The Commission further approved after full discussion a paper submitted by two members of the Anglican Church. This urged that an attempt to reach a common devotional understanding, and to share in the fundamental spirituality underlying the different traditions of Worship would be a valuable approach to the work of reunion, and supplementary to dogmatic and liturgical study. The practical steps proposed in this paper have now been begun, with the approval of the Executive Committee of the Commission on Faith and Order.

XVI

MARIOLOGY
(a) ROMAN CATHOLIC

★

Conrad Pepler, O.P.
(Great Britain)

'We should remember,' says St. Thomas Aquinas commenting
on the *Ave Maria*, 'that of old it was a very great thing for angels
to appear to men, and also was it the right thing for men to show
them reverence. Thus to the credit of Abraham it is written that
he showed hospitality to angels and reverenced them. But that
an angel had shown reverence to man was an unheard of thing
until the time when he reverently greeted the Blessed Virgin
saying: *Ave, Hail.*' Thus in the eyes of Catholic theologians the
veneration of our Lady began at the Annunciation when she was
accorded honour and respect by the messenger of God Himself.
And it is an undeniable fact that those first simple words of
Gabriel's have been taken up and repeated with such an increasing
volume and intensity that they become almost the hall mark of
the Catholic. These simple words of praise have found their echo
in every age. The third- and fourth-century pictures of the
Madonna surrounded in the glory of her nimbus, the excited cry
of the Ephesian populace when they learned that their veneration
of the Mother of God—*Theotokos*—was vindicated, the dedication
to the Blessed Virgin of some of the earliest churches after the
peace of Constantine, the consequent introduction of her feasts
into the calendar—all this reveals the fact not only of the close
association from early times between the sacred liturgy and the
veneration of the Virgin, but also that she was accorded a type
of honour and respect not apparently granted to any other human
being. To trace the development of this fact from those beginnings
until its mature intensity at the present time in the Catholic
Church need not occupy us here; it is too evident. The average
Catholic man or woman has shown his need for a spiritual Mother

not only in his private intercessions but also in his public worship of the Father, the Son and the Spirit.

This characteristic of Catholic life and worship came eventually to demand some explanation and some safeguards. The worship of the Virgin was evidently not to be confused with the worship in its strictest sense signifying the honour offered to God alone. By the thirteenth century Catholic theologians had invented a terminology to meet the facts. For it was clear that no Christian could worship the Virgin as he should worship God; it was clear equally that Christians as a general rule paid far greater respect to the Blessed Virgin than to any other individual appearing in the Church's calendar as worthy of veneration in the liturgy. To meet these facts the theologians said that the worship given to God was to be called *latria*, an adoration which was to be shown to God alone, or to the humanity of Christ as being one, with the divine person. The honour and worship paid to the saints was called *dulia*, a word adopted from the current Greek for veneration. And then, for lack of a better word, they called the type of greater respect shown to our Lady by the manufactured term *hyper-dulia*,[1] which simply means that the veneration shown to her is 'above' that shown to the ordinary saints. So far, then, as the facts are concerned it is obvious that Catholic veneration of the Virgin soars above and beyond that of any other saint.

These distinctions, however, were not invented as a kind of convenience to guard against idolatry on the one hand and to explain a quantitative difference in worship on the other. The honour paid to the Blessed Virgin and to the saints in the liturgy and devotion of the Church is one of the best examples of the union of prayer with dogma which is expressed by the phrase *lex orandi, lex credendi*. The distinctions between the different types of cult arise neither from a mere denial that the Christian adores our Lady, nor from a quantitative judgment of the actual extent of her cult compared with that of other saints; but they rest on the natures of those who are to be venerated and consequently upon the actual demands they make upon our respect. Almighty God does not—indeed cannot—leave us free to select what type of

---

[1] Not every Catholic theologian regards *hyper-dulia* as being different in kind from the *dulia* granted to the other saints. But in view of the great progress in the development of the doctrine concerning Mary's place in the redemption, it seems likely that those who deny it will become a minority.

honour we should show Him. He is man's creator, so that man depends on Him for the entirety of his being, his personality, and everything about him that is of any reality. Man is bound, there-fore, by the natural law according to which he is constructed and under which his life is to be conducted, to offer Him the complete subjection of all his powers of mind and will and of all his being. This he must do by means of an integral form of worship called 'sacrifice', rededicating his life to the author of life. No one but God may be offered this type of veneration, for no creature is, or could be, so subject to another creature, however elevated. Thus the sacrifice of the Mass, which is the most complete act of adoration, is never offered to our Lady, even though it is very frequently offered to God in her honour. This essential worship which springs from the roots of man's being has, as we have said, been called *latria* or adoration, rather as a scientist might decide to call a certain radiation 'alpha' as distinct from 'gamma'. The reality is there whatever the name, and no Christian in his senses would recognise the blessed Virgin Mary as the infinite author of his being, nor would the Church ever willingly permit such idolatry.

Creatures of God's making, however, have often some divine touch of beauty or holiness which entitles them to a special kind of respect. We must pass over here the veneration paid to the things that belong specifically to the Second Person of the Trinity, such as His humanity, or the cross upon which He died—created things which do receive some share of the adoration accorded to the Son of God; here we are concerned with a human creature, a human person. Now the nobility of a human person is something which is not simply an inanimate mirror of divine glory. We revere the memory of Shakespeare, not merely that of his 'muse'. For it is man's personal superiority or nobility that calls forth respect and esteem among his fellow human beings in different ways. The mayor's office as superior in a city entitles him to be called 'his worship'. So also just as a certain office or position demands honour, the presence of certain virtues in a person calls forth from his fellow men a respect which amounts to veneration. His holiness originates from God, but it is due in some measure also to his co-operation with God. So the saints gather round them the devotion and veneration of their fellow Christian creatures. These qualities can obviously never reach the independence and infinity which belong to God alone, but they can establish a man head and shoulders above his fellows. This honour or worship has been called, for the sake of a name, *dulia*; and, although it can be of all sorts according to the nature of the nobility revered, such as civil *dulia* or honour paid to a mayor or a king, we are speaking here of that special type of nobility which belongs to supernatural holiness. In this case particularly, the respect due to a person on account of the many graces he receives from God will be a respect which not only includes God in its orbit, but which also recognises a certain dependence upon the holy one under God.

Thus the veneration of a saint is not simply a question of telling him in respectful terms what a fine fellow he is, but also of asking him for certain favours which are his to share in some way with all who come to him. This is best seen in relation to the doctrine of the mystical body, without which neither liturgical worship nor the veneration of saints can be understood. Since these highly favoured men and women are so favoured precisely by reason of a greater share in the infinite life of God, their nobility is theirs not simply for themselves but also for all men who are joined to God in any way in this same divine life. The saints are, as it were, the particularly well-to-do members of a very closely knit and loyal family. The worship they receive, then, is one not only of praise but also of petition, so that the liturgy often pours forth a stream of prayers to them, as is often heard in the litany of the saints.

In such veneration our Lady very evidently shares. She is indeed a member of this heavenly nobility, and thus she necessarily enjoys great praise, and receives a great number of petitions. But it is also evident that, since her position in the plan of redemption is unique, her superiority must also be equally unique. We have seen how the Angel recognised the special veneration due to Mary even before she had become Mother of God. That was because, in Catholic belief, she was born immaculate and full of grace. But such nobility in Mary up to that moment might still have been regarded as being only in degree different from the nobility of other holy people who shared the same life, even though Mary had it to the fullest extent. But when she had become Mother of God and had become wholly bound up with her Son's work of redemption, beginning with her *Fiat* to the Angel and concluding with His *Fiat* on Calvary, shared so intimately by her, she had acquired nobility to which no other creature could attain. She became, in consequence, Mother of all Christians, and Queen of heaven; and as Catholics began to realise the uniqueness of her position, so veneration towards her deepened and expanded into something which was unique not merely quantitatively or in degree, as being accorded to her more than to any other saint, but also in its very nature. The liturgy became studded more and more with feasts of the Blessed Virgin Mary, a process which has continued to the present day as the theology of Mary's place in the plan of redemption continues still to develop. And Catholics naturally recognise a greater dependence upon their supernatural Mother than upon any other saint in heaven. They turn, therefore, in a unique way to their Mother, praising her for being the Mother of her Son, for being full of grace, for being the cause under Him of our joy and our salvation. For this reason, then, the Catholic worships our Lady in a way that he worships no one else[1]— certainly not in the way he worships God, but also not in the way he worships other creatures for God's sake. And this veneration arises not so much from anything in the worshipper, be it a psychological need for a 'universal Mother' or an emotional superstition stirred by visions and apparitions, but rather from the special veneration due to the qualities in herself, qualities which are of a different nature from those of other men. The Catholic does not worship the Virgin because the Church or his forefathers have urged him to do so, but because this unrivalled position and quality of the Mother of God calls out for a special veneration. Her honours and dignities are not put upon her from outside, as the idolater decorates his graven image with qualities from his own imagination. Mary the mother of Jesus radiates her special qualities from her person and draws this Catholic worship to herself. Catholic worship of the Virgin Mary, then, is something demanded, not something merely given. It is a unique type of *dulia* or honour which is called forth by the special nobility of the Mother of God and Queen of Heaven.

Yet that honour, in the eyes of the Catholic, can never be seen

[1] Many non-Catholics seem frightened of the word 'worship' as applied to our Lady. But it is an unwarranted restriction of its meaning to limit it to the idea of adoration. A glance at the Oxford English Dictionary will show that the word 'worship' may be used for any type of *dulia*.

as apart from God, still less as a rival to God's own honour. For Mary is the fairest of His creatures, and if she is praised for her beauty, so much the more praise and love does the Author receive. Every hymn to the Blessed Virgin leads the singer to the Father, and to her Son in the love of the Holy Spirit. *Corde et animo*, the Church says in her liturgy, 'In heart and spirit we sing glory to Christ in this celebration sacred to the super-excellent Mother of God—Mary.'

XVI

MARIOLOGY
(b) ORTHODOX

★

Vladimir Lossky[1]
(France)

I

It is very hard, if not impossible, for an Orthodox theologian who
has to speak about the Mother of God to limit himself to one of
the three groups of materials to be employed, and to be concerned
with *either* scriptural, *or* dogmatic, *or* devotional data. The three
are indissolubly linked together in the life of the Church, where
devotion, Scripture, and dogma are present simultaneously in
theological thought, as it seeks to be (as far as it can be) aware of
all that the Church has. The question which is our subject now
(her all-Holiness) is one about which the dogmatic and scriptural
data, taken by themselves, are inadequate for our purpose; on the
other hand, the devotional data are so rich and complex as to be
incomprehensible, if not treated in connection with the two other
groups of materials.

If we were to limit ourselves to the dogmatic data, in the strict
sense of the word, and were dealing only with dogmas affirmed by
the Councils, we should find nothing except the name *Theotokos*,
whereby the Church has solemnly confirmed the divine maternity
of the Holy Virgin.[2] The dogmatic subject of the *Theotokos*, as
the name was affirmed against the Nestorians, is Christological
before it is anything else; that which is thereby defended against
the gainsayers of the divine maternity is the hypostatic unity of

---

[1] This paper appeared in *The Mother of God*, edited by E. L. Mascall (Dacre
Press, 1949), and is reprinted by kind permission of author and publishers.

[2] The term 'ever-virgin', which is found in the Conciliar Acts from the
Fifth Council onwards, has not been expounded by the Councils which have
used it in any special sense.

the Son of God, when He had become the Son of Man. It is Christology which is directly envisaged here; it is indirectly that at the same time there is a dogmatic confirmation of the Church's devotion to her who bore God according to the flesh. It is said that all those who rise up against the appellation *Theotokos*, all who refuse to admit that Mary has this quality given to her, are not truly Christians, for they oppose the true doctrine of the Incarnation of the Word. This should demonstrate the close connection between dogma and devotion, which are inseparable in the Church. However, we know instances of Christians who, while recognising for purely Christological reasons the divine maternity of the Holy Virgin, abstain from all special devotion to the Mother of God for the same reasons, desiring to know no other Mediator between God and Man save the God-man, Jesus Christ. This suffices to demonstrate that the Christological dogma of the *Theotokos* by itself—taken in the abstract, apart from the vital connection between it and the devotion paid by the Church to the Mother of God—would not be enough to justify the unique position, above all created beings, assigned to the Queen of Heaven, to whom the Orthodox liturgy ascribes the glory which is appropriate to God ($\dot{\eta}$ Θεοπρεπὴς δόξα). It is therefore impossible to separate the dogmatic data, in the strict sense, from the data of the Church's cultus, in a theological exposition of the doctrine about the Mother of God. Here dogma should throw light on the cultus, and the cultus should enrich the dogmatic aspect of the subject with the Church's living experience.

II

We are in the same position in relation to the biblical data. If we desired to consider biblical evidence apart from the Church's devotion to the Mother of God, we should be obliged to limit ourselves to the few New Testament passages relating to Mary and the one Old Testament passage cited in the New Testament with reference to her (the prophecy of the Virgin-Birth of the Messiah in Isaiah). But, if we look at the Bible through the prism of the Church's devotion, or (to use the proper terms at last) in the *tradition* of the Church, then the sacred books of both Testaments will supply us with innumerable texts used by the Church to glorify the Mother of God.

However, here there is something that may seem to be trouble-some for us. Some passages in the Gospels, if viewed externally, from a point of view outside church tradition, seem to contradict quite flagrantly the extreme glorification and unlimited veneration of the *Theotokos* in the Church. Let us take two examples. Christ, when bearing witness to John the Baptist, calls him the greatest of them that are born of women. It is therefore to him, and not to Mary, that the highest position among human beings should belong (Matt. 11. 11; Luke 7. 28). Actually, in the practice of the Church, we find the Baptist with the Mother of God on the two sides of the Lord in the δέησις ikons: but the Church has never exalted St. John the Forerunner above the Seraphim, nor has she ever placed his ikon on a footing of equality with the ikon of Christ, as the ikon of the Mother of God and the ikon of Christ stand on the two sides of the entrance into the sanctuary in Orthodox churches.

Another passage in the Gospels shows us Christ publicly oppos-ing the glorification of His Mother. He answers the exclamation of the woman in the crowd who cries out, 'Blessed be the womb that bare thee, and the paps that thou hast sucked,' by saying, 'Yea, rather, Blessed are they that hear the Word of God, and keep it' (Luke 11. 27-28). But it is just this passage in St. Luke, seeming to abase the fact of the divine maternity below the quality of those who receive and keep the divine revelation—this very text which is read as the Gospel in the liturgy on the festivals of the Mother of God, as if under its seemingly negative form it hid an even greater act of praise.

Again we face the impossibility of separating dogma from life and Scripture from tradition. Christological dogma obliges us to recognise the divine maternity of the Virgin. Scriptural evidence teaches us that the glory of the Mother of God does not reside merely in her corporal maternity, in the fact of her having carried and fed the Incarnate Word. Then church tradition, the holy memory of those who 'hear the Word of God, and keep it', gives to the Church the assurance with which she exalts the Mother of God, ascribing to her an unlimited glory.

Apart from church tradition, theology would be dumb on this subject and unable to justify this astounding glorification. That is why Christian communities which reject the idea of tradition in every form are also alien to the cult of the Mother of God.

The close connection between tradition and all that concerns the Mother of God is not simply due to the fact that events of her earthly life, such as her nativity, her presentation in the Temple, and her assumption, are celebrated by the Church without being mentioned in the Bible. If the Gospel is silent about these facts, and if their poetical amplification is due to apocryphal books of late date, still the foundation theme which they signify belongs to the mystery of our faith and is not to be taken away from the Church's consciousness. The notion of tradition is richer than we habitually think. Tradition does not merely consist of an oral transmission of facts capable of supplementing the biblical narrative. It is the complement of the Bible, and above all it is the fulfilment of the Old Testament in the New Testament, as the Church becomes aware of it. It is tradition which confers the power of comprehension of the meaning of revealed truth (Luke 24. 45). Tradition tells us what we must hear and, still more important, how we must keep what we hear. In this general sense, tradition implies an incessant operation of the Holy Spirit, who could have His full outpouring and bear His fruits only in the Church, after the Day of Pentecost. It is only in the Church that we find that we are capable of tracing the inner connections between the sacred texts which make the Old Testament and the New Testament into a single living *corpus* of truth, wherein Christ is present in each word. It is only in the Church that the seed sown by the Word is not barren, but brings forth fruit, and this fruitfulness of truth, as well as its capacity for being fruitful, is called tradition. The cultus of the Mother of God which, viewed externally, might seem to be in contradiction with the biblical data, is spread far and wide in the tradition of the Church and is the most precious fruit of tradition.

But it is not only the fruit of tradition; it is also the germ and the stem of tradition. We can find a definite relationship between the person of the Mother of God and what we call the tradition of the Church. Let us try, in setting forth this relationship, to see the glory of the Mother of God beneath the veil of the silence of the Bible. We shall be led to this by an examination of the inner connection between the texts.

St. Luke, in a passage which is parallel to the one we have already quoted, shows us Christ refusing to see His Mother and His brethren, and declaring that 'My mother and my brethren are they that hear the word of God, and do it' (Luke 8. 19-21). The context is significant; in St. Luke, at the moment when the Mother of God desires to see her Son, He has just finished the parable of the Sower. In St. Mark and St. Matthew, the parable of the Sower follows immediately after the episode of the Mother and brethren of the Lord. The connection is equally evident (Matt. 12-13; Mark 3-4). 'The seed . . . on the good ground are they which in an honest and good heart, having heard the Word, keep it, and bring forth fruit with patience.' 'He that hath ears to hear, let him hear.' 'Take heed therefore how ye hear: for whosoever hath, to him shall be given; and whosoever hath not, from him shall be taken away even that which he seemeth to have' (Luke 8. 8, 15, 18). Now, it is the faculty of keeping the words heard concerning Christ in an honest and good heart, the faculty which elsewhere Christ exalted above the fact of her corporal maternity, which the Gospel attributes to no individual except the Mother of the Lord. St. Luke insists upon it, as he notices it twice in his Infancy narrative: 'Mary kept all these sayings, and gathered them in her heart' (Luke 2. 19, 51). She who gave birth to God Incarnate kept in her memory all the testimonies to the divine nature of her Son. We could say that we have here a personification of church tradition before the Church was, were it not that St. Luke is careful to tell us that Mary and Joseph did not understand the saying of the Child, that He must be about His Father's business (Luke 2. 49-50). Therefore the meaning of the sayings kept faithfully in her heart by the Mother of God had not been fully realised in her consciousness. Before the consummation of the work of Christ at the Day of Pentecost with the birth of the Church, even she upon whom the Holy Spirit had come down to fit her for her part in the Incarnation of the Word had not yet attained the fulness of life which it was her vocation to attain. All the same, it is already possible to see the connection between the Mother of God, as she keeps and collects together the prophetic sayings, and the Church, as she keeps tradition. One is the germinal form of the other reality. Only the Church, the complement of Christ's humanity, will be able to keep the fulness of revealed truth which, if it were entirely committed to writing, could not be contained within the space of the whole world (John 21. 25). Only the Mother of God, she who was chosen to carry God in her womb, could fully realise in her mind all the import of the Incarnation of the Word, which was also the fact of her own divine maternity.

Those sayings of Christ, which seem so harsh to His mother, are sayings which exalt the quality which she has in common with the sons of the Church. But while they, as guardians of tradition, can only more or less become conscious of the truth and make it fruitful in them, the Mother of God, by virtue of the unique relationship between her and God, whom she can call her Son, can alone rise here below to a complete consciousness of all that the Holy Spirit says to the Church, reaching this plenitude in her own person. But this complete consciousness of God, this acquisition of the fulness of grace appropriate to the age to come, could only happen to a deified being. This places before us a new question, which we shall try to answer so that the special character of the Orthodox Church's devotion to the Sovereign Queen of Heaven can be better understood.

III

Christ, when bearing witness to John the Baptist, called him 'the greatest of them that are born of women', but He added, 'He that is least in the Kingdom of Heaven is greater than he.' Here Old Testament holiness is contrasted with the holiness that could be realised when the redemptive work of Christ was done and when 'the promise of the Father' (Acts I. 2, 4), the descent of the Holy Spirit, had filled the Church with the fulness of deifying grace. St. John, although 'more than a prophet', because he baptised the Lord and saw the heavens opened and the Spirit like a dove descending on the Son of Man, died not having received the promise, like all the other witnesses in the faith, 'of whom the world was not worthy', who, according to the divine plan, 'could not be made perfect without us' (Heb. II. 37-40). 'Without us' means without the Church of Christ. It is only through the Church that the holiness of the Old Testament can receive its fulfilment in the age to come, in a perfection which was inaccessible to men before Christ.

Incontestably she who was chosen to be the Mother of God was at the summit of Old Testament holiness. If St. John the Baptist is called 'the greatest' of those before Christ, that is because the greatness of the most holy Mother of God belongs not only to

the Old Testament, where it is hidden and does not appear, but
also to the Church where it will be fully realised and manifested,
to be glorified by all generations (Luke 1. 48). The person of St.
John remains in the Old Testament dispensation; the most holy
Virgin passes from the Old Covenant to the New, and this transition in the person of the Mother of God shows us how the New
Covenant is the fulfilment of the Old.

The Old Testament is not only a series of prefigurations of
Christ, which become decipherable after the Good News has
come. Before it is that, it is the history of the preparation of the
human race for the coming of Christ, a story in which human
freedom is constantly put to the trial by God. The obedience of
Noah, the sacrifice of Abraham, the Exodus of God's people under
the leadership of Moses, the journey through the desert, the Law
and the Prophets, constitute a series of divine elections, in which
some human beings remain faithful to the promise made to them,
and others fail to be faithful, so that they suffer punishments (the
captivity and the destruction of the first temple). All the sacred
history and tradition of the Jews is the tale of the slow and
laborious journey of fallen humanity towards the 'fulness of
time', when the angel was to be sent to announce to the chosen
Virgin the coming Incarnation of God and to hear from her lips
the human act of consent to that which the divine plan of salvation
accomplishes. Thus, according to a saying of St. John of Damascus,
'The name of the Mother of God contains all the history of the
divine economy in this world' (*De Fid. Orth.*, III, 12, P.G. 94,
1029-32).

This divine economy preparing the human conditions for the
Incarnation of the Son of God is not a unilateral one; it is not a
matter of the will of God making a *tabula rasa* of human history.
In this saving economy Divine Wisdom is adapted to the fluctua-
tions of human wills and to the different responses of men to the
divine challenge. It is thus that Wisdom hath built herself a house
through the generations of the Old Testament righteous men;
her house is the all-pure nature of the Holy Virgin, whereby the
Word of God will become co-natural with us. The answer of
Mary to the angelic annunciation, 'Behold the handmaid of the
Lord; be it unto me according to thy word', resolves the tragic
problem of fallen humanity. All that God required of human
liberty since the Fall is accomplished. And now the work of re-

demption, which only the Incarnate Word can effect, may take place. Nicholas Cabasilas said, in his homily on the Annunciation, 'The Incarnation was not only the work of the Father and of His Virtue and His Spirit; it was also the work of the will and faith of the Virgin. Without the consent of the all-pure and the co-operation of her faith, this design would have been as unrealisable as it would have been without the intervention of the three Divine Persons themselves. Only after teaching and persuading her does God take her for His Mother and receive from her the flesh which she wills to offer to Him. Just as He voluntarily became Incarnate, so He willed that His Mother should bear Him freely, with her own full and free consent' (Jugie's edition, *Patr. Orient.* XIX, 2).

From St. Justin and St. Irenaeus onwards the Fathers have often drawn attention to the contrast between the 'two virgins', Eve and Mary. By the disobedience of the first, death entered into the world. By the obedience of the second Eve, the Author of life became Man and entered into the family of Adam. But between the two Eves lies all the story of the Old Testament, the past from which she who has become the Mother of God cannot be divided. If she was chosen to take a unique part in the work of the Incarnation, that choice followed and concluded a whole series of other acts of election and a line of chosen people by whom it was prepared. It is not for nothing that the Orthodox Church, in her liturgical texts, calls David 'the ancestor of God' and gives the same name of 'the holy and just ancestors of God' to Joachim and Anna. The Roman Catholic dogma of the Immaculate Conception, as it is unfortunately formulated, seems to break up this uninterrupted succession of instances of Old Testament holiness, which reaches its term at the moment of the Annunciation, when the Holy Spirit came down upon the Virgin to make her fit to receive the Word in her womb. The Orthodox Church does not admit the idea that the Holy Virgin was thus exempted from the lot of the rest of fallen humanity, the idea of a privilege making her into a being ransomed before the redemptive work, by virtue of the future merits of her Son. It is not in virtue of a privilege received at the moment of her conception by her parents that we venerate the Mother of God more than any other created being. She was holy and pure from her mother's womb, but not with a sanctity which places her outside the rest of humanity-before-Christ. She was not in a state analogous to that of Eve before the

Fall at the moment of the Annunciation. The first Eve, 'The mother of all living', lent her ear to the sayings of the seducer in the state of paradise, the state of innocent humanity. The second Eve, she who was chosen to become the Mother of God, heard and understood the angelic saying when she was in the state of fallen humanity. That is why this unique election does not separate her from the rest of humanity and from all her fathers, mothers, brothers, and sisters, whether saints or sinners, whose best part she represented.

Like other human beings, such as St. John the Baptist, whose conception and birth are festivals of the Church, the Holy Virgin was born under the law of original sin, sharing with all other human beings their common responsibility for the fall. But sin never could become actual in her person; the sinful heritage of the fall had no mastery over her right will. Here was the highest point of holiness that could be attained before Christ, in the conditions of the Old Covenant, by one of Adam's seed. She was without sin under the universal sovereignty of sin, pure from every seduction in a humanity enslaved by the prince of this world. She was not placed above history in order to serve a special divine decree; she realised her unique vocation while in the chains of history, sharing the common destiny of all men awaiting salvation. And yet, if in the person of the Mother of God we see the highest peak of Old Testament holiness, her own holiness is not limited thereby, for she also surpassed just as much the highest peaks of the holiness of the New Covenant, and realised the greatest sanctity which the Church can attain.

IV

The first Eve was taken out of Adam; she was one who, at the moment of her creation by God, took unto herself the nature of Adam, to be complementary to him. We find an inverse relationship in the case of the New Eve; through her the Son of God became the Last Adam, by taking unto Himself human nature. Adam was before Eve; the Last Adam was after the New Eve. But we cannot say that the humanity assumed by Christ was a complement of the humanity of His Mother. It is the humanity of a divine Person, that of the Heavenly Man (I Cor. 15. 47-48). The human nature of the Mother of God belongs to a created

person, who is engendered of the issue of the earthly man. It is
not the Mother of God, but her Son, who is the Head of the new
humanity, as 'he is the Head of the body, the Church, which is
his body'; the Church is the complement of His humanity (Eph.
1. 22-23). Therefore it is through her Son, and in His Church, that
the Mother of God could attain the perfection reserved for those
who should bear the image of the Heavenly Man (I Cor. 15. 49).

We have already indicated a close connection between the person of the Mother of God and the Church, when speaking of
tradition as personified, as it were, by her, before the Church
existed. She who bore God according to the flesh also kept in her
heart all the sayings that revealed the divine nature of her Son.
This is a testimony concerning the spiritual life of the Mother of
God. It shows us that she was not simply an instrument, who
willingly let herself be used in the Incarnation; she was also a person who sought to realise, in her own consciousness, the meaning
of the fact of her divine maternity. After having offered her human
nature to the Son of God, she sought to receive through Him that
which she did not yet have in common with Him, participation
in the divine nature. It is in her Son that the fulness of the Godhead dwelt bodily (Col. 2. 9). The natural connection which
linked her to the God-man did not, in itself, confer upon her
person the state and privilege of deification, although the Holy
Spirit came to her to make her fit to accomplish her unique task.
In this sense, the Mother of God, as she was before the day of
Pentecost, and before the Church was, still belonged to the
humanity of the Old Testament, and was among those who waited
for the promise of the Father, expecting to be baptised with the
Holy Spirit (Acts 1. 4-5).

Tradition shows us the Mother of God in the midst of the
disciples on the day of Pentecost, receiving with them the Holy
Spirit, who was communicated to each of them as a distinct
cloven tongue of fire. This agrees with the testimony of the Acts
(1. 14; 2. 1). After the ascension the apostles 'continued together
with one accord in prayer, with the women, and with Mary the
Mother of Jesus, and with his brethren'. 'They were all together
with one accord in one place on the day of Pentecost.' The Mother
of God received, with the Church, the last and only thing she
lacked, so that she might grow 'into a perfect man, to the measure
of the stature of the fulness of Christ' (Eph. 4. 13).

V

She who by the power of the Holy Spirit received the divine Person of the Son of God into her womb, now receives the Holy Spirit, as He is sent by the Son. The two descents of the Holy Spirit upon the Holy Virgin may be compared, in the one sense, to the two communications of the Spirit to the apostles, one on the evening of the day of Resurrection and the other on the day of Pentecost. The first of these conferred on the apostles the power to bind and to loose; this is a function independent of their subjective qualities; it is closely due to the divine decree which selects them to play this particular part in the life of the Church. The second communication of the Spirit, at Pentecost, gave to each of the receivers the possibility of realising his or her own personal sanctity; that will always depend on subjective personal conditions. But the two communications of the Spirit, that which is functional and that which is personal, are mutually complementary. One can see this in the apostles and their successors; no one can fulfil his function in the Church well, unless he is striving to acquire holiness; on the other hand, it is hard for anyone to attain holiness if he neglects the function in which God has placed him. The two should coincide more and more as life goes on; one's function (or vocation) normally becomes a way by which one acquires selflessness and personal sanctity. We can see something analogous in the otherwise unique instance of the Mother of God: the objective function of her divine maternity, in which she was placed on the day of her Annunciation, will be her personal way of sanctification. She will realise in her consciousness, and in all her personal life, the meaning of the fact of her having carried in her womb and having nourished at her breast the Son of God. It is thus that the words of Christ which appear to abase His Mother, in comparison with the Church, receive their true meaning as words spoken in supreme praise of her; blessed is she who not only was the Mother of God but also realised in her person the degree of holiness corresponding to that unique function. The person of the Mother of God is exalted more than her function, and the completion of her holiness receives more praise than its beginning.

The function of the divine maternity has been fulfilled in the past; but the Holy Virgin, still on earth after the Ascension of her

Son, remains, as much as ever, the Mother of Him who, in His glorious humanity, is seated at the right hand of the Father, 'far above all principalities and powers and dominions, and above every name that can be named, not only in this world, but also in that which is to come' (Eph. 1. 21). What degree of holiness, able to be realised here below, could possibly correspond to the unique relationship of the Mother of God to her Son, when as the Head of the Church He dwells in the heavenly places? Only the entire and total holiness of the Church, the complement of the glorified humanity of Christ, containing the plenitude of deifying grace, communicated ceaselessly since Pentecost to the Church by the Holy Spirit. The members of the Church can enter into a family relationship with Christ; they can be His mother, brothers, and sisters (Matt. 12. 50), in the measure of their accomplishment of their vocations. But only the Mother of God, through whom the Word was made flesh, will be able to receive the plenitude of grace and to attain an unlimited glory, by realising in her person all the holiness of which the Church is capable.

<h2 style="text-align:center">VI</h2>

The Son of God came down from heaven and was made man through the Holy Virgin, in order that men might be able to rise to deification by the grace of the Holy Spirit. 'To have by grace what God has by nature': that is the supreme vocation of created beings and the final destiny to which the sons of the Church aspire here below, the destiny of the Church in history. This destiny is already reached in the divine person of Christ, the Head of the Church, risen and ascended. If the Mother of God could truly realise, in her human and created person, the sanctity which corresponds to her unique role, then she cannot have failed to attain here below by grace all that her Son had by His divine nature. But, if it be so, then the destiny of the Church and the world has already been reached, not only in the uncreated person of the Son of God but also in the created person of His Mother. That is why St. Gregory Palamas calls the Mother of God 'the boundary between the created and the uncreated'. Beside the incarnate divine hypostasis there is a deified human hypostasis.

We have said above that in the person of the Mother of God it is possible to see the transition from the holiness of the Old

Testament to the holiness of the Church. But, if the all-Holy Mother of God has reached and consummated the holiness of the Church, and all holiness which is possible for a created being, we are now concerned with yet another transition: that is the transition from the world of becomings and historical destinies to the eternity of the Eighth Day, the passage from the Church to the Kingdom of God. This last glory of the Mother of God, the *eschaton* realised in a created person before the end of the world, places the Mother of God, now in this time, beyond death, beyond the resurrection, and beyond the Last Judgment. She participates in the glory of her Son, reigns with Him, presides at His side over the destinies of the Church in time, and intercedes on behalf of all before Him who will come again to judge the quick and the dead.

This supreme transition, by which the Mother of God rejoins her Son in His celestial glory, is celebrated by the Church on the day of the Feast of the Assumption; on that day the Church thinks of a death which, according to her inner conviction, could not but have been followed by the corporal resurrection and ascension of the Most-holy One. It is hard to speak and not less hard to think about the mysteries which the Church keeps in the hidden depths of her inner consciousness. Here every uttered word can seem crude; every attempt at formulation can seem sacrilegious. The authors of the apocryphal writings often alluded imprudently to mysteries about which the Church had maintained a prudent silence, for the sake of the salvation of those outside the Church. The Mother of God was never a theme of the public preaching of the apostles; while Christ was preached on the house-tops, and proclaimed for all to know in an initiatory teaching addressed to the whole world, the mystery of His Mother was revealed only to those who were within the Church, the faithful who had received the sayings of Christ and were pressing towards 'the high calling of God in Christ Jesus' (Phil. 3. 14). It is not so much an object of faith as a foundation of our hope, a fruit of faith, ripened in tradition.

Let us therefore keep silence, and let us not try to dogmatise about the supreme glory of the Mother of God. Let us not be too loquacious, like the Gnostics, who wanted to say far more than it was needful to say, because they had mingled their heretical tares with the pure wheat of the Christian tradition. Let us rather listen to St. Basil when he described that which appertains to tradition by saying that it was 'an unpublishable and ineffable teaching, which was preserved by our fathers in silence, so as to be inaccessible to all curiosity or indiscretion, for they had been healthily instructed how to protect, by silence, the holiness of the mystery. It would not be proper to publish in writing the teaching given about things which ought not to be seen by the eyes of the uninitiated. Apart from that, the reason for an unwritten tradition is that many people who often inspect what is contained in these teachings are in danger of losing their veneration for the things concerned by becoming used to them. For there is a difference between teaching and public preaching. Teachings are to be kept in silence; public preaching is to be made manifest. A certain obscurity in the language of the Scriptures is another way of keeping silence; thus the meaning of the teachings is made harder to understand, for the benefit of those who read them.'

If the teaching about the Mother of God appertains to tradition, it is only through our experience of life in the Church that we can adhere to the unlimited devotion which the Church offers to the Mother of God; the degree of our adhesion to this devotion will be the measure of the extent to which we belong to the body of Christ.

XVI

MARIOLOGY
(c) ANGLICAN

★

T. M. Parker[1]
(Great Britain)

If I were asked to name one thing upon which in devotional ethos
the Eastern Orthodox and the Western Catholic traditions were
most at one I think that I should choose Marian devotion as that
meeting point. In many matters there is a greater unity between
the central tradition of the East and the central tradition of the
West than appears at first sight, matters in which the very obvious
outward differences obscure a oneness which is really there. (This
is true, for example, in eucharistic practice, I should say.) There
are other matters in which a superficial resemblance cloaks a real
difference. (I think myself that this is probably the case in regard
to some sides of sacramental theology or of Trinitarian doctrine.)
But, if there is a field of Christian thought and life in which the
two outlooks and the ways of expressing them are fundamentally
one, it is, I would claim, to be found especially in devotion to our
Lady. That unity does not lie in detailed resemblance; there are
hardly two prayers to Mary common to East and West, and there
appears at first sight to be a real contrast between the popular
Western image of the Blessed Virgin and the ordinary type of
Eastern ikon of her. Yet those obvious divergencies are superficial
in the strictest sense of the word; they have no more significance
than the differences between two brothers' handwritings or the
various forms in which common features are transmitted in a
family. In general, I do not believe that the simple Western worshipper and the simple Eastern worshipper would find anything
strange or repugnant in the way in which the other approaches
their common Mother, were they to join in Marian devotions—a

[1] This paper appeared in *The Mother of God*, edited by E. L. Mascall (Dacre
Press, 1949), and is reprinted by kind permission of author and publishers.

conclusion which finds symbolic expression in those shrines in Eastern Europe which draw pilgrims from both communions.

I am speaking of course primarily of those parts of the West in which there has been no break in continuity of the popular tradition of Marian devotion, when I say that here there is the minimal difference between East and West. In the Anglican area of Western Christendom it would be idle to deny that there has been such a break, even though the tradition has never become quite extinct. There has never been any formal condemnation of devotion to the Mother of God by the Church of England; there have almost always been, from the sixteenth century onwards, a few who have practised it. Yet one swallow does not make a summer, and, if we are to look at the matter objectively and dispassionately as we should, we must face the fact that prayer to our Lady was, for something like three centuries, the exception rather than the rule in Anglican devotion. Such a gap is bound to have its effects, and consequently we cannot take England as a norm if we are considering the relationship of East and West in this matter. I shall have more to say about this later on, but, in order to remove misconceptions, it is necessary to make the point at once. I am not now therefore comparing specifically *Anglican* habits with Orthodox in the review I am making.

When this has been said, I maintain that I am justified in claiming that East and West have diverged less upon the matter of devotion to the Mother of God than upon many, or perhaps most, others. If so, to what are we to attribute the fact? I suggest that it results from two vital causes:

1. A unity in doctrine
2. A unity in religious instinct

1. The chief difficulty felt by any Protestant about both Orthodox and Catholic veneration for our Lady is that it seems to him a kind of excrescence upon Christian faith and Christian prayer. Even if he gets over the notion that other Christians regard Mary as a goddess and that their prayers to her are idolatrous, he still cannot see any necessity in them. If *he* can, as he thinks, live his spiritual life fervently and successfully without much thought of Christ's Mother, why should others find it necessary continually to mention her, still more to pray to her? How should we from our different backgrounds answer him? Surely by calling his

attention to the place of Mary in the economy of redemption. We should, I take it, say quite simply that, since in the fulness of time 'God sent forth his Son, made of a woman, . . . that we might receive the adoption of sons' (Gal. 4. 4-5), one cannot ignore that fact, least of all when one is praying the prayer of sonship. In other words, Mary of Nazareth was not just a dim figure in the story of redemption but a cardinal factor in it, since it was from her, and not from anyone or anything else, that God the Son took human nature. For, as Bede, the Englishman, points out, the true reading of the verse is '*Made* of a woman', not 'born of a woman', 'because, being conceived from the Virgin's womb, He did not take His flesh from nothingness, nor from some external source, but from His Mother's flesh. Otherwise He could not properly be called Son of man, if He did not have His origin from a human being.'[1] The Blessed Virgin then is not an extraneous figure in the story of human salvation, but a chief actress in the drama, who plays a key part. To forget her in the choric function of worship which we perform in the play is like ignoring Jocasta in *Oedipus Rex*.

Such, I take it, is the answer any Orthodox would make to a Protestant critic, just as it is the reply which any Western Catholic would return to him. But, if so, that argues a degree of doctrinal agreement which can only be termed complete unity of belief. We are alike in our practice because our faith is one and our comprehension of that faith is identical.

Yet equally, I believe that we should both make that answer with some astonishment at its necessity, however much experience might have shown us that it is constantly called for in all parts of Europe influenced by the Reformation. It is always surprising to find that someone else regards as abnormal something which seems to oneself the most natural thing in the world. We may know theoretically that there are communities in which family ties count for very little; yet it always comes as a shock to be asked such a question as: 'Why do you want to see your mother so often?' Something like this is the reaction of any Orthodox or Catholic to his Protestant brother's desire for a reason for his ikon of the *Theotokos* or his 'Hail Mary'; such things seem to us

[1] . . . *quia, conceptus ex utero virginali, carnem non de nihilo, non aliunde, sed materna traxit ex carne. Alioquin nec vere Filius hominis diceretur, qui originem non haberet ex homine.* (Lib. 4, cap. 49 in Luc. 11.)

the most obvious necessities of any Christian devotion, a necessary part of the worship of anyone who seriously believes in the Incarnation. This is what I mean when I speak of a unity of religious instinct between East and West upon this matter. It would seem abnormal to any of us brought up in these traditions *not* to bring Mary into our prayers; it would be omission, and not practice, of such devotion which would seem to us to need defence.

These considerations are of importance, not only in thinking about the relations of East and West, but also in trying to define the conditions of a sound devotion to Mary. For there are and have been false forms of such devotion. Ignoring such eccentricities of heresy as the cake offerings of the Collyridians (who did apparently do what we are accused of doing, and treated Mary as divine) we may notice a few aberrations of this age-long Christian practice.

(*a*) There is the type of Christian who treats devotion to our Lady as something apart from the rest of Christian prayer, who indulges in prayers to her only upon special occasions, and then without much reference to the mysteries of faith. This might be summed up as the attitude which thinks that prayers to our Lady are to be said only in the Lady Chapel or only upon feasts of our Lady. Such an outlook is perhaps rare—though one can detect it in some Anglicans, to whom Marian prayers are always 'occasional offices'—and is never fully conscious. But it does exist.

(*b*) Then there is the person who reveres Mary, not as the Mother of God, but as merely a type of ideal womanhood—to whom (once again to use a picturesque image) the figure of the Babe seems unnecessary in an image or ikon of her. Curiously enough this is the commonest error made by those who have just begun to advance beyond the Evangelical suspicion of all devotional mention of the Blessed Virgin. It usually takes the form of a delicate, but rather empty, pseudo-mediaeval chivalry and is, I think, the kind of attitude to which Chesterton was referring when he said that, in the Unitarian circles in which he was brought up, when Mary was mentioned she was always called 'the Madonna'.

(*c*) There is again the man who prays to Mary primarily for controversial purposes, because other people do not—rather as some of the Jews of old fasted 'for strife and debate, and to smite with the fist of wickedness' (Isa. 58. 4). . . . Occasionally one finds the person whose devotion to our Lady seems an argument rather than a prayer.

(*d*) Finally there are those who seem to pray to Mary simply for what they can get, and not primarily to honour her. There has been from time to time the lurking notion that our Lady is more easygoing than God and will obtain favours from Him which He would rather we did not have—a Mother who spoils her children and overcomes the wiser generosity of our Father. From this came probably the one justifiable criticism of popular devotion to Mary made at the Reformation, amongst many that were captious or untrue. But it cannot be denied that such a repulsive distortion of the idea of invocation of our Lady did exist in the Middle Ages and indeed still does exist.

All these aberrations are predominantly Western, and the first three to be found more often among Anglicans than among Roman Catholics. . . . I think that they can throw more light upon the true bases of devotion to Mary than anything else. For what have they all in common? Two things: a forgetfulness of dogma and a lack of naturalness. For, to take them one by one, to make of devotion to Mary a thing apart, or to reverence her merely as a type of the eternal feminine, or to treat her just as a symbol of Christian divisions, or to make use of her without loving her—all these errors come from forgetting that she is the Mother of God. And, equally, none of these false approaches to her is a natural one; each is highly artificial and perverse. And therefore I suggest that the two touchstones of genuine devotion to our Lady are, firstly, the proportion of faith, and secondly, childlike spontaneity. Whenever either of these is lacking, still more when both are absent, there is danger of wrong devotion and usually more than just danger. You must approach Mary as you approach God—with faith and as a little child.

Let us look a little more closely at this phrase, 'Mother of God' —for it seems to frighten many worthy people. It is quite extraordinary to what lengths they will go to avoid it without actually falling into heresy. Thus they will say that it has an un-English ring about it—and therefore try to substitute for it *Theotokos*, which explains what is meant so much better to the simple Englishman. Or they will invent uncouth neologisms like 'Birth-giver of God'. . . . Yet the expression 'Mother of God' conveys accurately, to anyone who is at all acquainted with Christian dogma, the unique privilege of Mary in a way that no other English expression does. The suggestion that its use will revive paganism, by causing the simple to imagine that Mary is the Mother of God in the sense that Juno was the mother of Mars, seems to me as far-fetched as the fears which beset Lewis Carroll's White Knight. (Indeed there is always a strong suggestion of the White Knight about some of the precautions of the more conventional moderate Anglicans—the White Knight with his mouse trap to catch mice which might run over his horse and the spiked anklets which guarded his charger from the bites of sharks. For they never try to protect us from really credible dangers. To anyone familiar with the Anglican layman, the notion that he might be beguiled into pagan theogonies is as heartily amusing as a suggestion that he needs to be guarded from ruining his health by undue asceticism.) It is noteworthy that Arabic-speaking Christians (who from their constant exposure to Moslem criticism might be expected to be more than usually sensitive to accusations of pagan anthropomorphism) quite roundly call Mary 'Mother of God' in a phrase which has the same connotation as the English one. The truth is that the ordinary simple Christian, if he has been at all adequately instructed in the simple truths of his religion, is far less likely to lapse into monstrous heresy than his mentors imagine. 'These things have I written unto you concerning them that seduce you. But the anointing which ye have received of him abideth in you, and ye need not that any man teach you: but as the same anointing teacheth you of all things, and is truth, and is no lie, and even as it hath taught you, ye shall abide in him' (I John 2. 26-27). St. John the Theologian knew and trusted his 'little children' better than do some would-be teachers of to-day.

The real danger is not that men should think too highly of Mary, but that they should think too lowly of her, or rather that they should think too lowly of Christ. It is, I think, no accident that absence of devotion to Mary commonly goes with luke-warmness of devotion to her Son. For I suspect that some of the objection to the words 'Mother of God' springs unconsciously from a lack of deep conviction about the Deity of Christ. This is more frequently met with than we think. I said just now that the laity can be trusted if well instructed; but in the Church of

England they are often not well instructed. And I sometimes wonder what the honest answer would be if one pressed upon certain Anglicans, not ordinarily suspected of unorthodoxy, the question, 'When you say that Christ is God, do you really mean that He is so in just the same sense as the Father is God?' Would they perhaps hedge, or at least hesitate? Too many do not realise that the logical consequence of the Incarnation is that Jesus of Nazareth, a character in history, was and is personally *God* in the fullest sense of the word, and therefore to be worshipped as such *sans phrase*. Not to be clear about this not only obscures the unique privilege of Mary and so makes men niggardly in honouring her. It also creates the risk that the throne which should be hers is given instead to the Son, in place of His rightful one. That is to say, our Lord, in men's minds, instead of occupying His place at the right hand of the Father, comes instead to be thought of as merely the highest of beings *after* God. The way to keep the proportion of faith is not to measure out nervously the devotion you give to Mary, but to be quite sure first that you have given to God the things that are God's. Just as, only if you do this, can you be quite sure of not defrauding Caesar, so equally you can be certain that, when God has been given His due, Mary will automatically take her proper place in the universe. The person who is most likely to fail in civil allegiance is the man who thinks of God as a limited monarch; in just the same way the Christian who is most likely to underestimate the Blessed Virgin is he who has an inadequate idea of the nature of Deity. Newman once spoke of the Arian Christ as usurping a throne in God's plan reserved for her who is really the highest of created beings, as the Arians thought their Saviour to be.

Here I am quite sure that the Orthodox Church has something to teach us in the West. For, to my mind, the weak spot in Western Marian devotion is the extent to which it is dominated by requests to our Lady. The Western so often has little to say to her beyond 'Pray for us.' The Eastern, on the other hand, *praises* Mary. I think that this fact comes out at once when one examines the Eastern liturgies. Not merely is Mary more frequently mentioned; she is mentioned precisely in order that we may proclaim her glory. 'More glorious than the Cherubim, and beyond compare exalted above the Seraphim . . .'—that is the key-note which keeps sounding in these prayers. Equivalent expressions are not unknown in the West, but they are far less prominent. It is interesting to note that the 'Hail Mary' began in the mediaeval West as a salutation to our Lady, but by the sixteenth century it was considered necessary to add to it the final petition for prayers. . . . It seems to me symptomatic that the Westerner cannot go on indefinitely merely praising our Lady; he must at all costs ask her for favours. I venture, indeed, to think that it is true of Western devotion to the saints, as of Western devotion to Mary, that it is too much concerned in practice with getting and too little with giving. 'Practical' in modern usage commonly means 'avaricious', and the 'practical' Westerner is too apt to think more of using the saints than of contemplating them. He is concerned too much with what he can get from them. This spiritual cupboard-love indeed is the besetting temptation of Western spirituality; it appears even where God is concerned, and is at the back of that craving for sensible devotion which was one of the causes of the Reformation and against which one has so constantly to warn those who desire to make spiritual progress. Worst when it affects man's approach to God, it is scarcely less undesirable when it colours our relationship to the Body of Christ Triumphant, and especially to Mary, that Body's Queen. There is, I believe, a kinship between devotion and art, which is nowhere more marked than in the fact that self-interest mars prayer scarcely less than it does art. If your approach to the universe is determined by the will to dominate and exploit, you will produce false art, as you try to translate the impact of the universe upon you into art forms. You cannot paint Niagara, whether photographically, impressionistically or surrealistically, if your predominant thought is the number of kilowatts you can extract from it to drive your factories. In a similar way you cannot worship well if your first and last thought is of the benefits you can derive from God, His Mother, or His saints. This can be said without falling into the Quietist heresy that the Christian should be completely unconcerned about his own salvation; it is our duty to wish for our salvation, and therefore for all gifts necessary to it, because our salvation will be to the glory of God. What spoils our prayer is to desire even spiritual goods, because they will become *ours* if granted. And the great safeguard against this is a plentiful admixture, or rather a predominance, of praise in our prayers. The point I wish to make is that this applies no less to devotion to Mary

and the saints than to direct worship of God; praise should be
our key-note here as well. It is therefore strange that praise of
Mary seems to be more suspect to some than are requests for
her prayers. Many who will cautiously admit the lawfulness of
invocation of the Blessed Virgin (in strictly guarded terms) shrink
from lauding her. Yet the former practice by itself would seem
to lead more directly to deification of Mary than the latter; merely
to ask for her intercession is more likely to make a man regard
her as, so to say, a separate agent from God, than is the extolling
of her greatness, which inevitably brings to mind that all that
Mary is comes wholly from Him who, being mighty, has magnified her. You can ask for the Virgin's prayers without stopping
too much to consider why they should be effective; you can
hardly praise her without considering your reasons for so doing,
and this leads inevitably to thoughts of God, and of His grace,
which exalts the humble and meek.

I stress this because the Englishman, and still more perhaps the
American, is of all Westerners the most likely to be infected by
the profit motive in all that he surveys. Inability to forget self-
interest in prayer is likely to be an especial temptation to English-
speaking people.

It is here that the other principle, which I suggested as a touchstone of pure Marian devotion, namely natural Christian instinct,
comes to our rescue. If Mary is our Mother, then we shall, if we
let ourselves behave naturally, no more approach her solely for
profit than we should our natural mothers. One of the earliest
nursery lessons, that a mother does not appreciate love which is
wholly self-regarding, is also a primary lesson of prayer. And I
venture to think that the Orthodox, who has throughout history
been less self-conscious at prayer than the Western Catholic, less
afraid to be natural, can help us much. Prayer should always be
theological, but not nervously so. Always to be stopping short in
praises of the Virgin lest we might overstep the bounds of exact
truth is to be like the man who is terrified lest he might say something extravagant about his mother. A good mother would not
mind if he did; still less, if I may use a daring, yet I hope not
irreverent, analogy, would a good father overhearing. So I for
one am not unduly shocked by the exuberance of Eastern prayers
to the Mother of God, or by their invasion of the Eucharistic
Liturgy; indeed I covet them, and I reflect, with some amusement

and not a little interest, that when the modern Roman Breviary wishes, as in the Octave of the Immaculate Conception, to say something really extreme about Mary, it has to raid Eastern writers in order to do so. And I regret, not merely the absence of any reference to Mary whatever outside the Creed in the unchanging parts of the Prayer Book Mass—otherwise she is mentioned only in seasonal prayers like the Christmas Preface or Collect—but the reticence of the Roman Mass, which contents itself at ordinary seasons with almost formal sentences in the Canon and some other prayers, without ordinarily using any direct address to her. As I have said, right devotion to Mary calls for a constant turning to her in every context of prayer. Just as the cultus of the Reserved Sacrament is falsified when it is divorced from the Liturgy by the segregation of the place of reservation from the altar of sacrifice, so the veneration of God's Mother is distorted when prayers to her are carefully isolated from the ordinary corporate or private devotions of the Christian. It is a sound instinct which has associated so closely in usage the Lord's Prayer and the Hail Mary. If an untrue devotion to our Lady is to be avoided, what is needed is not fewer prayers to her, but more. A form of prayer which does not mention her is to some degree incomplete. Not only does it make men think of God apart from the Incarnation and the Body of Christ: it also runs the risk that when we do turn to Mary we shall forget her relationship to God. Never to think of God without Mary and never of Mary without God is a safe rule.

It is, I know, startling to the average Westerner, and most of all to the Anglican, when he attends an Eastern Liturgy and hears the choir, almost immediately after the Consecration, break into an exuberant hymn to our Lady and continue with it during the pleading of the Sacrifice. Yet, if the doctrine of the common sacrifice of Christ and His Mystical Body means anything at all, the practice is not indefensible, and the real fault may well lie in the critic who has so divorced in his mind the ideas of the Incarnation and of the Heavenly Altar from his conception of the eucharistic action as to think it is. It may not seem to us all the ideally best prayer for that moment of the rite, but it is not a bad one. Nor need we applaud too unreservedly the opposite development in the West which turned Benediction of the Blessed Sacrament, in its origins a Marian service, into one directed more exclusively to our Lord. To my mind the danger signal in regard to devotion to

Mary is always isolation from other prayer, for that always means a tendency to divide the Faith, and that in turn leads normally to loss of the proportion of faith, which, as I have suggested, should be our first principle here. As long as one thinks of devotion to Mary—or to the Saints—as an optional extra in worship, there will always be the danger of devotional schizophrenia. Our praying minds will be split and the separate portions will almost certainly think wrongly. Wholeness, which means among other things 'togetherness', *sobornost*, must be the key-note of worship, as of theology. It has been said that the Faith is like a network rather than an assemblage of discrete dogmas; cut one strand and the whole pattern loses its meaning. It is not always appreciated that prayer, which is the expression of dogma and intimately related to it, is no less a complex whole which one divides at one's peril. The man who takes no notice of Mary and the whole company of heaven in his prayers will be in danger of a wrong approach to the God upon whom he desires to concentrate. That may not be his fault; past history, and the almost insuperable prejudices with which it infects the individual, may have robbed him of part of his devotional birthright. Nevertheless the objective fact remains that his whole vision of God will be to some degree defective, as if he were spiritually colour-blind. He will no doubt enter into life, but in this world at least, it will be (to vary the metaphor) with one eye only.

We Anglicans then, who have suffered much from just such a deprivation, have here, perhaps more than anywhere else, a lesson to learn from our Orthodox brethren. We can indeed learn much from our nearer neighbours in the West—and I personally am not one of those many who find an Orthodox cicerone *per se* an easier guide than a Latin—but I believe that here at least we shall be closer to first-hand experience if we turn to the East. For I think that it is not the Church of England only, but the whole West, which here needs to go to school in Byzantium. (I noticed with some interest that those shrewd folk, the English Dominicans, have recently republished an English translation of the Akathist Hymn.) Frederick the Great once said that but for the Reformation the Roman Church would have made the Blessed Virgin a Fourth Person of the Trinity. He perhaps spoke truer than he knew and, like Balaam, without being fully conscious of what he was saying, as was the habit with that monarch who, like our own James I, might have been described as 'the wisest fool in Christendom'. For it almost certainly is the case that the Protestant attack upon devotion to Mary made the Counter-Reformation too self-conscious in Marian devotion, too afraid on the one hand of letting itself go, lest it might invite more charges of idolatry, too deliberately controversial in 'extreme language' on the other. So it was that the natural, and despite its eccentricities fundamentally sound, mediaeval development of devotion to Mary in the West was blighted, even in those districts where it was not extinguished by Protestantism. Bremond has said, in reference to the court of Henry IV of France and its religious outlook, that it is always a mistake to learn your catechism controversially, against other people, and he points out the difficulty St. Francis de Sales had there in teaching a more natural Catholicism to those who were anti-Calvinists rather than Catholics. I suggest that devotion to Mary suffered in the same way by being carried out against a background of critical observation. If the childlike mind is a *sine qua non* of true devotion, we must remember that no child is natural when it knows that it is being watched. It is noteworthy that Western devotion to our Lady is most natural, healthy and best balanced in some of those peasant communities which are least conscious that others do not believe or act as they. It may run to odd forms which the sophisticated would not wish to share —and which indeed would do them harm—but I believe that it is more integrated with the whole of religion, less devotionally schizophrenic, there than in other parts of Western Europe. Be that as it may, I am quite sure that the best way to reinvigorate, deepen and reform Marian devotion will be found in a return to the East, not by way of mechanical borrowing (which would only introduce a different sort of artificiality), but by that reassurance and re-education which will result from an examination of a part of Christendom where this vital element in Christian prayer, as I believe it to be, has burgeoned undisturbed by gales and frosts. There it was that it first took root—for the East has always led the West in the matter. There, too, it has been most intimately intertwined with the general growth of Christian thought. And there we, who have endured such adverse climatic conditions in recent times, can learn peacefully to cultivate our spiritual garden in which Mary must be the Burning Bush which brings to us the presence of God.

XVI

MARIOLOGY
(d) REFORMED

*

Max Thurian
(France)

Introduction

The doctrine and the veneration of Mary in the Roman Church create extreme difficulties for ecumenical thought. Even though one can believe that in the doctrine of grace, of the sacraments or even of the Church, it is possible to hope for developments which would one day permit closer understanding, or even unity: though it is possible to think that the influence of a particular theological school or a liturgical renewal, or of the circumstances of the growing dechristianisation and of the necessary awakening, might hasten purification of use, or renouncement of error, thus leading to ecumenical solutions; one can see no way through the problem posed by Mariology and the veneration of the Blessed Virgin in the Church. True, prejudices can be dissipated in fraternal discussion, doctrine can be centred anew upon its truly Christological character, and worship can be modified, reformed, or spiritualised. Nevertheless, Catholic Mariology poses the most agonising problem for ecumenical thought. The labours and the conversations best disposed to sacrifice what is secondary and accidental bring little encouragement, and leave the problem fundamentally unchanged. A Protestant cannot understand how, on a silence as great as that of the first centuries of the Church with regard to Mary, Catholic Mariology has been able to build in all good faith. He cannot but be impressed by the considerable disproportion which exists between the attitude of the biblical writers with regard to the Virgin and the veneration sometimes tantamount to worship which is paid to her in Catholic piety. There is here something overwhelming for a mind which in other respects is ready to admit the incontestable values of pure Catholic theology and of the Roman liturgy. Such a mind must recognise the important place which Mariology has taken in theological instruction and the role of the veneration of Mary in piety and in the liturgy.

The *Dictionnaire de Théologie Catholique* has a total of rather more than five hundred columns under the two headings of Mary and the Immaculate Conception, while it allows a little less than four hundred for the corresponding articles on Jesus Christ and the Incarnation. It is clearly important not to base too many conclusions on facts of this kind. One can understand that X. Le Bachelet finds it important to defend and to support with many details the dogma of the Immaculate Conception, and that he needs three hundred and seventy columns for his exposition,[1] while in ninety-four columns A. Michel can find sufficient space to expound the Incarnation.[2] But this difficulty, this very minuteness, and the time taken to develop the argument, are all indeed revealing and prove the importance which attaches to the subject.

We ought also to voice the astonishment of the Protestant at the practice of telling beads, or the fuller devotion of the holy rosary with its fifteen decades of Ave Marias, each with a Pater Noster and a Gloria Patri. The liturgy itself, however fully centred on the person of Jesus Christ, has gradually given a fairly large place to devotion to Mary. Besides numerous feasts of the Virgin, of which some are biblical and legitimate (being observed also by Anglicans and certain Lutherans), the Offices are followed by an antiphon to the Blessed Virgin, whenever indeed the full office of the Blessed Virgin Mary is not said every day, alongside the canonical offices, as it is by Carthusian and Cistercian Orders. It would seem that Christian prayer was not felt to be complete if it did not finish with some intention in honour of the mother of Christ.

True, in the realm of piety as of liturgy, reforms are always possible. Mariology itself, often doubtful as a theological development, is susceptible of modification in theological faculties and in personal thought among theologians; but what is disquieting for non-Roman ecumenical theologians is that certain ideas reach the unchanging level of infallible dogma, which can never be repudiated so long as the Roman dogmatic position remains what it is. The dogma of the Immaculate Conception has now been followed by that of the Assumption. It is here that the most unshakable obstacles for all ecumenical thought occur, and the promulgation of the Assumption as a dogma *de fide* seems to be a serious error from the point of view of unity. It is thus very important to be quite clear as to what Mariology signifies in Catholic theology as a whole.

If it is true that the veneration of Mary shows most clearly the theological change which has taken place in the course of the centuries in the doctrine of the Mother of God, we must still not overstress the point, for there will always be completely orthodox theologians and priests who will disavow certain practices, and desire their reform or rejection. The origins of the veneration of Mary are more complex than those of the doctrine of Mary. It has its roots in the soil of the fourth, fifth and sixth centuries, when it was exposed to all sorts of pagan impurities.[3] It is made up of elements arising from the popular and natural religious sentiment which the Catholic Church—either from charity, or from an attempt to express charity in ecclesiastical policy—always finds it difficult to condemn. But doctrine is much surer ground, for if Mariology has been considerably influenced by Marian piety, it must be recognised that, thanks to the theologians, it has remained within the limits of the logic of the Roman Catholic mind. Each aspect of the doctrine of Mary is perfectly easy to explain when it is understood in the totality of Roman theology. There is not, in any essential points, one discordant note. The development is homogeneous. But it is precisely in the face of this logic and this homogeneity in the Roman dogmatic synthesis that the very question arises of the legitimacy of its theological method. The fact that the development of dogma, in the manner in which it is conceived in Catholic theology, can lead to definitions such as that of the Immaculate Conception or the perpetual virginity, which seem to us so far from the letter and the spirit of Scripture, raises quite naturally the question: 'Is this homogeneous dogmatic development legitimate, and are its theological premises well founded?'

We have no wish to stress the view that Marian devotion is contrary to the Gospel, nor to win an easy theological victory by describing excrescences in the cult of the Virgin. It seems to us necessary to study Roman Mariology in order to see the relationship of the doctrine (as found in the conciliar texts, the infallible definitions of the Roman *magisterium* and the leading theologians) to the theory of dogmatic development and the doctrine of living tradition. We shall then have, in a concrete example, a clearer revelation of the fundamental spiritual attitudes and theological methods which both characterise Roman Catholicism and most clearly illustrate our differences from it.

1. *Mariology and the Bible*

One is often very surprised to-day at the community of thought which is possible between Catholic and Protestant exegetes on numerous texts which formerly each used for his own purposes. Biblical criticism, before which each has had to bow in recognition of its scientific value, and which, far from ruining faith, has been able, on the contrary, to increase understanding of the sacred text, has greatly helped to bring theologians into agreement on a common interpretation. If Protestant theologians continue to think that every Reformed doctrine must proceed from a deductive interpretation of the documents which the primitive Christian faith has bequeathed to us, Roman Catholic theologians no longer seek to make the texts suit preconceived dogma, whether that of transubstantiation, the Immaculate Conception, or the perpetual virginity. They content themselves with showing that Catholic dogma is not contradicted, either explicitly or implicitly, by Scripture, but is in a direct line with apostolic meditation on the revealed fact, according to the principle of homogeneous development which operates in the living tradition, and which is recognised and defined by the infallible *magisterium* of the Church.

Biblical studies common to Catholics and Protestants to-day are able to reveal a very great unity of thought, so long as one remains on the level of scientific exegesis. The Catholic theologian will at most avoid certain possibilities of translation or interpretation which would contradict the dogma, and will choose the more suitable alternative; while the Protestant theologian can maintain a more 'scientific' liberty. It is thus, for example, with the text on the *adelphoi* of Jesus (Mark 3. 31 and parallels), which Catholic exegesis would wish to render only by the term 'relations' or 'cousins', while a Protestant can remain open to several possible translations, even to that of 'brothers', sons of Joseph and Mary, since he does not have to defend the perpetual virginity of Mary, which he does not find in Scripture.

This growing unity of thought, so far as exegesis and biblical study are concerned, makes us rejoice, but must not delude us. For the difficulties remain unchanged. If we cannot but applaud the renewal of scriptural studies in Catholicism, seeing therein a great promise for the unity of Christians, we must equally take into account that this renewal, and the rights of a scientific exegesis against tendentious interpretations of certain controversial texts, impels Catholic theologians to define even more clearly the role of living tradition and of the infallible *magisterium* in the formation of dogma, in order to give certain doctrines the sure and sufficient basis that they can no longer honestly find for them in Scripture. And it is then that the divergence of theological method becomes apparent, and that firmly established positions are strengthened. We are then no longer on the same ground. Our norms are no longer drawn from the same sources. And, when authorities have been cited from either side, nothing more is needed than to 'draw away the ladder'. '*I* base myself only on Scripture, as a document of the primitive Christian faith which alone is normative.' '*I* base myself on Scripture as it has been understood by living tradition, in the infallible decisions of the councils and of the Roman *magisterium.*' When once the theory of authorised sources is admitted, the doctrine regarding the relations of the Church, of Scripture and of unity is no longer anything more than a matter of ceaseless theological research in a predetermined direction, and in obedience to principles.

In spite of this *impasse* to which so many ecumenical encounters lead, we must not give up working together, for we must hope that the salutary misgivings which generate unity may arise in the minds of both sides when confronted with the thought of their separated brethren. What Catholic, in spite of the sureness of his theological principles, his faith in the infallible Church and the homogeneity of development, would be entirely unconcerned by the disturbing silence of the New Testament concerning the Virgin, both in doctrine and in veneration? What Protestant, in spite of his certitude that every norm of his faith can be found within the limits of the biblical canon, and that Scripture possesses sufficient light on the essential truths for the Church to be able to derive from them all the substance of her dogma, would be quite unmoved by the evolution of certain ideas and forms within the New Testament, and by the fact that the first extra-biblical Christian authors (certain of whose writings almost slipped into the canon) defend points of view which Reformed theology rejects as Catholic?

The study of Mariology and of the history of its development is therefore extremely revealing of the respective positions of Catholic and of Protestant theology. Newman and Pusey had already felt this deeply on the level of thought, and on the level of religious experience, since the former, having become a Roman Catholic, had no difficulty in legitimising Roman Mariology (though he minimised its significance); while the latter, remaining an Anglican, expressed the greatest reserves.[4] Recently Père Daniélou, in the volume *Protestantisme Français*, declared that 'the devotion to the Most Blessed Virgin and the dogma of the mediation of Mary, so dear to the Catholic heart', was one of the significant points in the struggle between Catholicism and Protestantism.[5] Finally, Prof. Maury in his opening lecture to the Faculty of Theology of Paris, in 1945, affirmed: '. . . the doctrine of Mary and the cult of the Virgin seem to me to pose with increasing precision and with an unmistakable clarity the real problems of our relations with the Roman Church'.[6] He saw Mariology as typical of the Roman position as much from the formal as from the material points of view, taking its theology as a whole, 'inasmuch as [this problem] implies a specific conception of authority in matters of faith, and also inasmuch as it expresses a specific conception of the content of the Christian faith, i.e. the divine redemption in Jesus Christ'.[7]

Our exegetical positions on the biblical texts which concern Mary, as on so many other controversial points, seem to-day less antagonistic because of the greater precision with which the problem of dogmatic development is judged. It is possible to admit agreement on the critical interpretation of the texts, and yet not to be united on the dogmatic level, because of a different conception of the Church, of its authority as regards faith, or of dogmatic development. The attempt is no longer made, for example, to defend the Immaculate Conception by invoking the text of the *Protevangelium* of Gen. 3. 15. The discussion on this subject in the *Dictionnaire de Théologie Catholique* is most significant. It is also willingly recognised that Scripture is extremely sober in its hints about Mary, and it was sometimes even admitted, as by St. Robert Bellarmine in a *Votum* to Paul V in 1617 on the subject of the Immaculate Conception: *In Scripturis nihil habemus*. But what always strikes a Protestant is that in all good faith the silence, or the very great sobriety of the sacred text is admitted, and so, equally easily, are the most extreme Mariological developments. Once again it is a total conception of theology which is involved.

2. *The Reticence of the First Three Centuries*

It is not only the silence of Scripture which strikes us, but also the astonishing reticence in the second and third centuries. It is not a sufficient justification of such reticence to say (as does Père Régamey in his presentation of the most beautiful texts on the Virgin[8]) that the Church, occupied in consolidating its Trinitarian and Christological faith against heresies, had not the leisure to go deeply into the Marian mystery. Indeed, is it not recognised in another connection that Mariology is closely linked to Christology and that the definition of the title of *theotokos* had a purely polemical aim against the Nestorian heresy, as the first antiphon of the third nocturn at Matins in the Office of the Virgin in the Roman liturgy still attests: 'Rejoice, O Virgin Mary, thou alone hast destroyed all heresies in the whole world.'

Apart from a few indications on the virginity of Mary (which are really no more than an echo of the Gospel) in St. Ignatius' Epistles to the Trallians (IX) and to the Ephesians (XIX), a Mariological statement is hardly to be found in the second century. St. Justin was the first, in the Dialogue with Trypho, to parallel 'Adam-Christ' with Eve-Mary, in terms of a wholly evangelical simplicity. St. Irenaeus takes up the comparison again, but still in the same evangelical tone: 'That which Eve-virgin has bound by her unbelief, Mary-Virgin has unloosed by her faith.'[9] After Clement of Alexandria, who gives a comparison, without great interest, and with little dogmatic significance, between the fruitful virginity of Mary and that of the Scriptures,[10] we must await the commentary of Origen on St. John (*circa* 240-250) before we find a more intense Marian note, where the idea of the spiritual motherhood of the Virgin already makes itself felt, however discreetly. 'No one will be able to understand the meaning [of the Gospel of St. John, that flower of gospels],' says Origen, 'if he has not leant on the breast of Jesus and received from Jesus the one who has become also his mother. But in order to be another John, one must have been shown, as John was, by Jesus in the capacity of Jesus. . . . Indeed, whosoever is brought to perfection

in Christ lives no longer, but Christ lives in him; and because
Christ lives in him, Jesus is saying to Mary of him also, "Behold
thy son," the Christ.' Our Protestant thought ought perhaps to
insert a question mark here; we feel ourselves less at ease. However, we ought not to commit the whole of Protestant thought
too readily to this hesitation, since the very last sentence of a
meditation on the Virgin by Pasteur de Saussure strikes exactly
the same note: '. . . Since she was Thy mother, how should she
not be ours, who are the members of Thy Body, who are but
one mind with Thee?'[11]

Up to the middle of the third century, then, the authors whom
we can consider as serious give only a very relative importance to
Mariology. Their reticence is that of the Gospel itself. An appeal
could be made to the *Protevangelium Jacobi*, an apocryphal writing
of the end of the second century, whose desire to supplement the
canonical Gospels on the history of Mary denotes a development
of Marian piety in certain Christian quarters at that date. But it
gives evidence of a very naïve imagination, and lapses into the
worst possible taste in its affirming of the virginity of Mary. Hence
it is not possible to accord the author any credit. He is no more
than the vague witness to a certain Marian state of mind at the
end of the second century, in a certain ecclesiastical circle. Before
the Council of Nicæa two further sources, however, can be quoted,
from the end of the third century, which foreshadow a more
marked Marian orientation. First there is the vision of St. Gregory
Thaumaturgus (bishop of Neo-Caesarea of the Bridge) related by
St. Gregory of Nyssa, where it is, moreover, very difficult to
distinguish between legend and history.[12]

He sees one night an old man, St. John, in company with Mary,
'full of a superhuman majesty, who confirms him in his faith'.
Then there is the prayer *Sub tuum praesidium* of which the original
was found in 1938 on a papyrus of the third century in Manchester:
'Under the shelter of thy mercy, we take refuge, O Mother of
God; lead our prayer not into temptation, but deliver us from
peril, thou alone chaste and blessed.'

We have thus had to come a long way into the third century
before we discover a serious text indicating the beginning of a
Marian development, which henceforward becomes increasingly
pronounced, and appears more and more to contradict the reticence of the Scriptures and of the first three centuries of the

Church. This is the fundamental reason for our misgivings, and for our doubt in the face of the Catholic Marian edifice. In the light of the sudden and unexpected flowering of Marian piety to which the apocryphal writings and the Fathers of the fourth and fifth centuries bear witness, one cannot help assuming, in the Mariological development, pagan and oriental influences which affect the conception of grace and of theology. The cults of goddesses, of divine mothers, of virgin mothers, and the great respect for virginity, became the ideal of the first ascetics, by a confusion of thought which identified it with purity and even with sanctity.

3. Mary in the Bible

The consideration of the fact that Mary finds little place in the literature of the first three centuries, and the spirit of anti-Marian polemics, must not, however, lead Reformed theology to minimise the significance of the Gospel texts where she appears associated with the history of her Son. It is necessary to go back to the Scriptures in order to make a few comments on certain controversial texts, and to supply a corrective to certain exegeses which have been falsified by polemics either from the Protestant or from the Catholic side.

St. Mark 3. 31-35; St. Matt. 12. 46-50; St. Luke 8. 19-21; 11. 27-28

First there are the texts which record the episode when His relatives come to lay hold of Jesus, saying that He has lost His mind. Mary is there with the brothers of Jesus, and, when their presence is made known to Him, He says: 'Who is my mother and my brethren?' Then pointing to the crowd He says: 'Behold, my mother and my brethren. For whosoever shall do the will of God, the same is my brother, and sister, and mother.' ('These which hear the Word of God and do it,' is the Lucan version.) It is possible to say, with Catholic apologists, that Mary is specially in mind in this gesture of Christ, and that she is doubly designated as His mother, carnal mother and spiritual mother, since she *par excellence* has heard and done His Word. However, one cannot but admit in all intellectual honesty that Christ here puts the importance of the carnal motherhood of Mary very much into the background in the order of the kingdom; He who will later say sternly that 'if any man cometh unto me and hateth not his

own father, and mother . . . he cannot be my disciple', does not
here seem to exclude Himself from that rule of the Kingdom of
God, which not only subordinates the realm of the carnal family
to the exigences of the Kingdom, but even requires that the preoccupations of the Christian, his very filial love, shall be put into
the background. This text cannot then be minimised, and the
Catholic insistence on the relations of the mother to the son which
are assumed between Mary and Jesus surprise us, when Christ
Himself seems to invite us not to cavil about the facts of the flesh
and of psychology, when He replies (to the woman who proclaimed the womb and the breasts of Mary blessed): 'Yea, rather,
blessed are they that hear the Word of God, and keep it.' In both
episodes, St. Luke records the same answer to Jesus. It is no other
than a providential caution to all Mariology which, abandoning
the purely theological ground of the Word of God, with its anti-
natural and illogical paradoxes, bases itself on a meditation of a
psychological and logical order, inspired by the proper filial
relations of the natural man with his mother. Not that we think
such a psychological meditation forbidden—it can be enlightening
from certain points of view, and can usefully moderate certain
Protestant anti-Marian extremes. But Christ twice puts us on our
guard against the danger of a natural Mariology and invites us
rather to hear the Word of God.

St. Luke 1 and 2

It is all the more interesting that it should be St. Luke who
twice records, and in a form peculiar to his writing, this warning
of Jesus, since it is he who, in another connection, has emphasised
the great importance of the role of the Virgin in the Incarnation.
There is first of all the annunciation with the angelic salutation:
'Hail, thou that art highly favoured; the Lord is with thee.' Mary
is not for us full of grace in the physical sense which Catholic
Mariology gives to this term. She is highly favoured, in that God
has fully enfolded her in His merciful regard; He has not regarded
the sin and misery of His handmaid, but He has regarded her
lowliness in order to clothe her with the cloak of His justice, to
overshadow her. The angel does not state an immaculate holiness
whose origin goes back to her conception; he declares to Mary
that the Lord is with her, and that He endues her with the most
wonderful grace, which He has given to no one before, since His

Son is to be born of her. To this unique grace corresponds a unique act of faith, on which the whole hope of the Old Covenant and the whole salvation of humanity depends: *Fiat*. 'Be it unto me according to Thy word.' Certainly Mary can only accomplish this act of faith because she is highly favoured by God, but it is nevertheless she who says the *Fiat*; it is the Holy Spirit in her, and that is why one cannot neglect this place in which the purpose of God is accomplished, this heart of Mary, in which resounds the echo of God's holy will, which becomes incarnate among us. God has not caused Christ to be born of Mary without her knowing it, He has desired her acceptance, and although it is He Himself in her who has said this 'yes', by the grace with which He had endowed her, He has none the less desired that she should pronounce it, and that the Incarnation should begin there. Thus we cannot regard Mary with indifference; we must in no way dismiss her personality, on the pretext of better attributing all glory to God alone; for God has desired that she should be an obedient servant and not a passive instrument of His purpose. Mary is then for us the example of pure faith, without hesitation or reserve—a faith which sums up that of the patriarchs and of the prophets, and on which the salvation of the world depends, thanks to the Incarnation which it inaugurates.

Karl Barth writes: 'All the angels of all the heavens now look only at this place where Mary is, that young girl, to whom, however, nothing has happened but this simple regard of God, cast on her lowliness. This short instance is full of eternity, of an ever-new eternity. There is nothing greater in heaven and on earth. If ever, in the history of the world, something of capital importance has happened, it is indeed this "regard".'[13]

As to the episode of the visitation of Mary to Elizabeth, we are obliged to recognise that Protestantism, in its exegesis of the sacred text, in its preaching and in its piety, does not take full account of the word of Elizabeth: 'Blessed art thou among women and blessed is the fruit of thy womb. And whence is this to me, that the mother of my Lord should come to me? For, behold, when the voice of thy salutation came into mine ears, the babe leaped in my womb for joy. And blessed is she that believed; for there shall be a fulfilment of those things which have been spoken to her from the Lord.'

The meeting with Mary has produced a supernatural impact on

Elizabeth, so great that the child that she bears leaps in her womb, and that she finds herself filled with the Holy Ghost. The evangelist does not need to tell us that it was Christ conceived in the womb of Mary who produced the miracle; Mary meets Elizabeth and the latter is filled with the Holy Ghost. Mary and Jesus are but one at this moment, and the mother is closely united to her son in this first miracle worked by Christ. The text even says that it is at the salutation of Mary that the event took place. The voice of the mother has carried the Word of the Son of God in her womb, and calls forth in Elizabeth an abundant outpouring of the Spirit. And it is by the Spirit that she declares Mary blessed among women, giving her, in fact, a unique place among her equals. She even raises Mary to the dignity of attributing to her the same qualification as to her Son: 'Blessed art thou . . . and blessed is the fruit of thy womb.' Then she speaks of the great honour that Mary's visit brings to her. She gives her, further, the magnificent title of 'The mother of my Lord': a solemn title which foreshadows the future declaration of the Council of Ephesus in 431: 'the mother of my lord . . . the mother of my God . . . the mother of God.' Then she declares that on hearing this voice of Mary, whose visit is for her a great honour, her child leapt in her womb. The voice of Mary has produced the marvel. Lastly, she calls blessed her who has believed, she praises the faith of Mary and by so doing makes of it one of the important elements in the mystery of the Incarnation.

The *Magnificat* which the Virgin then sings manifests both the humility of Mary and the splendour of the choice that God makes of her. Thus, she dares to prophesy that all generations will call her 'blessed'. Can we say that this title is really conferred in all truth by our Reformed piety? What Protestant does not tremble on hearing the phrase 'the blessed Virgin Mary'?

The incident of the presentation in the Temple and of the purification of the Virgin calls for remark. According to the law of Leviticus (12. 6-8), every woman, after the birth of a son or of a daughter, must go to the Temple and present to the priest a lamb of the first year for a burnt offering as a sacrifice of thanksgiving, and a young pigeon or a turtle dove as a sacrifice for sin, at the entrance to the tabernacle of the congregation. Poor people could replace the lamb by a second pigeon, and that is what Joseph and Mary do. Now the law says: 'The priest shall offer it before the

Lord and make an atonement for her (the woman), and she shall
be cleansed from the issue of her blood.' So Mary has brought
the young pigeon as a sacrifice for sin. She has need to be purified
like every woman here on earth and, although blessed among
them, she does not distinguish herself from their full humanity.
She is a sinner like the others. This precision of the text allows us
greatly to doubt the affirmation of the Immaculate Conception
and the perpetual virginity *in partu* and *post partum*.[14] Mary has
had need of the sacrifice for her sin and the purification of her
blood: she is not immaculate and she has borne Jesus like any
woman. Clearly, it may be said that she was unable or unwilling
to escape the law, just as Jesus willed to undergo Baptism. However, while the Evangelists strongly emphasise the different meaning of the Baptism of Jesus, which is a superabundant gift of the
Spirit for His ministry; and while St. Matthew records in addition
the hesitations of John the Baptist, stressing the holiness of Christ;
St. Luke does not hint at anything which might alter the significance of the sacrifice for sin which Mary accomplishes for her
purification.

St. Paul only accentuates further our certainty of Jesus' common
birth of a woman humanly like us all, although chosen and blessed
among all, in the single text where he makes allusion to Mary:
'God sent forth His Son, born of a woman, born under the law,
that he might redeem them which were under the Law . . .' If
the miraculous conception of Christ in the Virgin's womb through
the power of the Holy Ghost has manifested the divinity of our
Saviour, His ordinary and humble birth of a woman, in a poor
stable, under the Law, subject to all the exigences of nature and
religion, emphasises for our consolation and our faith His full
humanity that He shares with us all.

The prophecy of Simeon: 'A sword shall pierce through thy
own soul,' associates Mary not only with the mystery of the
Incarnation but also with that of the passion of Christ. 'A sword
shall pierce through thy own soul.' Mary present at the passion of
her Son, at His agony, at His painful death, will feel to the very
depths of her being the anguish of Him who has been one with
her, whom she has brought into the world, nourished, reared,
and loved. The Gospel descends here to the level of the psychology
of motherhood, and this authorises us to feel and to imagine the
pain of Mary to whom so many promises had been made, and

who now sees the life of her well-loved Son, whom her whole
faith had believed Son of God and Messiah, draw to so cruel an
end. She lives at the foot of the Cross the contradiction of the
Gospel, and sees Him who is at once her child and her God suffer
and die. She fills up in her own flesh, with all the sufferers of the
Church, 'that which is lacking of the afflictions of Christ . . . for
his body's sake which is the Church' (Col. 1. 24). That is to say,
that in this valiant and suffering *stabat Mater* which St. John shows
us, we see the repercussion of the power of faith which Christ's
passion wins for Mary, and for all who participate in His suffering
and in His death, and Mary reflects in her suffering the very
suffering of her Son and thus permits us to grasp all its depth.
Mary thus associated with all the martyrs and the sufferers of the
Church, erect and unrebelling beneath the Cross, becomes a living
testimony to the marvellous effects of the passion of her Son,
which are faith, patience and peace. Thus united with the sufferings of Christ, she is in a greater intimacy with this crucified Son;
she understands His whole being and His whole ministry, and
His prayer becomes more real, better understood, more efficacious. To reflect the passion of Jesus Christ and to gain in intimacy
with His whole person and thus to see His intercession becoming
one's very own, that is the meaning of this filling up of the
afflictions of Christ by the suffering and martyred Christian: Mary
at the foot of the Cross suffers thus, without taking away any
pain from her Son who lives in her and shines through her. She
unites herself thus to His function, which is the function of the
Church, of prayer and witness—unites herself to the redemptive
work of the unique Saviour. 'Yea, a sword shall pierce through
thy own soul also.'

One last episode of the Gospel of His childhood recorded by
St. Luke can further instruct us: it is when we see Jesus at twelve
years old remaining in the Temple, instructing the doctors without troubling about His parents who are seeking Him. To His
mother who reprimands Him He replies: 'How is it that ye sought
me? Wist ye not that I must be in my Father's house? . . .' And
the Gospel adds that His parents 'understood not the saying which
he spake unto them'. Mary, then, although supernaturally informed of the nature and of the mission of her Son, has not a
completely clear understanding of all these things. Certainly she
'ponders all these things in her heart', but without grasping all

their significance. She remains the humble handmaid of her Lord, retiring and submissive.

St. John

If the Gospel of St. Luke reveals to us a Mary highly favoured, and associated with the mystery of the Incarnation, but still insufficiently conscious of the great things that God has done for her, St. John marks a stage in the development of the understanding of the Virgin and thus in the deepening of the apostolic understanding concerning the person and the role of Mary. St. John calls Mary 'the mother of Jesus'; we see him more sensitive to the relations which unite the Virgin and Christ. Did he not take Mary to his home after Good Friday? It is legitimate for us to think that she must have told him a multitude of things concerning Jesus, which enables him, with the intimacy which linked him to his Master, to transmit to us the most profound message of the Saviour, though without being able to give us them all in detail: 'And there are also many other things which Jesus did, the which if they should be written every one, I suppose that even the world itself could not contain the books that should be written' (John 21. 25). All those sayings that the mother of Jesus pondered in her heart, are they not precisely those which cannot be 'written every one' without filling the universe—those things of which the Gospel of St. John is the echo? The Orthodox love to say that the Gospel of St. John is also that of Mary.

St. John presents Mary to us at two important moments in the life of Christ: at His first manifestation at the wedding of Cana (John 2. 1-12) and at the foot of His Cross (John 19. 25-27). At Cana, Mary as a sensitive and charitable woman has perceived the embarrassment of the hosts who, on account of the large number of the guests, see themselves suddenly short of wine. Mary gives proof on this occasion of a very sure faith in her Son, since after having informed Him of the situation, certain as she is that He will be able to do something ('they have no wine'), and after having met with a refusal, she says to the servants: 'Whatsoever he saith unto you, do it.' There has often been a desire to see in the reply of Jesus to His mother a certain hardness and a setting aside, and this text has been used polemically, with pleasure at having found a saying of Christ which really belittles His mother. Apart from the fact that the expression of which our text is the

echo probably does not mean what we make it mean by translating it literally, it is unworthy of us to suppose in Him feelings
of contempt towards His mother. The most probable translation
ought to be: 'Woman, does that concern us, me and thee?'[15]
Jesus has ascertained in the spirit of His mother the faith, and the
hope in a possible miracle, which her charity ardently desires in
order to extricate the hosts from difficulty. And He gives her to
understand that since His hour is not yet come, she must not
expect of Him a miracle which would manifest Him immediately
as Son of God and Messiah. Now Mary gives proof here of a very
great audacity, since she seems to disregard the refusal of Jesus
and, full of faith in His omnipotence, asks the servants to do all
that He tells them. Perhaps she has not understood the saying of
Jesus and commits a blunder? That seems improbable; Jesus has
been so clear! It seems rather that she wishes to impel Him to do
something, and in fact, through her intervention ('Whatsoever he
saith unto you, do it'), Jesus feels Himself constrained to perform
a miracle. Mary has then been the providential instrument of the
first manifestation of Christ and, after having brought Him into
the world on the day of His Incarnation, Mary causes Him to
enter upon the sorrowful career of His ministry: 'This beginning
of miracles did Jesus in Cana of Galilee, and manifested forth his
glory; and his disciples believed on him.' Is there not in this story,
which not one of the synoptic Gospels records, and where we see
the Virgin alone, full of faith, impelling Jesus to manifest Himself
—is there not here a fragment of that Gospel of Mary of which
we spoke earlier? Is there not here an event which she alone has
pondered in her heart in order to recall it to St. John, who has
transmitted it to us? Her faith in the divinity of her Son, her
authority, her role, appear important here, and here we see Mary
closely united to Jesus at the moment when He is about to begin
His work of salvation.

We have already spoken, in connection with the prophecy of
Simeon, of the meaning which must be given to the presence of
Mary at the foot of the Cross. We must also penetrate the meaning
of the words of the Crucified to His well-beloved disciple, when
He is about to entrust to him His mother: 'Behold thy mother.'
An extreme use has been made of these simple words to justify a
spiritual motherhood of the Virgin. Entrusting His disciple to
Mary, and Mary to His disciple, Jesus has on this view willed that

Mary should be considered as the mother of the Body of Christ, of the Church, of each Christian. We are unable to follow the exegetes, whether Catholic or Protestant, who see all that in these simple words.[16] It is really to remove to a mystical level facts which are extremely ordinary and commonplace. And the remark which, in the Gospel, follows this famous saying of Jesus, ought to suffice to bring us back again to more prosaic considerations. 'And from that hour,' the text says, 'that disciple took her unto his own home.' Jesus has not given Mary to John and to every Christian in him, as spiritual mother; He has simply asked him, and him personally, through love for this mother whom He abandons, to take care of her, to console her, to support her, to feed and house her to the end of her days.

The acts of the Apostles make only one mention of Mary, which indeed is proof that she played no apparent role in the primitive Church. If she has the respect and the affection of all Christians, she remains nevertheless in the shade, living by the invisible presence of her Son, always the humble handmaid who, her unprofitable work completed, retires and disappears in the body of her Christ. She has not even the first place in the nomenclature of the Acts of the Apostles. In the upper chamber the text mentions first the eleven, and then goes on: 'These all with one accord continued steadfastly in prayer, with the women, and Mary the mother of Jesus, and with his brethren' (Acts 1. 13-14). The sacred text, generally fairly careful to name the Apostles hierarchically, with Peter at their head, here places Mary between the women and the 'brethren'[17] of Jesus after all the apostles. It is vain to say that that is normal because Mary has not a hierarchical place in the Church, but simply a spiritual one. If to-day the list were to be rewritten, would not Catholic theologians unhesitatingly put her at the head of the apostolic college, the *Sanctissima regina apostolorum*,[18] or at least before the holy women. That is significant. The author of the Acts gives no evidence of a Mariological preoccupation. It is the same with all the writers of the Epistles.

Mary appears once more in the Book of Revelation (12) in the form of a pregnant and glorious woman, which links her both with Israel and the Church. The commentary which Père Féret has made of this text in his *Apocalypse*[19] seems on the whole acceptable. We cannot go into all the details of this exegesis. Let us simply say that the woman of the Apocalypse in verses 1 to 5

of Chapter 12 is at once Israel and Mary, who is the extreme point
of hope and of the expectation of the Old Covenant, at the same
time as the instrument willed by God for its realisation. From
verse 6 onwards, this woman is a figure of the persecuted Church.
The fact of this twofold reference to Mary in the vision of Israel
and of the Church leads to a further extension of her place as the
figure of the Church, which Pasteur de Saussure has made in his
beautiful and valid meditation on Mary, already quoted.[11]

4. *Mariology and the Doctrine of Grace*

If one wishes to grasp the very foundation of Catholic Mariology, it is essential to realise that the whole development of the
doctrine of Mary (if not of her veneration, which has more mixed
and obscure sources) finds its starting point in the dogma of the
Council of Ephesus concerning her divine motherhood (Mary,
mother of God) which we also acknowledge. Whence then does
it come that, starting from a confession of faith identical in its
terms, we see such divergent developments forming themselves in
the Catholic and Protestant traditions? This divergence is clearly
due to different conceptions of grace and of the Church, the two
chief grounds of our theological controversies.

'We call her the Mother of God, but do we think enough of
what that represents?' writes Père Henry. 'A creature who says
to her Creator: Thou art my Son. A mother who is truly mother,
but who has given nothing to her Son but what her Son has
already granted her the power to give, who has begotten nothing
but what God has taken and made in her.'[20]

A creature who says to her Creator: Thou art my Son! That is
the great wonder of Catholics concerning Mary—the basis on
which the whole development of Mariology will be found to rest.
But that wonder is also ours! Why then can we not continue on
similar lines and build an identical temple to Mary?

It is convenient to treat separately the explanation of these
divergent tendencies. The effects of grace in the individual and in
the Church are not conceived in the same manner, and consequently the effects of grace on Mary are differently recognised,
on one side and the other.

In order to understand the way in which the mystery of grace
is grasped in Reformed theology we must recall the passage in
Colossians which well characterises this form of thought and sums

it up in a few words: 'If ye then were raised with Christ, seek those things which are above, where Christ is, seated on the right hand of God. Set your mind on the things that are above, not on things that are upon the earth. For ye died, and your life is hid with Christ in God' (Col. 3. 1-3). For the whole of Protestant thought, the life of grace is conceived not so much as an incarnation of a divine power in man, as a raising of the Christian with Christ, human and Divine, seated now at the right hand of the Father, so that man may never dwell on 'things on the earth', but is always straining in search of a heavenly treasure. For this reason, Protestant faith and piety cannot ever rest content with considering Christ in the Church (e.g. reverence for tradition, the hierarchy, the Roman Pontiff), nor in His witnesses (veneration of the Virgin, of saints, of relics), nor in His sacraments (eucharistic worship, veneration of sacred or blessed things). All these realities, certain of which, at any rate, can have the value of a sign, are only the occasion or the means of looking above, the vehicles of an ascent with Christ in order to seek the life hid in God. Catholic thought and spirituality, on the contrary, dwells longer and more willingly on these signs, for it finds in them the fulness of Christ. Life with Christ is hidden, it would appear, not in God, but in the Church. The work of God's grace in each of us is, for the Protestant, essentially a merciful attitude of the Father who, in His love, deigns to look upon us in Jesus Christ, to forgive us, and to clothe us with His free and unconditional justice. The work of our salvation is essentially something which happens at this very moment in God, in the very heart of the Trinity, between the Son, the intercessor, through His Passion, and the just and merciful Father. The Psalmist gives an echo of this fundamental doctrine: 'Mercy shall be *built up for ever*; thy faithfulness shalt thou establish *in the very heavens*' (Ps. 89. 2). Grace, the work of our redemption and of our sanctification, is an abode which Christ prepares for us in God and where we can already live, by living in Christ, and that abiding life we shall find in its perfection on the day of our glorious manifestation with Him. This is indeed also what St. Paul declares to the Corinthians: 'For we know that if the earthly house of our tabernacle be dissolved, we have a building from God, a house not made with hands, eternal in the heavens. For verily in this we groan, longing to be clothed upon with our habitation which is from heaven: if so be that, being

clothed, we shall not be found naked' (II Cor. 5. 1-3). The tabernacle is the carnal body of man; the eternal house, the house
which is from heaven, is the sanctified and glorious body which
God prepares for each of us as a garment of perfect righteousness.
We shall be clothed upon with this if we are found 'clothed' (to
take the expression in the material sense)[21] with our carnal body,
that is, if we are not dead at the *parousia*. On the contrary, if we
are naked, we shall not need to be clothed upon, but simply
clothed; our spirit living in Christ will find anew its concrete,
sanctified and glorious form.

'For indeed we that are in this tabernacle,' continues the Apostle,
'do groan, being burdened; not for that we would be unclothed,
but that we would be clothed upon, that what is mortal may be
swallowed up of life' (II. Cor. 5. 4). St. Paul does not appear very
optimistic as regards his present sanctification; he groans under a
burden. If he looks 'at things of the earth', he has no grounds for
rejoicing. At any event, he does not wish, after the manner of
Platonists and Platonisers, to see his soul finally delivered from
the body, flying away like the dove from its cage. He wishes to
be clothed upon with the house which is from heaven, the work
of God's grace, the abode prepared by Christ, in order that his
mortal and sinful nature may at last be absorbed in the life of
Christ, wherein he has lived only in the hope, raising himself on
high in order to be with the Son and to live with Him in God.

This does not mean that Protestant theology fails to see that
the justice and holiness with which God presents us, out of His
pure grace, have a certain interior, immanent, concrete character.
The Reformed, and even the Lutheran, faith (but perhaps more
marked in Calvin than in Luther), believes in a *justitia domestica*.
The great German Catholic theologian Karl Adam has recently
peremptorily affirmed that 'interior justification, considered
generally by Catholics to be strange to Luther, has to-day been
secured for him by unbiassed historians.'[22]

However, Père Congar [23] persists in doubting the validity of
the Lutheran concept of forensic justice, in spite of the defence
which Pasteur L. Marchand has put forward.[24] It is admitted that
certain Protestant theologians have sometimes so expressed themselves as to lead to such a doubt. Thus Karl Barth, quoted by Père
Congar: 'We are holy, good (one hardly dares say it), not with
a justice, a holiness and a goodness interior to us, *emanating from*

our attitude and from our acts, but with a justice, holiness and goodness which are foreign, and given to us . . .'[25]. Père Congar points
out, justifiably, that the fact of considering justice as *interior* to
the Christian, does not necessarily imply that it '*emanates from our
attitude and from our acts*'. A *justitia domestica* can be, although
interior to us, entirely the gift of God.

The affirmation of a *justitia domestica* is unquestionable in Calvin.
We need only give as an example the Geneva Catechism. In the
preliminaries to the chapter 'On the Law', where Christian
obedience is about to be studied in the light of the Ten Commandments, the minister puts the question: 'But can we have the
justifying faith, without doing good works?' And the catechumen
must reply: 'That is impossible; because, to believe in Jesus Christ
is to receive Him just as He gives Himself to us. Now He promises
us not only to deliver us from death, and to bring us back into a
state of grace with God His Father, by the merit of His justice;
but, also, to regenerate us by His Spirit, in order that we may
live holy lives.'[26] There is, then, for Protestant theology a present
regeneration and a lived holiness, and not only an imputed justice.
In any case this regeneration and this holiness are not in any way
a matter of merit; they are the life of Christ in the Christian and
in the Church. Certainly, Christ takes and uses our nature, our
person, in order to make this life in us real, but it is He who is our
life, our regeneration and our holiness. Our nature remains sinful
always, and thus we can have no merit in ourselves. There is a
conflict between Christ and the self, and the temporary victories
of the Holy Spirit over our flesh are the intermittent moments of
holiness in us. Thus, divested of all inherent and permanent holiness, without any merit, neither the Christian, whoever he be,
nor the Church, can be the object of veneration. Only Christ in
them should receive honour, and not in any way their person,
their nature, their virtues, their faith.

But Christ cannot ever be separated from the Church and from
His witnesses, and a Protestant piety which rejects all veneration
of Christ in the Church, its hierarchy, and its saints, falls into an
individualist spirituality, wherein Christ is sought solely and
directly in the heart of the Trinity without the assembly and communion of the Church and of the saints. But the sign (Church,
saints, or sacraments) must not retain to itself the attention of the
faithful; it should be a pathway, an instrument, a vehicle, for the

coming of Christ to man and for the raising of man to God. The sign is necessary, but it must not claim for itself what can only be found as it leads men to Christ.

This divergence between Catholicism and Protestantism, on the question of the effects of grace, could be summed up by saying that for Catholicism the being is physically transformed by the Holy Spirit, and is thus brought physically (according to the change which takes place in his nature) into communion with Christ; while for Protestantism it is rather a question of the abiding of the Holy Spirit in a nature which remains sinful, and yet serves as the instrument for God's work of sanctification, allowing itself to be conquered and subjected by Him, while at the same time remaining attracted by rebellion.

In this perspective it can be understood that for Catholicism the individual Christian can participate in the very physical being of Christ. The Holy Spirit begets him to a new life, so that he becomes the son of God and brother of Christ, in the physical meaning of the terms. The Church is the body of Christ not only in an analogical sense, but in reality. The Church is the human body of Jesus Christ, His physical body, and it participates physically in His life. Now because the Church and the Christian are, through faith and sanctification, in a physical relation with Christ whose body they are, members and brothers, they participate naturally in His whole physical existence; Mary, the physical mother of Jesus, becomes the mother of the faithful in a very concrete and direct way. When Christ commits His beloved disciple to His mother, it is not simply a question of a particular gesture interesting no one but John; it signifies the universal motherhood of the Virgin. Thus the doctrine of the universal motherhood of Mary is directly based on the doctrine of grace, and on a physical participation of the Church and of the Christian in the life of Christ.

This same doctrine explains the way in which Catholic theology envisages also the person and the nature of Mary. If grace produces this physical sanctification, Mary, chosen in order to become the mother of the Saviour, and therefore receiving a superabundance of grace, is superabundantly sanctified. On the other hand, in order to be worthy of a physical participation with the Son of God as close as in the Incarnation, she has had to be physically prepared, whence her perfect holiness.

The doctrine of the Immaculate Conception means nothing other than this physical preparation of Mary to become the mother of God, being unable to receive Him in her womb except as in an abode perfectly intact. It is sometimes thought that the dogma of the Immaculate Conception is a sign of Pelagianism in Roman theology, because it would indicate that God can reveal Himself only where there has already been an effort towards Him. But the Immaculate Conception does not signify any effort of Mary to be worthy of her God. On the contrary, this dogma manifests the unique glory of God and takes all value of merit from Mary's very act of faith. From before her birth she has been preserved from sin, fully redeemed by Christ, prepared to receive God within her as her Son. A very predestination of the Virgin is being expressed. And that is most important and interesting to emphasise, for there is here revealed to us anew the divergence of our conceptions of grace. The predestination of Mary to become the mother of God implies for Catholic theology that she has been 'highly favoured' and consequently physically prepared, and perfectly so, in order to be worthy of participating in the physical life of her Son, and above all of having Him participate in hers. The Immaculate Conception of Mary is her predestination to be the instrument of the Incarnation, conceived as a physical preparation perfectly accomplished by the gift of a superabundance of grace.

Protestant theology sees this matter very differently. Predestination does not express itself in a man's being by sanctification, but is a merciful decision of the God of love which infallibly leads the sinful and forgiven elect soul, even through sin, to the end which He has chosen for him. Mary, then, predestined from the womb of her mother, has not been immaculately conceived, but infallibly directed by God, in spite of her sin, to the accomplishment of her role in the mystery of the Incarnation. The grandeur and the supereminent dignity of this role matter little. God does not measure the magnitude of the functions which He entrusts according to the dignity of His ministers, which is itself entirely conferred by Him. On the contrary, He wills that His glory should shine forth the more signally because it manifests itself in a being who is the least capable of attributing it to Himself. And such is Mary, the humble sinful handmaid who has found favour with God.

The place of the Virgin Mary is unique in the economy of the Kingdom of God. She is the culmination of the long procession of prophets of the Old Testament. In her reposes all the hope of Israel and all the consolation of the world. Her *Fiat* is to set in motion the historical work of redemption. She is a personage unique in history, but she remains a miserable sinner who has need of the forgiveness of her Son.

5. *The Presence of Mary in the Church*

Reformed theology wishes to keep Mary in the Church, and it accuses Catholicism of taking her out of it, and placing her above and over against the Church. If Mary walks at the head of those who have believed, she walks with them, turned with them towards her Son, from whom she awaits with them the redemption of her body and eternal glory, after having received, like them, the forgiveness of her sins, justification and sanctification.

The Catholic doctrines concerning Mary seem to Reformed theology all tending to banish Mary from the Church—the body of sinful men that we are. We have seen above how that is the case with the dogma of the Immaculate Conception. The perpetual virginity makes of her a woman different from others, the virginity *in partu* makes of the birth of her Son a singular mystery, the virginity *post partum* makes of her marriage with Joseph a false marriage. The question of knowing whether Mary had other children besides Jesus remains open, provided that one does not seek to defend the perpetual virginity of Mary and so to remove her from the common existence of every woman. Calvin himself will have it that she had no other children, and attacks Helvidius —not, it seems, in order to defend the perpetual virginity of Mary so much as to affirm the plenitude of the gift of God in Jesus Christ. 'Helvidius has shown himself too ignorant, in saying that Mary had several sons, because mention is made in some passages of the brothers of Christ.'[27] Calvin translates *adelphoi* by 'cousins' or 'relatives'. We have already said in another place, that according to the custom of the Hebrews all relatives are called brothers.'[27]

The new dogma of the Assumption, now promulgated as being *de fide*, completes the removal of Mary from the conditions of the Church. There, indeed, Mary passes from the temporal level of the Church and enters the level of eschatology. Her body has undergone glorification, has not known corruption, and has nothing more to wait for. She has passed through all the stages of the transformation 'from glory to glory'. She is alone in this state, between the Church which awaits the end and the Trinity which prepares for it: she is the Kingdom of God.

But if Reformed theology criticises the exaltation of the Virgin as making her a divine personage, outside human conditions, and if it defends the common presence of Mary in the Church, it does so only in negative criticism, and not positively in the framework of theology or liturgy, as is the case in the Anglican Church. If it is necessary to open in Reformed theology a chapter on Mariology which would illumine our conception of the incarnation and of grace, the role that Mary ought to play, like the apostles and all the saints, by her presence and her witness in the Church, must also be manifested in piety and in liturgy. A Church which despises the communion of saints, of all the saints, present and past, here and elsewhere, risks losing itself in individualism and sectarianism. The soul which seeks Christ only in the heart of the Trinity and in biblical history, and not in the Church and the witnesses of all ages, will know only an individualistic and cramped piety. A Church which does not renew itself in contact with the life of the saints and with tradition becomes sectarian and cuts itself off from the great body of Christians and from all the riches that it contains. 'But ye are come unto mount Sion,' says the author of the Epistle to the Hebrews (12. 22-23), 'and unto the city of the living God, the heavenly Jerusalem, and to innumerable hosts of angels, to the general assembly and church of the firstborn, who are enrolled in heaven, and to God the Judge of all, and to the spirits of just men made perfect, and to Jesus. . . .' To come unto God, to Jesus, is to come to the heavenly Jerusalem also, the city of the angels and the saints. Nothing is taken away from the love which one owes to Christ alone, from the adoration and obedience which are given to Him alone, nothing from His sacrifice and His intercession. It is He whom one loves in His saints, whom one adores in venerating them, whom one obeys in following their example. His sacrifice is fully sufficient, although it is reflected in living witness in the offering of their lives, and it is the Spirit which in them intercedes for us. The presence and the commemoration of the saints in the Church ought to be conceived in the light of the Johannine doctrine of the love of God. 'He that loveth not his brother whom he hath seen, cannot love

God whom he hath not seen? And this commandment have we from him, that he who loveth God love his brother also' (I John 4. 20-21). The commemoration of the saints in the Church is a form of perfect love. One cannot love God in Himself only. He must be loved in one's brothers, in the Church, in His saints. And if the profound meaning of the communion of saints has been understood, as truly uniting us to all those who are in Christ, of all ages and all places, we ought to consider this love of our brothers as embracing all the saints of tradition. The love of the brethren which makes perfect our love of God is not only the love of the brethren of my Church, but of all catholicity in space and time. It is the love for all the witnesses of Christ, and quite naturally for the best known in the Church, for Peter and for Paul, for Augustine and Francis, for Thomas and Bernard, for Calvin and Luther. Why, then, should the mother of the Saviour be excluded from this brotherly love, she whom St. John loved and took to his own home?

They all guide us and sustain us in each day's combat; in loving them we love Christ in them, whose perfect image they for their part reflect. 'Be ye imitators of me, even as I also am of Christ,' St. Paul says to us (I Cor. 11. 1). To imitate Paul or Mary is to imitate Christ, it is to understand an aspect of the Person of Christ shown forth in them and to apply it to oneself. The commemoration of the saints in the Church is the love and imitation of Christ, and also an act of thanksgiving for the gifts of God shown forth in them, for His power of resurrection and regeneration. 'Blessed is she that believed,' cries Elizabeth (Luke 1. 45); and Mary herself predicts the Church's praise of God on her account in the 'Magnificat': 'For, behold, from henceforth all generations shall call me blessed' (Luke 1. 48).

Thus Mary is present in the Church, at the head of all the saints, as mother of God and the first Christian; to be loved, and so to lead to the love of Christ; to be imitated and so to lead to the imitation of Christ; to be called happy and blessed among women, and so to lead to the praise of God: 'My soul doth magnify the Lord.'

The spiritual consequences of this presence of Mary in the Church are important:

Firstly, it shows the humble life hidden with Christ, the contemplation and mystical life which by her are restored to honour in the Church, against spiritual and ecclesiastical pride, against useless activism.

Secondly, it speaks of a corporate spirituality which is revived in the heart of the Church, the family of God, with all the tenderness of Jesus Christ, and His gentleness, and His friendship; as against that false virility and austerity which is too often the rule in Christian circles, the hardness and dryness of a certain kind of puritanism.

Finally it marks the role of woman in the Church, which is signified by the attitude of Mary towards her Son. She is not a priest as He is; she stands behind Him; she follows Him. Her function is to take care of Him, to love and warn Him. She is capable of intuition and audacity as at Cana; she can be the decisive cause of great events; she sympathises, she suffers at the foot of the Cross; she bears all things, believes all things, hopes all things. She is indispensable to the work of salvation. But in her proper place, like another Mary, she is seated at the feet of Jesus, listening to His words. Such is woman.

Very early, in the Church, we see Mary soberly associated with piety and the liturgy. Such are the oldest figures of the Virgin in the cemetery of Priscilla:[28] the Virgin mother and Isaiah, the first artistic representation of Mary; the Virgin of the adoration of the Magi, in the Greek chapel where Mary is seen crowned as an empress; the Virgin of the Oranto fresco where Mary is shown as an example to a virgin taking the veil. . . . In these three interesting cases, as in all the primitive representations, the Virgin figures with the child whom she presents. We are far from the Madonnas of the nineteenth century, with open arms, without Jesus, like that of the vision of St. Catherine Labouré in the Rue du Bac. But we are also far from the Protestant exclusion of any liturgical or pictured presence of Mary in the Church. How is she to be regarded to-day in accordance with the Gospel, in the Reformed Church, in view of all the theological and spiritual advantages of which we have spoken and in view of a new centering upon the great ecumenical tradition?

Reformed thought should first look at Anglicanism and Lutheranism.

From Anglican sources we see in the Book of Common Prayer sanctorals in the spirit we have indicated, with the Feasts of the Purification and the Annunciation, each with its Proper Collect,

Epistle and Gospel, and appointed Lessons for Matins and Even-song. The Calendar of 1662 makes simple mention also of the Visitation, the Nativity, and the Conception of the Virgin Mary.[29] The Revised Prayer Book of 1928 (as proposed) follows the same in its Alternative Calendar.[30] In the liturgies of communities or colleges of Catholic tendencies we find, moreover (as, for example, in the Cuddesdon Office Book), in addition to the above-named feasts, The Repose of the Blessed Virgin Mary on 15th August, with prayers, antiphons, chapters and proper responses.[31] The Collect of 15th August gives clearly the meaning of this presence of Mary in the worship of the Church, of Mary with the faithful, adoring her Son and revealing an aspect of His person. 'O almighty God, who hast favoured with a singular grace the Blessed Virgin Mary, the Mother of our Lord; deign we beseech Thee to sanctify our bodies in chastity, and our souls in humility and love, through the same Jesus Christ, Thy Son, our Lord. Amen.'[32] Luther had 'allowed the feast of the Purification and of the Annunciation of Mary to remain',[33] and the High Church Lutherans have maintained, following him, the observance of certain feasts of the sanctoral cycle. There is, for example, in Sweden the *Svenska Tidegärden*, the evangelical breviary, with the feasts of the Purification, the Annunciation and the Visitation.[34] The 'Common Service Book' of the Lutheran Church of America, reproduced in the 'Divine Office' of the Evangelical Lutheran Church of France (an unofficial publication),[35] likewise observes the same three festivals.

For the first time there has appeared in a book of Reformed prayer a sanctoral in the *Divine Office for each day*,[36] where the feasts of the Purification (under the name of the Presentation of our Lord Jesus Christ in the Temple), the 15th August (Mary, Mother of the Lord) and the Annunciation (the Tuesday of the third week in Advent) are provided for. Here, for example, is the second collect for 15th August: 'Holy God, eternal and almighty Father, who hast favoured the Blessed Virgin Mary with a full measure of Thy Grace, and hast adorned her with the spiritual gifts by which she prayed to Thee and magnified Thee, grant that Thy Holy Spirit may in like manner inflame our hearts and inspire continually in us the desire to hallow Thy great name, the blessed name of the Father and of the Son and of the Holy Ghost. Amen.'[37] This collect, like that quoted above, shows a Mariological spirit which in no way contradicts Reformed theology, but may well rather enrich it with the treasures of the communion of saints, and renew in it a more corporate and ecumenical conception of the Church. It is not a question of praying to Mary, nor even of asking her intercession, or of commending oneself to her intercession and to her merits with God. Such prayers would be foreign to Reformed tradition.

It may however be asked in passing, as though to pose a disturbing ecumenical question for our private satisfaction, whether any request for the intercession of the saints who have preceded us in Christ must necessarily be considered as foreign to the strict evangelical spirit. Are not prayers for one another, intercession and the request for intercession, the most significant manifestations of the mystery of the communion of saints in the Church? Intercession is, with the Word and the Eucharist, the most firm cement of the Christian community. The wider the field of intercession, the more the Church grows to the true dimensions of the Body of Christ. The more we pray for the other Churches and ask their intercession, the more our ecumenical consciousness is deepened. If we can ask the intercession of a living brother, why, in the certitude that we have of the life in Christ of those who have left their bodies, may we not ask dead saints to pray, when we ourselves are drawing near to the city of the living God and to innumerable hosts of angels and to the general assembly and Church of the firstborn? Will not this strengthen our faith in eternal life? And if it is true that the request for intercession is a powerful means of deepening our certainty of the total communion of the Body of Christ, does not this intimacy with St. John or St. Andrew, with St. Francis or Luther or Mary, and the request for their prayers, widen to infinite frontiers our faith in the fulness of the Church? The community of the Church feeds on the preached Word, on the eucharistic Communion and on intercession. If to-day we understand by the Church only the preached Word, our spiritual life remains limited; we must listen and see the Word preached and lived by all the saints of tradition, in order to benefit from the riches of all truth. In the Communion of the Holy Supper, we must be equally conscious that it unites us not only to our brothers communicating with us, but to the whole Church; such is the meaning of the commemoration of the saints in the Canon of the Mass. Finally, intercession strengthens the sense of the *koinonia*. It would not make sense for Reformed doctrine to pray for those who have died within the communion of the Church. We do not pray for saints who now rest in Christ; we do not pray for Christ. But just as we invoke the intercession of Christ, why do we not ask that of those who live close to Him? They are no more separated from us than when they were alive. St. Paul or St. Peter or Mary are as near to us as they were to their contemporaries in the Church. To ask their intercession with God no more devalues the unique intercession of Christ, than to ask here on earth the prayers of a brother for oneself, or to intercede for others. All true intercession is made in Christ and 'the Spirit itself maketh intercession for us with groanings which cannot be uttered' (Rom. 8. 26), in us, in our brothers living and dead, in all the saints, in the whole Church. And this request for intercession appears to have the extraordinary power of recalling to us the life of all who have preceded us in the Church, assembled in Christ, and never separated from us. The entire Church then becomes, in our consciousness, a living Church which does not believe in the death of its members, against which the gates of hell shall never prevail. The great litany of the saints is the most moving and the strongest ecumenical prayer. And Mary is present at the head of this general assembly and Church of the firstborn whose names are written in heaven.

Clearly the Church must always watch, and call to mind the uniqueness of Christ's sacrifice and intercession. For the doctrine of merit can easily be rooted in a too anthropocentric conception of intercession. Men have commended themselves to the intercession of the martyrs of the faith, believing that their sufferings gave them greater intimacy with Christ and rendered their intercession more powerful. This conception of suffering as intercession finds its justification in the thought of St. Paul (Col. 1. 24).

The offering of one's whole life to the service of Christ (Rom. 12. 1) may also be seen from the angle of intercession. In the same way, again, the offering of fasting and almsgiving (Acts 10. 4) can be seen as an intercession, a way of full identification with the supplication of God, not only in spirit and in word, but also with one's whole being, importuning the Lord like the widow in His parable. But from there to the doctrine of merit, rejected by Reformed theology, there is a possible and dangerous transition. Thus, to ask the intercession of the saints may lead to a belief in their merits and a desire to benefit from them. And it is to this error that the Roman Church seems to us to have fallen a prey: if so, the uniqueness of the sacrifice and of the merit of Christ is weakened. Intercession must always remain truly an intercession in Christ, by the Holy Spirit, whatever be its form (suffering, consecration, fasting, almsgiving) and be founded on the sole merit of Jesus Christ, since there is no other.

Conclusion

We will give in conclusion an office of Matins with Propers at a feast of Mary, mother of the Lord, on 15th August:

Introduction (O Lord, open thou . . .)

Psalm 95 with the invitatory:
> 'My soul doth magnify the Lord
> And my spirit rejoiceth in God my Saviour.'

Hymn (Reformed paraphrase of the Magnificat)[38]

Three psalms with antiphons:

Ps. 45, ant. v. 14 (the typological interpretation of this psalm referring to Mary)

Ps. 46, ant. v. 6 (Mary is here a figure of the New Jerusalem, of the Church)

Ps. 87, ant. v. 7 (Mary the figure of the Church, the source from which proceeds our redemption)

Versicle and Response:

℣. She shall be brought unto the King in raiment of needlework.

℟. With joy and gladness shall they be brought. (Ps. 45, 15a, 16a.)

Three Lessons on the Gospel of St. Luke:

(2: 41b-45) taken from Calvin's commentaries on harmony.
(Lesson I on v. 42, II on v. 45, first part, III on v. 45, second part).

Each followed by a response:

I

℟. Blessed art thou among women, and blessed is the fruit of thy womb.

✠

And whence is this to me, that the mother of my Lord should come to me?

℣. Blessed is she that believed; for there shall be a performance of those things which were told her from the Lord.

✠

And . . .

II

℟. He hath regarded the low estate of his handmaiden.

✠

For behold from henceforth all generations shall call me blessed.

℣. For he that is mighty hath done to me great things; and holy is his name. And his mercy is on them that fear him from generation to generation.

✠

For behold . . .

III

℟. Behold this child is set for the fall and rising again of many in Israel; and for a sign which shall be spoken against.

✠

Yea, a sword shall pierce through thy own soul also.

℣. That the thoughts of many hearts may be revealed. Glory be . . .

Te Deum

Collect (as p. 316 at note 32 or p. 316 at note 37).

NOTES

[1] *Dictionnaire de théologie catholique*, A. Vacant, etc., Vol. VII, p. 1, col. 845–1218.

[2] *Ibid.*, Vol. VII, p. 2, col. 1445–1539.

[3] Père Daniélou in an article on 'La Vierge et le Temps' does not deny this mysterious coincidence of the worship of heathen Virgins and Mothers with the worship of the Virgin-Mother of God; he even seems to make of it a ground of apologetic, an *Anknüpfungspunkt* for the heathen. 'India, the adorer of goddesses, of virgins—phenomenal aspects of the Advaita—will feel the human and cosmic grandeur of the Virgin-Mother . . .', 'Dieu Vivant', No. 10; Paris: Ed. du Seuil, 1948.

[4] Cf. 'On the worship of the Blessed Virgin in the Catholic Church', letter from J. H. Newman to Dr. Pusey, Paris, 1866.

[5] *Protestantisme français*, p. 439; Paris: Ed. Plon, 1945 (coll. 'Présences').

[6] *Bulletin de la Faculté libre de Théologie protestante de Paris*, No. 25, March 1946, p. 6.

[7] *Ibid.*, p. 7.

[8] *Les plus beaux textes sur la Vierge Marie*, présentés par le Père Pie Régamey; Paris: Ed. du Vieux Colombier, 1942.

[9] *St. Irenaeus: Against Heresies*, L. III, chap. XXII, n. 4; P.G., 7, col. 958–960. See also V. XIX, n. 1; *ibid.*, col. 1175.

[10] *St. Clement of Alexandria*, Strom., VII, cap. 16; P.G., 9, col. 529.

[11] *Contemplation de la Croix*, p. 74, Neuchâtel: Ed. Delachaux et Niestlé, 1944.

[12] P.G., 46, col. 909–912.

[13] *Foi et Vie*, Nos. 85–86, August–October, 1936, Paris, p. 509–510.

[14] A doctrine not of faith, but supported by the whole Roman Catholic tradition, according to which the virginity of Mary remains intact, before, during and after the birth of Christ, as is affirmed, among many other doctors of the Church, by St. Bonaventura in his *Commentarium in evangelium Lucae*, 2: 53 (Opera, Quaracchi, 1901, Vol. VII, p. 56). Speaking of Mary, he says: *. . . quae est porta clausa ante partum et post partum et in partu . . .* 'she who is a closed door before, after, and in her childbirth'.

[15] It is at bottom the ordinary expression of a refusal to intervene, He being the Christ. An imperative translation would give: 'Let us not concern ourselves with this, neither thou nor I!' Far from expressing, as Loisy would have it, a refusal of communion with His mother ('What have I to do with thee?'), Jesus begs His mother to remain quiet and not to compromise Him. The words which follow explain the meaning of this plea: 'mine hour is not yet come'. It must even be noticed that in these words Jesus associates His mother with a possible intervention and miracle, that He envisages a common action: 'What for thee and me.' The expression, which betrays its semitic origin, is to be found several times in the O.T. and the N.T. and always in order to mark the refusal

L

322 LITURGY AND DEVOTION

of an inopportune intervention (II Sam. 16. 10; 19. 22; II Kings 3. 13; Matt. 8. 29; Mark 1. 24; Luke 4. 34). 'Why should *we* concern ourselves in this affair?' would be another good translation. This is the opinion of Strack-Billerbeck (*Kommentar zum neuen Testament aus Talmud und Midrasch*, Münich, 1924), and recently taken up by P. Braun (*La Sainte Bible*, under the supervision of L. Pirot and A. Clamer, Vol. X, p. 328). In the same way the word 'Woman!' that Jesus addresses to His mother, and which can appear to us offensive, contains no irreverence but only emphasises the solemn nature of the words of Christ. It is in the same way that Jesus addresses Mary from the Cross, where He nevertheless shows Himself to be full of compassion and tenderness (John 19. 26).

[16] This tradition of seeing in these words of Christ the donation, in the person of John, of the whole Church and even of humanity to the motherhood of Mary, is a tradition which becomes general only very late in the twelfth century. Support is already to be found for it in Origen (Comm. in Joan. I, IV, 23). The Abbé Rupert de Deuts has greatly developed its mystical meaning (Rupertus, Comm. in Joan., P.L., CLXIX, 790).

This doctrine of the motherhood of Mary extending to the whole body of Christ, the Church, and finding its foundation in this text of St. John, has been sanctioned by Leo XIII (Encycl. *Quamquam pluries*, 25th August 1889; *Octobri mense adveniente*, 22nd September 1891; *Incundum semper*, 8th September 1894; *Adiutricem populi christiani*, September 1895, and by Pius XI in these terms: *Sanctissima regina apostolorum Maria, cum homines universos in Calvaria habuerit materno animo suo commandatos, non minus fovet ac diligit, qui se fuisse a Christo Jesu redemptos ignorant, qua, qui ipsius beneficiis fruuntur feliciter* . . . 'Mary, the most blessed queen of the apostles, does not choose and esteem less those who know not that they have been redeemed by Christ Jesus, than those who happily rejoice in His benefits, since all men were committed to her maternal soul on Calvary' (Encycl. *Rerum Ecclesiae*, 28th February 1926). Pasteur J. de Saussure equally supports in a certain sense the motherhood of Mary with this text of John (*Contemplation de la croix*, pp. 73-74, Neuchâtel: Ed. Delachaux et Niestlé, 1944).

[17] This is not the place to treat the problem of the 'brethren' of Jesus from the exegetical point of view. Let us say at the very outset (we shall come back to the question further on) that it is here a question of a delicate and perhaps insoluble historical problem, and that it is not possible to say honestly that those who are called in the New Testament 'brethren' of Jesus are really sons of Mary; Pasteur Ch. Brutsch has perhaps over-simplified the problem in his book, *La Vierge Marie*, pp. 53-54 (Neuchâtel: Delachaux et Niestlé, 1943).

[18] Pius XI, Encyclical *Rerum Ecclesiae*, 28th February 1926.

[19] H. M. Féret, *L'Apocalypse de Saint Jean, vision chrétienne de l'histoire*, pp. 231-241, Paris: Ed. Corréa, 1946.

[20] *La Vie Spirituelle*, May 1949, p. 472, Paris: Ed. du Cerf.

[21] The only possible meaning, since further on Paul wishes not for an 'unclothing' of his material body, but only a 'clothing upon'. If nakedness be taken in the spiritual sense, consisting in the absence of faith, one cannot see how the

apostle could desire a 'clothing upon' other than the justice of faith with such groans. It is in this way indeed that Père Spicq, O.P., interprets it in *La Sainte Bible*, Vol. XI, 2, p. 335, edited by L. Pirot and A. Clamer, Paris: Ed. Letouzey et Ané, 1948.

²² Karl Adam: *Vers L'Unité chrétienne, le point de vue catholique*, translated by F. de Bourbon-Busset, introduction by R. P. Bouyer, Paris: Ed. Aubier, 1949; quotation from the résumé made of it by R. P. Maurice Villain, S.M., in *Vers l'unité chrétienne*, Catholic monthly information bulletin, Paris: Istina, April 1949.

²³ 'Sainteté et péché dans l'Eglise', in *La Vie Intellectuelle*, November 1947, pp. 20-21.

²⁴ 'Le mystère du Christ et de l'Eglise', in *Foi et Vie*, May 1946, pp. 376-403.

²⁵ *La confession de foi de l'Eglise*, Cahiers théologiques de l'Actualité protestante, No. 2; Ed. Delachaux et Niestlé, Neuchâtel-Paris, 1943.

²⁶ John Calvin: *Le catéchisme de Genève*; Ed. Je Sers, Paris, 1934, p. 52.

²⁷ John Calvin: *Concordance qu'on appele Harmonie composée de trois évangélistes*, Geneva, 1555, p. 392.

²⁸ Since the first half of the second century.

²⁹ *The Book of Common Prayer . . .*, University Press, Oxford.

³⁰ *The Book of Common Prayer*, with the additions and alternatives proposed in 1928, University Press, Cambridge.

³¹ *The Cuddesdon College Office Book*, University Press, Oxford, 1940.

³² *Ibid.*, p. 115.

³³ *Von der Ordnung des Gottesdienstes in der Gemeinde* of 1523.

³⁴ *Den Svenska Tidegärden*, C.V. K. Gleerups Förlag, Lund, 1944.

³⁵ *L'Office Divin*, Ed. luthériennes, Paris-Strasbourg, 1948.

³⁶ *Eglise et Liturgie*, Communauté de Taizé-lès-Cluny, Communauté de Grandchamp, 'L'Office divin de chaque jour': Ed. Delachaux et Niestlé, Neuchâtel-Paris, 1949.

³⁷ *Ibid.*, p. 248.

³⁸ *Louange et Prière*, hymn book of the Reformed Churches of France: Ed. Delachaux et Niestlé, Paris, 1939; No. 88, p. 128.

XVII

AN APPROACH TO THE WORK
OF REUNION
THROUGH COMMON DEVOTIONAL
UNDERSTANDING

★

Gilbert S. Shaw and Eric Hayman
(Great Britain)

Introduction

The Unity of the Body of Christ is both the unity of the individual
members in their Head, through their realisation and experience
of relationship in Him: and also the unity of the Body itself in its
life and activity as an organism. This latter aspect, with the historic
breaches that have formed diverse and even rival Christian organisations, is the special concern of the Faith and Order Movement
as a whole. Doctrinal theology, and the nature and theory of the
Church, are its proper field. The results achieved, however, may
be significant and far-reaching, and may yet remain at the level
of scholarship, ineffective to move the main currents of Christian
living, unless attention be directed also to the wide differences in
the practice, method and customs of private devotion. As it is, in
divided Christendom the divergent traditions of devotional practice and emphasis do more to divide the generality of Christians
than differences of understanding in doctrinal concepts.

It is therefore proposed that there should be established a series
of discussions on a realistic and practical level, though also on a
level of serious and informed scholarship, between selected members of different communions who are well qualified by experience
and learning to explain the techniques and disciplines that belong
to the individual in personal devotional life. Such an enquiry
would obviously be closely woven with some of the existing pro-
jects of the Commission on Ways of Worship, and it would be

needlessly complicated to separate the strands completely. The dominant reason for the new study lies in the fact that the dispositions, both moral and spiritual, whether of individuals or of congregations, tend in practice to be formed by the pattern of worship to which they are accustomed, and by the types of private devotion which they understand and use, rather than by the intellectual appreciation of theological problems. It will be evident, in this psychological age, that the formative effect of emotional patterns of devotion, working in the unconscious, is the paramount factor in training the spiritual life.

It will be clear that in asking for a study of 'devotional theology', the appropriate terms should rather be 'ascetic theology'. The latter phrase is suspect owing to a common misunderstanding of its meaning. Ascetic theology implies the training of the whole man for his ultimate purpose of union with God, and it is so understood in the Anglican, Roman Catholic and Orthodox traditions. It has no relation to a negative or dehumanising process, for which it is often mistaken in Protestant thought, and for that reason rightly castigated. This paper is written from an Anglican background, with a full consciousness of the duty owed by its members to that communion. The writers believe in its integrity as a formal part of the undivided Body, both in Faith and in Order. But alongside this duty and conviction, and even as part of it, there is the deep consciousness of a duty of Christians as such to all their fellows, of whatever Christian communion and confession. Such a combined loyalty, neither forgetting nor exaggerating either aspect, is the characteristic temper of mind required in ecumenical work. In such a temper of mind it is possible to speak without apology out of the setting in which a man belongs, and from the fullness of his own convictions. In this paper, therefore, the problem of Christendom as a whole is not minimised by the use, mainly, of illustrations from Anglican experience.

It must be clear that theology and devotion are always closely allied, for the whole object of credal formulae is to safeguard the soul's approach and adherence to God. Theology, moreover, is essential for growth into a deeper knowledge of God. Such theology may be quite simple, and for the majority it must remain so. But precisely because of this simplicity it tends in history to isolate or to emphasise particular truths at different social and historical stages. There are economic, cultural, and even political reasons that cause some one theological truth to form a focus for popular devotion at a given time. It may even be said that dogma is primary, for it secures the right handing-down through tradition of revealed truth. So there is in these proposals no alternative—still less a rival—to dogmatic enquiry. They seek to recognise the complementary value of ascetic theology. There are deep mis-understandings in the latter field, as in the former. It is, however, from a common understanding of the fruitfulness of ascetic theo-logy in forming the life of union with God that a new inspiration for integral unity in worship may arise. Such a unity does not imply a rigid uniformity of type, but welcomes and expects the multiplicity of organic life. The purpose of dogma is to safeguard the relationship between God who reveals Himself, and man to whom the revelation is made. Ascetic theology is the understand-ing and study of the life of union which credal statements are concerned to protect. Thus dogma and devotional practice can only be complementary—never rivals. Both in their several ways illustrate and confirm one another to the sole end of man, which is to know God and to do His will.

Our Lord's appeal for unity does not imply merely a theological exactitude, but a full religious experience. The function of theo-logy is to guard the integrity of that experience. The historic creeds have grown up as signposts and warnings against those aberrations into which men seemed liable to stray from their intended relationship with God, found in the saving work of Christ and the sending of the Holy Spirit. Every question that concerns reunion requires the clarification of our understanding of the soul's total relationship to God. The practices of devotion either expand and enrich that understanding, or else they limit and fetter it. In different parts of the broken Body of Christ today, different traditions and uses have arisen which are not understood by Christians in other parts of the Church, and which even pre-vent the growth of understanding. The corporate aspect of this matter is the proper concern of the Commission on Ways of Worship. But there can be no contrast between personal and liturgical devotion. The two are inseparable and can hardly even be studied in isolation one from the other. A Christian is not a unit concerned with a private relation to God in Christ. He is a member of the Body of Christ. His prayer and his life in the Body will affect his individual prayer. This in turn will enrich or impoverish his life in the Body. The two aspects are not even complementary, but are one whole. It is the visible rupture of this wholeness which more than anything else has widened and perpetuated the divisions in Christendom. This becomes clear in history. The breach between East and West, for example, was doubtless contributed to by obstacles of understanding in Greek and Latin minds, and aggravated by the political conflicts between Old and New Rome. But it was widened and accentuated by divergences of devotional practice. The break-up of Christian unity in the West seems to spring directly from the devotional unrest of that turbulent age, in which feudalism was breaking up and nationalism was beginning—when reforming bodies broke from the traditional Church, and the 'counter-reformation' sought and found devotional renewal within that same tradition. The same forces were at work in both bodies, and both were conditioned by the political, economic and mental temper of their age. It was an age of the rise of individualism, and an age of intolerance. Devotional practices became the symbols of loyalties. My neighbours prayed in a way different from my own and became anathema for that reason. This temper of separateness was not only exaggerated by the stress of conflict, but also hardened by limitation of communications. The early English travellers to Russia could only criticise and despise what they could not understand in Eastern Orthodoxy. When, with the end of the religious wars, communications increased the facilities of contact, this was not yet enough to produce mutual understanding. The discovery of varieties in practice led to scepticism rather than to comprehension. The educated turned to philosophy and the common sense of humanity rather than to religion as their means of interchange.

The impact of the scientific method, and man's increasing mastery over the material, has produced a completely different temper of mind, and the difference is more apparent in the Protestant cultures. The spiritual concept of religion tends to be ignored under a guise of indifferent tolerance. This is the situation of the present day. There is a culture which is man-determined even to the seeking of a religion of man, whether through 'scientific humanism' or through 'naturalism'. In such a world, Christianity is regarded as one among many competing ideologies with or without political affiliations, and the natural man sees little or no distinction, nor any vital importance, in its divisions.

The Church is aware of these facts chiefly because of their effect in the sphere of evangelism. The competing loyalties and divergent practices within a single national unity or mission field prove grievously embarrassing. The pressure of modern times compels an emphasis on the corporate. Since the Church has failed to interpret the true nature of corporate life to modern industrialism, still less to the collective masses, the result is a purely humanist collective, which denies or ignores the dependence of man upon God. The consequent sense of urgency tends to foster a reunion in defence of Christian principle and morality, but only to weaken thereby the cause of reunion at the deeper and more integral level. If the work of reunion should stay on the relatively superficial plane, new and deeper divisions are bound to be formed. It is not man's intellect, but the depth of his soul, which binds the human being. No acknowledgment of Spirit can dispense with a life of Spirit.

The genius of the Faith and Order Movement can never be content with some external closing of ranks for a supposed immediate end. It cannot use some agreed propaganda which would conceal for practical purposes the major distinctions that still mark the divided state of Christendom. To act in such a way could only render existing differences irreconcilable. The setting up of what would prove only a Protestant ideology, based upon some common programme determined by expediency, and modelling its devotional life upon the residuum of doctrine that could survive, would, as is widely realised, not only perpetuate disunion and prevent understanding of the older traditions: it would imperil the devotional integrity of those who accepted such compromise. The true task is at a far more costly level. It involves the exercise of the fullest charity and patience in order to discover true principles of integration, not least among those bodies which feel impelled to claim their own self-sufficiency in undivided truth, and are therefore under no compulsion to re-examine their own standpoints.

This warning has been truly heard within the movement which has led to the creation of a World Council of Churches. Even were this not so, the signs of the times appear against any such hasty action. Within the Christian bodies of the divided West there are evidenced many signs of devotional recovery. The bodies concerned are not ignoring the special emphasis which has held them in separation, but are still steadily drawing towards a unity based upon Scripture and upon primitive practice. The special position of the Anglican Communion affords an example. The Anglican Church stands isolated among the Reforming bodies because it claims integral continuity both in doctrine and in order with the unbroken Body. It has found—not by copying other traditions but by a resurgence of the religious experience implicit in its own formulae and common practice—new understandings and powers through the recovery of the meaning of liturgy, the revival of personal religious life; the re-introduction of the dedicated life of religious communities; and a renewed attention to the sanctification of the temporal order through the ministry of the Body of Christ.

In several of the confessions which arise from a break with the historic order, there are likewise movements toward a new understanding of liturgy, and a feeling after the dedicated life of religion. The hard divisions are breaking down, not by some external compulsion causing a hasty union of expediency, but through an inner working of the Holy Spirit. The riches of the Church are being rediscovered, and there is a new willingness to understand the spiritual integrity of those who differ in outward forms, or in the less fundamental doctrinal emphases. It is to encourage this unity of spirit—not as a flight from reality into some vague 'mysticism', but as a real integration and understanding of practical Christian living—that this essay is directed. It envisages a steady and co-ordinated task of devotional research, probably undertaken by different groupings from time to time. Its work is not an academic exercise to provide information, but a living contribution to mutual understanding, to the increase of charity, and to the development of that integrity of God-centredness through which alone the union for which our Lord ever prays can be realised. Experience has proved that when groups from different communions are able to use in common, over a period of time, one or more types of devotional approach, and can enter in common into one or more types of spiritual tradition, they will be able far more easily to reach mutual understanding, and to overpass the instinctive and emotional frontiers which their long separation has produced. In this way one of the most serious obstacles to an organic reunion may be removed. It is common knowledge, for example, that even within the Anglican tradition there are misunderstandings caused by varieties of use and emphasis in devotional instruction. This is a source of difficulty not only to the convert, who may be expected to understand some diversity, but rather to the conservative and traditional elements which have matured in a partial separation, and have as it were built themselves into close patterns and into fixed associations of ideas and practices, which to them form the whole of religion. If that is so within one communion, how much more difficult will it be to achieve a living understanding between elements that are more widely separated by their historic past. This gulf can, however, be bridged by a mutual interchange of traditional practice and experience, to prepare the way for a reunion that might otherwise lack reality. It is essential in such an approach to avoid any tendency towards a common denominator of unoffending practice. Rather must the way be left open for the Holy Spirit to guide the participants into the richness of the Christian devotional way —not into its poverty. Thus may be recovered the landmarks of that devotion which is primarily Christian and which undoubtedly informed the growing life of the early centuries.

The Argument

In the foregoing section the groundwork for this concern has been made clear. It is now necessary to outline some of the considerations to which the enquiry must direct attention. It will be convenient to deal very briefly with the main lines of enquiry and then to develop in greater detail those which emerge as primary.

The first problem, which might be termed a study of differences, is patent on the surface. The present divergent practices have become independent to such an extent that even among praying Christians the conception of the very nature of prayer, and of its purposes and methods, varies so greatly in different parts of the Church as virtually to prevent any common basis of understanding. The first step might thus be to assess the present separations and study each historically, so as to ascertain when the particular divergence arose, and the special emphases that have been sustained during its historical development. Thus the present situation in any divergence could be assessed. This process would, of course, entail a study also of the common origins of the bodies in question at the various points of rupture, and would thus indicate the common devotional tradition as it existed at various stages. This common tradition could then be traced in history to determine its antiquity, and to decide how far its effective existence in any of the present forms of the Church could be proved. This would establish a certain pattern of relationships, in which the common elements could be separated from the divergent elements.[1]

The problem could, however, be approached by an immediate review of unquestioned origins. Instead of tracing back from divergence, the tree of Christian devotion could be traced up into its many branches. This form of approach is rather an historical and literary one, and would begin from a study of the light which is thrown by the New Testament documents, and by early church writings, upon the primitive devotional practices. It must also be asked to what extent the present divergences of devotional *ethos* and practice represent conscious and willed departures from the common tradition, as, for example, the disuse of all sacramental forms in certain periods of separation, which practice was newly adopted in the system of a much more recently established Christian body—the Salvation Army. To what extent, on the other hand, are some divergences the unconscious effects of a new pattern created by the separation?

Another main line of enquiry must analyse carefully the organic relationship of corporate and individual prayer, and must also study the relation of prayer to conduct. Prayer cannot be considered without perceiving that it is the expression and experience of the whole man, in and through the reformation of his will. It is not an alternative to his normal, natural activity: rather does it determine the whole character of that activity. It has already been pointed out that there are no rigid barriers between corporate and liturgical worship on the one hand, and the personal devotion of individuals on the other. Man is a member of the corporate body, but also an individual expression of that membership. The reconciliation of these complementary aspects is found in the ful-

---

[1] In the study of animal heredity, relationship of an otherwise somewhat divergent group is traced by observing in its members certain common factors derived from the parent stock from which the divergence was first made. The possession of these factors marks them out as being family groups within one species. It is thus, for example, established that all the breeds of domestic pigeon are of one stock, and, if allowed to interbreed freely, would ultimately revert to the type of their common ancestor.

ness of personality, which is also the fulness of charity. Man starts
as a separate individual in and through his fallen human nature.
Through grace he grows into a fulness of stature, at first by the
renewing of his mind into conformity with the mind of Christ;
and ultimately through the more direct action of God made
possible by man's dependence on Him, and culminating in that
transforming union which is the Glory of God expressed in His
creature.

We may now turn in closer detail to three main lines of enquiry,
recognising that much of the formal work of the Commission on
Ways of Worship underlies them, and has prepared their way.

(1) *The enquiry through history:* a study of the origins and development of Christian devotion.

(2) *Liturgy and personal devotion.*

(3) *Prayer in the life of the modern world:* a study of the problems
of man in relation to his society as they affect the devotional
life.

The Enquiry through History

This part of the enquiry cannot be content with any merely
academic portrayal of devotional customs in the earliest or in any
later period. What is significant is to establish norms of valid
Christian spiritual experience, and to trace their movement and
their growth (or it may be their distortion) in the life of the broken
Body, so that we may become aware of the fulness of Christian
tradition and practice. We must begin at the Christian beginning
and yet bear in mind that the foundations were laid in the Old
Dispensation, and are developed in the immediate situation of
New Testament Jewry. We see in our Lord not only the divine
Son, but also the fulfilment of all that is best in man. He therefore
sanctifies through the Holy Spirit and draws into the riches of His
Body the ways of thought and expression, and even the practices,
of the world into which His sanctifying power extends. So, for
example, the classical division of man's nature into body, soul and
spirit is taken up by St. Paul and used to illustrate and explain to
the Greek world the Hebrew psychology of the wholeness of man,
and his relation to God through God's gift of the divine Spirit
whereby man became a living soul—a person capable of prayer
as a relationship of dependence upon God. That fundamental

Hebrew stress is most germane to this enquiry, for it is so often questioned. Not only in early days, but through the long history of the Church, there have been Christians seeking to cut themselves off from their roots. The resulting tendency has always been to exalt the independence of man. The Hebrew emphasis demands a drastic reconsideration which is completely relevant to the devotional life. God is wholly other than us His creatures. He has, none the less, given us the means to communicate with Him, not by any limitation of Himself but as a gift of His grace. But He has done more. When through a deformation of his will man turned to his own ends as the supreme good, God brought mankind back through His own act of love, by the taking of human flesh, and accepting all the consequences thereof, and by this means restoring man to the divine glory. That which is of origin in God is, in man, only a derived quality. The Hebrew tradition, in which our Lord's own prayers are expressed, is concerned chiefly with man's responsibility to glorify God, both by worship and by affirmation of the divine nature: and his parallel responsibility to carry out the divine will whereby the unity of purpose between the Creator and His creatures is made operative.

This relationship is fully explicit in the Lord's Prayer, which is the norm in this respect of all Christian prayer. Yet the Hebrew emphasis does not preclude the Church from taking into the ultimate glory of creation the riches of the nations. The Beatitudes, which give the pattern of the blessed life of dependence upon God in a fallen world, were supplemented by the classical moral concepts of the cardinal virtues, and also by the concepts of philosophy, so far as these were applicable to convey the divine truth to others. Plato, and later Aristotle have a significant part in the riches and practice of Christian prayer. But they are used only in so far as they may illustrate or rightly extend the primary principles of the Revelation. The danger of the errors which arose in later practice, and the origin of divisions and confusions, arise in part from excessive interest in methods or concepts which derive from the secondary source alone, and are of value only as means of communication. In such a way an undue interest in the techniques of the search for the reality of Absolute Being may lead to a false emphasis on isolated elements in the mystical tradition, such as those drawn from the 'pseudo-Dionysus'.

Man is inclined, apart from Revelation, to make his own con-

cepts of Deity. He may try to understand too much, in a desire
to escape the elements of mystery and the necessity of faith. Such
a course leads into a virtual Arianism, where the Son's humanity
is so emphasised that the Father is left in isolation: or to a devotion
so Christ-centred that it forms a virtual monotheism in which the
Father is obscured by a beneficent Son. In either form of error the
work of the Holy Spirit is effectively ignored. There is also a
possible drift into a pantheism in which God is lost in His creation.
This tendency was normally more eastern than western, but it has
reappeared in the West with the present revival of pseudo-philo-
sophies and the theology which is constructed to support them.

We are thus concerned with theology, but in terms of the
devotion by which it is strengthened and confirmed. Such an
expression in either aspect demands a medium of thought and
language in which it may be manifested.

The Primitive Church extended its message to all parts of the
world. Secure in the commission and promise of its Founder,
it presented to the common needs of mankind a gospel in which
was embodied an answer universal in its scope and character.
Just in proportion as the faith took deep root in different places,
it underwent certain inevitable transformations. The Gospel
must needs be translated, and as the process of translation involved more than merely turning a meaning in one language to
its nearest equivalent in another, the translation of the Church's
message effected certain differences in emphasis, brought to
light new aspects of meaning, and involved subtle variations in
the kind and degree of its apprehension on the part of different
peoples.[1]

In this first dispersion—the exodus of the new race led by the
Spirit of God into all the world—the three major divisions are
evident, Semitic, Greek and Latin, 'in essence fundamentally the
same, but strongly marked and almost personal in their own
individuality and character'.[2]

As we have rediscovered the importance of the Old Testament
in illuminating the New, so also must we rediscover the importance of understanding the Semitic tradition, both in its Jewish
elements and in the definitely Christian contribution as seen in

[1] Gavin: *Some Aspects of Contemporary Greek Thought*, Preface, p. xix.
[2] *Ibid.*

available manuscripts. In this tradition there has been little or no development. In the Greek and Latin traditions, however, with which this enquiry is specially concerned, the differences are so marked that we are inclined to lose sight of the conformities, more especially as the two traditions have tended to grow away from each other. There is, however, a certain general unity up to the time of St. Augustine in the West, which may be regarded as a norm. The spiritual masters of that age disclose its character in their writings. There is in this reference no real danger of a leadership divorced from the common life. The sermons and homilies of St. Augustine and St. John Chrysostom, for example, indicate both the general level of spiritual apprehension among their congregations, and also the methods and the content of the spiritual instruction on which the prayer life of the Church was built up. St. Augustine's volume on the Psalms demonstrates not only the truths he was setting forth, but also the way in which the praying Christian was taught to train himself in that understanding of God which is the basis of all prayer truly so-called. Beyond this homiletic material there is valuable evidence in the actual liturgies of the day. The devotional atmosphere for the individual soul was created and purified by his participation in the liturgy. The place of congregational response, and the active sharing in the work of adoration and thanksgiving, gave to these liturgies a popular origin, and a popular understanding far more intelligent than that which exists among the average laity of today.

> Religion and piety swayed men's lives . . . Not only for its foundations, but also . . . in the development of its worship, the Christian Church levied on Jewish practice. Psalms, hymns, prayers, intercessions, instructions, and Bible reading—all these . . . received their chief significance and culminated in the Eucharist itself.[1]

The character of this obvious living tradition is further seen in St. Benedict's insistence upon the balance of essential elements in all prayer. Supplication, oblation, intercession, and thanksgiving underlie both the popular instruction and the more formal ordering of Monastic devotion in later years.

The rapid expansion of the Church, both within the Roman Empire and beyond it, caused an inevitable dilution of spiritual

---

[1] Gavin: *Liturgy and Worship*, SPCK, 1932, p. 109.

purity. This impoverishment, denounced in unmeasured terms by St. Jerome and others, led first to the individualism of the desert, and then by a necessary reaction to the earlier monastic rules. Finally there came the balanced order of the Benedictine practice in the West, and that of the disciples of St. Basil in the East. Inevitably what has survived in writing from these early days has been more for the religious than for the secular, though the sermons are in the main an exception. It is clear from the time of St. Augustine that the conception of 'the two lives' was in the current coin of the Church's thought, and was later strongly emphasised with the development of feudalism. Its proper value today is seen not in some 'double standard', but in the differences of function within the one Body. For the secular Christian there was thus developed under the impetus and experience of monastic life a largely systematised popular devotion for public use. In its simplest forms, and for the least educated elements in the Church, this framework may have been limited to the Lord's Prayer and the Creed. But from that 'minimum rule' personal tendencies and temperament led into various paths, thus opening the way for the divergences of tradition which are here considered. Space will not permit the tracing of the Eastern development, save to note that the later Western emphasis upon formal discursive meditation is there unknown, and that the whole tendency is towards a sometimes extreme detachment formed through ascetic practice, and at the same time to a warmth of devotion. This *affective* devotion is fully recognised as a necessary part of the Holy Spirit's guidance, but it can be marred by overemphasis and strain, to the neglect of other balancing elements. The fulness of prayer, which is union with the divine in the derived glory of the heavenly order, was to be sought by seclusion and retirement. Yet those who attained were not to be separated from, but to serve, their brethren. The higher rungs of the ladder may appear to be leading to seclusion, but the highest of all is the return. Such is also the tradition of the Russian Church in modern times as evidenced in the person of the Starets. The story of the Blessed Serafim, and some indications in *Russian Letters of Direction*, make this ideal clear. The perfection granted in solitude is fulfilled in the return to the service of mankind.

The mark of Eastern devotion is in the tenacity with which the tradition is maintained, and in the elaboration of that tradition.

By contrast, the West tends so to simplify and modernise that nothing may be left unexplained. This insistence on 'utility' is marked in the West from the first, although it was romanticised in Gaul and in the Northern traditions. The emotional and aesthetic aspects of devotion are far less prominent in the direct Latin tradition. The intellectual groundwork of prayer became increasingly emphasised. Meditation gradually monopolised the field, and with the marked growth of intellectualisation in later years, the affective and contemplative aspects of prayer fell into virtual disuse. The very necessary stress upon self-knowledge was so marked that it virtually excluded the primary emphasis upon the knowledge of God which is the *summum bonum* of the Gospel.

This divergence is of special importance for our present purpose, since it was in a similar manner (though with a different purpose and upon different historical grounds) that the Northern tradition came to stress aspects of supplication and petition—even of demand upon God—which had the similar effect of concentrating the devotional life upon the needs and activity of the praying soul rather than upon the reality of God Himself. The marked distrust of mysticism in the Lutheran Reformation—however necessary to correct the excesses of popular devotion in the Latin tradition—closed for Northern Christianity many paths which are essential to the realisation of a true ecumenical progress.[1] Up to

---

[1] A good deal of Lutheran distrust of mysticism (shared also in Reformed theology) rests on a misconception of the connotation of the word in Western or Eastern use. The difficulty will certainly arise in groups working on the lines of this essay, and was therefore rightly explored by the sub-committee of the Commission on Ways of Worship. During preliminary discussion both Lutheran and Anglican members reached complete agreement on the basic facts. They were further agreed in condemning as false a 'mysticism' which so laid stress on immanence as to end in a complete depersonalising as the result of a quest for 'absorption' and loss of identity in the divine. It was pointed out that not only in the higher forms of non-Christian religion (i.e. those which have passed beyond an instinctive level) but also in the synthetic systems, now widely advocated, which are based upon these non-Christian forms, there are different forms of 'mysticism', generally exalted into some form of self-willed attainment. For Christianity, however, it was cordially agreed that the goal of the spiritual life was concurrence of will with the will of Christ, which by contrast could only integrate and enrich human personality.

It was therefore agreed that, as far as may be, the term 'mysticism' (even when rightly understood) should be set aside. The response of the individual to imparted grace should rather be discussed in terms of *ascesis*, though it would

the time of Luther there was still a common intellectual basis
between North and South, and this fact somewhat delayed the
full sweep of the Reform in the devotional field. The same common heritage probably explains the fact that the recovery of the
great tradition by the counter-Reformation has informed the
prayer-life of widely separated areas of the Christian world. Even
where history has brought deep cleavages there is still a common
devotional atmosphere created by the spiritual certainties of *The
Imitation of Christ* and *The Practice of the Presence of God*.

We in the West may look back thankfully to a common heritage with the saints of the middle ages, interpreting them with
our modern knowledge of the historical and mental climate of
the age. But it is equally certain that we are the descendants of
those divisions which the convulsions of the renaissance created.
The common life of men was so broken that they were forced to
live within themselves in defence against the corruption and
worldly compromise that surrounded them. A French Roman
Catholic—Père Pourrat—has said:

> The priest, the monk, and the faithful layman who wanted to
> do his duty could hardly discover anywhere outside his own
> interior life the means of protecting or freeing himself from the
> evil influence of popular opinion. More than anything they
> wanted a thoroughly Christian mentality and unshakable con-

be admitted that this approach does not cover the whole ground of contemporary Christian experience. It is further necessary to observe the distinction
between the normal graces and those which belong to infused states, since both
the evidence for the latter, and their complete orthodoxy, are unquestionable.

Having thus distinguished Christian mysticism (and the mystical theology
which is concerned strictly with these infused states, and with contemplative
prayer) from the false systems and techniques of a supposed 'science', one further distinction remains to be noted. It is necessary to preserve the special use
of the term *mystical body* to express the fact of the Body of Christ embracing
both time and space. This term does not denote the search for God, but the
givenness of the total life of Christ to all who are being transformed into the
fulness of His stature. It is in this sense that the Anglican Order of Holy Communion offers thanks to God

> for that Thou dost vouchsafe to feed us, who have duly received these holy
> mysteries, with the spiritual food of the most precious Body and Blood of
> thy Son our Saviour Jesus Christ; and dost assure us thereby of thy favour
> and goodness toward us, and that we are very members incorporate of
> *the mystical body of thy Son*, which is the blessed company of all faithful
> people. . . .

victions to set against the maxims of paganism. They wanted the mind of Christ and not the fancies of the crowd. The example and the words of Christ are the sole rule of right: to wander from them is inevitably to go astray. A man must be really convinced of this, whatever he may see or hear around him in the world, or even in the Church and her rulers.[1]

The same thing is true of the passion of devotion of those who had broken with what to them was a corrupt body—the historical and visible Church. Both in Roman Catholic and in Protestant circles, therefore, the same motive of reform was active, and in both cases it tended towards an individual piety. It would be profitable to study in closer detail the various types that evolved from that critical age. Pourrat has done this so far as the Roman Communion is concerned. The Anglican Communion, always maintaining its intention of continuity with the past, re-emphasised in its Book of Common Prayer the mutual relation of Scripture and Psalter as the basis both of public and private prayer. This is well brought out in the *Preces Privatae* of Bishop Lancelot Andrewes. But during the period of the Civil Wars the Anglican Church suffered through the imposition of alien forms, and of persons nourished in other traditions. In the next generation came the loss of the Non-Jurors, and the deadening results of church membership being regarded as a test of political conformity, whereby movements of genuine spiritual revival were lost to the Church. The Methodist revival was indeed born within the Anglican communion but was finally driven out by conservative indifference. This new discipline stressed the systematic study of Scripture, and based its prayer both upon Scripture and upon a wealth of affective material in a Scriptural hymnology, which on its eucharistic side preserved the undivided tradition of the Church in a manner insufficiently realised today. It was on the European continent that the change of emphasis already noted was most obvious and formative. The stress in private prayer was that of vocal affirmation, with a marked emphasis on supplication, and somewhat on thanksgiving. There were, however, important emotional and mystical tendencies, which as usual led to overemphasis and exaggeration. Some attempted to reach to contemplation without the essential groundwork and the ordered discipline of the three

[1] Pourrat: *Christian Spirituality*, Vol. III, p. 3.

ways—purgation, illumination and union—by which the imperfection of human nature is gradually made able to live the life of prayer. Consequently there grew up in many quarters a dislike and suspicion of 'enthusiasm'.[1] Such individualism has now largely broken down, though it still persists in certain sects. Notably in the nineteenth century, however, there was a renewed realisation of the need for corporate expression and renewed willingness to try to understand the prayer of others.

In such a perspective the present stage of ecumenical work requires a growth of understanding in the devotional field, as well as in the field of dogmatic theology. Without this corresponding understanding, no realisation of unity in the dogmatic field will bear its proper fruit in the life and service of the Body of Christ. In our devotional life the divergences are at present grave. Even where the various traditions of corporate worship become formally understood, the springs of spiritual life are still far from bringing the Christian family into one joyful participation in that unity for which our Lord offered His deepest intercession. At the present time, without any clear appreciation of the reasons which

[1] The growth of sectarian movements, seeking for religious reality in a supposed return to primitive Christianity behind the accepted tradition, produced a twofold effect. It is now recognised that there are two strains affecting devotional life. There is a tension between the 'horizontal' and the 'vertical' emphasis. The 'vertical' acknowledges that the soul is under the Word of God. The 'horizontal' is conscious rather of the relationships in the world around. Neither need deny the other, but in practice a conflict arises. In one sense the 'vertical' can never be overstressed, but it may tend to ignore the 'horizontal' in a false other-worldliness, or to suppress the claims of a sinful world in a pharisaic Puritanism. If, on the other hand, there is overemphasis upon outward conditions, such as is very natural to fallen man, attention may be withdrawn entirely from the 'vertical', thus producing a godless humanism: or else the 'vertical' may become solely a personal safeguard to ensure personal prosperity in outward affairs. In the latter case, religion becomes a self-centred and even hypocritical emotion, and gives ground for the accusation that 'religion is the opium of the people'.

The true resolution of this dual emphasis is the balance of Withdrawal and Return, which Professor Arnold Toynbee (*Study of History*, Vol. V, *passim*) sees as the characteristic of Christianity. Because of the Incarnation the 'horizontal' cannot be ignored. It must, however, be held subject to the light of God, and controlled by a constant 'vertical' regard. 'In Thy light shall we see light.' The history of the devotional life shows many defections from this true balance, which can be used as a test or estimate of the due relationship between private and corporate religious practice.

lie behind, prayer for some is limited to a rather formal intellectual exercise, while for others it is confined to the necessity for a warmth of love. Should this warmth fail them, their spiritual life appears lost and unstable. For others again, though few, prayer implies only a contemplation in which, by misunderstanding its purpose and relation to the spiritual life as a whole, they may easily fail to understand and to love their brethren.

Liturgy and Personal Prayer

The growing secular demand for the collective, and the recovered Christian demand for the realisation of unity, combine to produce a condition in which liturgy can be more readily appreciated. Liturgy, as the means of coming together in a common worship, implies a corporate intention, and acknowledges a common dependence upon God, and a common relationship among those who are thus dependent. The mutual relationship of individuals is extended and enhanced in a unity of relationship. This mutuality is more than brotherhood. It is marked by the emotional and volitional activity of family life. A family has a continuous life. It is not only a unity in space but a unity in time—a unity which is organic in and through its members.

In the broken Body this desire for corporateness can, however, misunderstand the meaning of liturgy unless it looks back into the history of corporate prayer, and into the relationship of corporate and individual prayer. We have many corporate devotional expressions in modern times, but they are not liturgy. As a simple example, corporate observances proposed for ecumenical worship are for use on occasions of united intercession with a common intention. But they are special expressions of the deep concern of various parts of the divided Body for its healing. Liturgy, on the other hand, is essentially the common prayer of the whole Body and has as its sole purpose the expression and sharing of a common action. The note of action is paramount. Liturgy does not replace private prayer, though this will never reach its fullest expression until it shares in the common action wherein the whole Body is united. This dependence of personal prayer upon the common prayer is most clearly seen in the Jewish background of Christian worship, and in the practice of the early Church. The mental prayer of individual members was drawn from and extended by the study of the sacred books read in the corporate service. In the same way the Psalmody of the Temple had provided the private affective prayer, gathered up and held into a unity through the one Altar in the one Temple.

The prophetic promise of the Old Testament was that the *Shechinah* of that Temple would come to dwell in each heart. The many sacrifices of the Temple have been superseded by the 'full, perfect and sufficient sacrifice, once offered' on Calvary. The corporate worship of the early Christians grew out of the Jewish background with the use of lesson and psalm. Its focus of attention was not the earthly Temple to which the synagogues looked, but the heavenly unity where He who is the conqueror over sin and death has sat down at the right hand of the Father, for ever making intercession for us, and offering the worship of His members. In Him alone are we acceptable, since we must receive His life in our bodies through our partaking of the fruits of sacrifice. Around that central theme of the breaking of the Bread and the sharing of the Cup, the Church built up its regular system of prayer to sanctify the whole of life in the Divine Office, later known as being supremely *Opus Dei*.

We are here concerned with the practice rather than with its theology. It is now clear that this coming together was considered essential from the earliest times. Even with the immediate expectation of the *Parousia*, and the consequent emphasis upon the individual relationship to Jesus and on the expectation of His coming, we find also the insistence upon the common service offered by the common family. That family looks back in time to the great company of witnesses who have gone before, who 'apart from us . . . should not be made perfect' (Heb. 11. 40). It also faces the immediate conflict of the present time, wherein 'we may offer service well-pleasing to God with reverence and godly fear' (Heb. 12. 28), and so, in Him who is our justification, may be brought eternally into that glory to which we give ourselves in the liturgy, as the centre of all our worship and activity.

Liturgy implies a continuity. If, in spite of the continuing rite, the meaning has become obscured, its significance must be recovered. Where the form has been lost it must be restored through an understanding of its origin. No mere corporateness will assure this continuity of action and understanding if in the coming together there is any contradiction regarding the meaning of the unity. The truly corporate union may thus have to wait for many

years, since it can only be reached through the painful discerning
of what the broken parts of Christendom mean by their several
expressions of devotion. Such a discerning will not be content
with mere outward conformity, but will demand an inner understanding and common intention. This will be helped by every
real attempt to experience liturgical action in the deep places of
the spirit as well as in the formal pattern. Such a movement as
that in the Reformed Church of the Netherlands must help in
making alive the significance of the family in Christ, and also in
strengthening and invigorating private prayer through the use of
the liturgical material of Scripture and Psalmody. In a contributed
paper upon this development the Revd. W. Vos writes:

> It is the whole Church which is praying in worship, not the
> minister alone. The actual liturgy of the Dutch Reformed
> Church does not take sufficient account of this. The prayers are
> long and *ex tempore*; one is never sure that 'the whole state of
> Christ's Church' will be prayed for, that the needs of the con-
> gregation will be brought before God; neither is one sure that
> the essential elements of worship will find their proper place in
> every service: confession of sins, thanksgiving, etc. The litur-
> gical style is lost. Therefore set forms of prayer are introduced
> again, partly the classically Reformed prayers, and partly
> prayers borrowed from other Churches: collects, litanies, etc.

Universality implies a common action of word and form which
belongs to the family, so that all can make their offering. The
individual offerings will be enhanced and made particular in so far
as the private prayer of the individual contains its own development. The common liturgy must be such that the simplest begin-
ner in Christian experience and the greatest saint—the simplest
active and the most advanced contemplative can all take their part
as instruments in a great orchestra. They are not there as spectators
and audience, but as executants in a common harmony.

Many of the bodies which have, for one reason or another,
concentrated upon their corporate gathering for worship being an
exercise of private prayer in which others join, are now finding
the necessity of returning to set forms. Just as with the communions which have never lost their practice of liturgy, its
recovery does not mean submitting to a dull uniformity but finds
room for many diverse liturgical expressions. It does not follow

that the study of liturgy should aim at a loss of diversity. Rather should it seek to recover the sense of principle, and so return again to the theological concept underlying the service. The question is as of old: 'What mean ye by this service?' (Ex. 12. 27). Here it is especially important to realise the sense of continuity, not only in the visible body but in the invisible. The worship of God, and the activity of the family in that worship, is a greater thing than any earthly congregation. We are come not to an earthly mountain, but to the glory of the Lamb upon the throne. The historical reasons for the Protestant departure from the recognition of the saints are understandable, but that departure involves a lessening of the total recognition of the glory—an impoverishment in the common sense of the family.

> I suggest, in fact, that when the veneration of saints has lost its due proportion in the life of Christian devotion, either by excess or by defect, it is not so much because Catholics have had an exaggerated notion of the worthiness of the saints as because Catholics and Protestants have only too often had a much impoverished notion of the splendour of God. The right course is, surely, to admit in their fullness without fear or grudging, the glories that God manifests in His creatures, in both the natural and the supernatural order, and then to reflect: 'If even this is infinitely exceeded by God's own perfection, how much more glorious must He be than in our wildest dreams we could have supposed.'[1]

There are deep inherited prejudices that may make it hard for some to appreciate this view. Yet it must be insistently maintained if there is to be any organic reunion in Liturgy, since the whole emphasis is upon the timeless reality.

> Therefore with Angels and Archangels, and with all
> the company of heaven, we laud and magnify Thy glorious
> Name, evermore praising Thee and saying:
> HOLY, HOLY, HOLY, Lord GOD of Hosts;
> Heaven and earth are full of Thy Glory;
> Glory be to Thee, O Lord most High;
> Blessed is He that cometh in the Name of the Lord;
> Hosanna in the highest.

[1] E. L. Mascall, D.D.: *Existence & Analogy*, p. 140.

In this connection it may be well to note a finding recorded by an Orthodox Youth Conference held at Geneva:

> The Orthodox participate in the Ecumenical Movement with the consciousness of their Christian responsibility, to be a living and effective witness to Orthodoxy, ready to explain those of its dogmas which are least understood by other Christians, particularly the place of the Holy Virgin and Mother of God in the life of the Church.[1]

The private prayer of the early Christian grew naturally out of the liturgical framework. The later divergence came in the West, in that over-intellectual age which led into the Reformation. It is easier to assess this within the historic continuity of Roman Catholicism, although it could be worked out within the Anglican communion, and in much greater detail within the Reformed bodies which are now seeking to recover a sense of liturgy. Dom Cuthbert Butler estimates the influence of Fr. Augustine Baker and the counter-reaction to it in later times:

> Still, it cannot be gainsaid that in Fr. Baker's estimation interior private prayer held the first place, and he undisguisedly proclaims its superiority over the public recitation of the Office (cf. *Sancta Sophia*, esp. the chapters 'State of Introversion the end of Religion': 'Vocal Prayer': 'Internal Affective Prayer'). Here it may be profitable to suggest that Fr. Baker and Abbot Guéranger, who in his excellent and suggestive General Preface to the *Liturgical Year* (Advent Volume) seems equally to exalt the liturgical prayer of the Church to the depreciation of private personal prayer, are each of them reacting against opposite tendencies that had run to extremes at the times when they wrote.[2]

Before leaving this main question there are two further aspects that may be noted. The first concerns the general relation and difference between the Eastern and the Western attitudes taken as a whole. In the East the sense of the total organism of the Church and of all prayer is strongly marked, in accordance with the earliest traditions. In the West the tendency is towards organisation rather than organism. 'Dogma, liturgy and personal devotion are pigeon-

---

[1] *Sobornost*, Summer, 1949, p. 214.
[2] Butler: *Benedictine Monachism*, p. 72 (2nd ed. 1924).

holed into separate compartments of life, and their organic bond
is obscured. Faith becomes imposed and not elicited. . . . The
Mother of God loses her solidarity with mankind.' This fact conditions personal prayer in the two main divisions of Christendom,
for Eastern personal devotion has always kept close to the liturgy,
and the private prayer of its individual members finds expression
in prayers drawn from liturgical sources. There is also a stress on
acts of devotion in relation to the different parts of the liturgical
action and to the actual structure of the Church. This may be
illustrated by St. Serafim's teaching to the laity that they should
use a few prayers really well, and by the common Eastern practice
of long private devotions before the Iconostasis. In the West, on
the other hand, organisation and particular method becomes the
aim, although here also for a long period (as is shown by the
medieval primers) private prayer drew from the setting of liturgy.
With the break-up of the renaissance period even the corporate
prayer of the Reformed bodies tends to become methodised,
since congregational prayer is secured by the guidance of a leader,
to whose utterance the congregation is assumed to assent. The
reaction against a lack of personal expression in corporate worship
resulted in a large variety of pattern. In place of a common form
in which the congregation could make a common and recognised
response, the unity has to be preserved by the attention of the
particular congregation to a succession of ideas presented to them
at the time. The result has been a widely different conception of
what corporateness in worship should mean. The Anglican,
accustomed to regular responses shared by the congregation with
the minister, finds himself at a loss in—say—Congregational worship, wherein the attention has to be secured by following the
words of a long didactic prayer. The Congregationalist, likewise,
is unsatisfied in the Anglican setting by what appears to him as
formalism.

The second aspect is due to the fact that in the Western development of private prayer there has been a strong tendency to divide
the more expert in method from those less learned. Where this is
done, learning, rather than the strength of a simple surrender,
becomes the standard of excellence. In corporate worship apart
from the liturgical norm, the communication of the reality of
Spirit has to be sought through an emotional stimulus which emphasises the differences of level. Hymns reflecting deep affective

experience, and a general insistence upon the existential emotional state, leads to the stress being laid on the consciousness of experimental search rather than on a solid acceptance of faith, through which deeper wisdom may be reached.

Man and Society

Christian man is not only a member of Christ but also of the natural human society in which he must manifest his Christianity, and to which he owes a Christian duty. The aspect of his duty which is here relevant is the moral and spiritual responsibility that he owes to the world around him. Here again history has brought about a distortion in men's minds by distinguishing too sharply between the categories of 'secular' and 'religious', and between spiritual and active works of mercy. The whole mental outlook inherited from the Greek attempt to rationalise reality has tended to separate the thinker from the experimenter. The ideal of the most perfect life was that of the philosopher or of the forest hermit. Religion was a specialisation, and though work was necessary in order to secure the balance of life, the working world as a whole owed a duty to religion rather than the reverse process.

The essential claim of Christianity is to sanctify the whole of man's life; but in practice the mental temper from the classical age onwards has been largely affected by the tendency just noted, so that a good deal of church history can be interpreted as attempts to correct or master it. Christianity frankly assumes the necessity of 'two lives', since some measure of specialisation is inevitable in human affairs. But this assumption is made in order to secure a total enrichment of life, so that the worship of God, and the ordering of the world in accordance with the will of God, shall be more completely realised. The story of the Desert Fathers, and of the later growth of coenobitic monasticism, is essentially a penitential expression, not only for the individuals but for the community of mankind, for whom they make reparation. In later times the active orders were developed in order that the work of nursing, or teaching, or the care of the poor might be compassed more effectively. In order to deal with the intolerable weight of sin in the world, with the deficiency of the human will, and with the perversion of man's own self-seeking, there was need of a movement that would present a reversal of the evil process. The monastic stress on unity, on obedience, and on self-abandonment to the utmost limit, was designed to reverse and to rectify that which was deficient in the world. The world that forgets God must be held together by those who remember God. Their whole life, however active, or seemingly passive, its outward appearance, is a work of worship and intercession—a turning back to God of the process of disintegration and loss. The Palestine hermit—when describing the passing of St. Antony—could speak of him as 'the father of men', although Antony had remained hidden in the Egyptian desert. In the first days of monasticism, and in the first Benedictine Rule—which later became the norm for the West— there was a close association of physical labour with the work of the choir. In the middle ages the pattern was lost, restored, and lost again. In the renaissance, while the mental outlook of the age was changing to the experimental and scientific, and assuming the short-term tests of immediate practical value, the Reformation in non-Catholic areas resulted in the suppression of monastic life rather than in rectification. But the principle of the unity of life remains, and is showing signs of revival as being essential in a united Christendom. In the Anglican communion the religious life is now firmly established after tentative beginnings. The Continental Reformed Churches are also sharing in the same development. Works of mercy (such as the work for the care of children and of the poor, inaugurated by Sister Eva of Friedenshort in the last century, and still surviving in Germany despite the material chaos of two wars) or the present movements among French Lutherans provide clear indications. This is an indirect means of expressing the Church's impact on the world, though, since it is the most complete expression of dependence on God, it may well prove the most fundamental means. When the financial security of her hospitals was wiped out during the economic crisis, Sister Eva's reflection would find many parallels in the hardships of the Cistercian and Carmelite foundations. 'Now we have no one and no resources but God.' Remedial works of this quality can be carried out most effectively in the discipline of a dedicated community, just as the life of prayer may also demand that discipline for its fullest perfection. Thus the connection between the religious life and the total situation of the world is an intimate one.

The major relations of the Church with the social order are recorded fully elsewhere and cannot be summarised in a brief space. The essence is that the Church has never accepted the view that Christianity has no responsibility for the social order, though this has been a characteristic tendency in some Lutheran and Calvinist developments. Resistance to the state has aimed rather at liberty of conscience than at the sanctification of the secular. It must not be forgotten that this preoccupation with liberty of conscience is fundamental in the American way of life, and is so embodied in the constitution of the United States. So much of the development of religion in America reflects the fact that until the influx of Southern European and Irish elements, the founders of American life were those who had left Europe in the intolerant age for conscience sake. Religion for them was largely a personal morality, and all they asked of the state was freedom to practise their particular tenets. Therefore, in the Protestant areas of the West, the recovery of the sense of Christian obligation to a Christian social order has been slow, and often neglected as actually irrelevant or harmful to true religion. Great Christian movements, such as the campaign against slavery, have made an effective protest, but bad conditions rather than a governing principle have brought the stimulus for the recent Christian impact on the political and economic situation. This has been evidenced in the work of reformers such as Wilberforce and Shaftesbury in England, or John Woolman in America. An important contribution of a rather different character has come through successive Papal Encyclicals, and has given rise to such movements as *Catholic Action* and *Jeunesse Ouvrière Chrétienne* — known largely as 'Jocisme'. The situation of today has increased the influence of this latter trend, since from the Resistance movements—particularly that in France —there has arisen the identification of the Church with the daily life of the people, with a closer consequent understanding between Catholic and Protestant concern. An actual new missionary technique has developed in the movement of the Catholic priest-workers in France. This new realisation of the solidarity of man as man, and the need for its sanctification, is the most dominant factor of the present day. It raises real problems in devotion, both liturgical, corporate and personal. We stand as it were at the beginning of a new epoch in human living, in which the concept and philosophy of the classical age is not only being challenged, but seems to have worked itself out in Christian experience. The Church can only take over into the new climate its fundamental principles, and it may have to modify the customs and practices to which it has become accustomed, though nothing vital can be jettisoned in this process. The challenge of today is simply that the material is the sole criterion of life. Such a notion demands

> a complete break with the past, and the creation of a new social order entirely based on the mechanical organisation of life. Anything that stands in the way of this—religion, personal liberty, traditions of culture or moral standards—is to be ruthlessly thrown on to the scrap-heap, and we are to make a fresh start without the inheritance of the past.[1]

That is the radical solution, and it is leading to the political conflict of today, in which a God-denying materialism is meeting a weakened civilisation, torn politically and economically by internal stresses. Part of the dilemma is that there are, in all the falsehood, unquestionable Christian demands, however divorced from their true source. The danger for Christianity in such a struggle is lest the outward expressions of the faith should be used as the rallying point of conservatism, with all its diverse concomitants of particular prejudices and self-expressions. The hope, on the other hand, is that the inner life of Christendom may be renewed by the pressure, so that a fresh Christian understanding of man's social needs, and of true personal-corporate life will result from the world's challenge.

Conclusion

The Church is thrown back into a historical situation very like that of the fourth century, when it stood as a small but growing body against the still active political power of a dying paganism, which was content to tolerate the Church if it could be used for the ends of the State. In this setting an appeal for the re-studying of the early practice becomes relevant and important. In the mission-field, particularly in the Far East with its own long tradition of culture, and its renascent sense of solidarity, it is proving impossible to dictate those elements of Christian tradition which belong to our particular Western history. The work must begin again from the Gospels, from the faith as built upon the Gospels, and from the writings of the early Fathers, which date before the particular applications that formed Christendom in the West. Europe and the civilisation dependent upon Europe may be in

[1] Dawson: *The Modern Dilemma*, p. 39.

eclipse, but Christianity will not die. Whatever is vital in it, since it is the very revelation of God, will bring new witnesses to declare His glory, and to wrestle with the deficiencies in the situation. 'The things which are shaken' are being removed 'that those things which are not shaken may remain' (Heb. 12. 27). We need to develop such an understanding both of corporate and personal devotion that Church and Christian alike may be able to bear faithful witness in this time of judgment. The ecumenical movement itself, with the interest now being shown in it not only by the Orthodox Church but also in personal contacts with the Roman Catholic Communion, is a symptom of this common concern. Without common understanding of the meaning and practice of prayer in our various divisions, the growing unity of the Church will be hindered by its inability to express its common witness to the reality of the supernatural. There is need to study not only the different expressions of devotional life, but also to enter into the spiritual warfare against the spirit of confusion and darkness which has enslaved the soul of modern man.

In the first age of persecution the unknown author of the *Epistle to Diognetus* expressed the task of the Christian. 'What the soul is in the body, this the Christians are in the world.' There is an organic unity in all men, in the Adam which dies and must be made alive, reborn in the second Adam who is Christ. The recovery of that organic unity in Christ is the task of the Christian in all times and in all places. We dare not lay aside that task, because it is committed to us by God. As we give ourselves to witness to this fundamental unity we shall inevitably be drawn more and more into His unity, and shall learn one from another. Whether the struggle be one of soul, or an economic adversity used as a penance, or a white martyrdom, or even the fiercer call to witness before the rulers of this world, and perhaps to find the glory of that witness in a martyrdom unto death, the issue is unknown, but the devotion and patience are the same in all.

The conclusion of this essay is thus to plead for effective action in establishing a relatively expert enquiry among those from all parts of the Church who have the necessary knowledge and experience, and above all a deep concern to enter as fully as they are able into the spiritual traditions which are feeding the lives of their Christian brethren. Expert knowledge is of special importance at the present stage, owing to the necessity of testing the various *attraits*, particularly in popular devotion, so as to discriminate between factors which are truly Christian, and others which may have derived from purely natural sources (such as the modern quest for psychological self-realisation) or from the long traditions of paganism and of non-Christian religious systems. It is essential that, preferably in small and carefully chosen representative groups, the inwardness of the several devotional and liturgical traditions should be shared in practice and discussed in great sympathy and charity. It is necessary to 'feel the life' as well as to know the biological theory of the Body of Christ. The Report of the World Conference of Faith and Order meeting at Edinburgh in 1937 pointed to a conception of corporate union—of organic unity—in these words:

> Our task is to find in GOD, to receive from GOD as His gift, a unity which can take up and preserve in one beloved community all the varied spiritual gifts which He has given us in our separations . . . The visible Unity of the Body of Christ can issue only from the Living GOD through the work of the life-giving Spirit.[1]

But as the full understanding of an orchestra rests upon practical knowledge of all the varied instruments in their separate functions, purposes and range, so this diversity of the soul's approach to God in worship and in prayer must be more fully understood in its variety before it can be rediscovered in its wholeness.

The Commission on Faith and Order has already realised other and impalpable elements which cause embarrassment and mutual criticism in ecumenical relations. These are not least evident when Christians share the experience of their most fundamental approaches to God. This enquiry is in no sense an attempt to evade either the intellectual tension of our divisions or their deep moral pain. The development of the spiritual life in the undivided Church, and in the later centuries, and the resultant growth of the ascetic and mystical theology of the Church, is a matter of historic fact and one suited to expert study. The historic course of that growth is at least as clear as is the pattern of liturgical development, though we have urged that both are but aspects of a living whole. The two aspects require different techniques of study, but the aspect now being considered is fully as precise and

[1] *Faith and Order*, Edinburgh, 1937, pp. 252 f.

expert a matter. It is believed that two considerations of great importance for the ecumenical purpose will arise:

(1) For centuries the traditional pattern of the spiritual life developed through the undivided Church and continued to grow and to be enriched up to the time of the Reformation. It has already been pointed out above that the separation of East and West had led to the strengthening of two separate aspects of the spiritual life, which became exaggerated in their separation. Without it, the growth of the whole might have been more healthy and balanced.

The balance was further disturbed at the time of the Reformation and in the events that immediately followed. For the undivided tradition the Vision of God was the summit of Christian hope. It could be longed for, but never commanded. It was a heavenly fruiting which might in the mercy of God be given to crown the serious resolve of the Christian will to correspond with graces already bestowed on the soul during its time on earth. This vision, said our Lord, was possible only to purity of heart—to a singleness of will united with His own. Such a transformation of being demanded a very rich and integral conception of prayer.

The elements of 'prophetic prayer', which Heiler contrasts with what he condemns as 'mystical prayer', are entirely essential to any Christian understanding. But they are not the whole. Similarly, a distorted notion that the practice of meditation was 'a means to advance ourselves in perfection' vitiated the first attempts of the Counter-Reformation to restore the balance. It has been well said that 'the uniform Christian tradition condemns as of the nature of blasphemy every attempt or desire to bend the divine will to our own'. Such partial understandings of the spiritual life appear the probable major cause of the lamentable fact that some Christians are repelled by the devotional expression and practice of others. We are no longer at one in understanding the very purpose of the spiritual life.

(2) But if that divergence besets us, there is another and far more hopeful fact. When small groups of people, with a knowledge of the problems they are to face, and also with a firm intention to offer themselves and their common work to the will of God, set themselves with leisure, and in the atmosphere of spiritual conference and retreat, to live into devotional traditions other than

M

their own—to enter as fully as our common sin allows into the deepest worship of those traditions—then barriers are removed and there is understanding below the level of initial prejudice. This understanding grows with the absence of self-consciousness in true worship, and thus into a greater comprehension of the faith as it informs life. A new sense of proportion enters into the hardest ecumenical thinking and study. The obvious example of this development is almost common knowledge today. No one can habitually use the classical devotions of the Roman Church, or the eucharistic prayers of the Divine Liturgy in the Orthodox Church, without acknowledging gifts that transcend confessional boundaries and enrich the life of *Una Sancta*.

Practical Considerations of Method

It may be well to indicate briefly the lines of working consistent with these proposals.

(1) Retreat conferences must first review the existing norms and types of devotional practice, and study the circumstances in which they grew up, and their relation to the primitive norms and types in the undivided Church.

(2) But for the special task of the approach to the work of reunion through a common devotional understanding, something more than a purely critical faculty will be needed. In the past, divisions have been accentuated and hardened because members of one tradition have been critical of the modes of expression in another, since they could not understand the foreign devotional language. It is obvious that a complete objectivity in the devotional field is at present unlikely. Even scholars working within the normal fields of scholarship tend to find in the records of the primitive Church only material to support their own pre-conceptions, rather than entering into the wholeness of early practice so as to grasp the entirety of the devotion by which the Church has lived. Whenever the wholeness is missed, the divergences cannot be properly estimated.

(3) The only fruitful approach will lie in an integral devotion to the simple fundamentals of Christian experience as shown in the New Testament, respecting and accepting the sincerity of the varied Christian practices which have gradually emerged, and

which form the contemporary Christian pattern. The New Testament must not be used as a mine of proof-texts to justify existing practice, but used rather to gain a deeper common understanding of the wholeness of Christian life and experience. Without the critical faculty there can, of course, be no standards of truth. But its exercise must relate to those standards without overmuch regard to the special pleading of any one particular tradition. Yet the various traditions exist, and they stand for living facts in living practice.

(4) The question of church order is of special importance. We have not sought to minimise the differences nor to ignore the regulations of different church orders. It is not the task of the Committee to draw up new standards, nor to seek some minimum form of devotion which might excite unrepresentative minorities but could never commend itself to the Church as a whole. The task in this field, as in that of Liturgics, is to search out the reasons for divergence, to emphasise that which is common and to promote mutual understanding. But throughout, the whole task will be related to the *grande tradition* which emerges in every form from the earliest days of the Church.

(5) Devotion informs and demonstrates theology, but is itself dependent on theology. There must therefore be a general theological agreement amongst those engaged on this task. A firm grasp of the Trinitarian doctrine as it is expressed in the New Testament, and as it was wrought out in the decisions of the early Councils in opposition to the speculations of successive heresies, is clearly fundamental. There can be no integral devotional understanding between the Arian and the Christian outlook. The whole basis of the soul's approach to God, and of God's approach to man, would be vitiated at its foundation if the Arian view were considered admissible in the discussion. Even among those, moreover, who do accept the Trinitarian position, there may be in practice great difficulties in devotional understanding, more especially where there has been a strong emphasis on some partial aspect of devotional truth, and consequent estrangement from other traditions. But the fundamental ground is still secure.

In all the work it will be of the highest importance that the spirit and purpose of the whole undertaking is made very clear. Without a personal devotion, and a real submission to God's will for the unity of His Church, there can be little hope of progress. With that devotion and that desire, and in complete dependence upon the Holy Spirit, the individuals who give themselves to this discipline will find their own lives enriched through the Spirit, and may thus become interpreters of God's holy will to the Church at large.

INDEX

ABSOLUTION
  public, 90, 106
      priestly authority denied, 168;
      survival in, 131
  sacramental, prerequisite for Com-
      munion, 62, 73; retained in *Conf.
      Augustana*, 93
ADORATION, 69, 106, 119 f., 167,
      198
  chief end of worship, 49, 69; dis-
      trusted, 135 f.,; grows with mystical
      perception, 220
AGNUS DEI, 90, 107, 118
ANAMNESIS
  Dominical, 193; Eucharist as, 47,
      52, 82; Genevan formulary of, 246;
      new understanding of, 235; tradi-
      tional intention of, 239 f.
ANAPHORA, 60
ANGLICAN CHURCH, cf. Chs. III,
      XII, XVIc, XVII *passim*
  'Anglicanism' a misnomer, 188;
      eucharistic tradition in 189, 191;
      integral continuity of, 325, 329;
      revival of Religious life in, 348
ANNUNCIATION, 257, 270 f.
  in Book of Common Prayer, 315 f.
ANTE-COMMUNION
  definition, 31 f.; in Dutch Reform,
      225; preaching at, 130
ARCHITECTURE
  Church, Liturgical indications in,
      226
ASSUMPTION
  in Book of Common Prayer, 275,
      315; difficulties from definition,
      266, 290 f.; as isolating BVM, 312
AUGUSTINE, SAINT
  and Eucharist, 201

BAPTISM
  admission by (*sacramentum initii*), 35,
      61, 71; adult, 91 f., 141; Barth on,
      93; Calvinist rejections of, 91;
      developing thought on, 36, 143 f.;
      disused by Society of Friends, 173;
      elements alone emphasised, 237;
      immersion, not confined to Bap-

tists, 140; infant, rejected, 143;
      public worship, administration du-
      ring, 146; in Scotland, 119; in
      Sweden, 105; subjective tendency,
      92; spiritual efficacy alone in, 244
  theology of, Roman Catholic, 48;
      Orthodox, 185; Anglican, 71 f.
  Trinitarian formula in, 146
BENEDICTUS, 90, 118, 229
BODY OF CHRIST (cf. CHURCH,
      UNA SANCTA), Ch. XVII
      passim
  a sacrificial Body, 200 f.; Unity of,
      324 ff., 340
BURIAL, 73, 96, 163

CANON OF MASS, 52
  adaptations of, 190; commemora-
      tions in, 317
CANONICON, 55 ff., Chs. V, XIV,
      XVId *passim*
  Baptism, doctrine rejected, 143 f.;
      influence on Anglican worship, 189
CALVIN
  Institutes of, 236; Lausanne liturgy
      goes beyond, 244; Nestorianism in,
      243; Sacraments integral with
      Word in, 119; on Symbol, 115;
      transformation of liturgy by, 225
CATECHISM
  as confessional standard, 128; West-
      minster, 68
CATHOLICISM
  Old, Ch. XV; Roman, Ch. I,
      XVIa
CHURCH
  the Universal (cf. BODY OF
      CHRIST, *UNA SANCTA*), 23,
      25, 51, 60 f., 77, 99 f., 110, 122,
      136 f., 156 f., 168, 177 f., 187, 202,
      312 ff., 317
CHURCH ORDER
  Books of, Service forms, etc.
  Agenda (ed. Brunner), 81; Book of
      Common Order, 111, 113, 115 ff.,
      123 f.; Book of Common Prayer,
      72, 76, 149 f., 163, 190, 202, 339;
      Canonicon, 55; Evangeliebok, 105,

357